THE MYSTERY OF CHRISTIAN FAITH

A Tangible Union with the Invisible God

An Apologetic on the Borderline of Theology, Medicine, and Philosophy

---

Paul Ungar

University Press of America,® Inc.
Lanham · Boulder · New York · Toronto · Plymouth, UK

Copyright © 2008 by
University Press of America®, Inc.
4501 Forbes Boulevard
Suite 200
Lanham, Maryland 20706
UPA Acquisitions Department (301) 459-3366

Estover Road
Plymouth PL6 7PY
United Kingdom

All rights reserved
Printed in the United States of America
British Library Cataloging in Publication Information Available

Library of Congress Control Number: 2007938471
ISBN-13: 978-0-7618-3957-6 (paperback : alk. paper)
ISBN-10: 0-7618-3957-7 (paperback : alk. paper)

∞™ The paper used in this publication meets the minimum
requirements of American National Standard for Information
Sciences—Permanence of Paper for Printed Library Materials,
ANSI Z39.48—1984

Dedication

This book is dedicated to my dear children, Maria, Julia, Paul, Joseph, Andrew, Marta, and Thomas, to the memory of my Theology Professor, Dr. J. Fucak, who was very helpful in writing Part One of the book, and to Msgr. Dr. P. Lopez-Gallo, who was especially kind in reviewing the manuscript, and helping with his sharp theological insights in correcting it.

Contents

Part 4: Living in a Tangible Union with the Invisible God

Preface

The Roman Emperor Diocletian made a vow to exterminate Christians. However, on the ruins where his palace once lay (in Split, Croatia), stands the cathedral of the local bishop today. The history of Christianity is full of similar challenges. The church confronted different challenges in times of early persecutions: at Constantine's turnover, during the Middle Ages, the Renaissance, Enlightenment, the French Revolution, the subsequent secularism and modernism, the rise of fascism, and the downfall of communism.

In spite of changing times, threats, and challenges, Christianity persisted. It grew inch by inch, approaching its purpose of promoting God's kingdom. It is worth asking, "What gave the church and believers such persistence to overcome all potentially fatal historical trials?" The thesis of this book is that Christianity's vitality comes from perhaps the deepest mystery of faith itself: *From the believer's tangible experience of union with the invisible God.*

In our postmodern age, the church faces a new challenge—collective estrangement from God. What may be the reason behind widespread agnosticism, religious indifference, apathy, and loss of interest in God, which prevail in our time like never before in history?

I confronted the very reason of such a collective distrust in God in the spring of 1975 when I attended a conference as a young MD. In one workshop, a lecturer attempted to distinguish disordered from "normal" behavior with an example, which I translate as follows: If someone would suddenly spring to his or her feet crying out in a panic, "Help! A tiger is attacking me!" obviously he or she would be in need of psychiatric treatment. The lecturer concluded that "If somebody is discerning, experiencing, communicating with, or is afraid of something which exists only in his or her mind, then this person is mentally ill and suffering from a delusion."

But then another participant spoke out, complicating the matter. "Things are not so simple," he said. "For instance, religious people imagine and fear something like the attacking tiger—something which has never been seen, touched, or measured by anyone—they fear God." He further stated, "Faith is one instance of a socially tolerated delusion."

Although I was already a firm believer at that time, on the spur of the moment, I was unable to appropriately object to, or to answer for myself (much less for the public) the question provoked by the participant. However, I realized that he very clearly expressed one of the reputed challenges to faith in our time: reductionism, which entails explaining trust in God away, downgrading faith to a socially-learned behavior pattern, or even proclaiming it as nothing more than a deception, illusion, or delusion. Since the seventeenth century Enlightenment, scientific reductionism has been on the rise, while interest in God has shown a parallel decline in Western cultures. This trend is particularly challenging in our time.

Having been so directly and powerfully confronted with the mystery of faith, my interest in theology began to sprout. After specializing in neurology and psychiatry, completing a master of science degree in psychodynamics, and a doctor of philosophy degree in existential psychotherapy (Viktor E. Frankl's "Logotherapy"), in 1985 I began studying theology. One of my interests was to come up with a counter to the overwhelming theological question raised some ten years earlier by my agnostic colleague: Do believers truly experience the reality of the invisible and scientifically unverifiable, but still existing, "living God,"—or is Christian faith a delusion-like self-deception.

I quickly realized that most theologians have neither an easy nor a simple explanation to this question, because the answer to it lies on the borderlines of theology, psychology, psychiatry, and philosophy. However, during my studies, I also realized the fact that faith is God's gift; it is a genuine internal psychological experience and evidence for a believer that is stronger than any external, purely technical proof or disproof. Nothing is more essential to healthy or sick, rich or poor, young or old, clerics or lay people, than living in an intimate union with the invisible but "almighty, eternal, and ultimate love," namely God, as experienced by believers.

In 1991, after I completed my studies in theology, my family and I moved from Europe to Canada. Here I continued to explore the same topic—to search for a synthesis of theological and psychological insights in order to better understand how people of faith experience, communicate with, and live in relationship (union) with the invisible God. This book is the result of my research.

My book attempts to accomplish the previous goal in the following order:

- Part 1 examines the question of who God is, and what are experientially, for people of faith, his "personal characteristics" that emerge from Biblical description.
- Part 2 discusses the anthropological characteristics enabling believers to communicate with the spiritual, transcendental, and "quite other" God.
- Part 3 explores when, how, and through which psychological functions believers experience the biblical "personal characteristics" of the invisible and immeasurable God.
- Part 4 focuses on the question of whether Christian believers are able to substantiate, tangibly communicate with, and live in union with the "Almighty, Eternal, and Ultimate Love,"— the Biblical God.

Acknowledgment

Scripture taken from the HOLY BIBLE: NEW INTERNATIONAL VERSION®. NIV®. Copyright © 1973, 1978, 1984 by International Bible Society. Used by permission of The Zondervan Corporation.

The "NIV" and "New International Version" trademarks are registered in the United States Patent and Trademark Office by International Bible Society."

Part 1

Who Is God?—What are God's "Personal Characteristics" as they Emerge from a Biblical Description?

Chapter 1

Introductory Clarifications

Although all of us live in the same world, each of us judges that reality differently. Some absolutely deny the existence of God while others, just as resolutely, claim that they live in union with God, and that God is the most important reality in their lives. What causes this huge disagreement concerning the question that is probably the most important in human life?

Simply put, the reason is that devoted believers do definitely experience, through faith, living in a relationship with God, while for nonbelievers, living in a tangible union with an invisible God is an absurd notion—indeed, an impossibility.

How is it possible that people living in the same world experience it so differently?

Let us answer this question with a true story. According to Lajos Kardos, the gestalt psychologist Wolfgang Kohler believed that a monkey trying to reach a banana gets an "insight" to use the stick inside of his cage as a tool.[1] On the other hand the behaviorist Edward C. Tolman thought only "trial and error" helps the monkey to reach his goal. A group of psychologists who belonged to these two different schools of thought undertook an experiment to solve the dispute. When they observed the same monkey trying to grab the banana with the stick, some of the psychologists stated positively that the monkey had insight. The other group determined resolutely that the monkey did not reason.

How could psychologists observing the same monkey, in the same environment, at the same time, come up with such contradictory conclusions? The problem was not with the eyesight of the observers, but with their understanding and interpretation of what they had seen. Everyone recognized what he or she was trained in, or simply what he or she wanted to see. This story demonstrates how the same observation can be interpreted in different ways. It explains why people living in the same world experience it so differently. What could be done then to enhance mutual agreement in our understanding of natural and supernatural events, or even biblical truth?

The place to start is by defining our terminology, because disagreement can arise especially if multiple ideas are understood by the same words, or if the same words are understood in a different sense. We need to clarify our terms before we start researching what enables believers to live in a relationship with God and what prevents non-believers from communicating with God. Thus, let us first clearly define our terminology.

1.1. What Does It Mean to Live in a "Tangible Union" with the Invisible God?

Christian mystics, saints, and ordinary believers speak of their relationship, and sometimes of their union, with God. Is, however, their relationship with an invisible and untouchable God "tangible?"

This issue came up while I was discussing the manuscript with one of my dear and respected critics. He remarked that saying an experience of the divine can be tangible is a contradiction in terms. God himself, he argued, does not possess the qualities that can affect our five senses. Therefore, the sensations some saints and mystics have felt throughout the Church's history, or the experience each one of us has had or could have of God (e.g., a vision, ecstasy, or some other tangible signs of his existence), represent illusions. The only exception is our speech about the Incarnate Word, who was able to use his humanity to communicate with his contemporaries in a way that was literally tangible.

To avoid possible misunderstandings, let us clarify the meaning of the word "tangible" as used in the title of this book. Indeed, God is spiritual, non-corporeal, and therefore, not recognizable through the senses. However, in this book we are focusing not so much on the transcendental mystery of God, but rather on how believers experience and communicate with (the biblical) God.

Let me illustrate the difference between the two objectives with biblical examples. Moses, when approaching a burning bush that was not consumed by the flames (Exod. 3:2), heard the voice of God, saying "Do not come any closer," and, "Take off your sandals, for the place where you are standing is holy ground." Moses was afraid to look at God and hid his face, fearing he would die if he saw God, who told him, "I am who I am" (Exod. 3:5-14). These words of God revealed that God is a mystery comprehensible only to himself and that God is known to himself alone—that God cannot be experienced in a sensory way.

From this biblical example we realize that Moses did communicate with God despite the invisible, non-sensory, and—for humans—inexplicable, nature of God. Although he did not fully grasp the transcendental God's mystery, Moses accepted his revelation with faith, and thus, Yahweh's message was clear, definite, and intelligible to him. Our purpose is somewhat similar to that of Moses: not primarily to focus on the impenetrable mystery of God's deity, but to accept it with faith and discuss the believer's experiential and "tangible" communication and living in union with the invisible God.

Although nobody has seen God, it is a biblical fact that Christ appeared to Saul on the road to Damascus. Despite the fact that Jesus' intervention was non-sensory, it made Saul physically fall off the horse and become blind. Furthermore, in this encounter, Jesus not only communicated his identity to Saul, but also shared with him, almost in the blink of an eye, all that the other apostles learned (through the senses) from being disciples of Jesus for almost three years (See Gal. 1:11-12). Evidently to St. Paul, his communication with Jesus was not insecure or elusive, but experiential, evident, and "tangible"—the paramount truth of his life.

We could, commenting on Saul's encounter, repeat our conclusion drawn from Moses' example: we do not know how the transcendental God,—the Risen Jesus—appeared to Saul: this is a mystery. We are, however, interested in discussing how a human person like Saul experiences—and through which psychological functions acknowledges—communication with the invisible God.

The experience that St. Teresa of Ávila recounts is the best piece of evidence. She describes the vision and the phenomenon of her transfixion with these words:

> I saw an angel beside me toward the left side, in bodily form, something I very seldom see. Although angels are often represented to me, it is without seeing them, except in the sort of vision I have already referred to. But in this one, it pleased the Lord that I should see him thus: he was not large, but small, very beautiful, his face so suffused with light that he seemed to be one of the very highest angels, who

appear all on fire. They must be those they call Cherubim, who do not tell me their names; but I see plainly that in heaven there is much difference of some angels to others, and of others to others, that I don't know how to say it. I saw in his hands a long dart of gold, and at the end of the iron, there seemed to me to be a little fire. This I thought he thrust through my heart several times, and that it reached my very entrails. As he withdrew it, I thought it brought them with it, and left me all burning with a great love of God. So great was the pain that it made me to give those moans; and so utter the sweetness that this sharpest of pains gave me, that there was no wanting it to stop, nor is there any contenting of the soul with less than God. The pain is not physical but spiritual, although the body does not fail to share in it somewhat, and indeed plenty. It is such delightful language of love that passes between the soul and God that I beg of His goodness that He give the enjoyment of it to him who may think I die. The days that this lasted, I went about as if distracted: I did not wish to see or to speak, but to burn myself with my pain, which greater glory to me than anything there is in all creation.[2]

From the three examples, we conclude that Moses, Saul, and Teresa of Avila did in fact communicate with God, when God intervened in their lives. Similarly, believers do not experience God as touchable through their senses (except in miracles). Rather, people of faith communicate with the invisible God through psychologically experienced processes and functions that are very different from the senses or sensory discernment. Thus, we pose this question: can the paramount reliability and validity of such a discernment, which enables the believer's relationship and union with God, possibly be referred to as "tangible," despite the fact that God is invisible and untouchable? In other words, is the believer's encounter with God so evident that it could be described as metaphorically "tangible?"

According to the *Concise Oxford Dictionary*, the word "tangible" has two meanings.[3] First, it is defined as something "perceptible by touch;" second, as something "definite; clearly intelligible; not elusive or visionary." In the latter definition, the words "definite" and "intelligible" signify an experience or message that is clear, evident, and understandable. "Definite" and "intelligible" mean something factually and unmistakably personally experienced, such as their encounter with God and the received message were for Moses, Saul, and Teresa of Avila.

From the example of the disciples and the saints, as well as from the self-revelations and behavior patterns of exemplary mystics, we may deduce that this second, metaphorical meaning of the word "tangible" may accurately describe the experience of their communication with God. For people of faith, evidence for God's presence is not vague or dubious. Moses, Paul, and Theresa of Avila realized without a doubt that they communicated with the *quite other*, unknowable God. Their encounter may not be humanly understandable, but from a biblical perspective, it is clearly intelligible. Thus, in this book when we say that union with God is "tangible" for committed believers, we mean that it is an explicit, convincing, reliable, and paramount biblical experience, and not merely an elusive, visionary, or arbitrary fantasy, and definitely not the perception of something that does not exist (i.e., a hallucination) or a mistaken perception of an existing entity (i.e., an illusion).

The term signifies what I wish to assert in this book: that the invisible, untouchable, and transcendental (God) may become experientially and tangibly more close to the committed believer through his or her faith than anything that could be perceived by the senses.

Consequently, we will express two very different realities by using two similar terms. The term "touchable" will refer to that which one can see, touch, and measure in inches, pounds, or seconds. The term "tangible" will mean a non-sensory, (but, as John Paul II called it, "trans-empirical") invisible, and untouchable, but nonetheless evident and unmistakably true reality—like that experienced by Moses, St. Paul, and Teresa of Avila.[4] As the reader may notice from the biblical descriptions, something that is non-sensory can still be tangible and experiential!

In addition, our definition of "tangibility" implicitly leads to the conclusion that an enduring self-deceptive or fantasized union with an arbitrarily invented god is not possible. Such a relationship, like every forgery, has to end in disillusionment. Only a true God may permanently become tangible and experientially present through an authentic believer's faith.

We will now turn our attention to the following: Who is this God with whom believers are able to live in a tangible union, and what are His distinguishing characteristics?

1.2. "God" or "god"

Undoubtedly, there are many reasons why people experience all spheres of reality, including God, differently. One important and common reason is that people have different concepts of what is meant by the notion

"God." What sort of understanding of God can we come away with from this very general word? According to the *Concise Oxford Dictionary*, "god" signifies in many religions "a superhuman being or spirit worshipped as having power over nature, human fortunes, etc.; a deity." In contrast to this definition, according to the same dictionary, "God" (in Christian and other monotheistic religions) is "the creator and ruler of the universe; the supreme being."

Does such a definition adequately explain who God is for Christians? True, God is a "superhuman being," and he is the creator and ruler of the universe. However, in the Christian understanding, God's "personality,"—the nature and essence of who he is—is not defined solely by his superiority to the universe which is dependent on him. Rather, God's unique and *quite other* love and goodness are equally important manifestations of who God is. In fact, for believers, God's experiential "personal characteristics" reveal much more about him than do impersonal abstractions, such as "creator and ruler of the universe; the Supreme Being."

In this book, the term "God" means the one who, through the Bible, reveals his very self, and who is simultaneously experienced by both the church and believers in the sense that people of faith live in an experiential and tangible union with him.

Throughout history, theological books drafting God's "personal profile" were either more biblically or more philosophically oriented. This book connects both revelation and philosophy, combined with the believer's experience, emphasizing that only the biblical God is experiential. Disappointment in an arbitrarily imagined, "self-created" or misinterpreted image of God or gods is inevitable, because

Their idols are silver and gold, made by the hands of men,
They have mouths, but cannot speak, eyes, but cannot see;
They have ears but cannot hear, noses, but they cannot smell;
They have hands but they cannot feel, feet, but they cannot walk;
Nor can they utter a sound with their throats.
Those who make them will be like them, and so will all who trust in them. (Psalm 115:4-9)

The psalm clearly expresses the insurmountable difference between faith and idolatry. Namely, the genuine form of human existence is in relationship with God. Humans are destined to progress and mature as persons, emotionally, intellectually, morally, and spiritually—to act as someone created in God's image and likeness. In attempting to reduce the revealed Deity to the level of idols or human invention, humanity jeopardizes its own spiritual growth in a "transcendental"—Godly—direction. Even if practiced by religious people, idolatry (like the worship of money, luxury, or power) promotes a moral and spiritual regression, and it reduces *Homo religious'* self-understanding and self-esteem from someone created to ultimately become what the Bible calls "a disciple," to a spiritless "thing"—a worthless toy in the hands of blind and indifferent cosmic powers. As the last verse of the psalm notes, "Those who make them will be like them, and so will all who trust in them."

This millennia-old truth, which is as valid in the postmodern era as it was in Biblical times, is evident in the idolater's experience of coming from meaninglessness and going towards nothingness. It leads to the intellectual, behavioral and social effects described by the psychiatrist Viktor E. Frankl as "suffering from a meaningless life," and its symptoms are abundantly present in our modern idolatrous climate.[5]

1.3. God's "Personality"

Greek mythology, like most ancient and modern religions that are not based on revelation, imagined the gods in an anthropomorphic way. The Greek gods were greedy, lusty, or bloodthirsty, indiscriminately expressing sadistic personality traits by taking pleasure in humans' wars, catastrophes, or suffering. Humans experienced helplessness toward the overpowering forces of a "fate" that was directed by the gods' whims and pleasure. Faith was not needed to communicate with or relate to the gods, but manipulation, bribery, and deception were the language worshippers of that period used and the means of interaction between humans and gods.

The Judeo-Christian understanding of God is very different. As Fritz Rotschild formulates, while "in primitive religion divine wrath was often a primary and ultimate phenomenon and the enigma of divine power was experienced as constant threat," in revealed religion God's anger does "not come 'out of the blue,' so to speak, but is itself a reaction of God to the behavior of man."[6] Thus, in revealed religions people are not helpless puppets in God's hand, but have their own responsibility. By good and godly behavior, (which is linked to "lived faith"), God's anger can be avoided and turned into love.

Furthermore, in revealed religions God is not only seen as good and loving, but as a being completely different from all of creation. In Exodus 33:19-20, for example, we read,

> And the Lord said, "I will cause all my goodness to pass in front of you, and I will proclaim my name, the LORD in your presence. I will have mercy on whom I will have mercy, and I will have compassion on whom I will have compassion." But he said, "you cannot see my face, for no one may see me and live."

The unimaginable splendor of God, which no human eyes were permitted to see, signifies that God is different from that which human senses, feelings and ideas are able to comprehend. That is, God is transcendent.

Christians have always believed that human thinking is insufficient to grasp God's mystery. This belief was clearly expressed in the creeds of the first Ecumenical Synods (see August Franzen[7]). These synods dealt with two crucial issues. The first was the Christological question concerning Jesus' person; the final understanding reached stated that Jesus had two natures, human and divine, which are neither divided nor mixed. The second issue was the Trinitarian question which resulted in the claim that God is one in His essence, but exists as three persons. Observed from human perspective, and using human logic, these statements are difficult to understand or visualize.

Through the centuries, writers have continued to use philosophy to understand something of the mystery of God. According to Walter Kasper, for example, Anselm of Canterbury defined God as "that than which nothing greater can be thought."[8] Thomas Aquinas (according to the same author) in his *Summa Theologiae* talks about "God, the supreme Good in which all finite goods participate." Indeed such "supreme Good" is, as Ferenc Szabo formulates, "quite different" from what we finite humans are able to recognize.[9] The idea of the ineffability of God is even more clearly and dramatically expressed by Søren Kierkegaard in *Philosophical Fragments—Johannes Climacus*.[10] Here God is described as "absolutely different" from any human being and indeed from anything that one can understand or imagine. Finally, the theologian Karl Rahner expresses the idea of the ineffable God (as noted by Kasper) as "the holy mystery."[11] Our whole book is focused on discussing one and the same issue: how believers are able to tangibly experience their relationship and communication with such an "absolutely different being," who—

according to the Christian understanding of God—is nonetheless a "person."

Keeping all this in mind, when speaking of God's "personality," we are aware that God is absolutely different from what humans understand by the notion of personality. When we use the phrase "God's personality," we transfer the infinite and "ultimately different" from transcendental into human concepts, thereby inevitably conceiving of God as he is not. On the other hand, we are unable to experience or imagine God without abstractions. The very idea of "God's personality" is abstract; it is also an anthropomorphism (i.e., an attribution of a human characteristic to a nonhuman being). More precisely, it is a metaphor. (Metaphors like the "angry," "demanding," or "jealous" God helped Old Testament authors to conceptualize him.)

To Christian believers, God's distinct personality is revealed especially through Jesus Christ's ministry. The purpose of our examination of Jesus' personality is to psychologically and experientially profile and conceptualize the unimaginable God. Having acknowledged that God's "personality" is an anthropomorphism, we will no longer place the term "personality" in quotation marks when using it of God.

When we endeavor to apply the modern conception of "personality" to revelation, we come upon a difficulty. In the Bible, there is no exact psychological analysis of God's or Jesus' personality. However, almost everything Jesus taught or preached during his entire ministry is a revelation about God's personality, expressed most often through explanations of the rules of "God's kingdom." By revealing God's kingdom, Jesus revealed its king's (God's) personality.

Biblical revelation will not be easy to interpret. The Bible was written by and for people who lived in cultures that held ideas different from those of today. Inevitably, biblical terms and ideas often no longer carry the same content they once had. For us, for example, the important term "God's kingdom" has a somewhat unclear meaning because of cultural disparity. Therefore, we need to return to those times when the expression was in common use. Let us trace the evolution of the idea of the kingdom of God from ancient times.

Notes

1. Lajos Kardos, *Behaviorizmus* (Budapest: Gondolat Konyvkiado, 1970), 147-49.

2. William Thomas Walsh, *Saint Teresa of Avila* (Rockford, IL: Tan Books, 1977), 135-36.

3. R. E. Allan, *The Concise Oxford Dictionary* (Oxford: Clarendon Press, 1990), 1246

4. John Paul II, *Crossing the Threshold of Hope* (New York: Alfred A. Knopf, 1994), 34.

5. Viktor E. Frankl, *The Unheard Cry for Meaning* (New York: Washington Square Press, 1985), 20.

6. Abraham J. Heschel, *Between God and Man* (New York: The Free Press, 1959), 24.

7. August Franzen, *Kleine Kirchengeschichte* (Freiburg: Herder Bücherei, 1968), 60-70.

8. Walter Kasper, *The God of Jesus Christ* (New York: Crossroad, 1992), 5.

9. Ferenc Szabo, *Az ember es vilaga* (Rome: Self-published, 1969), 94.

10. Søren Kierkegaard, *Philosophical Fragments Johannes Climacus,* edited and translated by Howard V. Hong and Edna H. Hong (Princeton: Princeton University Press, 1985), 46.

11. Kasper, *Jesus Christ,* 5.

Chapter 2

Concepts Preceding God's Self-Revelation

The message of *Man and His Symbols,* by the well-known Swiss psychiatrist Carl Gustav Jung could be summarized in one sentence for
our purposes: the consciousness of past generations is present in the
thoughts, feelings, and notions of people today.[1] Therefore, in every one
of us living today dwells an "Old Testament" person, with his or her
reasoning, religion, and behavior, and we can discern in ourselves traces
of these prehistoric human traits. The deepest, most ancient layers of
reasoning and understanding influence, and sometimes determine,
humankind's most recent thoughts, feelings, and behavior patterns, as in
cases of road rage, in satanic cults, or in the conduct of a "total war."
Let us explore the relevance of this gloomy legacy for our topic.

2.1. Stone Age Spirituality

The conception of god is one of our most ancient ideas. It reaches back
into the gloomy past of humankind's legacy. From their burial sites we
know that Paleolithic (older Stone Age) people already had religious
belief systems. However, if we wish to research the first elaborate ideas
of gods, we need to go back some forty-thousand years to Neolithic
(recent Stone Age) times.

At that time our ancient ancestors became agriculturalists and realized their dependence on sovereign powers beyond their world and capa-
bilities. The idea that powers exist beyond the human world and realm,
which we call "supernatural" today, stems from observation. The Neolithic
peoples observed that the weather and the harvest—thus their very exist-

ence—depended not only on their own efforts, but also on powers out-side of and greater than themselves. Those more powerful forces deter-mined their fate. All that happened in their world was in some way inter-related with something bigger than they were. However, unlike our concept of natural forces, these powers were not abstract, lifeless, and imper-sonal. Natural science, or the idea of inanimate objects, did not exist at that time. Everything, including the wind, stones, and water, was be-lieved to possess some qualities of the human mind, while governed by its own spirit.

According to art historian Arnold Hauser, in the Neolithic peoples' mind there emerged a confused, fluid picture of the world, bred from the inability to draw a clear distinction between the self and that which ex-isted outside of and apart from the self.[2] For our prehistoric ancestors, it seemed inconceivable that these beings and powers, so central in their lives, would not behave, feel, desire, like they did. Everything, the whole of natural and supernatural reality, was imagined as "human," acting in a similar manner and with a similar personality to that of the human being.

Consequently, Neolithic man and woman constructed a two-world picture: the "upper world" or the "hereafter" and the "lower world." The former was one in which mysterious animated forces lived; the latter comprised the known world, which was increasingly being dominated by humans. The upper world (invisible to humans) was viewed as superior but not in a transcendental dimension (like the Christian concept of heaven). The upper world of the Neolithic people existed in the same time frame and worldly reality as the lower world (they shared a com-mon space-time continuum); thus, the two realms were only vaguely separated.

Since the way in which the Neolithic peoples understood themselves depended on the benevolence of this humanized upper world, they made early attempts to appease it, in the hope that it would be benign and helpful to them. This magic-centered, formal type of worship was the precursor of primitive religious ritual. The Neolithic peoples' view of the world was the by-product of their need to explain and understand. This need made them human, distinguishing them from animals, and was the motivator and expression of ancient religious interest and ritual as well.

Motivated by such interests, which I term "God's call" (discussed in the fourth part of this book), humans, including Neolithic peoples, have searched for a connection and closeness to the unknown God from the very beginning of their existence. They did this to the extent to which their religious, cultural, and social environments enabled them. In summary, during prehistoric times, specific methods (typical for that era) were used to establish friendly relations with the other world, mostly under the direction of an initiated medium. It was believed that this intercessor knew how to communicate with the gods and spirits, that by magical rituals the shaman could influence the inhabitants of the upper world, thereby gaining their sympathy on behalf of others. The shaman was a mediator between the upper and lower worlds. Thus, the idea of important mediators between the two worlds (like miracle workers, healers, conjurers, and later priests) was more or less spontaneously, and later institutionally, established.

2.2. Religion at the Dawn of Civilization

The next important turning point occurred in Mesopotamia more than three thousand years before the birth of Christ. It was Mesopotamia that gave rise to the idea of the god's relationship with the king or kingship, and from there it spread to other cultures of the ancient world. As we shall see, this development had an important impact on the development of the idea of the kingdom of God that became so key to Jesus' preaching.

The people of this time were preoccupied with the question of what the supernatural, upper world of the gods was like. For thinkers of the time, the answer was obvious: if earthly occurrences were indeed mere consequences of what occurred in the upper world, then occurrences in the realm of the gods were possible to discern from occurrences here on earth. Thus, earthly events (storms, droughts, and lightning strikes for instance) reflected to some degree the dynamics that unfolded in the mysterious upper world.

Yet besides natural phenomena, social events were also connected to those in the upper world. The formation of the first great empires and earthly kingdoms, the conquering campaigns of the monarchs, successes, glory, pomp, and ceremony were only a shadow of the events taking place in the realm of the gods. Furthermore, all economic and political events also mirrored what happened in the upper worlds—the consequences of rivalries, wars, love, or hatred among the gods. It was assumed that the psychological characteristics of the gods did not differ much from those of men/women, since gods were like human beings—more powerful, but not better in nature.

Thus, the secret of the successes of the first great kingdoms and kings lay in their contemporaries' understanding of the impact of the gods and in the kings' demand for divine rights. The kings' claim was that the power of the great god supported their power and supremacy. Alternatively, the king who was defeated by his enemies, who was humbled, who lost his kingdom, also mirrored the loss of good will and support from the upper world in the eyes of his contemporaries.

The royal court itself, with the king at its pinnacle, followed by the high priests, the chief of staff, the chief dignitary, and then the noble, the rich, the simple people, and finally slaves in the lowest position, also mirrored the pattern of the ruling powers in the upper world. The greatness of the highest gods, followed by their subordinate but still powerful gods and half-gods, then spirits, and—at the bottom of the hierarchy—the masses of souls, served as a blueprint of how the royal court was to be set up. The greater the power of the patron god of the king in the upper world, the more powerful would be the king's court and, therefore, the more illustrious and luxurious his court entourage.

Since the will and judgment of the great gods were revealed through the actions of the great king, it was an honor to serve the king. Serving the king was deemed as almost equal to serving the gods, or the most powerful god himself, in ancient Egyptian, Assyrian, Babylonian, or Persian cultures. This is why, when making important decisions, the king always tried to secure the consensus and support of the great gods and high priests; hence the reasoning that to be an enemy of the king equals being an enemy of god.

2.3. The Relevance of the Ancient Legacy in Modern Times

Interconnections between the crown and church were practiced for centuries in European history in the politics of great kings and queens. The belief that great kings represented the choice and will of God was challenged seriously for the first time in 1792, during the French Revolution. However, right up to the end of World War I in 1918 with the fall of the Russian Romanovs, German Hohenzollerns, and Austro-Hungarian Habsburgs, many emperors, along with their people, held the conviction that their sovereigns represented the living image of God and his will.

So, if we consider these historic connections between great kings and gods, we can truly see how correct, and indeed prophetic, Carl G. Jung was. These connections live on in our cultures and in us as well. How ancient they are, and yet how modern! It seems that with little change they survived the old, the middle, and the modern and postmodern ages; they remain influential today and will continue to be so in the foreseeable future.

Much blood was shed needlessly due to prehistoric motives and stereotypes. It is understandable that in times prior to God's self-revelation, people mostly searched for union with their gods—in actuality with the ultimate God—in ways that their environment and cultural and social backgrounds enabled them to. Sadly, however, people continued to search for God unproductively after Abraham, Moses, and even Jesus. If people had believed, and above all practiced, the biblical principles of the kingdom of God, human history should have taken a very different course. However, this did not happen before 1918, nor afterwards unfortunately. Many once-great emperors have disappeared, but the fulfillment of or even the effort toward the realization of the kingdom of God in its biblical form has not emerged powerfully enough to determine the course of history or to replace the ungodly ideology of fallen emperors with a biblical one.

For the believer, however, those historical experiences serve as a warning to be critical and overrule the requirements of any zeitgeist, culture, or human establishment. The "world" seldom attempts to realize Godly truth, and following its requirements is most often a mistake from the ultimate truth's (God's) perspective. For, to paraphrase the apostle John's verses 17:11 and 17:16, "You are in the world but not of it." Because of the significance of these verses, we will return to them repeatedly throughout this book.

Notes

1. Carl Gustav Jung, *Man and His Symbols* (New York: Bantam, 1968).
2. Arnold Hauser, *Socijalna Istorija Umetnosti i Knjizevnosti* (Beograd: Kultura, 1966), 46-48.

Chapter 3

Ideas of God's Personality in the Old Testament

According to Adrian Hastings, the God in whom Christians believe cannot be conceived in any way other than that of the Hebrew Scripture, a God who intervened through history, a person who could be addressed as "thou."[1] Nothing is more integral to early Christian orthodoxy. What most absolutely holds the two covenants together is precisely God. Let us now discuss the Old Testament ideas and messages relevant to our topic.

3.1. Foundations of the Judeo-Christian Confession of the Almighty, Eternal, and Ultimate God

Although different groups within the Hebrew tradition (such as the jahwist, elohist, wisdom, or priestly) understood God's personality slightly differently, all agreed and proclaimed that God is the one "before the beginning," therefore, the first, eternal, almighty, and ultimate (as we read in Gen. 1:1-31). According to Isaiah 41:4, 44:6, and 48:12, God is the first and he is the last, God is absolute splendor and glory, he is the LORD. We read in Isaiah 6:1-7:

> In the year that King Uzziah died, I saw the Lord seated on a throne, high and exalted, and the train of his robe filled the temple. Above him were seraphs, each with six wings: With two wings they covered their faces, with two their feet, and with two they were flying. And they

were calling to one another: "Holy, holy, holy is the LORD Almighty;
the whole earth is full of his glory." At the sound of their voices the
doorposts and thresholds shook and the temple was filled with smoke.
"Woe to me!" I cried. "I am ruined! For I am a man of unclean lips,
and I live among a people of unclean lips, and my eyes have seen the
King, the LORD Almighty."

Then one of the seraphs flew to me with a live coal in his hand, which
he had taken with tongs from the altar. With it he touched my mouth
and said, "See, this has touched your lips; your guilt is taken away and
your sin atoned for."

The Lord God is almighty. The whole world is his creation. However, he is not an unapproachable or unknown God and is only very
seldom addressed, as in 1 Kings 18:36-37, simply as "God." More often
he is portrayed as the "merciful God" (as in Isa. 41:10 and 43:3). Perhaps he is most properly and accurately described as the one impossible
to define or compare (as in Isa. 40:25). To know God, according to
Amos 3:2, is possible only by being known to him, or as Fritz Rothschild
(in his introduction to Abraham J. Heschel's book *Between God and
Man*[2]) puts it, "being the object of his love." Even though he is hidden
and awesome, beyond the human ability to grasp his nature, Yahweh
always insists on justice, mercy, and love, and has a special, gentle, and
caring relationship with his people. According to Exodus 3:6, he re-
members Abraham and his successors; he is attentive to the suffering of
the Jews in Egypt (as in Exod.3:7), and is helpful in saving them, according to Exodus 3:8. He is the God of life and holiness; however, he is
also a jealous and a demanding God.

Because the human mind is unable to imagine or grasp the "first and
the last," the almighty, eternal, and ultimate facets of God, the Old Testament uses mostly metaphorical attributes to describe God's personality
(such as the all-annihilating fire in Exod. 3:1-15). All of those metaphors
represent, on one hand, the common foundation of the Judeo-Christian
understanding of God and, on the other, many of the logically substantiated concepts of God formed by philosophers.

However, since we are interested in a more subtle profile of the
ultimately mysterious Almighty, our aim is to probe more intimately into
God's personality. Therefore, let us now discuss a more personal aspect
of the relationship between Yahweh and his people that developed through
the second millennium of Hebrew history. From this relationship we

may deduce some aspects of God's intimate personality and how the almighty, eternal, and ultimate Deity revealed his love through the ensuing centuries.

3.2. Pre-Messianic Hebrew Ideas, Theology, and History

The word "theology" is composed of two Greek terms: *theos* (God) and *logos* (knowledge); thus, theology is a science concerned with the knowledge of God. Around the year 1100 BC, in the early monarchic period of Jewish history, the knowledge of God and the monarchy were interconnected. The Jews, according to John McKenzie, held the idea, more or less in common with the Palestinians and Mesopotamians, that the king was God's chosen one.[3] Nevertheless, this idea of God as the true ruler of Israel can be traced back to much earlier times than the establishment of Israel as a kingdom. The Book of Judges, asserts, for example: "But Gideon told them, 'I will not rule over you, nor will my son rule over you. The LORD will rule over you'." (Judg. 8:23) The First Book of Samuel expresses the same sentiment, "And the LORD told him: 'Listen to all that the people are saying to you; it is not you they have rejected as their king, but me'." (1 Sam. 8:7)

With the establishment of the kingdom, however, the idea of the king representing Yahweh obtained a new momentum. The king, as Fucak noted, had to be the promulgator, the implementer of God's will. Therefore, the real king of the Jews was not the flesh and blood king who sits in Jerusalem. He is only the representative of the true King, Yahweh, the God. Indeed, all the people of Israel are his people, and the intensity of their bond with God remains unequalled by any other group or nation. God is the true king, and the true king is God.[4]

It is quite obvious that, first, if God is the only true lord, then the Jewish people must serve God on earth as the angels and cherubim do in heaven; second, the earthly king should be honored only to the degree to which he carries out the will of God. After all, the king in Jerusalem is also a servant of God. Accordingly, the king may participate in the honor that is due to God, but there are limits, depending on his obedience to Yahweh.

There is another more significant and uniquely distinct idea that Israel maintains for itself. It is that the Israelites, the chosen people, are wholly the possession of God. The Jews differed from their neighbors in the belief that not only the king but the entire nation is God's chosen one. We read in Exodus, "You will be for me the kingdom of priests and a holy nation. These are the words you are to speak to the Israelites." (Exod. 19:6)

But what does this message from God to the Israelites, the holy people, mean? According to Fuèak, since Israel is "holy," meaning dedicated to God, it cannot be servant to any earthly entity nor to the personified entities of this world. Neither are earthly life and existence the sole objectives of this people. The Jewish people serve a different purpose; their main duties are serving God and keeping the Covenant. The Israelites belong to God especially by fulfilling his objectives, ideas, laws, and Covenant, even when these are in opposition to worldly rules, customs, and interests.[5]

What are the concrete implications of such a relationship? Jewish kings had not only the military, administrative, and secular powers that other kings had, but moral powers and obligations as well. The king's prime concern was not to enlarge his domain, but to preserve the purity of faith, to maintain belief in the one God, to reject idol worship, and to keep the Ten Commandments. These obligations seemed more important in the eyes of a religious Jew than the accumulation of worldly wealth, even though they were the sole duty of the kings in the surrounding kingdoms. Because the kings were Yahweh's chosen ones—his envoys— their greatness and effectiveness were measured by how faithfully they carried out their mission. In return for their fidelity to Yahweh, the kings received a promise of Yahweh's mighty and lasting support. The Second Book of Samuel confirms this as follows:

> When your days are over and you rest with your fathers, I will raise up your offspring to succeed you, who will come from your own body, and I will establish his kingdom. He is the one who will build a house for my Name, and I will establish the throne of his kingdom forever. I will be his father, and he will be my son. When he does wrong, I will punish him with the rod of men, with floggings inflicted by men. But my love will never be taken away from him, as I took it away from Saul, whom I removed from before you. Your house and your kingdom will endure forever before me; your throne will be established forever. (2 Sam. 7:12-16)

In summary, the duty of the Jewish king and all of his people, the chosen ones, was to emulate, witness to, and glorify Yahweh and the ethical and spiritual requirements that reflect God's personal characteristics.

The Jews had truly great kings between 1000 and 900 BC. The greatness of David and Solomon, for instance, was not due to greed, but to their being exemplary envoys and committed servants of God. Their successors to the throne should have followed in their footsteps. However, being imperfect as all humans are, Jewish kings did not always live up to the expectations of them laid out in the Old Testament.

Greed, selfishness, and hunger for power grew during the ensuing centuries. The kings did not strive to serve only Yahweh but also pursued worldly powers, alliances, and politics. Tension increased between rules set in the spirit of the Ten Commandments and rules necessitated by the spirit of politics. Social differences, injustices, and tension grew among the people. Assassinations of kings and betrayals became more frequent, and faithfulness to Yahweh ceased as well.

From the Bible we know that Yahweh, through his prophets, warned that political interests were being given a higher priority than the Covenant with God and that however important political principles were, they had to be placed second to morality, faith, and loyalty to God. These warnings proved fruitless, and the difference between royal authority based on morality and that based on greed became more pronounced. God's punishment did not take long to come. Religious Jews understood that the destruction of Jerusalem, the downfall of its kings, and the exile to Babylon were punishments from God. They afflicted the entire people, whom the unfaithful kings had led into ruin. As Jeremiah wrote: "The shepherds are senseless and do not inquire of the LORD; so they do not prosper and their flock is scattered." (Jer. 10:21)

The theocratic monarchy did not keep the faith entrusted to it. Paradoxically, its downfall did not destroy trust in Yahweh. Rather, the Babylonian captivity gave the Jews "time to re-think." These events opened their eyes. After the fall of the monarchy, the prophets returned to old, pre-monarchical ideals, and expectation of the Messiah, a new and true Savior, gained momentum.

According to Fucak, the Hebrew word "Messiah" means "anointed."6 Therefore, the word "Messiah" in the Hebrew language means the same as the Greek word "Christ." Originally, to be anointed was the king's privilege. For the Jews this was a symbol of the spirit descending on the anointed king, and by this act the king became worthy of the mission which he carried out to represent God on earth. He became Yahweh's anointed one and thus, through him and by him, Yahweh acted in this world. However, from that time on, it was not the ruling king but the coming of the Messiah that became one of the authoritative endorsements which inspired the piety and longing for the coming of God to his people. Furthermore, Christ revealed much more of God's personal characteristics than all of the authors of the Old Testament combined, because he was not only a real king, but also the real God.

Next, let us focus on God's even more prominent, concrete personal characteristics, connected to people's expectations of a Messiah in the last centuries before Christ and at the time of his birth. The expectations of the Messiah are the fulfillment of a long process spanning many centuries, and the end result of the progression of the divine revelation that, according to Christian perspective, culminated in and was fulfilled by Jesus Christ's incarnation.

3.3. Messianic Prophecies and Expectations

After the tragedy of 587 BC, the Jews in Babylon were faced with a difficult problem: How could the monarchy have fallen when Yahweh had promised that the House of David would never cease? It was Zerubbabel's hope (despite the prophesies of Zech. 6:9-14) that the dynasty could still be revived. However, another glorious king did not establish a new dynasty, and it became quite obvious that the dynasty would never be re-established.

Still, according to McKenzie, it was unimaginable for the prophets that Yahweh would not keep his word, that the prophecies would remain only empty promises. At this time, many religious Jews, in response to the fallen dynasties, turned their attention to a Messiah, someone who would be descended from the House of David, someone who would bring the promised deliverance of well-being and renewal to Israel.[7] The uncertainty was tormenting and the questions numerous. Who would this person be? How would it be known that this person was the Messiah? When would the Messiah come?

The prophecies of Isaiah and Daniel helped answer these questions. The prophecies of Isaiah began between 546 and 539 BC, the latter being the year Babylon fell. One of Isaiah's prophecies states, "Here is my servant, whom I uphold, my chosen one in whom I delight; I will put my spirit on him and he will bring justice to the nations." (Isa. 42:1)

Isaiah's answer to the nature of the Messiah's mission, is "to open the eyes that are blind, to free captives from prison and to release from the dungeon those who sit in darkness." (Isa. 42:7) In Isaiah, the fate of this person, and the way in which these events will be realized, is described in this way, "I offered my back to those who beat me, my cheeks to those who pulled out my beard; I did not hide my face from mocking and spitting." (Isa. 50:6)

Finally, Isaiah addresses the matter of whether this person will be successful in conquering his enemies: "Because the Sovereign LORD helps me, I will not be disgraced. Therefore, have I set my face like flint, and I know I will not be put to shame." (Isa. 50:7) Isaiah then brings the entire prophecy together.

> Therefore I will give him a portion among the great, and he will divide the spoils with the strong, because he poured out his life unto death, and was numbered with the transgressors. For he bore the sins of many, and made intercession for the transgressors. (Isa. 53:12)

Based on these few verses we cannot reconstruct exactly what kind of person this future Messiah would be. However, the fact is that a completely new type of Messiah is depicted, about whom it is said that he will be a servant and savior. This was in complete contrast to previous ideas of the Messiah—the glorious kings who most Jews expected would make them into a powerful nation that would be victorious over all their enemies. Obviously, the kingdom of God that such a Messiah would represent would be quite unlike the one based on the image of the return of the glorious kings. Many Jews did not want to accept such a Messiah, and Isaiah's greatness is, in part, that despite the fact that his vision was so unlike the one most Jews had, he saw it and dared to proclaim it. History unfolded as he foresaw. The Messiah was not a Jewish king, yet was more powerful than any earthly ruler in witnessing to God's personality.

Isaiah foresaw that the Messiah would be merciful and have a forgiving heart (Matthew would testify to this later in 11:29). He foresaw that he would come to serve and would be humbled, that he would show, through his very life, what the kingdom of God is truly like. (Luke writes about this in 22:27.) Isaiah foresaw also that the Messiah would be a king, a teacher, and a lord of the New Kingdom. (Luke 22:37)

The most surprising fact that Isaiah foresaw was that the Messiah would be persecuted and tortured, but would get a "portion among the great" again. Luke re-affirms this in 18:31-33. Would it not be bewildering to someone who does not believe in divine revelation that Isaiah saw all this ever so clearly, and furthermore, wrote about it 500 years before the birth of Christ? Moreover, take note that Isaiah wrote his prophecies in a completely strange environment that was awaiting a Messiah entirely different from the one he described.

The other prophet whose teachings we will discuss briefly is Daniel. Understanding the writings of Daniel is difficult, not only because he wrote partly in Hebrew and partly in Aramaic (a Palestinian language), but also because of his abundant and copious use of Greek idioms. It is not easy to pinpoint Daniel's exact place and time in Jewish religious history. Daniel himself mentions very little about the times in which he lived, so one can learn little about his period by studying his writings. According to Norman Geisler, conservative scholars have maintained that Daniel wrote in the sixth century. However, today it is thought by many critical scholars that he lived at the time of Antiochus IV Epiphanes, the Seleucid king who fought against the Maccabees and reigned between 175 and 163 BC. According to Geisler, "The book of Daniel contains an incredible amount of detailed predictive prophecy."[8] In parts of Daniel's second book (following verse 12 of chapter 6) the author writes about the future events that signify the "near end" or the time of the coming of the kingdom of God. These events and times are near to the coming of the Messiah. In allegory, Daniel explains that Yahweh will wipe off the face of the earth four great kingdoms—Babylon, Medea, Persia, and Greece—as well as the king from whom all evil comes (Antiochus IV Epiphanes). After this event will come the Messiah, whose mission will be to establish the kingdom of God on earth.

What sort of person did Daniel predict this future Messiah to be? His prophecies indicated that after the punishment of Antiochus IV Epiphanes there would appear someone who would be the "son of man." According to Fucak, in those days, the expression "son of man" was common in the Aramaic language and meant man in the general sense.[9] Therefore, the Messiah will be a man. But Daniel does not mean just any kind of man. Indeed, he asserts that God will give this son of man all possible power and glory." He writes:

> In my vision at night I looked, and there before me was one like a son of man, coming on the clouds of heaven. He approached the Ancient of Days and was led into his presence. He was given authority, glory, and sovereign power; all peoples, nations and men of every language worshipped him. His dominion is an everlasting dominion that will not

pass away, and his kingdom is one that will never be destroyed. (Daniel 7:13-14)

Humankind has always been interested in how the future would turn out. It seems that this wonder about the unknown stems from an ancient lesson, namely, that outside events—more powerful than we and therefore veiled in mystery—determine our lives. The coming of the Messiah is one such example. There never was a more significant event for all of humanity than the one Daniel foresaw. Never before did any one event burst into our world so radically as at the coming of the Son of Man. For the Son of Man, while being a man like us, is simultaneously God—totally different from us, or from what we know. Through Him the divine, or the "completely distinct" as philosophers have termed it, broke into our world. This is, and will forever be, the most significant event in the course of history.

Such an event was totally unknown to the Jewish tradition of that day. It seemed implausible that the son of man, a flesh and blood person, could come to earth "on the clouds of heaven." In Hebrew usage, "coming on heavenly clouds" was indicative of God; only God had the ability to travel on heavenly clouds. The future Messiah, therefore, was to be true man and true God at the same time.

Daniel foresaw interesting details about the mysterious mission and objectives of this Messiah. His objective would be to deal a deathblow to sin and death on behalf of humankind. This is a profound perception, the meaning of which can be understood only in light of the New Testament.

If we were not Christians, it would be difficult for us now to find an acceptable explanation for the event that was to happen. It would be difficult to understand the mystery that a true man who would also be God's anointed—in fact God Himself—was to be born in the person of the Messiah. It becomes quite obvious, as we read the prophecies of the Old Testament, that prophets like Isaiah and Daniel were the principal foreseers of the amazing events that would unfold. However, other prophets had something to say about the Messiah as well.

3.4. Some Other Messianic Prophecies

In the Book of Micah, we find more information about the Messiah, as in the following verse: "One who breaks open the way will go up before them; they will break through the gate and go out. Their king will pass through before them, the LORD at their head." (Mic. 2:13)

Zechariah also mentions some distinct characteristics of the Savior:

I will bend Judah as I bend my bow, I will fit it with Ephraim. I will
rouse your sons, O Zion, against your sons, O Greece, and make you
as a warrior's sword. The Lord shall appear over them; his arrow will
flash as lightning; the Sovereign Lord will sound the trumpet; he will
march in the storms of the south. The Lord Almighty will shield them.
They will destroy and overcome with sling stones. They will drink and
roar as with wine; they will be full like a bowl used for sprinkling the
corners of the altar. The Lord their God, will save them on that day,
as the flock of his people. They will sparkle in his land like jewels in
his crown. How attractive and beautiful they will be! Grain will make
the young man thrive, and new wine the young women! (Zech. 9:13-17)

Later, Zechariah goes on:

This is the plague with which the Lord will strike all the nations that
fought against Jerusalem: Their flesh shall rot while they are still standing on their feet, and their eyes will rot in their sockets, and their
tongues will rot in their mouths. On that day men will be stricken by
the Lord with great panic. Each man shall seize the hand of another,
and they will attack each other. Judah too will fight at Jerusalem. The
wealth of all the surrounding nations will be collected—great quanti-
ties of gold, silver and clothing. A similar plague will strike the horses
and mules, the camel and donkeys, and all the animals in those camps.
Then the survivors from all the nations that have attacked Jerusalem
will go year after year to worship the King, the Lord Almighty, and to
celebrate the feast of Tabernacles. If any of the peoples of the earth do
not go up to Jerusalem to worship the King, the Lord Almighty, they
will have no rain. (Zech. 14:12-17)

As Fucak noted, many Jews at the time of Jesus' birth tragically
misunderstood Micah's and Zechariah's words. Christ is indeed the great
King, Lord, and Deliverer of his people. But, although Jesus defeated
the greatest enemies of Israel—sin and death—the prophecies of Zechariah
and Micah should not have been interpreted as many contemporary Jews
interpreted them: that Yahweh will come and He will pass through this
world as a revengeful warrior at the head of his people, annihilating all
the enemies of Israel and making all those who tormented the Jews their
captives and slaves.[10]

The first step in understanding a Biblical message is to understand its *genus literarum*, roughly translated from the Latin as its "literal sense." If the text is in prose, then it may usually be understood literally. In poetry, which uses metaphors—words or phrases used to express something other than what they mean—the interpreter should search for a poetic meaning. But in an allegory, which uses a surface story to express an abstract, underlying meaning, only discerning this deeper meaning helps to understand the true message.

If we know the original Jewish ethos, we see that Micah and Zechariah predicted a defeat that would decimate the Messiah's enemies. Zechariah portrayed the glorious triumph of the coming Messiah over all his enemies and his rule over all peoples. He made clear neither where nor how his predictions would come to pass, nor the exact time of the fulfillment of his prophesies. However, if interpreted literally, not allegorically as they ought to be, these and similar writings were more agreeable for many Jews of that time than the unpopular prophecies about the coming of a suffering, humble Messiah. It is more appealing to human nature to take part in a victorious march than to accept the humble, forgiving Messiah. This is true especially for the Jews of that time, who did not comprehend that God's personality is different from their expectations, that his grace is much greater than a triumphant, euphoric enthusiasm such as is found in petty earthly kingdoms. When the Messiah did come, he brought about the realization of another kind of kingdom, the kingdom of God on earth, a different, much more prominent kind of fulfillment of Micah's and Zechariah's prophecies than many Jews understood and hoped for.

The triumph, for which many Jews longed, never came to pass. However, a completely different triumph and victory over estrangement from God, sin and death—the true enemies of Israel and all of humanity—did occur with the appearance of Christ. Still, many Jews could not comprehend that more had taken place than they expected, just as they did not comprehend (though this is still not easy to understand) that the prophecies of Isaiah and Daniel were much greater and more meaningful in revealing God's true personality than many interpretations of the prophecies of Micah and Zechariah by contemporary Jews.

3.5. The Distinction between
True and False Prophets

In general, true prophecies were never popular, nor commonly understood or accepted by the Jewish people in quite the same way we understand and accept them in our time. How did the ancient Jews make a distinction between a "true" and a "false" prophet?

This can be demonstrated with an anecdote: The false prophet would introduce himself at exactly noon by standing on the main square. In a sonorous voice, he would say, "Listen, people! It is exactly noon now, the sun is at its zenith." In contrast, the true prophet would stand in the square and say, "Listen, people! It is exactly midnight; it is completely dark around us now." Those nearby would be appalled and say, "Away with him, he is lying. What he says is not true. He does not know what he is saying."

Why is it that the one who speaks fallacy is considered the "true" prophet, and vice versa? The false prophet did not share anything new. He just loudly expressed what was already known—this is why he is not a true prophet. In fact, he is not a prophet at all. Meanwhile, the true prophet stated things that no one accepted or knew. However, some ten, a hundred, or five hundred years later, we might discover that (as in the case of Isaiah and Daniel) he was right. It was truly "midnight" at that time of Isaiah's and Daniel's prophesying about the coming Messiah and their contemporaries were truly surrounded by spiritual darkness. But how did the prophets know about the coming Messiah? It would be difficult to give an answer to this without acknowledging divine inspiration.

Let us summarize what the Old Testament revealed about God's personality. God is the almighty creator of heaven and earth, "the first and the last," the ultimate and eternal. However, he is also a compassionate, merciful, "person," willing to serve, endure suffering, persecution, and torture for the sake of all of humanity. And yet he is the Lord, having "a portion among the great," descending to earth "on clouds of heaven" in full glory. These attributes, from a human perspective, were very contradictory, but were confirmed nonetheless by Jesus' work and ministry, as well as by the still-unbroken union between Christians and Christ himself.

Notes

1. Adrian Hastings, "Schism," in *The Oxford Companion to Christian Thought*, ed. Adrian Hastings, Alistair Mason, and Hugh Pyper (New York: Oxford University Press, 2000), 643.

2. Abraham J. Heschel, *Between God and Man* (New York: The Free Press, 1959), 24.

3. John L. McKenzie, "Biblical Theology of the Old Testament" in *The Jerome Biblical Commentary*, ed. R. E. Brown, J. J. Castelot, J. L. McKenzie el al. (Englewood Cliffs, NJ: Prentice Hall), 175, 180, and 215.

4. Marijan Jerko Fucak, *Biblijska Teologija Novog Aavjeta* (Zagreb: Unpublished Presentations at the Institut Za Teolosku Kulturu Laika, 1986).

5. Fucak, *Biblijska Teologija.*

6. Marijan Jerko Fucak, *Dogadjaj Isus Krist* (Zagreb: Institut Za Teolosku Kulturu Laika, 1989), 21.

7. McKenzie, *Biblical Theology*, 216.

8. Geisler, L. Norman, *Baker Encyclopedia of Christian Apologetics.* (Grand Rapids, MI: Baker Books, 2000), 178-180.

9. Fucak, *Dogadjaj Isuskrist*, 59.

10. Fucak, *Biblijska Teologija.*

Chapter 4

The Personality of God as Revealed by Jesus Christ

In Mark 11:27 we read, "No one knows the Son except the Father, and no one knows the Father except the Son and those to whom the Son chooses to reveal him." There are pragmatic and commercial images that modern Christian culture promotes around Christmas time, as well as abstract, merely theoretical or philosophical concepts of God. However, if we want a personal, intimate relationship with him, then the only way to "know" God personally is with the help of his son Jesus Christ and by belonging to his body—the church. For us there is no other way to know God except by Jesus' revelation and his gift of faith.

In this chapter, we will focus on those characteristics that are relevant to our topic—those characteristics of Jesus' and God's personality that are "empirical," that is, experienced by believers. Our focus will be on two of God's personality traits that appear mutually exclusive from a human perspective: Jesus' extreme humility and his ultimate glory. Can we even conceptualize these characteristics as unified and part of one being?

First, before we observe how these seemingly incommensurable personality traits are realized through Jesus' ministry, let us examine the meaning behind the idea of "the kingdom of God."

4.1. Difficulties in Understanding the Expression "Kingdom of God"

Even a superficial reading of the Bible makes it obvious that Jesus seldom speaks of himself; rather, he focuses on "God's kingdom." It is not easy to agree on the meaning of this New Testament expression. The Bible uses "kingdom of God," in many places, but nowhere does it define its exact meaning in a precise and unmistakable way.

Could it be that Christ deliberately avoided explaining exactly what he meant by this phrase? If we want an answer, it is best to begin with the Bible itself, examining statements made in connection with the kingdom of God, and the King of the kingdom—Christ. Even after a quick reading of the Bible, according to Stanley and Brown (in *The Jerome Biblical Commentary*), we can ascertain that the idea of the kingdom of God is one of the main themes discussed.[1] It is found 14 times in Mark, 3 times in Matthew, and 31 times in Luke. (Luke was writing to Jewish Christians and for them the phrase was more significant than for Gentile Christians.)

Based on these numbers, it is easy to recognize that the heavenly kingdom was one of Christ's favorite topics, the center of his teaching from the very beginning of his ministry. In fact, Mark begins his gospel with this theme. Immediately after recording John the Baptist's imprisonment, Mark continues as follows: "Jesus went into Galilee, proclaiming the good news of God, 'The time has come,' he said. 'The kingdom of God is near! Repent and believe the good news!'" (Mark 1:14-15)

Fucak quotes Wolfgang Knorzer, an expert in Bible study, who points out that we find these very words not only in Mark but also in Matthew at least twice.[2] In the first instance, Matthew testifies, "Jesus went throughout Galilee, teaching in their synagogues, preaching the good news of the kingdom, and healing every disease and sickness among the people." (Matt. 4:23) His second reference reads, "Jesus went through all the towns and villages, teaching in their synagogues, preaching the good news of the kingdom and healing every disease and sickness." (Matt. 9:35)

According to the same author, words are rarely repeated in the Gospel. Such repetition is not accidental; rather, it indicates what is of prime importance in Christ's message. Yet, despite all of Christ's teaching, preaching, and healing, despite his fight against sin, sickness, and evil, our primary difficulty is our inability to comprehend precisely the idea of

God's kingdom, and subsequently the personality of its king: Jesus Christ. Nowhere are we given its exact description or analysis. Nowhere can we find an explanation that would satisfy our discursive thinking. We need to recognize that Christ did not submit his sermons to any logical analysis, but instead let the accumulation of his parables tell us the essence of his spiritual teachings.

We may wonder why Jesus chose to teach in this manner. Apart from Jesus' speaking a contemporary Hebrew vernacular strange to our Western way of thinking, part of the answer lies in the fact that not theory but experience is important in "knowing" Jesus, the king of God's kingdom, and "knowing" the triune God as well. Therefore, Jesus spoke about God's (his father's) and his own Godly personality, not explicitly and clearly, not as in a good owner's manual. Rather, Jesus gave comparisons, examples, or parables.

We humans are unable to grasp God's "psychological and theological profile" in the way we would a blueprint or mathematical equation. The information God gave us is quite different from anything humans experience or can visualize using everyday logic. As a consequence, to know God personally (as much as is possible for humans) excludes taking a rational shortcut as do agnostic philosophers, who pay no attention to Jesus' biblical self-revelation. We are not searching for God as conceptualized by those philosophers, but for a biblical God. Consequently, we will follow Jesus' examples, parables, and explanations as he reveals himself in Scripture.

4.2. A Brief History of Jesus' Ministry

A quick look at the history of Jesus' ministry will highlight some of his revelation of God's person. According to Mark, immediately after Christ announces that the kingdom of God is near at hand he makes another important announcement. He proclaims himself as the "Son of Man."

Read in the light of the prophet Daniel (7:13-14), this is an extremely important messianic proclamation. Christ proclaims himself as the promised Messiah! This is then followed by his baptism. Then after forty days in the desert, Christ begins to preach in the synagogue about the good news of the kingdom of God and heals the sick and afflicted who are brought to him.

According to Mark (1:9-21, 23, 28, and 3:1), Jesus first began teaching in synagogues, but shortly thereafter moved to the Sea of Galilee, where he became very popular. Then, suddenly, he withdrew from the region of Galilee and went to the northwest frontier, Caesarea, where, again according to Mark (8:27-30), he began to teach his disciples about crucial matters. He started to instruct them about the future. He told them that the Messiah would suffer a great deal and would be punished for the sins of others, all in accordance with the prophecies in the Old Testament. His disciples did not fully comprehend him.

According to Mark (9:2), a wonderful transfiguration took place six days after this teaching, after which Jesus started his journey toward his mission's final location: Jerusalem. (Mark 10:32-33) This is where Christ was arrested and judged, and, finally, where he suffered his death on the cross. However, as his disciples affirmed, three days later he was resurrected. He appeared to them and continued encouraging and teaching them.

What can we observe from this scenario? According to Fucak, in Jesus' ministry we can see a purposeful activity which progressed according to a plan, but which can be seen as significant only by observing it from afar.[3] First we see Christ introducing himself as the "Son of Man," the promised Messiah, which is confirmed at his baptism. Then, we see Christ begin his work, first in Galilee where he performed pleasant, desirable deeds such as curing, teaching, and preaching, all of which were expected of a Messiah and made him popular quickly.

The next phase of Christ's career occurred outside of Galilee, where he did not achieve the same degree of popularity. Moreover, he did not receive complete understanding even from his disciples. This is not surprising, since he now spoke about another aspect of the kingdom of God, about which no one wanted to hear. He spoke of the suffering and injustices that would befall the "Son of Man."

His disciples rebelled because they did not understand him. The mystery for them began with the recognition that the kingdom of God, and an essential characteristic of God's personality, consist not only of healing, forgiveness of sins, and teaching. They did not yet understand that the fundamental characteristics of God include something much bigger: the acceptance of suffering for others, the sacrifice of self for the sins of others. Naturally, the populace as well as Jesus' disciples hesitated to accept such a Messiah, since they knew that the same virtues were expected of them if this really was the kingdom of God.

Next in the scenario comes the most agonizing stage—the unjust condemnation of Christ, his silent suffering, and his death on the cross. All of these serve as examples to his followers through all ages. This is when Christ, the King of God's kingdom, was most gravely despised, most unjustly accused, and most cruelly condemned. However, this was part of the realization of the kingdom of God.

Then comes the final stage: the Resurrection, the Ascension, the highest level of attainable and describable glory. This, too, is a part of the fulfillment of the kingdom of God and a reflection of the characteristics of God.

We can try to analyze in detail some of the typical references in order to formulate a consensus about the properties of the kingdom of God. However, first let us try to define who the revealer of God's kingdom is. This may shed further light on the question of what God is like.

4.3. Who is Jesus Christ, the Revealer of God's Personality?

As Fucak notes, to find an answer to this question, we should stop at the first essential attestation—the voice of God himself as recorded by Mark: "You are my son, whom I love; with you I am well pleased."[4] (Mark 1:11) We can find similar words in Psalm 2:7, where they are spoken in relation to a different event—the coronation of the Jewish king. In a third instance, we find a similar message spoken some five hundred years earlier by the prophet Isaiah (42:1), though in yet a different context. Here the words refer to the servant of Yahweh. As we have said, the repetition of phrases in the Bible always expresses something very important. In this case, it means that God's son is identical to the real King of Israel, who is in turn identical with Yahweh's servant.

Now, another question arises: Why was the descent of the Holy Spirit so important? First Isaiah (6:1), then Luke (4:18) wrote about this descent as an exceptionally important event. It was also an important event during the coronation of kings. The presence of the Holy Spirit signifies the presence of God. This implies that God will work through that person, that he will be present through her or him. Thus, in all three—the Jewish kings, the servant of Yahweh, and the beloved son—God is present in a particular and unique way.

To contemporary Christian culture, all this seems self-evident. However, it was not so clear nearly two thousand years ago when the great majority of people awaited, and would have liked, a completely different Messiah from the one Christ turned out to be. Let us consider another quotation from Mark that is important to our understanding of the person of Jesus: "The time has come," he said. "The kingdom of God is near. Repent and believe the good news!" (Mark 1:15)

Again, according to Fucak, the person who hears these words must urgently decide whether he or she will recognize this important and decisive moment in his or her life. What is this moment? If we refer back five hundred years earlier, when Isaiah was active, we read: "How beautiful on the mountains are the feet of those who bring good news, who proclaim peace, who bring good tidings, who proclaim salvation, who say to Zion, 'Your God reigns!'" (Isa. 52:7)

People witnessing these events must recognize and accept that these promised foretold events have now come to pass. God himself, during the time of Tiberius Augustus, stood at the head of his people and now something truly new would begin: the kingdom of God. God's presence among his people had now begun in the person of Jesus Christ.

Undoubtedly, this present realm (the existing kingdom of God) is quite unlike the one which so many were eagerly envisioning. God is unlike their dreams. The Messiah who would enslave the enemy did not appear; nevertheless, a triumphal period in human history ensued. In the two thousand years of human history since that time, a new ethos has arisen—an ethos that expresses simultaneously both the humility of Isaiah and Daniel and also the triumphant imagination in Zechariah and Micah. These prophets declared that by being humble, loving, forgiving, patient, and self-sacrificing, the Messiah would become triumphant and victorious in this world. Two characteristics are united in the person of Jesus: the exceedingly humble and the exceedingly glorious; such is God's personality as well.

Many Jews could not comprehend that the greatness of God is manifested precisely through humility and by the willingness to suffer for the sake of others. These concepts are incomprehensibly greater than, and separate from, what the average person can grasp. However, if we really want to know God, then we need to cast away a considerable part of our rationale, which was shaped by our social environment.

4.4. Jesus' Revelation of God's Person in Galilee

Fucak notes that it may seem at first glance that Jesus' work in Galilee was the most successful phase of his career.[5] It was during this time that he was most popular and his life least problematic. At that time, it must have looked as if the kingdom of God had started off exactly as it should have. This was the time when, unexpectedly, his enthusiastic followers wanted to proclaim him king—so much so that, as John relates in 6:15, the Messiah had to hide. He did not want to be a king. He was one already!

However, according the same author, if we study this Galilean period more, we find it was not a "Sabbath time of leisure" for the Messiah, but throughout we notice something other than the popularity of Jesus. It was filled with working against, fighting against sin and evil. It was in Galilee that Christ fought his first great battle for his kingdom. He had just begun to fulfill his mission, as Luke explains, "The Spirit of the Lord is on me, because He has anointed me to preach the good news to the poor. He has sent me to proclaim freedom for the prisoners and recovery of sight for the blind, to release the oppressed."(Luke 4:18)

This was not an ideal period to preach to an enthusiastic crowd, but part of God's kingdom also includes persistent, strenuous fighting against sin and the power of the devil. The whole Galilean period of Jesus' ministry was a struggle against sin, evil, and the power of Satan. This fact also comes through in the writings of Luke, "You will be betrayed by parents, brothers, relatives, and friends, and they will put some of you to death. All men will hate you because of me. But not a hair of your head will perish." (Luke 21:16-18)

Another significant aspect of the seriousness of this period was that no one could be neutral in the fight. The outcome meant either escaping or being burdened and trapped by the predicament that, "whoever is not with me is against me." This period was difficult and exhausting, not only for Christ, but also for the people of Galilee. It was not easy for them to listen to their teacher and do what he asked. It was a time of difficult decision-making, which involved not only them, but all of humankind. No one could remain completely neutral. Challenges such as this are typical of God's personality. Luke reported Jesus' stance regarding this dilemma as follows:

> I have come to bring fire on the earth, and how I wish it were already kindled! But I have a baptism to undergo, and how distressed I am until it is completed! Do you think I came to bring peace on earth? No. I tell you, but division. From now on there will be five in one family divided against each other, three against two and two against three. They will be divided, father against son and son against father, mother against daughter and daughter against mother, mother-in-law against

daughter-in-law and daughter-in-law against mother-in-law. (Luke
12:49-53)

Luke shows Jesus using ordinary events to emphasize the importance
of this decision.

He said to the crowd, "When you see a cloud rising in the west, immediately you say, 'It's going to rain,' and it does. And when the south
wind blows, you say, 'It's going to be hot,' and it is. Hypocrites! You
know how to interpret the appearance of the earth and the sky. How is
it that you don't know how to interpret this present time? Why don't
you judge for yourselves what is right? As you are going with your
adversary to the magistrate, try hard to be reconciled to him on the
way, or he may drag you off to the judge, and the judge turn you over
to the officer, and the officer throw you into prison. I tell you, you
will not get out until you have paid the last penny." (Luke 12:49-59)

We find many similar passages in the synoptic gospels (Luke 9:60,
62; 17:21; Matt. 11:13; John 3:8). Undoubtedly, it was during that time
that the Son of God showed that he was able to conquer Satan—paradoxically, by his love for people. Most of these events took place in Galilee
during the glorious days in the life of Jesus. This hard-working, serving,
calling, teaching behavior is an important aspect of God's personality.

4.5. Jesus' Revelation of God's
Person Outside of Galilee

As Fucak observed, Jesus disappeared from Galilee unexpectedly in the
midst of triumph, and in the northwest region of the country he began a
new period in the history of the kingdom of God. We may regard this
time as the preparation period.[6] It was there that Jesus prepared his disciples for the final combat for the kingdom of God. It was there that
Jesus tested and probed his disciples as to whether they understood who
he really was, what the implications of his identity were, and what kind
of life awaited those who wanted to live in the kingdom of God. The
disciples had to know that they were destined to follow in the footsteps of
the Master. According to Mark (8:27-31), this period of preparation
began when Jesus and his disciples left Caesarea Philippi and he began to
ask his disciples, "Who do people say I am?" The disciples told him that
differing opinions had circulated among the people about him. Jesus asked

them directly, "Who do you say I am?" It was Peter who declared, "You are the Christ—you are the long-expected Messiah!"

This was the correct answer, but it was followed by many consequences. When discussing Jesus' teachings, Mark revealed probably the most important characteristics of God's personality: "He then began to teach them that the Son of Man must suffer many things and be rejected by the elders, chief priests and teachers of the law, and that He must be killed and after three days, rise again." (8:31) Here again Christ called himself the "Son of Man" who had been foretold by Daniel (7:13-14), and he reminded the disciples of the meaning of that title. The title does not refer to just any man, but to one particular man who has a special mission, one who will gain all the power and glory from God and who will be the judge over the world. And here Christ identified with this man. Therefore, his glory would be the greatest imaginable. However, suffering and humiliation would also be his, including torture and death on the cross.

The disciples could not imagine that Christ would die under such ignominious circumstances. For many of them it seemed that people neither needed nor wanted to be followers of such a Messiah. Nevertheless, this is the only way to the kingdom of God, and thus Christ's answer to many was: "If anyone would come after me, he must deny himself and take up his cross and follow Me." (Mark 8:34) Naturally, this disturbed the apostles who were awaiting a triumphal Messiah. Their fear was completely understandable. We ourselves would feel similar fear and confusion under these circumstances. Christ also understood this because in addition to being God, he was also a man.

Why was it necessary for the Messiah to suffer and die? Could he not have fulfilled his mission in some other way? According to Fucak's explanation, Jesus might have explained his mission and destiny to Peter as follows:

All of you, and you, too, Peter, find it difficult to visualize the image of a suffering Messiah, yet this is exactly how the kingdom of God will be realized on earth. The reason for this is that, although I am God's anointed, although I am the King of Israel, the true King, at the same time I am also the servant, the suffering servant, of Yahweh. There is no other way that leads to the kingdom of God. My divinity is not in conflict with showing others how to take on the sins of others and how to suffer for their sake. It is not in conflict with showing them what life is like in the kingdom of God. Surely, this is the essence: to love our fellow human beings in such a way that we are willing to suffer for them, and even give our lives willingly for them, in order to lead them into the kingdom of God.[7]

This passage condenses what Jesus may have said to his apostles in the conversation Mark alludes to in 8:34. It was obvious to Christ that, even after such an explanation, it was not easy for his hearers to bind their own lives to his and follow him. Possibly our own present-day reluctance to follow Christ is caused by this very same fear of the inconvenience and sacrifice that inevitably accompany serving God. Although Christ understands our fear, he likely does not approve our passivity. Surely it is obvious that he, too, was afraid.

Six days later, as Luke relates, another event took place that seems inexplicable at first glance.

As he was praying, the appearance of his face changed, and his clothes became as bright as a flash of lightening. Two men, Moses and Elijah, appeared in glorious splendor, talking with Jesus. They spoke about his departure, which he was about to bring to fulfillment at Jerusalem. (Luke 9:29-31)

This was followed by the same voice that spoke at the Baptism of Jesus at the River Jordan: "A voice came from the cloud, saying, 'This is my Son, whom I have chosen; listen to him.'" (Luke 9:35)

God's intervention at the outset of Jesus' ministry, his testimony that he is the Christ and that what he says is the truth is repeated: Christ is declared again as the Son of God. Maybe now we can better understand the ministry of Christ, his mystery, his divine power, and human strength, all of which even suffering and the certainty of death could not break. Christ's persistence was greater than his fear of death because through it he could become the example and Savior of humankind and the messenger of the kingdom of God. Such persistence is one of God's essential characteristics due to his never-ending love for humanity.

Jesus' (and God's) strength and power are rooted not only in his status as almighty creator and sustainer of everything existing, nor in glory or triumphal expectations, although these also express the power of God. Jesus' power and strength also lie in the fact that no suffering or threats discouraged him from doing good for humankind, bearing witness to the kingdom of God, and fighting for the spiritual salvation of all people. Perhaps this is the greatest strength and benevolence of God, and herein lies the difference between the kingdom of God and the reality of our earthly world. It was always difficult for humans to accept and identify themselves with the dichotomy of an almighty, but at the same time tender, God. Nonetheless, this dichotomy exists in God.

4.6. The Last Supper

Based on Mark's description (14:22-25), we can easily reconstruct the final days of Christ before his passion. Jesus appears unassuming as he proceeds into Jerusalem riding on a donkey. Yet the people welcome him in exultation. Soon thereafter, he clears the temple and is anointed by a woman whose name we do not know. This is how the days passed until about Wednesday or Thursday, when the Jews were preparing to celebrate the Feast of Passover, their exodus from Egypt. (Exod. 12:21-27) They were celebrating the covenant God made with Moses while Jesus and his little band of disciples prepared to celebrate the making of a new covenant. The last supper for us means a turning point, the inauguration of a new covenant that, as Mark points out, is now nearing its culmination and could be summarized as follows: "For even the Son of Man did not come to be served, but to serve, and to give His life as a ransom for many." (Mark 10:45)

Now Christ made a new covenant with the people of God. It is not easy to understand the meaning of this new covenant. Christ talked about his body and blood. It is difficult to understand these symbols, even if we already know that through them Christ has shown us his very own self-sacrifice. By the very act of the last supper, the New Covenant was inaugurated, and the disciples came to experience the inexplicable and unimaginable, yet real, nearness of Christ.

Jesus used symbols to make visible his mysterious presence. He was probably aware that the most important messages we receive we are ultimately unable to describe or define exactly. We use visible symbols to express important invisible meanings. For example, flying a flag is a sign of patriotism, love of one's country, one's willingness to make sacrifices for it. Wearing a ring is a symbol of love, attachment, fidelity, and similar emotions and commitments which cannot be easily and simply defined. Through symbols, a particular message is communicated to people already trained and conditioned by culture to understand it, even though it is impossible for them to pinpoint the exact meaning of the message.

According to Aldo Staric we use three types of symbols:

1. "Signs," which loosely represent the "reality beyond," but
   are the same for everyone. For example, traffic signs are
   symbols set by a collective consensus and therefore are
   changeable.
2. So-called "real symbols," which are part of the reality they
   represent. They are not arbitrarily established and, therefore, not changeable. For example, smoke as a symbol of
   fire.
3. Sacraments, which are visible signs (like bread and wine)
   that are not conventional or natural, but established by Jesus.
   These visible symbols are used by the resurrected Jesus to
   make possible a meeting between living humans and his transcendental reality. Of course, a meeting with Jesus, if we
   will experience it as he intended, is dependent on our being
   prepared to understand him beyond these symbols.[8]

Why did Jesus choose bread and wine as signs of his presence? We
do not know. However, we associate eating bread with the sustenance of
life, and drinking wine with experiencing happiness. Eternal life and joy
are the gifts of God for his people.

By partaking of the sacrament we are not only experiencing union
with Jesus, but also remembering and participating in the same ritual he
set in motion only a few hours after establishing the New Covenant. It
follows, therefore, that the Holy Eucharist is a tangible experience of
Jesus' presence for Christians. Participating in Jesus' mystery means
that we identify with him also in his suffering and sacrifice for others
through our own, thus making our destiny resemble his. In our own way,
we are ready to participate in the building of God's kingdom, even if it
means risking what happened to Christ.

With the establishment of the last supper, the New Covenant was
inaugurated and the disciples came to experience the mysterious nearness of Jesus Christ. By way of the sacrament of holy communion, contemporary believers all participate in an inexplicable mystery, in a transcendental reality of God that can be experienced, but not fully understood
or explained. This is the ultimate way of experiencing God's personality,
equally open to all believers.

4.7. The Last Battles of Christ in Revealing God's Personality: Jesus' Death and Resurrection

At this point, let us stop and question one of the most mysterious characteristics of God and his kingdom.

The chief priest asked Jesus, "Are you the Christ (the Messiah)? "Jesus answered, "Yes." Shortly afterwards, he added, "And you will see the power of the Son of Man who will come on the heavenly clouds." According to Fucak, at that moment, Jesus was certain that he had accomplished his mission.[9] He knew the verdict the judges would impose upon him, but he also knew the Resurrection would follow! That is why he declared what every Jew knew from the prophet Daniel (7:14) and from Psalm 110:1—that he is truly the "Son of Man," the Messiah. All this was incomprehensible to the people listening. They still did not understand the messianic mystery—why Christ must do what he did and why he was ready even to die. They asked, "If he is God, why must God suffer? Why must Christ die if he is truly God, if he is truly the Messiah?"

It took almost half a century before the early church was able to see the cross definitely as Christ's glory, not his humiliation. It was only then that the disciples seemed to comprehend that it is not unusual for God to show, or more precisely live, an example of sacrifice and suffering for others. This is perhaps the essential law of the kingdom, and characteristic of God's personality. Indeed, the Almighty can create different worlds with their own unique histories, events, and laws. He could have created a history where the bearing of the cross and suffering of his Son would be avoided and the salvation of humankind would still be accomplished. History would then have taken a different course. But would the consequences of Jesus' ministry for us be the same? Would our faith in Jesus inspire as much selflessness and love as it currently does? Would we take the same stand towards our own ministry and God-given mission in the world?

In Romans 1:4. we read that Jesus, "was declared the Son of God with power by the resurrection from the dead." This phrase refers to the consequence of the suffering and resurrection. The coming of God's kingdom in power was made possible by the cross, and the suffering is the pre-condition of this. Therefore, we can say that God, the Almighty, could have avoided Jesus' suffering and could still have accomplished our salvation. But if he had, we people living two thousand years later would not believe his "coming with power" as stated in Mark 9:1. His teachings and the example he taught us, our entire understanding of God's kingdom and personality, the essence of our self-understanding as Christians, the unique mission we have as his people, would all be very different then.

As Christ's suffering is a mystery, so is his resurrection. According to Fucak, the resurrection itself was a "metahistorical happening." "Metahistorical" refers to a real occurrence in space and time, but one that was and is not uniformly registered by all indifferent and impartial sources. The Napoleonic wars serve as examples of the opposite: namely, historical events, about which all historians agree.[10] Jesus' resurrection happened just as evidently as did the Napoleonic wars but was not acknowledged and/or witnessed by Jesus' enemies or by (seemingly) indifferent, and therefore "objective," observers. This is what makes it metahistorical—beyond history.

The metahistorical nature of the resurrection is evident in that after it occurred Jesus was not present for everyone in the same way. Only his disciples and followers were able to recognize and meet him, talk to him, see his wonders, and experience his presence. The Resurrection was a definite occurrence in space and time that clearly separated those who recognized and understood its significance from those who did not acknowledge the uniqueness of this eminent moment in human history.

The mystery of the resurrection is compounded by the dichotomous description of the resurrected Jesus in the Bible. He was, on one hand, a spirit, and accordingly the laws of nature did not apply to him because he existed at least part of the time outside of space and time. On the other hand, he spoke, ate, and acted in our world as we humans do. He dwelled in the same time as we, but also simultaneously outside of it.

Despite these difficult contradictions, it is a historical fact that the members of the early church were deeply convinced that Jesus had risen. They were ready even to give their own lives as proof of their conviction. The witness by the martyrs of the early church was a phenomenon that seldom occurred through history. They gave their lives not because of anger or because they sought revenge, but to bear witness to God's truth and kingdom.

Notes

1. David M. Stanley and Raymond E. Brown, "The Essential Elements of New Testament Thought," in *The Jerome Biblical Commentary*, ed. R. E. Brown, J. J. Castelot, J. L. McKenzie et al, (Englewood Cliffs, NJ: Prentice Hall, 1968), 308.

2. Marijan Jerko Fucak, *Dogadjaj Isus Krist* (Zagreb: Institut Za Teolosku Kulturu Laika, 1989), 56.

3. Fucak, *Dogadjaj Isus Krist*, 54.

4. Fucak, *Dogadjaj Isus Krist*, 57.

5. Fucak, *Dogadjaj Isus Krist*, 58.

6. Marijan Jerko Fucak, Biblijska Teologija Novog Zavjeta (Zagreb: Unpublished presentations at the Institut Za Teolosku Kultura Laika, 1986).

7. Fucak, *Dogadjaj Isus Krist*, 58.

8. Aldo Staric, *Susret S Kristom U Sakramentima Crkve* (Zagreb: Institut Za Teolosku Kulturu Laika, 1988), 3.

9. Fucak, *Dogadjaj Isus Krist*, 60.

10. Fucak, *Dogadjaj Isus Krist*, 139.

Chapter 5

Further Characteristics of God, the "Quite Other"

With this historical overview of the establishment of the kingdom of God, God's personality slowly unfolds before our eyes. Our understanding and "experiential knowledge" of him progressively evolve. Until now, we have looked at many aspects of our subject, but in little depth, as a medical general practitioner would: the GP keeps in mind only a few essential facts about many diseases, while a specialist knows only few diseases but many facts about them. Now we will say a great deal about a few things, as a specialist would. We will advance only a few lines of reasoning, from among those in the Bible as indicators of the personality of God. Even among these, we will discuss in depth—although necessarily briefly—only the most significant ones.

5.1. The Love of God

The Gospel of Mark reads:

> One of the teachers of the law came and heard them debating. Noticing that Jesus had given them a good answer, he asked him, "Of all the commandments, which is most important?"

> "The most important one," answered Jesus, "is this: 'Hear, O Israel, the Lord our God, the Lord is one. Love the Lord your God with all your heart and all your strength.' The second is this: 'Love your neighbor as yourself.' There is no commandment greater than these."

"Well said, teacher," the man replied. "You are right in saying that God is one and there is no other but Him. To love Him with all your heart, with all your strength and love your neighbor as yourself is more important than all burnt offerings and sacrifices."

When Jesus saw that he had answered wisely, he said to him, "You are not far from the Kingdom of God," and from then on no one dared ask him any more questions. (Mark 12:28-34)

Indeed, love is the new form of being, the new form of life, which characterizes the unchanging behavior of Jesus. In Jesus' case, love is not merely a feeling. Rather, it encompasses the fundamental characteristics of God, whose concern is not only for his friends (whom it is easy to love), but also for his enemies. Such love challenges the biological, psychological, and sociological foundations on which human love is based. It challenges the psychological dogma that human love always consists of the mutual interplay between give and take and that where there is no such reciprocation there is no possibility of authentic or lasting love.

The Bible portrays Jesus' love as distinct, unconditional, and absolute and makes it clear that Jesus demanded a similar attitude from his disciples. Since Jesus' love as well as his standards of behavior directly contradict human logic and instinct, they are not ideas that a biblical author would originate. Quite obviously, inspiration, or even more, the direct experience of Jesus' "quite different" love, was needed by the authors of the Scriptures to be able to describe such a mysterious personality as that of Jesus. Jesus' unusual personality traits and behaviors were as yet unknown to the world and ran contrary to the nature and healthy behavior patterns of humankind.

5.2. Suffering and Joy When Living in Union with God

Probably the main difficulty in knowing Jesus is that, for us, two mutually exclusive traits are mysteriously connected in God's personality: namely, joy and suffering. This is yet another way by which God sets himself apart from us.

Fucak discusses Goguel's view of the extent of the interconnection of these two personality traits.[1] According to Goguel, Jesus was confirmed in his conviction that he was the Messiah precisely because he had to suffer intensely when fulfilling his mission. This statement may seem at first glance paradoxical. However, upon more careful consideration, we realize its meaning—that suffering was for Jesus proof of his success as Messiah. The disciples understood to some degree, after Jesus' resurrection, that the carrying of the cross was a crucial and necessary part of Christ's ministry. They also understood that their suffering for the sake of others made them Christ-like, and in turn, their identification with Christ made them feel less alone in their suffering. This deep insight into Christ and their intimate connection with him gave the disciples strength to accept and endure lightheartedly their suffering and humiliation. We read in 1 Peter 4:13-14 as follows:

> But rejoice that you participate in the sufferings of Christ, so that you may be overjoyed when his glory is revealed. If you are insulted because of the name of Christ, you are blessed, for the Spirit of glory and of God rests on you.

The lifestyle of modern and postmodern Christian disciples also brings with it suffering, poverty, and sometimes even hatred. Those whose life is truly focused on love and on fulfilling Christian ideals cannot be as successful in worldly matters as those whose sole interest is pursuing materialism. A Christian must be "other-worldly." Such a person does not seek poverty, a simple lifestyle, or suffering. Rather, these are the results of a life that does not focus on money or worldly success at any cost. Perhaps such a life is the most powerful form of Christian witnessing.

On the other hand, from biblical descriptions, it is obvious that pleasure, happiness, and joy are unique characteristics. evident among all citizens of the Kingdom—from the babe John in the womb of Elizabeth, the cherubim and angels in heaven, Mary and the first disciples of Christ, the members of the first Church, the first martyrs, the first saints, and others, right through to the truly religious people of today. Everyone living by his faith in God's kingdom is joyful. What is it that makes those faithful people content, no matter what horrors await them, even those who know they may end their lives as martyrs? How can faith make them joyful despite all the suffering?

The answer has many components, some of which we've already mentioned, while others we may be unable to formulate or express concretely. Nevertheless, in John 15:9-15, closeness with Jesus means the realization of God's love. It means, as described in John 16:7, biblical peace and hope. These gifts were given by Jesus when he walked the earth, and, as John asserts in 14:13 and 16:20-24, nobody could take them away. Moreover, they lasted even when the Lord was no longer physically present to the disciples after his ascension as described in Lk 24:52. Theirs was not a selfish or profane happiness resulting from success, wealth, or victory, such as what Jesus' enemies felt beneath the cross according to Lk 23:35, or what Herod or Pilate may have felt. Rather, the disciples felt biblical joy, love and peace, the "quite other" gifts of the Holy Spirit.

A devil's advocate could try to explain the idea of the "Quite Other" God as an expression of an arbitrary, irrational, and imaginary human wish fulfillment, satisfying a universal need for a loving, forgiving, and almighty father figure and protector. It is, however, impossible even for a devil's advocate to attribute to wish fulfillment Jesus' acceptance of suffering for the sake of others, or his followers' acceptance of suffering. There is in fact no wish fulfillment in Christian discipleship, which requires an acceptance of a Christ-like lifestyle, one that sometimes involves enduring humiliation, poverty, and all that which psychologically-sound people instinctively try to avoid.

5.3. The Judgment of God

When we think of the judgment of God, all of us experience a *mysterium tremendum*. We wonder how judgment on us will be passed. Who can explain this to us better than Christ himself, the Judge, the Son of God? Let us consider Luke 15:11-34, and see how the father judges the prodigal son. This is a familiar story: the younger son was rebellious, wanted to be "free" and to live as he pleased. By leaving his father's house, he caused the father great sorrow. The father patiently waited for his son to "come to his senses." When the prodigal son repented, the father forgave and rejoiced, but for the older brother it was hard to accept his father's unconditional love. The forgiveness of this magnanimous father should not surprise us. Surely, Jesus is not talking here about a flesh and blood father, but about the ideal father: God. Who knows God better than Jesus?

How does God judge? Christ uses not abstract arguments but concrete examples that vividly and precisely illustrate the universal concept of an ideal father. He is forgiving, loving, and merciful, especially towards those who need it most. The mercy of God is wonderfully different from what we, the logical beings that we are, surmise it to be.

It is natural for us to echo the younger son's self-incrimination. From our viewpoint, he is perfectly correct in saying he is not worthy of his father's love and the party his father throws for him. However, we might also instinctively feel that the father acted unjustly towards his older son, who stayed with him at all times. However, God's criterion is completely different from our well-balanced sense of justice. He expects that all citizens of the kingdom of God grow to understand that the love of God is something more than mere justice. The father in the story loves both of his sons equally, even though they did not merit this love to the same extent, according to our judgment. It is not his love that is at fault, but ours, which is based on awarding everyone what he/she deserves, rather than on true forgiveness. This is the reason we often shut ourselves off from God's forgiveness, and in doing so, from the kingdom of God as well as a union with him. As Jesus knew and taught, love and forgiveness are an integral part of God's "quite different" personality.

5.4. To Whom Did Jesus Pay the "Redemption" and "Ransom" For Delivering Humankind?

All mainstream Christians believe that Jesus is the savior. However, what is the meaning of the biblical terms "redemption" (buying back slaves) and "ransom" that the New Testament uses to speak of Jesus' role as savior? These terms contributed to the shaping of early Christian theology. However, we are confronted twenty centuries later with difficult theological questions: how did Jesus "redeem" fallen humankind by his suffering? Who demanded "payment" with Jesus' suffering for humankind's redemption? And lastly, to whom did Jesus pay the "ransom" for "buying humankind back" from the power of sin?

I venture to say that nothing may influence our conception of God's personality more than the answers to these questions. In formulating the right responses, the most appropriate approach may be to start with an overview of humankind's interpretation of the biblical message through the centuries. Some of the theological concepts and explanations we are going to discuss here may seem outdated or overly speculative from modern perspective. However, let us not forget that we are dealing with one of the greatest mysteries of our faith and one of the most difficult questions in theology, to which is difficult to give a definite answer.

1. Philip H. Quinn explains how the early church and its first great theologians (e.g., Augustine) understood the death of Jesus and its sig-

nificance. "Christ's death was taken to be a ransom paid to the devil to liberate human sinners." Moreover, it was understood that the devil had the right to keep sinners under his power. It was believed that after his redemptive death, Jesus descended into hell. There the devil thought that he had the right to claim Jesus, but he was mistaken, for Christ was sinless. Thus, by descending into hell despite being sinless, Jesus redeemed the real sinners, namely, all of humankind.[2]

Gerald O'Collins, however, disputes the notion that the devil can claim the souls of sinners for his own. He argues that biblical ideas expressed in Romans 8:18-23, Galatians 3:13, 1 Corinthians 7:23 and 6:20, 1 Peter 1:18-19, Titus 2:14, Mark 10:45, and Timothy 2:6, do not "accept or imply that Satan has any rights over human beings," that such rights were ever given to him by God, or that Jesus' death was a ransom paid to the devil for sinners.[3]

2. According to Quinn, medieval theologians preferred "satisfaction" theories.[4] Since these concepts are of special importance for many contemporary Christians, let us discuss them in detail.

Sin and atonement were always a focus of Jewish religious interest. Consequently, the Hebrews developed an elaborate ritual sacrifice for atonement centuries before the birth of the Messiah. The Hebrew atonement system was unreflective; the accent was on fulfilling the ritual rather than on repentance and internal change. Through the sacrificial ritual, the Hebrews "covered their sins," by metaphorically placing the prescribed sacrificial animal between the sinner and Yahweh. When the sinner laid his hands on the sacrificial animal, it "took on himself" the person's sins. The high priest then placed his hand on the animal, thus offering it to Yahweh, and it was then sacrificed.

With Jesus' redemptive mission, this practice became meaningless. In Galatians 4:4-5, Paul wrote: "But when the time had fully come, God sent his Son, born of woman born under the law, to redeem those under the law, that we might receive the full rights of sons." Jesus did not come to abolish, but to perfect the law (Matt. 5:17-19), and he introduced the "law of love" in place of the "love of law." Similar to the way in which the Decalogue was revered by the Hebrews, respect for the law of love was paramount for Christians. According to Millard J. Erickson, the law does express God's person and will.[5] Therefore, for Christians, offending the "law of love" equals offending God; it is what we call sin.

Similar to the way in which the Hebrews were interested in atonement practice and the early Christian theologians were interested in Jesus' redemptive mission, scholastic philosophers were interested in explaining the meaning of redemption from sin. Satisfaction theories placed Jesus' redemptive work within a legalistic context typical of the Middle Ages' zeitgeist.

Anselm of Canterbury, according to Quinn, asserted, "Human sin offends God's honor."[6] In medieval understanding, the adequacy of satisfaction for an offense depended both on the severity of the offense and on the dignity of the person offended. Therefore Anselm reasoned that because "God's dignity is infinite, the debt each sinner owes is infinite as well." Hence it would be impossible for humans to pay adequate satisfaction to God.[7]

Consequently Anselm taught that "only someone both human and divine can both owe and pay the debt." Anselm set the direction for many generations of theologians who revised and further developed his concepts. For example, according to the modern theologian Millard Erickson, "Jesus' humanity means that his atoning death is applicable to human beings.[8] Because Jesus was really one of us, he was really able to redeem us," by offering himself as a sacrifice to propitiate the Father. Thus according to Erickson, the satisfaction theory explains Christ's atoning work: "Christ died to satisfy the justice of God's nature. However, since Jesus is also God, his death is a sufficient propitiation for the whole humankind."

The popularity of satisfaction theories through later Christian history was increased by the interpretation of various Old Testament prophecies (like Isa. 53:12) which hinted at a future Messiah who would replace the sacrificial animals and take on himself the sins of humanity. Luke 22:37 echoes Isaiah in Jesus' words at the Last Supper. In addition, in passages like John 17:19, we can see that Jesus saw himself as the substitute for humans sins. "For them I sanctify myself, that they too may be truly sanctified." According to John 1:29, John the Baptist cried out: "Look at the lamb of God, who takes away the sin of the world!"

It is a biblical and theological fact that Christ consciously took our place on the cross, and he vicariously died in place of sinners. His death has a sacrificial role, a reconciliatory role in humankind's deliverance, and a propitiatory role. He died that we might live, paying the "ransom" for our "deliverance" as his propitiation for humankind's offences. All this substantiates the necessity of Jesus' incarnation, suffering, death, and resurrection as part of God's redemptive plan.

However, satisfaction theories leave some question open. From a common sense perspective, does the forgiving and merciful law of love not exclude satisfaction in (or by) suffering? Does a payment for satisfaction by suffering, which may seem strange (even sadistic) to most biological fathers, not conflict with the almighty, eternal, and ultimate love of the heavenly Father?

From theological perspective, one could note that the word "justice" means that "everyone gets what he or she deserves." However, does the injustice of accepting the ransom paid by an innocent (Jesus) not conflict with "the justice of God's nature"? More importantly, would pursuing such legalistic justice not conflict with Jesus' teaching? In countless biblical examples Jesus demonstrated a different pattern; the prodigal son was immediately and wholeheartedly forgiven by his father (representing the Father), when his psychological choices and behavioral changes indicated that "he came to his senses." There is only one "limiting factor" to God's forgiveness: a person's willing exclusion of him or herself from Jesus' love. The problem then, is not with the unforgiving God, but the unrepentant sinner. Repentant sinners (like king David or the sinner crucified beside Jesus) were never excluded from God's closeness.

O'Collins offers a critique from a biblical perspective noting that nowhere do the Scriptures "speak about this price of ransom being literally or metaphorically paid to someone (e.g., God) or to something (e.g., the law)." According to O'Collins, in the Scriptures there is no mention of any law that would limit or compel God to show evidence of his loving and forgiving personality by forcing him to demand suffering as a payment for his propitiation.[9]

Yes, the Scriptures do talk about a "ransom" and a "deliverance." But could ransom and deliverance only be paid to what Erickson has called "the justice of God's nature"? Is there another possible explanation for 1 John 4:10: "This is love: not that we loved God, but that he loved us and sent his Son as an atoning sacrifice for our sins"? Before we answer this question, let us get an overview of other ideas.

3. Thomas Aquinas' teachings could be summarized thus, according to Quinn: "Christ's Passion is a sufficient and superabundant satisfaction for the sins of the whole human race; but it also ransoms us from the devil, though the price is paid to God, to whom it is owed, and not the devil."[10]

O'Collins refutes this interpretation, stating that the Bible nowhere reveals or suggests that the loving, forgiving, and merciful God ever demanded a ransom to be paid to him (or anybody else) for humankind to be released.[11]

4. Later "penal substitution" theories held, according to Quinn, that the essence of redemption is transferring the debt of sin onto Jesus. Jesus became, as Luther formulated, "the greatest of all sinners" and he then "substituted his own suffering in place of the sinner's," making us free of the bondage of sin.[12]

However, according to O'Collins, Jesus was not only a "substitute" for human sins, but humans "are invited to agree to this redemptive representation."[13] Thus, because faith, trust, and discipleship are conditions humans must meet to receive Jesus' redemption, redemption is not a one-sided action on the part of God, but also involves human action and will. On the other hand, two questions remain unanswered: Who demanded that Jesus' suffering be substituted for the suffering of sinners? And who assessed the intensity and extent of suffering necessary for the redemption of sinners?

5. During the Enlightenment "exemplar" theories were popular, which, according to Philip H. Quinn, claimed that "Christ's life and death are nothing more than an inspiring example of love and obedience," a living example of a life lived in true union with God.[14] This concept, according to Erickson, was first proposed by the Scholastic philosopher Peter Abelard, (a contemporary of St. Anselm).[15] Abelard built his theology on trust in God's love. In his understanding, Christ did not make a payment to his Father "to satisfy his offended dignity. Rather Jesus demonstrated to man the full extent of the love of God for him. This was accomplished by Christ's death. So the major effect of Christ's death was upon man rather than upon God."

The Bible does affirm that Jesus' ministry was an example, but at the same time unimaginably more than that—it is redemptive and produces evident effects of salvation and sanctification. Thus, Jesus' suffering is a model but also a vehicle of eternal salvation and fulfillment. By taking on himself our sins (and their consequence: death), by allowing himself to be killed by humans, Jesus killed human mortality, thus redeeming humankind from death.

6. Gerald O'Collins[16] states that twentieth-century theologians have amalgamated most of the aforementioned theories. We accept that position and will discuss the question raised by the title of this section by an amalgamation of the aforementioned theories.

The crucial claim that unites all the modern theological concepts is that sin is the primary obstacle that alienates humans from God. Evidently humans are unable to free themselves of sin and its consequence, death; therefore God accomplished this through Jesus' ministry, suffering, death, and resurrection. We know also that Jesus paid the ransom, and redeemed fallen humanity, establishing for us a new Gateway to God. We noted that Jesus saw himself as the substitute for humans' sins, but the Bible does not define to whom Jesus paid with his death for our life. However, we also know (according to O'Collins' observation) that when "the non-violent Christ, through his self-sacrificing death as our representative, removed the defilement of sin and restored a disturbed moral order," he was "victimized by human violence and not by a vindictive God."[17] The difference between Anselm's satisfaction theory and modern amalgamated concepts starts with the question: To whom did Jesus pay the "ransom" and "redemption" for our deliverance? The answer to that question is paradoxical and is composed like a mosaic of most of the concepts we have discussed.

First, let us ask whether it is possible that by his complete obedience to God's will, by accepting suffering and death for sake of humankind, Jesus paid the "redemption" and "ransom price" for the release of sinful humankind not to the Father, not to the Spirit, not to the devil and not to the law, but to sinful humankind itself. In this context St. Paul in Hebrews 9:14 wrote, "How much more, then, will the blood of Christ who through the eternal Spirit offered himself unblemished to God, cleanse our consciences from acts that lead to death, so that we may serve the living God." Thus, Jesus, "offered himself to God," knowing that such offering would "cleanse our consciences." Because of Jesus' sacrifice, Christians' "consciences are cleansed" making it possible for believers to "offer themselves to God"—and act in everything for God's glory. The Bible does not say—and it would be blasphemy to think—that the Father ever made a deal with Jesus to this effect: "If you suffer enough, then I will forgive." Such an arrangement would require that the amount of Jesus' suffering would be dictated by the amount of human sin. The recipients of Jesus' payment are Christians, i.e., humankind.

Indeed, Jesus' accomplished redemption and paid ransom is not only a nice example. It has a transcendental dimension as well, because Jesus objectively delivered humankind from the original sin and reconciled them with God. On the other hand, the explanation discussed here is not the only truth, and may not even be the whole truth. However, it is an eminent part of the truth which is tangibly experienced by people of faith.

I could note that many times good parents put superhuman effort and love into the upbringing of their offspring. Later, the love "invested" in their children acts efficiently through the children's conscience. Metaphorically, through the payment of love to their children, parents pay for the children's healthy attachment and "deliver" them from estrangement from family, traditions, faith, and God. By paying with their love, parents enable children's adherence to positive biblical, spiritual, moral, and community standards. God, through Jesus, did something absolutely more then this example. By his ministry, by offering for all time a single sacrifice for our sins (Heb.10:11), by his vicarious death (1 Peter 2:24), and by his resurrection, Jesus opened the gates of heaven for his people. Although this occurred in the transcendental realm, Christians already experience the reality of it through the possibility of cleansing their conscience and entering into a consequent tangible union with the invisible God. In fact, never through history were people of faith so close to God as they are after Jesus has paid the commensurable "redemption" and "ransom price" for us, to us.

Jesus was fully aware from the very beginning of his ministry that his life, teaching, preaching, ultimate love, and efforts to save humankind from sin would be met with rejection, animosity, suffering, and ultimately death. Being God and human simultaneously, he was prepared to pay the price, turning suffering caused by sin into the triumph of love, thereby providing hope and a living example for many. This was the ultimate demonstration of the personality of God—not only through words, parables, and examples, but also through his personal life, death, and resurrection.

5.5. Jesus' Blessings

How ought we best approach what we have been calling a "union" with God? If we read through the following verses, known as the Beatitudes (taken from the Latin word *beatus* meaning "blessed"), we shall have the answer:

Now when he saw the crowd, he went up on the mountain and sat down. His disciples came to him, and he began to teach them saying:

"Blessed are the poor in spirit, for theirs is the kingdom of heaven.

Blessed are those who mourn, for they will be comforted.

Blessed are the meek, for they will inherit the earth.

Blessed are those who hunger and thirst for righteousness, for they will be filled.

Blessed are the merciful, for they will be shown mercy.

Blessed are the pure in heart, for they will see God.

Blessed are the peacemakers, for they will be called the children of God.

Blessed are those who are persecuted for the sake of justice, for theirs is the kingdom of heaven. Blessed are you when people insult you, persecute you, and falsely say all kinds of evil against you because of me. Rejoice and be glad, because great is your reward in heaven, for in the same way they persecuted the prophets who were before you." (Matthew 5:1-12)

Such overturning of all values and goals that pragmatic, "normal" humans strive for is experienced by the self-denying persons who sacrifice everything and receive something worth more than what they have given up: they receive a union with God in return! Blessedness is a union with God, and a union with God is a blessing indeed. It is quite possible that they might be poor, might receive unjust treatment, might be persecuted; and yet, God is beside them. God's closeness to such believers certainly means much more than what the world offers—revenge, victory, wealth, security or success—for God's personality is "quite different" from the world.

Living in union with such a God helps Christians prove to the world that joy, despite all of the suffering in the world, is attainable. More precisely, biblical joy, peace, and love are reached through accepting unjust treatment, persecution, and even poverty for being Christ's disciple.

5.6. The Message of Christ's Miracles in Relation to God's "Quite Other" Personality

Let us begin this topic with the following question: Could Jesus really have performed the miracles described in the Bible? Before answering, let us review one. The following is described in the Gospel according to Mark:

> Another time he went into the synagogue, and a man with a shriveled hand was there. Some of them were looking for a reason to accuse Jesus, so they watched him closely to see if he would heal him on the Sabbath. Jesus said to the man with the shriveled hand, "Stand up in front of everyone."
>
> Then Jesus asked them, "Which is lawful on the Sabbath: to do good or to do evil, to save life or to kill?" But they remained silent. He looked around at them in anger and, deeply distressed at their stubborn hearts, said to the man, "Stretch out your hand." He stretched it out, and his hand was completely restored. Then the Pharisees went out and began to plot with the Herodians how they might kill Jesus. (Mark 3:1-6)

Did Jesus in fact perform such miracles? Christ was so feared and hated by Jewish leaders that, even during the bustle just before Passover, they sought a way to get rid of him as soon as possible. In spite of the fast approach of Passover and contrary to their usual legal procedures, they passed judgment against him with unprecedented swiftness. Why? What was it that frightened the priests and Pharisees so much?

Let us summarize Fucak's explanation.[18] In Jesus' time a "profane miracle"—an event that was inexplicable or unusual—was not an altogether exceptional occurrence. In the cities of Palestine as part of holiday celebrations, it was quite common to meet miracle workers or magicians who were able to perform remarkable deeds. So far, no one had been condemned for it. If Christ were such an impostor, a swindler whom any shrewd person could expose, then he would not have caused such turmoil in the minds of many Pharisees and priests, and they would not have passed judgment against him under such unprecedented circumstances. Christ must have performed some very crucial deeds to make some Pharisees and Herodians so fearful.

But what could possibly have made some Jews so frightened on that Sabbath day when Christ peacefully healed the man with the shriveled hand? Perhaps Christ was not just another unknown miracle worker after all. Perhaps he did indeed perform miracles. Through his act of healing on the Sabbath, most Pharisees saw the possibility that their perception of God was erroneous and discerned Jesus' warning against their religious smugness. Yet, instead of waking to the obsolescence of their observations and recognizing their need to amend their own grandiose self-image, the Jewish potentates chose to turn against Christ. It follows, then, that part of the evidence for the authenticity of Jesus' miracles lies in the intensity and swiftness with which the Jews reacted to them.

Jesus' miracles had conveyed a sign, a proof of God's action among his people. They were what I term "special statements" (i.e., revelations about the living standards, customs, and rules of living in union with God, and even about God's personality). What "special statements" regarding God's personality does the story in Mark 3:1-6 reveal? Before we can adequately answer the question, we need to compare early Christian and ancient Jewish perspectives regarding the relevance of health and sickness to one's closeness to God, concepts which prevailed in Jesus' time.

To early Christians, it was not of greatest importance whether they were healthy or sick, but how they could serve God in either condition. Someone with this perspective understood that God does not always give success, power, money, or health, but gives consolation, hope, and meaning whether a believer is sick or healthy. Health or sickness was for Christians not a criterion of closeness to God.

In contrast to this, most Jews considered sickness a natural condition: a punishment after Adam and Eve's fall. Furthermore, health or sickness was directly related to either a holy or a sinful life. Health and holiness were almost synonyms, as were sin and sickness. This is the reason the Jews awaited the Messiah who was to heal all their infirmities, as asserted in Isaiah: "No one living in Zion will say, 'I am ill'; and the sins of those who dwell there will be forgiven." (33:24) In such a context, it becomes obvious that the focus lies not only on the healing, but also the factor that made the miracle possible—the forgiveness of sins.

The other point of Mark's story is that Christ helped the man on the Sabbath. Since God himself gave Moses the strict commandment to observe the Sabbath, and since the Jewish Pharisees scrupulously observed the myriad of sabbatical prohibitions, no one except God had the power to nullify those laws publicly. That Christ dared to do so, that he disregarded such prohibitions, and, that he was able to cure the sick on the Sabbath proved that he is God, the one who gives and rescinds commands and that he stood above the commandments of the Decalogue.

Clearly, for a religious observer, this Sabbath healing described by Mark was not merely a holiday spectacle made by a common miracle worker. Many Pharisees and Herodians clearly saw it as a threat. It proved that God was at work in a manner very different from their understanding.

It is imperative that we remember that most often it is not the miracle that makes it possible to have faith; rather, faith makes it possible to see the miracle. In fact, it was their faith that caused some Pharisees and Herodians to acknowledge the miracle in its true value and meaning. Even so, they did not accept it as Jesus had proclaimed it to them. We, too, are faced with a similar choice. Will we recognize and have trust in a God who supplies us primarily with spiritual riches, or will we expect mostly profane gifts from God as did many people in Jesus' time?

Notes

1. Marijan Jerko Fucak, *Dogadjaj Isus Krist* (Zagreb: Institut Za Teolosku Kulturu Laika, 1989), 130.

2. Philip L. Quinn, "Theories of Atonement" in *The Oxford Companion to Christian Thought*, ed. Adrian Hastings, Alistair Mason, and Hugh Pyper (New York: Oxford University Press, 2000) 51-52.

3. O'Collins, Gerald. "Redemption" in *The Oxford Companion to Christian Thought*, ed. Adrian Hastings, Alistair Mason, and Hugh Pyper (New York: Oxford University Press, 2000) 598-601.

4. Quinn, "Atonement."

5. Millard Erickson, *Christian Theology* (Grand Rapids, MI: Baker Book House, 1995) 803.

6. O'Collins, "Redemption."

7. Quinn, "Atonement."

8. Erickson, *Christian Theology*, 812-813.

9. O'Collins, "Redemption."

10. Quinn, "Atonement."

11. O'Collins, "Redemption."

12. Quinn, "Atonement."

13. O'Collins, "Redemption."

14. Quinn, "Atonement."

15. Erickson, *Christian Theology*, 785.

16. O'Collins, "Redemption."

17. O'Collins, "Redemption."

18. Fucak, *Dogadjaj Isus Krist*, 82-102.

Chapter 6

God's Personality: Witnessing after Jesus' Ascension

H.G. Wells, a historian skeptical of Christianity, ended his description of the probable scene of Jesus' death with a sentence I summarize as follows: When the twilight of the early spring day on which Jesus was executed covered the hill where the three crosses stood and the Jews in Jerusalem started to prepare for the Passover celebration, perhaps few, if any, were interested to know Jesus' condition—whether he was still dying or was already dead.[1]

Wells' description is likely historically accurate. Biblical descriptions also inform us that Jesus' ministry seemed unsuccessful—his disciples were dispersed, his teaching defeated, and he himself was buried in the tomb immediately after his execution.

6.1. What Caused Christianity's Rapid Spread after Jesus' Ascension?

Jesus did not liberate his disciples from slavery, did not promise military victories or conquests, and did not justify bloody religious wars to ransack resources or to enslave and exterminate those who do not share the beliefs of most populist leaders. He did not even promise a worldly kingdom flowing with milk and honey or consistent, complete social justice, as have so many other religious and profane leaders. On the contrary, he proclaimed to his disciples, "You are in the world, but not of it," (as we summarized John 17:11 and 17:16). In other words, fun, wealth, justice, or respect, as a genuine purpose to live for, are out of the question for his followers. He requires people to take up their cross and follow him, which contradicts worldly criteria of desirability.

Despite the highly demanding challenges which Jesus dared us to achieve, both Christianity and the Christian church prospered and thrived. Church historian August Franzen chronicles the expansion of Christianity, explaining that sixty years after Jesus' ascension, at the end of the first century, Christians numbered only in the tens of thousands.[2] However, around the year 200, there were probably many hundreds of thousands, and near the year 300, before Constantine's conversion to Christianity in 312, Christians numbered from six to eight million. The entire Roman Empire at that time had no more than fifty million inhabitants.

Thus, in the first 300 years of its history, Christianity grew from a few decimated, devastated groups of fugitive disciples disappointed by Jesus' death into a rapidly spreading, enthusiastic faith community. Many of the same Jews who previously demanded Jesus' death became zealous Christians a short time later. For H.G. Wells, this explosive expansion of Christianity is attributable to the enthusiastic self-deceptive zeal of early Christians.

It is worth asking whether self-deception can be that lasting and successful (especially if such "self-deception" promises no lucrative or political gain) and whether it can bring as much optimism and joy as did Christianity. Observed from a professional perspective, the true cause of the lasting love, hope, and peace which the early Christians enjoyed definitely had to be something other than self-deception, something that was real despite being invisible, that is, the gifts of the Holy Spirit.

6.2. The Holy Spirit's Revelation of God's Person

St. Paul, in Romans 12:6-8 and Ephesians 4:7-13, and St. Peter in 1 Peter 4:10-11 discuss some seventeen spiritual gifts that are enabling members of the early church to serve each other in the common building of God's kingdom. These gifts include, among others, teaching, healing, and prophesying.

In Colossians 1:11, gifts of the Spirit are defined more broadly, and the Apostle talks about endurance, patience, and giving thanks with joy to the Father. Indeed, those more broadly defined spiritual gifts synchronize with the classic ones, such as the gifts of teaching, preaching, healing. Teaching, healing, and preaching provided opportunities to reflect biblical joy, meaning, peace, love, and the other gifts which are the essence of God's kingdom and which authenticate the witness of Jesus' disciples.

Gifts of the spirit may be understood on an even broader level, however. In the last sentence of Luke's Gospel we read, "Then they worshipped him and returned to Jerusalem with great joy. And they stayed continually at the temple praising God." (Luke 24:52-53)

What Luke means to say here is that the disciples were aware that Christ, despite his ascension, did not abandon them, even though he was invisible and untouchable. To his disciples, he was still experientially with them, and nothing and no one could take away from them their union with God! The behaviors described in Luke 24:52-53 are the "gifts of faith." They are a by-product of faith. The term "gifts of faith" includes the gifts of the Spirit, but these gifts of faith are available to, and experienced by, believers only.

Jesus' disciples experienced discipleship by receiving these gifts even in times when their understanding of his teachings was probably not much deeper than the perspective of his enemies. However, what made the faith of the previously insecure disciples so enthusiastic and strong after Pentecost, was what the Bible calls the "Holy Spirit." In John 16:12-13, Jesus, in his farewell talk, says to his disciples, "I have much more to say to you, more than you can now bear. But when he, the Spirit of truth comes, he will guide you into all truth." This takes place on the road (see John 13:31), and the talk is about the road and guidance. Jesus is discussing the meaning of "all truth." According to the theologian Xavier Léon-Dufour, the word "all truth" here does not have a metaphysical or an abstract meaning, but means Jesus himself.[3] Jesus is the full truth, but for the disciples this was difficult to understand before Pentecost: the descent of the Holy Spirit.

The Bible uses concrete terms to describe the Spirit. They are mostly connected with ideas that describe activities. Such metaphors include "water that gives life" (to the Jews in Moses' time), "everlasting life" (as in John 7:37-39), "Paraclete," (defender, helper, consoler), or the fire and storm which mobilize witness to Jesus Christ (as in Luke 12:49 and Acts 2:3). This refers to the Power, which mobilizes the preaching of the Gospel, as in Acts 1:8. My final example is the One who transforms us into Jesus' likeness, as in 2 Corinthians 3:18.

Recognition of the relevance of these metaphors was already evident in the first catechisms of the church. The congregation of the early church accepted Jesus' resurrection not only because there were people who testified to it, nor only because there were disciples who "saw" evidence that it occurred. The first and most important condition was within themselves, within their congregation, particularly in the Spirit's mysterious guidance as helper (*paracletos*) in striving for union with the resurrected Jesus, despite his invisibility after ascension. In fact, Jesus' ministry of revealing God's nature was fulfilled by the arrival of the Holy Spirit. Pentecost meant the fulfillment of the paschal mystery, as we may conclude from reading Acts 2:32-33, but it was also the beginning of a new era in God's revelation of his own person through Christians—God's people—to the world.

6.3. The Spirit's Guidance to Christians in Witnessing to God's Person

The ancient Hebrews maintained a nomadic lifestyle for a long time. This is why being "on the road" had such a special meaning for them. After their covenant with Yahweh, the idea of "road" and the expression, "to be on the road" ("on the journey") had a new meaning: to follow Yahweh, to travel in the ways of Yahweh—God's ways.

With the ministry of Christ, this idea of being on the road took on a new meaning. Now it came to denote a typical Christian way of living, a pilgrimage, a Christian lifestyle—the Way. In fact, this is the very name the first Christians were called, as recorded in the Acts of the Apostles.

> Meanwhile, Saul was still breathing out murderous threats against the Lord's disciples. He went to the high priest and asked him for letters to the synagogues in Damascus, so that if he found any there who belonged to the Way, whether men or women, he might take them as prisoners to Jerusalem. (9:1-2)

Christians "on the Way" (on the journey with Christ, guided by the Holy Spirit) were almost always easy to recognize. The "Way" for early Christians had a characteristic moral quest. We can find references to this fact in Paul's letters (1 Thess. 4:1; 2 Thess. 3:6, and Rom. 6:17-18). The Christian journey meant a complete transformation of one's personality. It meant a rebirth which enabled believers to enjoy the peace, joy, and glory of becoming a redeemed member of the church. It meant the experience of union with the Father and Jesus through the Holy Spirit. The assured internal union with the triune God externally gave rise to the traditional optimism, zeal, modesty, love, power, solidarity, and good family life which characterized early Christian communities. Such were the gifts of the Spirit to those "on the Way." Persecutions, tribulations, or suffering could not diminish Biblical enthusiasm. On the contrary, as one contemporary observed, "On the blood of martyrs grew the church."

The Spirit's giving witness to God's person through Christians supplements the testimony of Jesus. With the coming of the Holy Spirit, God reveals his own personality in a new way through the witness of God's people—the church, as well.

6.4. The Church's Witnessing of God's Person on Christmas Day in the Year 455

According to Franzen, in 455 the Vandals from North Africa invaded the city of Rome.[4] Their stay was brief—an orgy of ransacking and plundering followed by a triumphant return to Africa with their galleys laden with booty. The city of Rome was free again, but the fear lingered on. What if the Vandals or other pillagers should return? Desperate for a savior, the people of Rome turned to the church, the only authority they now found worthy of respect. They begged the pope, Leo the Great, for help. But the pope's power lay in the realm of morals, not in military might. Nonetheless he took action. On Christmas Day in 455, he spoke memorably about the peace of God. I summarize and paraphrase his message as follows: He resolutely pronounced that, "With the birth of the Lord, peace was also born into the world." Therefore, "God's people, do not be afraid; a worldly threat like Vandals cannot harm the spiritual peace of the citizens in God's kingdom." (This homily of Leo the Great is extolled as a masterpiece of rhetoric even in our time).

Indeed, the agnostics of the day were not impressed because they were convinced words would not save them. Obviously, they had a different idea about the savior, God's kingdom, and the peace he brings. They were not disciples and so were not interested in receiving gifts of faith; thus, they could not experience the power, peace, freedom, and joy unique to the faithful.

However, for those for whom living in God's kingdom meant not the pleasures of eating and drinking, but happiness and joy in the Holy Spirit, living in the invisible kingdom was an unequivocal reality. Christians, transformed by the Holy Spirit, demonstrated what gifts of faith involve in practice—living in and with Jesus and maintaining a joyful hope of a complete union with Jesus in heaven, greater than the fear of plundering or suffering caused by Vandals.

Fritz Rotschild stated, "One has to be inspired to understand inspiration." In my own words, the Holy Spirit inspires us to be like the "inspirer"—the triune God.[5] With the help of the Spirit, God's personality is mirrored in Christians, which continues to contribute to humankind's knowledge of God's personality.

Notes

1. Herbert George Wells, *A Világtörténelem Alapvonalai* (Budapest: Genius, 1925), 308.

2. August Franzen, *Kleine Kirchengeschichte* (Freiburg: Herder Bücherei, 1968), 24.

3. Xavier Léon-Dufour, *Rjecnik Biblijske Teologije*, ed. Josip Turcinovic, (Zagreb: Krščanska Sadašnjost, 1988), 342

4. Franzen, *Kirchengeschichte*, 98.

5. Abraham J. Heschel, *Between God and Man* (New York: The Free Press, A Division of Simon & Shuster Inc., 1959), 10.

Chapter 7

The Definition of God's Personality

The church historian August Franzen notes that according to the ecumenical Councils of Ephesus in 431 and Chalcedon in 451 AD, Jesus Christ possesses two personalities.[1] Existing in a "hypostatic union," the human and divine natures in Jesus are neither separate nor merged. This would be impossible according to Aristotelian logic, but not for Jesus, considering his "quite other" personality. From this conception of Jesus' personality, it follows that Jesus is fully God and human and that by knowing Jesus Christ's personality we may come to a deeper understanding of the personality of God, as far as this is possible for humans.

After discussing the biblical descriptions, we have a lot of information and knowledge about the King of God's kingdom, Jesus Christ. But do we now really understand God's personality? Or, would we agree with the dictum that, "If you do not ask me then I know; if you ask me then I do not know"? Why this mixture of knowing and not knowing in our mind?

Perhaps because of our ("Western") way of thinking and reasoning, we have the feeling that until we define something, or define it exactly, we do not understand its essence. Can we even begin to grasp God's essence? And, if indeed we can, how can we clearly and simply summarize his characteristics? One word expressing all of the qualities belonging to God discussed so far is "glory." We can accurately say that God is the ultimate glory. How can God's glory be adequately defined?

According to the theologian Packer, "Our gracious God has determined to glorify himself by blessing his people."[2] Thus, God's glory is expressed through the creation and sustenance of the universe and everything in it (including all life), by his love, providence, care, and forgiveness. But above all, God manifests his love through redeeming his people. Indeed, the same glory also belongs to Jesus Christ, according to Acts 3:13-15, Romans 6:4, Philippians 3:21, Matthew 24:30, and John 17:24.

From a human perspective, the idea of God glorifying himself may be a stumbling block. According to Packer, "A volume, they say, that depicts God so persistently as a 'jealous' Being, concerned first and foremost about his 'honor' cannot be regarded as divine truth." Some people may consider a God depicted in such a manner as blasphemy. However, Packer adds that, "those who insist that God should not seek his glory in all things are really asking that he cease to be a God. And there is no greater blasphemy than to will that."[3]

On the other hand, we may need to understand the term "glory" not from a human, but from a biblical perspective.

According to Xavier Léon-Dufour, the Hebrew word (*kabód*) meaning "glory" does not express fame or celebrity at all, but the "weight" of one's true value and worth.[4] God has the greatest possible "weight," thus glory, because he is the creator of the universe, dispensing love, providence, and forgiveness to his people; giving his own Son to redeem us; enabling humans to live in an experiential, tangible union with him; and granting us the eschatological hope that we will see him face-to-face in eternity. Thus, God's glorifying himself is the expression not of selfishness or pathological narcissism (as such self-glorification through creation, sustenance—even love—would be for humans), but the expression of his "quite other" love. By manifesting his deity, God showers us all with abundant blessing.

Glory is one of God's fundamental characteristics. It encompasses all of God's deeds in all spheres of time—past, present, and future. At the same time, it expresses the essence of God's magnificent splendor. However, does not our use of such an abstract term that needs semantic/ philosophical/ theological clarification hinder our attempt to find a simple and usable definition for it? Yes, it does. Therefore, let us break down this abstract term of God's "glory" into simpler, more concrete biblical terms.

A good starting point is 1 John 4, 8:16, which states, "God is love." According to G.W. Jeanrond, not only John's letter but the whole of John's gospel (written around the end of the first century) "depicts love as a communication between God and human beings in which God's essence is revealed."[5] Starting with the words "In the beginning was the

Word. . . ." and ending with the verse "The Word became flesh," verses 1-14 in the first chapter of the gospel of John are a hymn glorifying God's love.

From the very beginning, the disciples always "knew"—that is, they experienced God's love. Their "hearts were burning" when they talked with Jesus on the road to Emmaus. But this was not the only experience of God's love. As Paul in Rom 8:38-39 so fervently declares,

> I am convinced that neither death nor life, neither angels nor demons, neither the present nor the future, nor any powers, neither height nor depth, nor anything else in all creation, will be able to separate us from the love of God that is in Christ Jesus our Lord.

Love is one of the most typical characteristics of God's personality. The creation of the world and the first humans (as described in the Bible), Jesus' incarnation, teaching and preaching, forgiveness of sins, suffering and dying on the cross for our sake, indeed all characteristics of Jesus' personality, are manifestations of God's love. At the same time, however, God is the one whom we are unable to grasp precisely, to profile psychologically or theologically. He is the almighty and eternal, the first and the last, the Alpha and Omega, the LORD as we read in Genesis 2:1-21. In Exodus 15:11, human wonderment at God's awesome mystery is expressed as follows: "Who among the gods is like you, O LORD? Who is like you—majestic in holiness, awesome in glory, working wonders?"

God is the almighty. "Through him all things were made; without him nothing was made that has been made. In him was life and that light was the light of men. The light shines in the darkness, but the darkness has not understood it." (John 1:3-5)

If we connect these fundamental "quite other" characteristics with the all-encompassing love discussed in 1 John 4:8-16, then we can confidently define God's personality as "the almighty, eternal, and ultimate love." The first three traits, "almighty," "eternal," and "ultimate" are transcendental characteristics of God's personality. They reflect the fact that God is "quite different" from anything humans can imagine or grasp. The fourth characteristic, his love, can be experienced by humans. It is a strictly empirical (experienced) key characteristic, enabling Christians (as we will subsequently discuss) to encounter the personality and presence of the almighty, eternal, and ultimate Deity.

But let us also give voice to our doubts. Are we not deceiving our-selves by accepting that which we can neither see, nor touch, nor feel, therefore that which does not really exist for our senses? Could there not be just one flaw in the beautifully written idea of the love of God, namely, that such love does not exist anywhere because God himself does not?"

According to the Bible, God is present to his people now. But is this really so? How can we know and experience that he is really living with us, that nothing is closer to us than Jesus, whose existence cannot be scientifically explored and proven?

Which is the "real" reality—what the Scriptures envision or what we see and experience everywhere around us? God's kingdom or the cruel and selfish world of injustice where Vandals rule? How do we know that everything the Scriptures describe is really fulfilled in Jesus Christ? Yes, our faith enables us to believe and accept Jesus as the Messiah and sav-ior; but what compels us to believe the Scriptures and not the Communist Manifesto or some other belief system? To answer these questions will be our task in the second part of this book.

Notes

1. August Franzen, *Kleine Kirchengeschichte* (Freiburg: Herder Bücherei, 1968), 60-71.

2. J. I. Packer, *God's Plans for You* (Wheaton, IL: Crossway Books, 2001), 27.

3. Packer, *God's Plans*, 28.

4. Xavier Léon-Dufour, *Rjecnik Biblijske Teologije*, ed. Josip Turcinovic (Zagreb: Krscanska Sadasnjost, 1988), 1180-1182.

5. G. W. Jeanrond, "Love," in *The Oxford Companion to Christian Thought*, ed. Adrian Hastings, Alistair Mason, and Hugh Pyper (New York: Oxford University Press, 2000), 394-97.

Part 2

The Anthropological Characteristics that Enable Believers' Communication with the Biblical God

Chapter 8

The Problem Arising from God's Transcendence

According to one anecdotal story, the preacher John Wesley preached one morning in his church in a loud voice, "Jesus is alive!" Unexpectedly, from the very back pew one cynical voice asked, "And how do you know this?" Wesley responded, "Because I talked to him for a half an hour this morning!"

For a skeptical, or at least non-enthusiastic, believer such as the one sitting in the back of the church, it would be difficult to communicate with God as Wesley had done. Indeed, it would be equally as difficult to record Wesley's communication with God. But this would not mean that such communication did not take place, because the psychological evidence for it, as well as Wesley's experience of the encounter, could be objectively verified. For example, we could corroborate Wesley's experience by registering changes in his EEG rhythm, breathing, pulse, muscle tone, or confirm his experience of having spoken with God by a polygraph, a lie detector test. This would prove that Wesley in fact did, as many believers do, experience such communication, which for positivists, agnostics, or atheists, seems impossible.

Agnostics' difficulty in experiencing God's presence stems from his fundamental characteristics. God, according to biblical revelations, is the absolute. Since he is the absolute, God is "quite other," therefore different from anything in our world. Moreover, he is transcendent. Let us discuss what those attributes mean philosophically.

According to Ferenc Szabo, in the broadest sense, a philosophical "absolute" is that which in no way depends on the existence of anything other than itself. Given this definition, we can safely say that God—the absolute—is incomparable to anything known to humans and impossible to deduce, define, or imagine with the aid of familiar ideas and experiences. [1]

Because God is "absolute," logical constructs such as space and time have no validity in reference to him—God is literally "quite different" from that which human attributes can express. The phrase "quite different" also describes God's personal qualities, his love, forgiveness, fidelity, and acceptance of suffering for the sake of humankind. In short, God's "quite other"-ness is captured perfectly in Isaiah 40:25, "To whom will you compare me? Or who is my equal?"

The fact that God is a "quite different" being can also be expressed by the idea of transcendence. The word "transcendent" in this context means that what is impossible to experience through the senses does not exist according to physics, chemistry, mathematics, biology, or law. Since God is transcendent, humans have no means by which to scientifically study him or substantiate his existence; thus, he is "non-existent" for positivists, agnostics, and atheists, but "quite differently" present for his believers.

If then the biblical God is so different from anything we know or are able to realize, how do we know that he really does exist? If he is so different from anything we know or are able to realize, how was Wesley able to communicate with God experientially and tangibly? In the second part of the book, this will be our main focus. We will analyze the psychological discernment process that enabled Wesley, and continues to enable billions of other believers, to experience and communicate with the invisible God.

Note

1. Ferenc Szabo, *Az Ember es Vilaga* (Roma: Self-published, 1969), 78.

Chapter 9

What Happened to Thomas?

Our rationale in searching for the answers to the questions we asked in the previous chapter could be summarized thus: if believers experience God's closeness despite his transcendence, then in spite of his "quite other"-ness, something must exist in our make-up, and in God's, that makes communication with him possible. Let us search for such a hypothetical common denominator.

9.1. The "Common Denominator" Enabling Communication between the Infinite God and Finite Humans

Throughout his ministry Jesus challenged his listeners by his words and deeds to ". . . believe the good news." (Mark 1:15) The early preaching of the apostles, as recorded in Acts and in the letters of Paul, makes it clear that a categorical choice is being offered: accept with faith or reject without faith the person and the message of Christ. Can we then define faith as the factor that enables our experiencing of God and his characteristics? Is faith the common denominator that connects the two realms of the finite human and the infinite God?

Everyday experience confirms that this is indeed so. Only by faith can believers experience God's personality. They communicate with God despite his being invisible and untouchable and experience his love as realistically as agnostics experience the visible and touchable world. Faith is the prerequisite for communicating with God, and for experiencing God's personality, especially his love. As a telescope or microscope enables the human eye to observe either distant galaxies or viruses, so faith opens the eyes of the mind and heart to the realization of God's closeness and love, as it did for the disciples on the road to Emmaus, or for Saul on the road to Damascus. Thus, faith is the "common denominator" connecting finite and infinite; it is the eminent way of experiencing the existence and presence of the transcendent God.

Here faith operates epistemologically; (epistemology is a discipline analyzing the theory of knowledge). Epistemologically, faith is not only a common denominator where the infinite and finite meet, but is also a unique "recognition process"—it enables recognition of, communication with, and the "knowledge of" God.

How does faith enable us to recognize and "know" God?

Let us first discuss the general principles of the unique "recognition process" made possible by faith, based on the examples we have mentioned previously. We have noted that since God is invisible, transcendental, and "quite other," communication with him is not sensorial, as it is with natural objects. Nevertheless, we have seen that Moses, Paul, or Teresa of Ávila clearly understood that something exceptional and awesome was going on and that they were in fact experiencing and communicating with the almighty, eternal, and ultimate loving God. Communication with God, while remaining an incomprehensible mystery, was for Moses, Paul, or Teresa—as well as for contemporary people of faith—paradoxically also an intelligible, clear, evident, and comprehensible biblical experience. With the help of faith, these saints were able to place their encounter with the unknown God into a context of revelation. Such placement clarified their experience of this non-sensory and awesome communication and made it intelligible—"tangible" for them, not in a human or psychological sense but in a biblical sense.

This explains why a personal communication with the living God is possible only to people of faith. God's calls are mostly non-sensorial, personal, unique, and intimate, clearly intelligible only to the addressed believer, who is able, with the help of faith, to place the awesome God's call within a biblical context. Without faith, the scriptural placement is not possible, and the non-sensorial communication seems nonsensical.

We answer one question, but we are immediately confronted with the next problem: what is faith?

Faith is a mystery, in the sense that psychology cannot explain why some people accept God's call, while others ignore or reject it. Psychology, philosophy, or psychiatry cannot explain, give, or take away faith.

At the same time, although faith itself is a mystery, communication between God and believers is not unregistered but is experienced through such psychological functions as attention, will, thought, feelings, and memory.

From this point on, our task will be to find out and discuss a hypothetical "model" of how the common denominator of faith connects God and believers: more specifically, where, when, and how faith enables believers to experience closeness to the invisible and untouchable, but in the believers' life tangibly present, God. Since an example speaks more eloquently than any theoretical explanation, we will explore the problems relating to faith on the basis of the Bible's description of Thomas.

9.2. Thomas' Story

Let us turn to the Scriptures and analyze a biblical message that may explain how the expression of God's greatest gift—faith—enabled the disciples, to experience, not only theoretically or metaphorically but concretely, communication and union with the almighty, eternal, and ultimate love. This may be what makes such communication and union possible for us modern people as well.

In John 20:24-29, the following well-known story of St. Thomas presents itself:

Now Thomas (called Didymus), one of the Twelve, was not with the disciples when Jesus came. So the other disciples told him, "We have seen the Lord!"

But he said to them, "Unless I see the nail marks in his hands and put my finger where the nails were, and put my hand in his side, I will not believe it."

A week later his disciples were in the house again, and Thomas was with them. Though the doors were locked, Jesus came and stood among them and said, "Peace be with you!" Then he said to Thomas, "Put your finger here; see my hands. Reach out your hands and put them into my side. Stop doubting and believe."

Thomas said to him, "My Lord and my God!"

Then Jesus told him, "Because you have seen me, you have believed; blessed are those who have not seen and yet have believed."

In the first verses, a description of the typical behavior pattern of an agnostic is apparent. Yet in the second part of the story (which describes events a week later, and after Jesus' intervention), there emerges the profile of an enthusiastic and devoted believer to whom Jesus' resurrection and presence is the most experiential and important reality. From the biblical description, we realize that Thomas unequivocally experienced the almighty, eternal, and ultimately loving God's presence in the resurrected Jesus. The revival of Thomas's faith was the consequence of Jesus' intervention. So, we have no choice but to acquiesce in the fact that God's people, enabled by faith, are able to really and evidently pinpoint and experience God's existence, presence, and love. Such internal evidence is visible in a believer's behavior and even measurable, because Thomas' behavior and that of billions of contemporary believers would be different if he (and they) had not had an internal, convincing, experience of God's presence. Indeed, the same is valid for Wesley—we have to accept that he really experienced his communication with God within himself through his faith.

To come to such a conclusion is not difficult when we read John's testimony and observe the events in Thomas' life from a distance. However, to pinpoint the exact "touchstone" of the existence and closeness of the Almighty (but invisible) Father experienced by believers through their faith certainly seems more difficult. For now, we have only a partial answer: There is no natural way of discerning God. Faith is always the consequence first of God, the Spirit, miraculously intervening in the lives of believers and secondly of their reply to God's intervention: his call.

Can we understand how Jesus' miraculous transformation of Thomas' personality happened? No, this, too, is a mystery for us. But we can do something else. From the description of Thomas' reactions, we can deduce the probable psychological experiences and thoughts of Didymus that motivated his behavior and words as recorded by John. Thus, we will analyze not how Jesus performed his miracle in Thomas, but how Thomas experienced God's intervention and love in himself. As noted earlier, we will consistently use this methodology throughout this book. Using such an approach will enable us also to answer the questions of how modern people of faith experience God's personality and love, facilitated by his intervention, as well as how faith enables "seeing the invisible."

To do this, however, we need a closer analysis of the revival of Thomas' faith, a deeper insight into Thomas' mind. We shall do this in the next chapter. However, to do so, we must slowly shift our attention from focusing on the messages of Scripture to analyzing the experiential trustworthiness of these biblical messages.

Chapter 10

What Can We Establish from the Biblical Account of Thomas' Conversion?

After viewing Thomas' well-known biblical story from a bird's-eye perspective, let us summarize some important facts that are obvious even without a deeper biblical or psychological analysis.

10.1. What the Bible Does Not Say

Thomas' hesitation should not surprise us. During his life Christ was not always popular; he did not receive complete understanding even from his disciples. In the post-Galilean period when he warned of the suffering, trials, tribulations, and injustices that would befall the "Son of Man," almost all of Jesus' disciples became hesitant, disappointed, and even skeptical. Then after Jesus' death, they were unexpectedly in a situation where sustaining their faith was difficult for numerous reasons. The first of these was the crucifixion. Thomas, like the other disciples, was left alone with the thought that since Jesus was dead, God's kingdom no longer existed. Moreover, most of Jesus' disciples likely concluded that Jesus was not the promised Messiah after all.

In addition, Thomas was struck with terror by the thought that what happened to Jesus would likely happen to him too. The optimism of the coming kingship had passed. He experienced only unknown danger and the inescapable threat of the future as the consequence of his trust in Jesus.

In this state of mind, it is understandable why Thomas did not believe in the rumor of Christ's resurrection. Other disciples also doubted. Why would Thomas be different? At this stage, he did not want faith, but rather knowledge and solid, provable fact. He wanted to see and touch the resurrected Jesus. He, like the skeptic speaking out to Wesley from the back pew, sought material proof that would confirm the truth for him and for everyone,

When the resurrected Jesus Christ came to his disciples the second time and called on Thomas, he provided Thomas with the opportunity for certainty. Thomas could put his hands in Christ's side and get all the touchable proofs he needed. But did he do this? Note that after Jesus' offer of proof and his command to Thomas to "stop doubting and believe," the Bible does not tell us that Thomas put his hands in Jesus' side. But Thomas says, (or according to other translations he cries out), "My Lord and my God" with all his faith! This is the essence of John's description of Thomas's transformation relevant to our topic. The Scriptures do not ascertain that Thomas got the required proof of Jesus' resurrection by touching him—but by some other way.

10.2. What, Then, Enabled Thomas to Regain His Faith?

How did Thomas get the needed proof to regain his faith if not by touching Jesus' side? What gave him such strong certainty about Jesus that he no longer needed evidence? The simplest explanation would be that Thomas saw Jesus, recognized him, and further proof was unnecessary.

Although this is an attractive explanation, it does not coincide with other biblical accounts. Luke 24:13-35, for example, describes the disciples traveling with Jesus on the road to Emmaus. They were in contact with him and spoke to him much longer than Thomas did. Obviously, they had the opportunity not only to see, but also to observe, the resurrected Jesus. Yet they did not recognize him until "their eyes were opened" in a special way—by explaining Scripture and breaking bread with them, thus awakening their faith. Merely seeing the resurrected Lord is insufficient. Note that it is only regained faith that awakens conscious recognition of what the eyes have seen.

On the other hand, it is improbable that only his disciples were present every time the resurrected Jesus appeared. What really happened might have been that only his disciples recognized him. According to the oldest biblical report of Christ's resurrection as described in 1 Corinthians 15:6, Jesus "appeared to more than five hundred of the brothers at the same time." Indeed, the expression literally means not only five hundred males but a greater number of people—a crowd, a public appearance. At this time (and there may be other times) the public saw Jesus, but not everyone recognized him. Only "brothers" were able to recognize whom they saw, because their faith enabled their recognition. What happened at that time is similar to what is happening in postmodern society: only people of faith can "recognize," (i.e., acknowledge and live in a tangible union with) the invisible God.

This explanation is supported by the fact that not a word can be found, either in the Bible or in any other historical source, about how to recognize the resurrected Jesus. No one knew how, not the Roman soldiers and officers, not the Jewish priests or Pharisees, not Herod's uniformed and secret police. Neither in the Roman jurisdiction nor in the hostile Jewish environment could the resurrected and incredibly famous Lord have simply disappeared for the rest of his ministry if he appeared even once publicly as reported by St. Paul, if he was a real man and person after his resurrection. This is even more improbable if we keep in mind that the Jewish priests were informed about his resurrection (see Matt. 28:11-15)—they would not simply let him go after a public appearance. We assume that many could see, but few, with the exception of the faithful, could recognize the resurrected Jesus.

We have already mentioned that according to Fucak, the resurrection itself and Christ's appearance after his death were "meta-historical" events. This means that Jesus' resurrection actually did happen in history, but it was not equally noted among sympathizers and opponents. After his resurrection Jesus did not have a biological/natural body like Lazarus after his revival, but a pneumatic/spiritual body. The apathetic witness who was not a *pneumaticus*—("a spiritual man" in St. Paul's terminology) did not register contact with Jesus (see 1 Cor. 2:13-16 in reference to "non-spiritual people"). Apathetic, doubtful, "realistic" people—agnostics like Thomas before Jesus' second appearance—may have been frightened when they heard rumors that he had risen. They just did not want to acknowledge his resurrection. Because of their resistance to following Jesus on his "Way," they did not have "the mind of Christ" (1 Cor. 2:16) and therefore did not recognize what was clearly visible to committed disciples. Opening someone's eyes, making him or her not only see but understand in a meaningful biblical and spiritual context what he or she witnessed, was essential for that person's recognition of Jesus.

The events described in John 20:10-18 surrounding the "empty tomb" confirm this explanation. Mary Magdalene herself did not recognize the resurrected Lord while she was talking to him. She was convinced that Jesus was dead and that the person she was speaking to could not be her Teacher. Jesus' intervention by calling her name, as described in John 20:16, was needed for Mary to recognize her Redeemer and cry out "Rabboni" (Teacher)!

In summary then, it was not seeing Christ that made faith possible, but rather faith that made recognizing the resurrected Christ possible. What was really going on in Jesus' public appearances was a division between those who realized God's call to believe and those who did not. Now we understand the practical importance of defining faith as the "common denominator" between the transcendent God and finite humans, enabling us to discern his presence, existence, and love. Skeptical, indifferent people, despite having seen the resurrected Jesus, did not recognize or acknowledge him because they lacked faith. As Luke emphasizes in 24:13-35, eyesight alone—without having one's eyes opened and realizing what one saw—was insufficient to recognize the resurrected Jesus.

10.3. A Controversial Verse: John 20:29

Here we arrive at a seemingly controversial verse that can raise objections. In John 20:29, Jesus says to Thomas, "Do you believe because you see me? How happy are those who believe without seeing me." This at first seems to contradict what we have said. It seems as if Thomas became a believer again not through the miracle that Jesus created in him, but through his ability to recognize Jesus on seeing him. So was Thomas' great change really due to his seeing something visible and measurable that persuaded him of Jesus Christ's identity, thereby taking away his need to touch him?

On this issue, Marijan J. Fucak quotes the position of Donatien Molat.[1] According to Molat, the fourth Gospel is filled with a gradual growth of one event—the certainty of the Resurrection. The account of the Resurrection in John 20:1-10 starts with the discovery of the empty tomb when one person, the beloved disciple, "started to believe." According to verse 8, "He saw and believed." But according to verse 9, he and another disciple "still did not understand from Scripture that Jesus had to rise from the dead." Next, Jesus appears to Mary Magdalene and later to his disciples. With each appearance the certainty of Jesus' resurrection grows stronger in the reader. John finishes these gradations with Jesus' appearance to Thomas, concluding with the maxim: "Blessed are those who have not seen and yet have believed."

Those who "saw" were Jesus' contemporaries. Those who "believe without seeing" are also the disciples of JesusCbut those who came after the Christians of the early church. According to Xavier Léon-Dufour, "Starting with chapter 6 of the Acts of the Apostles, the name 'disciple' signifies every Christian, independent of whether he or she knew Jesus during his earthly life."[2] From this perspective, all believers are in some way equal to the apostles in their mission, despite their possessing different gifts than the Twelve.

Accordingly, the meaning of John 20:29 is that the disciples of the post-apostolic period are blessed because they believe by reason of the disciples' testimony. Jesus' sentence, "Because you have seen me, you have believed," means, "Because you are my disciple, you have believed." The emphasis is not on Thomas' eyesight, but on his discipleship.

Léon-Dufour further explains that discipleship meant to accept Christ as one's teacher and master, the God and Lord himself, to have a sense of vocation awakened by Jesus, and to follow him in his destiny of suffering and glory. It meant a permanent and lasting relationship with Christ. It was this sense of being a disciple that was the precondition of recognizing the resurrected Jesus.

St. Paul's explanation in Hebrew's 11:1 again indicates how irrelevant physiological eyesight is to faith: "Now faith is being sure of what we hope for and certain of what we do not see." Being sure of what we hope for and certain of what we do not see makes even us, 2000 years later, acknowledge not only Jesus' resurrection, but also our communication and connection with God.

Let us now return to Thomas' case. Thomas was not a shy person. He was not the type to hide his doubts and uncertainty or to be ashamed of them in front of the other disciples or Jesus Christ himself. If he could not get the evidence he needed by simply seeing and recognizing Christ, then there must have been a reason why he did not act on Jesus' invitation to touch his side. The reason for this could be that Thomas obtained certain evidence that was even more convincing than seeing or touching the resurrected Lord.

However, we have no clues as to what that evidence might have been. The Bible does not describe when and how Thomas got the needed proof; we are only able to discern that Jesus somehow intervened in Thomas' psyche. Neither psychiatry nor psychology can explain what Jesus did in the soul of Thomas. From his cry, "My Lord and my God!" however, it becomes obvious that he realized the change in his own personality, understood the reality of this event, and gained a new attitude toward Jesus.

How did he experience this new attitude? And how did Jesus make him experience it? To discuss these questions, we now have to leave the known and defined domains of theology and psychology. We are approaching the misty borderline between psychology and theology, the borderline between the natural and supernatural, between the experienced and the revealed. How can we test the validity of our ideas in an area beyond scientific exploration, and what will be the criterion of our accuracy? In the following chapters, we will use revelation to explain psychological experience and use the psychological experience of believers to verify revelation. At the end of this second part of the book, we will again return to Thomas and use the acquired knowledge to put the missing links together.

Notes

1. Marijan Jerko Fucak, *Evandjelje Ljubljenog Ucenika* (Zagreb: Institut Za Teolosku Kulturu Laika, 1986), 59-60.

2. Xavier Léon-Dufour, *Rjecnik Biblijske Teologije*, ed. Josip Turcinovic (Zagreb: Krscanska Sadasnjost, 1988), 1376.

Chapter 11

How Did Thomas Experience the Reality of Jesus' Resurrection?

Our earlier conclusion that Thomas did not acquire his security of Jesus' resurrection through sensory information raises several new questions. How and from what sources did Thomas gain his information? What was his psychological experience and what convinced him psychologically of the reality of Jesus' resurrection? The following section will attempt to answer these questions.

11.1. Thomas' Epistemological Problem

Everything we know, feel, remember, or generally experience of reality, outside and in ourselves, is registered by our mind. Even spiritual matters, including God's closeness with us, we register in our mind/psyche. Where does the information in our mind come from? John Paul II noted:

> The fact that human knowledge is primarily sensory surprises no one. Neither Plato nor Aristotle nor any of the classical philosophers questioned this. Cognitive realism, both so-called naïve realism and critical realism, agrees that *"nihil est in intellectu, quod prius non fuerit in sensu."* ("Nothing is in the intellect, which was not first in the senses")[1]

This famous sentence, written some 300 years ago by the philosopher John Locke in an *Essay Concerning Human Understanding*, changed the whole human theory of knowledge. Without sensory information, the human mind would be a "tabula rasa," a blank slate, thought Locke.

Here we are confronted with a controversy. Thomas' faith, as we concluded in our previous discussion, was intellectually (psychologically) experienced, in the sense that he knew, felt, and experienced his own trust in Jesus. However, we also concluded that Jesus' intervention was not received through Thomas' senses. How, then, did he "hear," register, and experience God's intervention and call, and more specifically, how did Thomas' mind register Jesus' resurrection?

The simplest answer is this: God is almighty, so he could make this happen. The resurrected Jesus somehow intervened in Thomas' mind and psyche, causing his conversion. That is factually true. But the question raised in the previous chapter still remains: how did Thomas experience the effect or change that God had instigated in his mind, which enabled him to consciously and freely regain his faith and cry out, "My Lord and my God?" Even if Jesus performed an inexplicable miracle, we are still left with the puzzle of how Thomas experienced it in his mind.

Though we cannot discuss God's miraculous transformation of Thomas, we can analyze Thomas' psychological reaction to God's intervention. Our first task will be to understand how Thomas' recognition functioned (and how recognition functions in the human mind in general).

11.2. The "Blueprint" and Functioning of Thomas' Mind

In everyday life, sensation and perception are the first sources of information about external and internal reality. The next step, as we know from medicine and psychology, is the assessment and evaluation of acquired perceptions. This happens by comparing the perceived to other already experienced information. Something similar had to happen in Thomas' mind while he was pondering the surprising verbal reports of his peers about Jesus' resurrection.

The psychological functions involved in assessing newly acquired sensory information (for example visible or touchable stimuli) include perception, consciousness, thought, feeling, attention, memory, will, instinct, and conscience. These functions are connected to the physiological functioning of particular areas and centers in the brain, and their integration within a new psychological functional unit—the self—enables one to function as a person. What we call personality is the end-result of an integration of all mental functions in one unit: the self. We can diagram this in Figure 11-1.

The figure illustrates the psychological functions produced by particular brain centers. A functional integration of the mental functions drawn inside the circle represents the conscious self, while those drawn outside the circle represent the preconscious content of the mind. The summing up of past and recent perceptions, thoughts, feelings, memories, and other contents of the mind enables one to form his or her opinion.

Figure 11-1

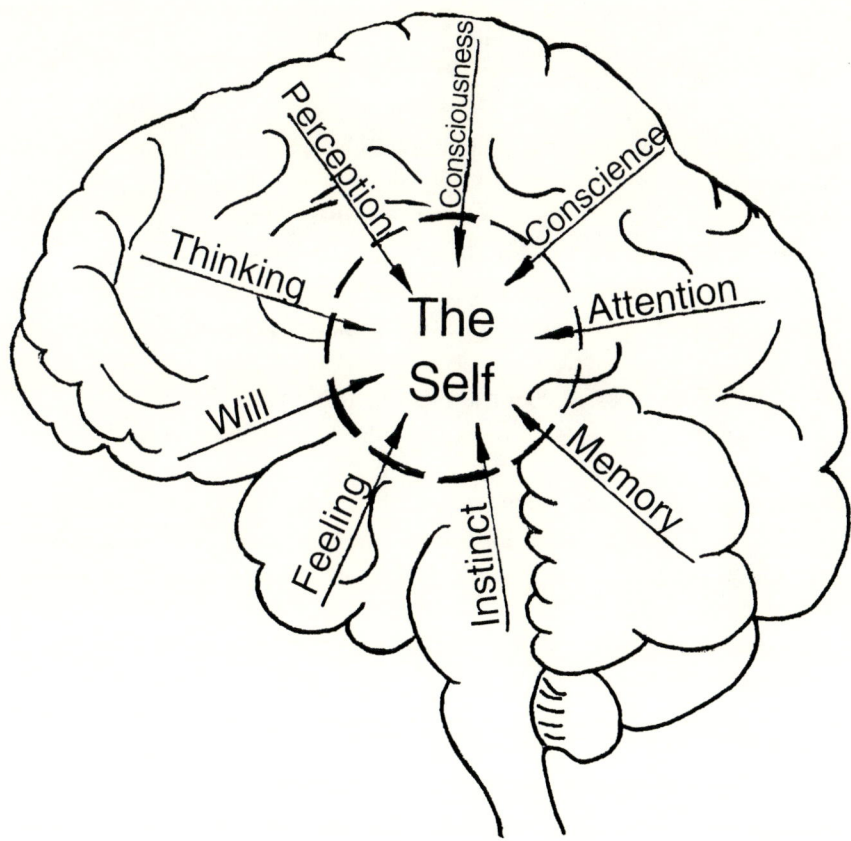

Such a process of integration in Thomas' mind influenced his reaction when the other disciples told him, "We have seen the Lord!" Thomas evaluated the new information (that Jesus was seen alive), comparing it with previously acquired evidence (that Jesus is dead). He mistakenly concluded that he now knew that this resurrected Jesus couldn't exist and asked for more convincing proof, namely, to see and touch him. As a final step typical of all evaluations, and as a consequence of this particular one, Thomas made up his own mind, adopting an almost positivist/atheist rejection of belief. If we were in his situation, who among us would behave differently?

In the next verses, Jesus' re-appearance is described. He intervened and Thomas regained his faith. From a psychological perspective, which mental functions enabled this? Furthermore, how did Thomas experience that Jesus had intervened in his personality, which led to the change in his behavior described in John 20:24-29?

Let us analyze Thomas' mental functions, one by one. Some of his psychological functions are easy to exclude, for example Thomas' perception. We concluded earlier that sight or even focused attention when talking to Jesus was insufficient for the disciples to acknowledge his resurrection on the road to Emmaus. Accordingly, even Thomas, before Jesus' intervention, did not recognize the resurrected Lord only by sight. We can also exclude Thomas' instinct, because there is no instinct in or related to faith. Faith was a free and responsible choice that Thomas made. In addition, any subconscious or conscious volition on Thomas' part can be excluded. He so blatantly refused to believe in the resurrection, that any conscious or subconscious deliberation underlying his utterances would be difficult to detect. From John's description we can conclude that his logic and reasoning, most probably heavily supported by emotion and memory, were sharply turned against acknowledging the resurrection.

Let us review. Jesus' intervention did not happen by engaging in some long, logical or emotional persuasion or by evoking memories of past revelations (as in the case of the disciples traveling to Emmaus). From John's description we have the impression that Thomas, like other disciples, did not ponder at length over whether the resurrection happened; instead, his conversion was an almost immediate transformation. First, Thomas rejected Jesus' resurrection without hesitation; then, seemingly immediately afterwards, he accepted it. Obviously there must have been a very important reason for such a radical change in his behavior which, as we discern from the biblical report, was connected to Jesus' appearance, words, and activities, but it was not an instance of simple recognition. How could this almost instantaneous reawakening of faith have happened if not through Thomas' perception, memory, will, feelings, consciousness, thoughts, or instinct?

Something had to change in his mind; his revival could not have occurred without a firm reason. This mysterious "something" would still remain unknown if we looked simply at the psychological functions discussed so far. It had to have occurred through a function on which we have not yet focused. The colloquial word for this psychological function is "conscience."

From our everyday experience, we know that conscience is especially important in resolving questions of faith. Common sense and biblical theology are in agreement with this. In Rom. 9:1, St. Paul declares, "I speak the truth in Christ—I am not lying, my conscience confirms it in the Holy Spirit—. . ." Theologically speaking, conscience reflects and confirms God's requests and guidance; it is a "bridge" connecting the apostle Paul and us, his successors, to the resurrected Jesus and the Holy Spirit.

Psychologically speaking, conscience is a peculiar function. Its function always involves evaluation of one's behavior from an ethical perspective. Although conscience neither reflects nor perceives reality as do the senses nor reacts to perceived reality as do feelings, thoughts, and other psychological functions, it enables a person to take a morally responsible stand.

Another peculiarity in the functioning of conscience is that it neither helps us to understand reality nor come to some pragmatic position on it as do all other psychological functions. Conscience only enables the subject's moral and ethical principles to perceive reality via other mental functions. In Thomas' case, it enabled him to connect the natural with the supernatural: events foretold in revelation with actual events; Jesus' intervention as he experienced it with his acknowledgment of the reality of his Master's resurrection.

All of this still does not explain how Jesus altered Thomas' mind. If we are to even come close to an answer, we must assume that Thomas likely experienced Jesus' transformation of him through his conscience and not through his other psychological functions. For this reason we will next examine this puzzling psychological function we call conscience.

first from the agnostic's, and then from the believer's perspective. We will then reconstruct the possible dynamics of Thomas' conversion.

11.3. Can an Agnostic Model Explain Thomas' Conversion?

We will use Sigmund Freud's teachings as representative of different agnostic explanations of human behavior. We will, however, focus even more on what agnostics cannot explain, either in Thomas' behavior or in that of contemporary believers. Is faith merely the "theorizing of a neurotic," as Freud labeled it, according to Viktor Frankl's *Ärztliche Seelsorge*?[2] Or, is it an authentic and true means of human communication with the almighty, eternal, and ultimate loving God, which agnostics are unable to grasp? That is what we aim to find out in the following discussion.

Summarizing Freud's concepts, Joseph Schwarz compares the human mind to a glass of water.[3] What is below the surface of the water represents the "id,"—the instinct. What is above the surface represents the "superego." (The concept of superego in Freud's model is most comparable to "conscience" in everyday language.) Only that which is on the surface of the water represents the responsible "ego"—the self. This is illustrated in Figure 11-2.

Figure 11-2

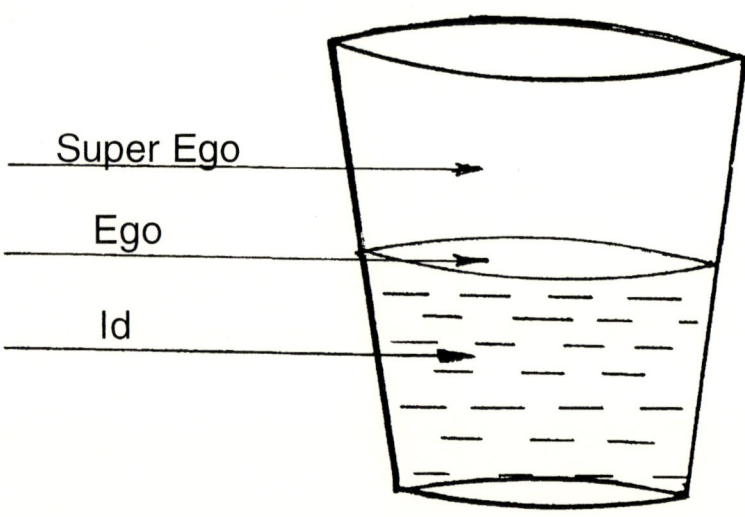

Super Ego

Ego

Id

According to the same author, we can summarize Freud's understanding of instinct as follows. Instinct is the dark side of the human personality which does not know logic, space, time, or reality outside itself, but has only one goal: to direct behavior. Its task is to defend and multiply life through whatever means possible. The ego, despite its limited power, has an important task. It has the task of fulfilling (as much as possible) the demands of the instinct while avoiding a collision with the superego (and the societal standards it represents), and at the same time remaining cognizant of natural and social reality. It has to balance instinct and superego, respecting that reality. The ego, then, is accountable for responsible behavior in humans, for instance by making choices and coming to conclusions in religious matters, as we saw Thomas do in the previous chapter.

At what point in a person's life does the superego, the conscience-like function, kick in? According to Otto Fenichel, the functions of the instincts are sufficient for self-preservation immediately after birth.[4] The ego's functioning begins later, brought on by communication with the external world. The turning point instigating the development of the superego occurs at between eighteen and twenty-four months of life, when potty training begins. At this age, the child's parents let him or her know that if he or she learns to regulate urination and defecation, they will show love to the child; if not, they will scold the child. The small child feels that he or she cannot exist without the parents' love. This makes him or her willing to control their instincts. He or she learns to trade the pleasure of satisfying instinct for the parents' love, so to speak. This developmental achievement contributes to the evolution of the superego. According to Fenichel, Ferenczi, one of Freud's early followers, referred to this early "conscience" as "sphincter morals."[5]

During subsequent development, the newly formed superego incorporates parental images, as well as the ethical requirements of society. This enables the superego to select, control, suppress, and censure dangerous, "sinful," and "shameful" instincts compromising social functioning. In this way, the superego contributes security. Its role, observed from this perspective, is the same as that of other psychological functions like perception, thought, or instinct, namely, the preservation of life.

Even agnostic psychological theories that differ markedly from Freud's—for example, cognitive-behavioral approaches—commonly describe conscience as an "internal inhibitor" and share the idea that psychological functions adjust life to social reality, enhance the individual's safety and security, and contribute to the preservation of life. The better that psychological mechanisms such as the superego work, the greater the chances for a safe, successful, and prosperous life. From this perspective, there is no relevant difference between the teachings of Freud, of a behaviorist, or a proponent of any other agnostic school of thought.

How can we apply agnostic views of conscience and its role to Thomas' encounter with Jesus? Like every normal man or woman, Thomas had a healthy, well-functioning "superego," or,in behaviorist terminology, an "internal inhibitor." Its role was to protect and make Thomas' life safer by controlling antisocial instincts and accepting socially required behavior. Nevertheless, to be a disciple of Jesus, especially immediately after his execution, was neither socially desired nor acceptable. Faith in the resurrected Jesus was an explicit threat to Thomas' safety and security, and therefore his superego demanded extreme caution in accepting the passionate claim of the other disciples: "We have seen the Lord!" Thomas' superego likely fully supported his response: "Unless I see the nail marks in his hands and put my finger where the nails were and put my hand in his side, I will not believe it." There is no way that a "healthy" superego would support Thomas' renewed faith.

In fact, any agnostic psychological concept can explain the behavior of an agnostic or atheist. It can even explain Thomas' refusal and reluctance to believe, but not the revival of his faith. However, even though Thomas' id, ego, or superego neither supported his conversion nor initiated it, Thomas' conversion occurred. The conclusion is inevitable: without the approval of his ego, instinct, or superego, Thomas had a conscious experience of his renewed relationship to God by psychological mechanisms that are not acknowledged by agnostic psychologists and psychiatrists.

11.4. Can a Christian Model of Conscience Account for Thomas' Conversion Experience?

A positive answer to the above question comes almost spontaneously. If Thomas' revived faith was not due to the previously discussed psychological functions or to his superego, then a different kind of conscience, a moral or Christian conscience, remains the only possible explanation for his crying out, "My Lord and my God!" Even though the logic of this reasoning appears self-evident, let us discuss in detail the evidence that supports the claim that (in contrast to the agnostic models) such a Christian conscience actually exists and is active in people of faith. In our discussion we will start from observed facts, then explain these philosophically. In turn, we will explain philosophical insights psychologically, and finally clarify psychological explanations theologically.

A. Observational Facts

Writers and poets had described the redemptive transformation of the human psyche, similar to that of Thomas, long before professionals recognized it. For example, Victor Hugo's well-known novel *Les Misérables*[6] depicts such an experience. The convict Jean Valjean, after having been granted his wish to stay in a retired bishop's house overnight, stole two silver candleholders. Caught by the police, then questioned about the goods in his possession, Valjean explained that his benefactor had given them to him. The suspicious policemen took Valjean back to the clergyman to corroborate his story. The old priest immediately understood the situation and surprised everyone by crying out the following, which I've rephrased, "O my dear friend, why did you leave behind the other things I gave you? Here they are; take them." He exclaimed this while putting some additional silver plates into Valjean's bag. By such unexpected and superhuman benevolence, the old bishop not only showed an exemplary Christian mind-set, but also awakened and inspired Valjean's conscience and changed his lifestyle forever.

This narrative is fiction; nonetheless, it portrays the human behavior pattern characterized by love, forgiveness, and unselfishness, all of which are quite inexplicable from the perspective of the superego, internal inhibitor, or similar type of conscience. Was the old bishop insane? Not according to the DSM-IV (Diagnostic and Statistical Manual of the American Psychiatric Association), in which there are no diagnoses that fit the description of the old clergyman's behavior.

Of greater immediate and concrete significance than fictional stories are the real life experiences which illustrate time and again that in the human mind psychological functions are at work acknowledging and enabling a real relationship with a real God. Such behavior as that exhibited by the old priest, or later by Valjean himself (or Thomas), are inappropriate and forbidden from the ego's, and especially from the superego's, perspective. How much more inappropriate and forbidden, from a Freudian or other non-religious theoretical framework, are the behaviors exhibited by Jesus, great prophets, church fathers and teachers, martyrs, and saints. They failed at, and moreover were uninterested in, making their lives safe or lucrative, and they ultimately sacrificed their well-being, not because they disregarded the superego and indulged in uncontrolled or antisocial behavior, but because they obeyed meanings, objectives, and values that differed greatly from those required by the superego, or by any other psychological function we have discussed.

We know this because behavior reflects one's mental processes and psychological make-up. If human behavior were regulated only by the psychological functions that agnostics recognize, then the model behaviors exhibited by prophets, by the disciples, by modern exemplary believers like Don Bosco, Maximilian Kolbe, or Mother Teresa, by billions of Christian believers, and even by many non-Christians, would not be realized. Ruled by their instinct, ego, and superego, humans would serve only worldly needs and goals. They would be little more than gifted animals possessing sophisticated cognitive functions and uninterested in the search for ideals, morality, or God. However, writers and poets present us with very different personalities, heroes, and behavior, almost as though there were two different kind of human personalities in the world.

B. Philosophical Explanation of Observational Facts

Hugo's novel depicts a universal human experience. Billions of Christians and billions of non-Christian religious people have searched for God, as their self-understanding and behavior prove. This fact (according to Ferenc Szabo) inspired the philosopher Pauler to describe humans as a "race searching for God."[7] However, if we really are a race searching for God, then, as Viktor Frankl terms it, a *Sinn Organ*—an "organ of purpose" (or an organ searching for ultimate purpose)—must exist not only in Christians but in every human person.[8] This "organ of faith"—a moral, religious, or Christian conscience—enables us to consciously strive not only for survival, but also for ultimate meaning—that is, God. It also enables us to freely and responsively declare like Thomas, "My Lord and my God."

One of the main differences between animals and humans is that every *Homo sapiens* is constantly evaluating or self-justifying, asking: "Am I making the right choice or fulfilling the right meaning in this situation—or in my entire life?" But we do not assess ourselves by a relative or arbitrary standard. We could translate Teilhard de Chardin's teaching (see *Le Milieu Divin*): The moral conscience is "in us," but "without us."9 It does not take its standard from the world we live in, but from the Absolute. This is the moral principle by which *Homo sapiens*, and *homo religious* judge themselves.

However, the absolute moral principle valid in one's own personal case may be assessed correctly or incorrectly. The accuracy of the assessment is not the point. The real criterion for self-evaluation is assessing one's personal reflections, circumstances, etc., by an absolute natural, moral law, which Immanuel Kant described as existing in every human mind.

Philosophically, any moral comparison is impossible without an absolute standard. However, the only Absolute is God. We compare any morality, meaning, or value according to natural laws reflecting the Absolute. This is how the human mind is created, and how God, through the standards of moral law, is unconsciously present even in non-believers. Even more evidently, he is present in the minds of his people of faith, through what we have called Christian conscience. This "organ of faith" enables the human person to consciously strive for a genuine form of human existence, which can be realized only in a relationship with God.

Next, let us continue outlining the characteristics of the "organ of faith," and then in the following chapters, see how it enables a conscious, psychologically experienced relationship with God.

C. A Psychological Explanation of Philosophers' Insights

Paraphrasing Freud's terminology, we may refer to Christian conscience as a "hyperego" (meaning "above, over, more powerful then superego") and using Frankl's teaching we may describe it as an "organ of faith" (enabling a psychological experience of God's call and one's own trust in him). Such a moral conscience cannot be reduced to a function of the superego. It cannot be labeled an internal inhibitor reflecting any model of "survival of the fittest" serving either a worldly or natural psychological function. In the following section, we will discuss this "hyperego conscience" (synonymous with moral and Christian conscience) in relation to Freud's superego conscience.

As noted, the Christian conscience's anthropological, or more exactly psychological, location can be thought of as existing as a hyperego, "above" the superego, the self, and instinct in Freud's model. What we are calling the hyperego conscience (or the Christian, or moral conscience) is a psychological function enabling the experiencing of the ultimate (God's) meaning, love, hope, trust, and above all, God's call, which is more important than every other worldly goal or value represented by the superego, ego, or instinct.

If antisocial instincts (which obviously do exist in humans) can be (and are) controlled, then obviously a censor such as the superego must, and does, exist. According to the same logic, however, if "quite other" spiritual ideals and morals are reflected in the behavior of people of faith, then a function enabling conscious experience of faith, and of the Spirit's teaching also has to exist. Thus it is possible to use the superego to explain the behavior of agnostics or atheists, but not that of Christians, or even non-Christian religious people. They apparently obey a different, supreme, or more exactly, ultimate "supervisor" that exceeds the superego.

There are other differences as well. While the superego serves the preservation of biological life at all costs, the Christian conscience preserves everlasting life at all costs. While the former requires security and a prosperous life at all costs, the latter requires service to and union with God, even if this makes one's life insecure. While the superego serves as an internal inhibitor, censoring antisocial or dangerous instincts and impulses, the moral conscience acts as an "internal stimulator." It does not inhibit, but rather motivates, requiring and stimulating spiritual, biblical behavior, and in so doing, enabling the attainment of the gifts of faith as consequences of a union with God.

In contrast to the superego, which promotes obedience and submission to external and internal standards of survival, the Christian conscience has as its main role the promotion of freedom. The moral conscience encourages not slavery to the law or to societal standards and expectations as does the superego, but rather freedom—the ability to discern new, responsible, and individual ways of doing good. The Spirit's roles of freedom and leadership become operational in the Christian conscience.

It is possible to psychologically analyze, understand, or in some cases "fix" the functioning of the superego, the internal inhibitor, or similar control mechanisms. The religious conscience, or as Kant termed it the absolute moral law, is generally off-limits in psychotherapy.

A blind or mentally retarded person cannot be taught or "conditioned" to eyesight or intelligence. Similarly, conscience (or the absolute moral law) can only be awakened, educated, or inspired; it cannot be caused, given, or taken away even by the best of parents, educators, or psychotherapists.

The superego preserves life well if it is flexible and adaptable. "If you live in Rome, live like a Roman," goes the saying. In practice, this often means accepting one's environment and behavioral constraints. In contrast, the requirement of moral conscience to do what is morally good is probably the deepest and most unchangeable imprint humans possess. The requirement to do what is morally good (independently of that which one discerns as "good") never changes, never loses validity. Philosophers from Plato through Kant to Frankl have been amazed by this immanent quality of conscience, possessed by all humans, and requiring the fulfillment of the most paramount of natural laws: to do good.

D. A Theological Clarification of the Psychological Explanation

The role and task of conscience, as St. Paul describes it in many instances (Rom. 2:14-16, 2 Cor. 4:2, 1 Tim. 3:9, 2 Tim. 1:3, and Heb. 13:18) is to reflect God in the human mind. Paul wrote:

> Indeed, when Gentiles who do not have the law, do by nature things required by the law, they are a law for themselves, even though they do not have the law, since they show that the requirements of the law are written on their hearts, their consciences also bearing witness, and their thoughts now accusing, now even defending them. (Rom. 2:14-15)

What we have here is the Apostle's conviction that gentiles, as well as other non-Christians, despite their lack of Moses' law, behave similarly to Jews because they are obeying the natural law written in their hearts. Agnostics, atheists, and people altogether indifferent to religion have written on their hearts God's natural law as well. Paul summarizes this natural law in Romans 13.9: "Love is the fulfillment of law;" and in Galatians 5:14 he states, "The entire law is summed up in a single command: 'Love your neighbor as yourself.'" According to Ferenc Szabo, Thomas Aquinas goes so far as to assert that, in revelation, the natural law is fulfilled.[10]

However, the role of the hyperego conscience (a moral conscience) lies not only in hearing the requirements of the natural law but also in registering God's presence and in hearing God's call with its invitation to respond. Empirically and psychologically, there is no other mental human function enabling either an experience of and union with God or behavior that runs contrary to worldly wisdom.

On the other hand, this is exactly what conscience requires: being "in the world, but not of it," to paraphrase John 17:11 and 17:16. In this regard, St Paul wrote in 2 Corinthians 1:12:

> Now this is our boast: Our conscience testifies that we have conducted ourselves in the world, and especially in our relationship with you, in the holiness and sincerity that are from God. We have done so not according to worldly wisdom but according to God's grace.

The requirement of living according to the natural law, and even more according to God's law (especially as Christ taught and exemplified it), is how we will define conscience in this book. Thus, the hyperego conscience (Christian, moral, or religious conscience—four terms for the same concept) is comprised of the characteristics in one's personality that reflect "holiness and sincerity that are from God" (2 Cor. 1:12). This is what we will understand by the term "conscience."

The Christian way of life was never acceptable to the world, and the world in turn always presented a challenge to it. What made Christians (I mean true Christians, not "Christian-Pharisees") such insufferable and abhorrent people in the eyes of the world? We use the term "world" to include people directed by instinct, superego, and ego, who accept biological, psychological, and sociological rules, laws, and customs, but who do not strive to transcend their nature, to be different from and more than just a "social animal."

The answer lies in the fact that Christians respected and emphasized their conscience, which does not serve worldly success, fun, or survival of the fittest. Christian conscience does not reflect selfishness—the prized principle of the world—but a Christ-like lifestyle that is and always has been repulsive to communist or radical capitalist ideologists, led by "human animal" principles. Christians were always strangers in such a world. Rather Christians have always listened to and acted on conscience. This has enabled them to receive God's grace, to live with and experience God, and to dwell in a different world: God's kingdom.

11.5. Do We Have The Explanation Now?

We started this chapter by asking the question: If not through his senses, how did Thomas discern the reality of Jesus' resurrection? To answer this question we first analyzed Thomas' mental functions one by one. We concluded that psychologically there was no other possibility for Thomas' mind than to first obtain the reality of Jesus' resurrection through his conscience. Thus, it was through Thomas' conscience that Jesus intervened to enable him to regain his faith and cry out, "My Lord and my God!"

We then discussed what Christian conscience is and how it functions. By discussing observational facts and psychological and theological explanations, we concluded that Christian conscience is a unique function that assesses reality differently from any other structure in the human mind. We then deduced that, primarily through his conscience, Thomas had experienced the reality of Jesus' intervention and his resurrection.

Thus, Christian conscience is the "organ" that not only communicates with the natural world, but also receives "quite other" information, since in Thomas' case it was able to recognize Jesus' transcendental, non-sensory message.

However, if we define conscience as that which does not so much reflect the rules of the natural world we live in, but rather the holiness and sincerity that come from God, then we are confronted with new and difficult questions.

Where does the believer's ethical knowledge reflecting non-material Spiritual inspiration come from? How does the everyday, experiential psychological function of conscience receive information of the spiritual, "quite other" God? And inversely, how can our psychological Christian conscience contact God's "quite other" reality? How is the believer's finite mind able to contact and communicate with infinite reality?

Was something more than just Thomas' mind and psychologically experiential conscience involved in the communication between Thomas and the resurrected Jesus?

We realize that there ought to be a "missing link" between the psychological function of Christian conscience and the supernatural God, between the brain and the spiritual realm, and between the human and the transcendental.

One well-known philosopher writing during the Enlightenment was concerned that all of the mysteries perplexing people would sooner or later be solved. We see, however, the opposite occurring: with every question that is answered, innumerable new mysteries emerge.

Notes

1. John Paul II, *Crossing the Threshold of Hope* (New York: Alfred A. Knopf, 1994), 33.

2. Viktor E. Frankl, *Ärztliche Seelsorge* (Wien: Franz Deuticke, 1965), 29.

3. Joseph Schwarz, *Argumente fur Gottes Existenz* (Eisenstadt: 1988), 80.

4. Otto Fenichel, *The Psychoanalytic Theory of Neuroses* (New York: Norton, 1972), 103-6.

5. Fenichel, *Theory*, 102.

6. Victor Hugo, *Les Misérables* (London: Penguin Books, 1976).

7. Ferenc Szabo, *Az Ember es vilaga* (Rome: Self-published, 1969), 68 and 86.

8. Viktor E. Frankl, *Antropologische Grundlagen der Psychoterapie* (Wien: Hans Huber, 1976), 21.

9. Pierre Teilhard de Chardin, *Le Milieu Divin* (Paris: Seuil, 1957), 197.

10. Ferenc Szabo, *Az Ember*, 174.

Chapter 12

The "Missing Link" between Believers' Conscience and the Spiritual God

At the doorstep of the Faculty of Theology where I studied was posted the well-known sentence of St. Anselm of Canterbury: *Fides quaerens intelectum* ("Faith searches reason"). Probably nowhere is our reasoning more questioned than in the topics we are going to discuss in this chapter and the next. Are humans comprised of a spirit and body, as many believers think, or a body and mind only, or a combination of spirit, mind, and body? From a philosophical, moral, and practical perspective, nothing is more important than how we answer those questions.

Nobody doubts that we are or have a body. Due to the progress of psychiatry and psychology, the mind is also accepted as a real component of the human constitution. It is different for the idea of the human spirit. Even believers sometimes find it difficult to incorporate soul and spirit into their professional ways of thinking. On the other hand, despite the agnostic/positivist mental climate we live in, one hears much talk of "spirituality." Often the idea is used in an ancient magical, animistic, and mythical context. Even more surprisingly, archaic magical, mechanic/materialist, and positivistic concepts often coexist in the minds of some postmodern people.

For example, despite general acceptance of the concept that the human mind is a product of the brain and despite such mythical spiritual ideas as those mentioned above, the concepts of spirit and mind are still envisioned by many as interrelated. Often, even non-religious agnostics and positivists have a vague sense of something awesome and indefinable—in short, spiritual—acting and influencing their personality, feelings, or behavior.

According to Norman Geisler, the following confession is attributed to Bertrand Russell:

> even when one feels nearest to other people, something in one seems obstinately to belong to God, and to refuse to enter into any earthly communion—at least that is how I should express it if I thought there was a God. It is odd, isn't it? I care passionately for this world and many things and people in it, and yet . . . what is it all? There must be something more important, one feels, though I don't believe there is.[1]

In such "natural," non-religious concepts of spirituality, the very old and essential problem with which we ended the previous chapter remains unanswered: how can the immaterial spirit and the material brain work together? Modern science understands that the human brain produces the contents of the mind—sort of like a computer—in a strictly causal and deterministically regulated manner. How could such a mechanically functioning brain be truly interconnected with a non-material spirit?

A typical Enlightenment answer emerged in the now controversial ideas of Gottfried W. Leibniz. According to Leibniz non-material spirit could not interact with the material body or brain. We only have the impression that such interaction occurs because God set up the body and spirit in a fashion comparable to two clocks that show the same time, but function independently of each other. "In the body everything happens as though it were directed by a spirit, and in the spirit everything happens as though it were connected to a body," thought Leibniz in his 1710 *Théodicée*, according to Mihail Jarosevski.[2]

In contrast to the proponents of mythical spirituality stand other contemporary professionals. These include positivist and materialist behavioral scientists, neurologists, physiologists, and brain researchers. They will find measurable physical, chemical, biochemical, or neurological processes which are always and only regulated by the principle of cause-and-effect in the body and the brain, the organ of psychological life. However, a materialist viewpoint cannot explain a believer's conscientious spiritual behavior of "being in the world, but not of it." Nor can it explain Christian love and faith, the "gifts of faith," and other biblical behaviors that so plainly contradict the view of the brain's serving only biological survival. Indeed, Wesley's experience of "speaking for half an hour with God" cannot be explained by those thinking in materialistic and positivistic concepts.

This will be our agenda as we search for a hypothetical "missing link" that may bridge the transcendental gap between the psychological conscience and the transcendental God.

First we will discuss the relevant teachings of past philosophers who are still important sources of human knowledge about "metaphysics"— that is, reality beyond the physical, visible, and touchable.

Then we will discuss revelation, which was, is, and always will be (for believers) the most important source of knowledge about the spiritual (God's) realm. In doing so, we will discuss the anthropological concepts of the ancient Hebrews and those of St. Paul.

Thirdly, we will, from a neurological and psychological perspective, supplemented with philosophical and biblical concepts, observe how the human soul, mind, and brain are able to experience God's "quite other" spiritual reality—how and through which brain and psychological functions believers communicate with God.

In subsequent chapters, we have to be especially humble. The topic of our discussion borders on mystery, first because we cannot see, touch, and measure what we are trying to understand, and even more because God does not reveal exactly how communication occurs between the transcendent spirit and scientifically established brain processes. For these reasons, our knowledge cannot reach metaphysical certainty; nor can it always be based on evidence "beyond a reasonable doubt." Sometimes we have to use metaphors or work with a balance of probabilities, while hoping that different, better explanations will emerge in the future. We know for sure that somehow the interaction between spirit, mind, and body occurs, and that God "touches" the human mind and personality. The following discussion is a small step towards understanding how.

Notes

1. Norman L. Geisler, *Baker Encyclopedia of Christian Apologetics* (Grand Rapids, MI: Baker Books, 2000), 676.

2. Mihail Jarosevski, *Istoria Psihologii* (Moskva: Izdatelstvo Misl, 1966), 186.

Chapter 13

Theologians' and Philosophers' Explanations

In our overview, we will focus only on those relevant philosophical ideas that can help us understand how the believers' experiential union with the invisible God occurs. The concepts we will now discuss cover some two-and-a-half thousand years of human intellectual history.

13.1. From Plato to Augustine

The Jews had great, divinely-inspired kings, judges, and prophets, but they had no great philosophers. In contrast, the ancient Greeks had great philosophers, but no great spiritual leaders or theologians. The reason for this is that the Hebrews trusted revelation to answer the questions that the Greeks hoped their philosophers would. The friendly interaction between Jesus' followers, the early apologists, church teachers and fathers, and pagan philosophers may be surprising to us. However, what may surprise us even more is the profundity of the insights of Greek thinkers, which were later often adopted and used by Christian philosophers.

The first great philosopher who explicitly divided material appearance from spiritual essence, was Plato (427-347 BC). According to Will Durant, Plato realized that human behavior "flows from three main sources: desire, emotion and knowledge."[1] In his understanding "desire has its seat in the loins," emotions are connected to the heart, while "knowledge has its seat in the head." How is knowledge acquired? According to Mihail Jarosevski, while studying with the mathematician

Pythagoras, Plato realized that mathematicians use geometrical ideas like the line, triangle, or circle to research the rules of the world.[2] Even though geometric ideas do not exist anywhere in nature, geometrical ideas best explain the functioning of the natural world. Plato concluded that truth lies not in sensory experience, but in ideas that explain relationships and happenings in sensorial reality and steer natural events, according to his well known metaphor, as a seaman steers his ship. When we think, Plato explained in *Theatetus,* the soul is talking to itself about recollections gathered in an existence prior to birth, in a world of ideas. The world of ideas is ideal and eternal, like non-material geometrical ideas themselves. Humans too are an "idea" temporarily imprisoned in a material body, the "prison of the soul." Plato also described conscience (*sineidesis*) as a motivator in striving for goodness. In *Phaedo,* Plato discussed the eternal, immortal, and ultimate idea: God. Plato was the first to bring these themes into philosophical discourse. He discussed god as the creator of the universe ("cosmos"); but, unlike the Judeo-Christian God, Plato's was anonymous, more a "divinity" than a personal God.

Plato's influence was, and is, enormous on Christian thought. It is evident in the works of everyone from Saints Paul and Luke, to Plotinus and St. Augustine, to Scholastics like Albert the Great and Bonaventure, to contemporary Neo-Platonic philosophers.

Yet another prominent philosopher with challenging ideas was Aristotle, a thinker of the fourth century BC (384-322). As Will Durant explains, Aristotle's metaphysics "grew out of his biology. Everything in the world is moved by an inner urge to become something greater than it is." So matter—a mere potential—becomes "something greater" by taking on a specific form. To Aristotle, explains Durant, form was "not merely the shape, but the shaping force, an inner necessity and impulse which moulds mere material to a specific figure and purpose."[3] In his understanding, this particular form or shaping force that moulds matter into a living body in living creatures is the spirit, the principle of life. Therefore, every living being has a unique shaping form (i.e., spirit). There are vegetative (plant), vital (animal), and rational (human) spirits. The forms of things, their spirits, do not exist independently of matter.

Humans manifest a particular human spiritual form, expressed through the matter of the body. According to Jarosevski, Aristotle was the first to describe the psyche (mind) as distinct from all other entities. He identified mind with the rational human spirit, which is able to contemplate and perceive things. Aristotle explained perception with a creative comparison: just as wax is able to retain the imprint of a ring, so the spirit is able to "retain imprints" of things. The human spirit is able to meditate about absolute form, which is god. God, in the Aristotelian sense, inspires humans to imitate his perfection.[4] However, according to F. L. Cross and E. A. Livingstone, Aristotle's sense of the divine "did not hold to be personal in a Christian sense;" his god is a "god of the philosophers"—the primary reason that everything exists.[5] According to Durant, god for Aristotle

> is absolutely perfect; therefore he cannot desire anything; therefore he does nothing. His only occupation is to contemplate the essence of things; and since he himself is the essence of all things, the form of all forms, his sole employment is the contemplation of himself.

Most of Aristotle's writings were virtually lost during the turmoil of the next 1500 years. After the great Scholastic philosopher Thomas Aquinas became familiar with Aristotle's ideas through Arabian sources, "The Philosopher," as Aquinas reverentially called Aristotle in his *Summa Theologiae*, became prominent once more in Western philosophy. While early Scholasticism was neo-Platonic, late Scholasticism was Aristotelian because of Aquinas' efforts. Before moving ahead to Scholasticism, however, let us continue chronologically with Augustine, the greatest Christian philosopher of antiquity.

13.2. From Augustine to Kant

St. Augustine (354-430) was one of the most controversial of thinkers, both rejected and respected. He admired reason but also realized that "there exists something above human reason," According to Norman Geisler, although Augustine used reason to substantiate his faith, he also said, "I believe in order that I may understand."[6] Augustine's dynamic experience and knowledge, especially in philosophy-theology, is interesting and amusing. First, he was a Greek pagan, then joined a cult of Manicheism which he later replaced with Neo-Platonism, after which he became a zealous Christian, and finally became the bishop of Hippo, in North Africa. His abundant psychological and theological insights are interesting even today, both to lay and professional persons.

Augustine's contribution to contemporary culture worldwide is enormous. According to Jarosevski, he was the first to describe introspection, an internally acquired self-understanding of the subject.[7] Augustine's concept is widely used in modern psychology from Freud to Frankl and from Beck to Shapiro. What we experience internally as the most important and most evident truth within our self is experienced introspectively.

Almost five hundred years after Augustine, Christianity encountered a radically new way of connecting theology and philosophy. This was accomplished by the Scholastics. The greatest Scholastic theologian, and the greatest saint/church teacher and philosopher, Thomas Aquinas (1225-1274), "The Angelic Doctor," in his *Summa Theologiae* (which contains three parts, 38 tracts, 631 Questions, 3016 articulations, and approximately 15,000 proofs) expanded the teachings of Aristotle and connected them to a Christian context. In his understanding, humans are composed of corporeal and spiritual substance. Although the soul has many characteristics which we may call psychological, it is not material but spiritual. Or inversely, the intellect which the modern vernacular calls mind, is incorporeal and spiritual—it is of the soul.[8]

We may attempt to give a taste of Aquinas' understanding of the human spirit as follows:

1. The spirit is the first principle of life.
2. The spirit has to be non-material because, if not, then matter would be the origin of life.
3. The spirit is independent of the material world because it is non-material.
4. Because it is independent of matter, the spirit is immortal.
5. Because the spirit is immortal and non-material, it stems from God.

To a modern professional, Aquinas' arguments and reasoning may seem speculative. Despite the deep cultural gap between the mental climate of the Middle Ages and that of the twenty-first century, many facets of modern Christian theological anthropology nevertheless reflect the paradigms of Thomism. For example, Aquinas contributed to our understanding that intellect and other mental functions are correlated to the soul's activity.

An example of modern Thomism is found in the work of René Le Trocquer. In *What is Man*, he asserts that intelligence seeks understanding of reality, of being, of that which is. In this pursuit, intelligence deals with both the existing and non-existing. It transcends space and time, discerns the universal and general, but is simultaneously able to withdraw into itself, thereby distinguishing self from non-self.[9]

This capacity of the mind "is linked to a deliverance from everything material, to the mind's situation beyond space and time." The fact that man is "not enclosed within himself" but able to "step out" of himself "is a sure sign of the immaterial nature of the knowing subject." Le Trocquer further explains that "matter, indeed, makes the subject one particular fragment of a species, one part of the universe; it cuts him off from all else."

However, he goes on to say that the ability of the human intellect to contact reality outside of the person is a "sure sign of the immaterial nature of the knowing subject [who] in so far as he thinks, must be spiritual." Such "illuminative power in the intelligence" is "like a reflection in us of the divine intelligence." Thus, Le Trocquer concludes that the soul is a spirit situated beyond space and time, essentially impervious to change, and transcending the body. The soul is therefore naturally immune from corruptibility and there is nothing within that can cause its fragmentation; in other words it is immortal.

Gradually after the high Middle Ages, scholasticism fell into decline. Although Aquinas' thought was used extensively in theology, there was little scholarly expansion. Fortunately, Thomism underwent a revival between the middle of the nineteenth and twentieth centuries. The result is that some seven hundred years following Aquinas' death, some of his ideas—rephrased by Jacques Maritain, Joseph Marechal, Karl Rahner, Bernard Lonergan, the philosopher Henry Bergson and the psychiatrist López-Ibor—are still very much present in the modern Zeitgeist.

However, in those seven hundred years there have been other important philosophical developments. The first sophisticated post-Scholastic philosopher relevant to our discussion, René Descartes (1596-1650), built his philosophy from scratch. According to Cross and Livingstone, Descartes first "rejected everything in which one can imagine the least doubt." Then, by proclaiming, "I think, therefore I exist," he established a secure foothold. He then proved God's existence. Descartes found the idea of God within himself—since he, Descartes, had the idea of God, and since "this idea must have all the perfections that are represented in the idea," it (the idea of God) does not stem from the imperfect world, but from God himself.[10]

Unlike the Scholastics' understanding of soul, Descartes' soul had nothing to do with directing the body or behavior. He imagined the functions of the body working mechanically, like a clock; but instead of springs and gears, the body moves by muscles and bones so that the spirit's role becomes unnecessary. Descartes' dualism, so typical of Enlightenment thinkers, is close to Leibniz' speculation which we already discussed. He signaled a turning point in philosophy. Nevertheless, the next in a series of almost mortal blows to metaphysical philosophy came in the century that followed, through the writings of Immanuel Kant.

13.3. From Kant to Rahner

The publication of *The Critique of Pure Reason* by Immanuel Kant (1724-1804) in 1781 marks a turning point in philosophy.

Kant's work posed a significant challenge to the extreme skepticism introduced into philosophy some sixty years earlier by David Hume. Hume had proclaimed that no causal relationship could be proven rationally between natural occurrences. According to Will Durant, he argued that we perceive events only and then "infer causation or necessity."[11] So, according to Geisler, "after the constant conjunction of two objects, heat and flame, for instance . . . we are determined by custom alone to expect the one from the appearance of the other."[12] Hume's skepticism is so all encompassing that, if we were to follow him, we could not, without first testing our assumption, be sure even that "the sun will rise tomorrow."

Kant, however, realized that there are facts we know without any prior testing. For example, we know with absolute certainty that the sum of the internal angles in every triangle always equals 180 degrees, or that the sum of the angles in a square equal 360 degrees. According to human logic and knowledge, these geometrical figures cannot be otherwise. Also, the laws of Newtonian physics have a similar universal a priori validity; that is, we know their relevance in advance without prior testing. According to Cross and Livingstone, Kant "felt that there could be only one solution, namely that it was the understanding (*Verstand*) which prescribed to nature her laws."[13] In other words, "the validity of the causal law ('every event has a cause') rests not on some constraining principle in the external world of nature, but in the fact that consciousness is so constituted that it cannot but so interpret the empirical data which it receives." The brain's functional characteristics determine how we perceive perceptions and, ultimately, reality. Therefore, in studying reality, we discover in it our own brain's functional principles beyond every perception. By this, according to Cross and Livingstone, "Kant cut at the root of traditional metaphysics, with its claim to provide knowledge of subjects which wholly transcended nature." Most philosophers after Kant agree not only that they are unable to rationally discuss or explore metaphysical reality, but also that humanity cannot even know the essence of reality. We can only appreciate how reality appears to us.

As a fervent Lutheran, Kant substantiated his own faith in God by discerning, according to Cross and Livingstone, that "the stern voice of conscience in man assures him of truths reason is impotent to establish." Relying not on metaphysical reasoning but on his conscience, Kant found his way to God. However, widespread skepticism had been unleashed by Kant's ideas. After the year 1781, metaphysical philosophy, despite numerous attempts to revitalize itself, never again became a universally accepted school of thought.

Subsequently, philosophers of the nineteenth and twentieth centuries actively sought a solution to the controversy raised by Kant. The early existentialist Søren A. Kierkegaard (1813-1855) expanded Kant's "Copernican Revolution." According to Millard. J. Erickson, the essence of Kierkegaard's philosophy is a revolt against the metaphysical, where, in the search for ultimate truth, a subject's individuality has no role. But for him truth exists always in the subject's personal experience, in which spirit, soul and conscience have a prominent role and responsibility.[14]

According to Erickson, Kierkegaard rejected Hegel's impersonal and universal concept of logic. (According to Hegel, even angels and God must respect logic if they, indeed, think or act logically.) According to Kierkegaard, however,

> The difference between God and man is not merely one of degree. God is not merely like man but more so. They are of fundamental different kinds. Thus God cannot be known by taking the highest and the best elements within man and amplifying them. Being qualitatively distinct, God cannot be extrapolated from the ideas that man has nor from the qualities of man's personality or character.

Since God is "absolutely different," his logic must be different as well. By analyzing God's behavior described in the Scriptures, Kierkegaard developed a system of "paradoxical logic" to help illuminate God's way of thinking. Here are some freely quoted examples, given by Bernard Rahm.

- Humans need to use reason; however, they are unable to understand God through reason.
- Humans are responsible for sins; however, they are unable to willfully avoid sinning.
- One must lose life to find it.
- To save oneself, one must take up his or her cross.
- The greatest is the smallest.
- Some of the first become the last.
- God is at the same time everywhere and nowhere.[15]

Other philosophers did try to revive metaphysical philosophy. According to Erickson, the pragmatist William James (1842-1910), together with Charles. S. Pierce (1839-1914), established the so-called Metaphysical Club in Cambridge, Massachusetts, with the purpose of developing a "scientific metaphysics." However, their ideas shifted focus. While metaphysical philosophy was concerned with discerning absolute truth, pragmatism emphasized (according to Erickson) that "the meaning of an idea lies solely in its practical results." Accordingly, "We should be concerned not with how God is, but with the effects, 'the phenomenology of him'."[16] As Armand A. Maurer states, "Faith and trust in God is helpful," therefore true. According to the same source, we can summarize the message of James' *The Varieties of Religious Experience*, as follows: Only what is in harmony with reality is useful. Therefore, "This supreme reality, which Christians call God, is real because he produces real effects."[17]

Maurice Blondel (1861-1949) turned to Neo-Platonism. In his understanding (according to Etienne Gilson) only the "concrete is real." Nevertheless, the abstract and the concrete are interconnected through will, because "the will is always tending toward something else beyond what it wills," and so "will can carry us beyond our present self" from the realm of the concrete into the area of the abstract.[18] We could summarize the message of Blondel's book *L'Action,* as follows: Blondel distinguished between two expressions of will; one could be identified as the concrete "willed will" (for example, the intention to read this book), while the other is the abstract "willing will," which is present beyond every act of will (i.e., the will to get new information, to know more). The "willing will" intends to change the existing, to expand, and to reach out and grow. The willing will is a unique human characteristic—

an expression of the soul. The soul, according to Blondel, is the source of human determination for change, improvement, and progress toward the ultimate—God.[19]

The existentialist/neo-Thomist Joseph Maréchal (1878-1944) turned to Aristotle and developed (according to Copleston) a so-called transcendental Thomism. He described as unique to our species the persistent human need to be what we have not yet become, to transcend limits and goals. The call to transcend, to get closer to the infinite—to God—is a spiritual expression. God is "everything," the complete fulfillment, the last goal of all human activity. Being human involves being engaged in a permanent search for the absolute and ultimate, who is God.[20]

Karl Rahner (1904-1984), in *Spirit in the World,* described the purpose that coordinates theological thinking as "connatural" or a "preapprehensive" (*Vorgriff*). It directs striving for the ultimate, the first and the last, the perfect truth. Discerning "signs of God" in all existing "realized reality," humans gain "analogous knowledge" of the unknowable God. The idea of God is the ultimate abstraction of which the constituent parts are also all existing beings, and in which every particular form of existence has its reason and source.[21]

On the other hand (according to Erickson) in his ecclesiology, Rahner explained, "There is no such thing as being totally apart from grace. Grace is present even within nature itself. Man experiences grace as part of his own self." Such an approach makes it possible for Rahner to recognize "anonymous Christians." These people may include non-Christians who are indirectly related to the church by their search for ultimate selflessness, benevolence, and justice, incorporating and indeed embodying Christian values. They are not entirely "apart from the grace of God. Christ died for them as well."[22]

Ferenc Szabo says that "death is the moment of total freedom, and total conscientiousness for Rahner." It is the last moment when the immanent choice for or against Jesus can be proclaimed.[23] Consequently, the act of death has an almost privileged, central position in human life, as P. Boros, one of Rahner's students, described it.

We have just reviewed some history of philosophical teachings. But what is the importance and place of philosophy for a theologian of our time?

13.4. The Contemporary Relationship between Philosophy and Theology

Many modern Christian and non-Christian readers alike are interested less in the philosophy of Aristotle or Saint Thomas than in promoting acceptance of what the Scriptures reveal. Such skepticism toward the philosopher's ability to explain questions of faith was, from the very beginning, present in the minds of God's people.

For example, profane philosophy was never popular among Eastern Orthodox theologians. Their attitude was: No pagan or even Christian philosopher can explain God's characteristics or the laws of his kingdom, better than Jesus Christ could. So, should we even be thinking philosophically at all?

Nevertheless, speculative/philosophical thought is difficult to separate from Christian reasoning for at least two reasons. On the one hand, willingly or not, consciously or not, even the most evangelical Christians often use Christian philosophical terms and ideas to appreciate Scripture and revelation. For example, "conscience" is, for all Christians, an idea of distinguished interest. However, according to C. Williams, one will barely find the idea of conscience as we use it today, or even the term itself, in the O.T. Scriptures and N.T. Gospels. The only exception to this is Proverbs 17:11, but Proverbs is a Hellenistically influenced document.[24]

The reason for this, according to E.R. Callahan, is that the Hebrew people were "theocentric, unreflective, and lacking of introspection." They were extremely behaviorally oriented even in their religious life, excessively emphasizing ritual, while the paramount importance of internal motivation was increasingly neglected. As a result, cultic and ethical activities tended to become increasingly formalistic and to be judged solely on the basis of their external conformity with the Law.[25]

Nevertheless, according to the same author, "Perhaps nowhere else in the world of literature is remorse of conscience so superbly described as in the recounting of the reaction of Adam and Eve to their disobeying God (Gen. 3:7-11)."

Reflection of conscience was in the minds of the Hebrews connected to the heart, loins, kidneys, and other somatic/sensitive experiences. The Hebrews felt, but did not know, conscience.

However, (according to Williams) the term conscience

is met some "30 times in the rest of the New Testament: 20 times in the Epistles of St. Paul, five times in the Epistle to the Hebrews, three times in the first Epistle of St. Peter and twice in the Acts of Apostles." Why is this so? Because the Gospels retain the terminology of the Old Testament, [while] St. Paul and other New Testament authors took over the term "*sineidesis*" which they found in the Hellenistic culture of the day both as a popular concept and even as a technical term in the writings of the Stoics.

As a consequence of how the New Testament used philosophical terminology, today it is difficult to think theologically without using Greek, Augustinian, Thomist, scholastic, and even modern philosophical terms and ideas. As the Hebrew and Hellenist sources are synergistically interconnected in Paul's letters, so biblical and philosophical thought is necessary for postmodern believers to understand God's message.

The other reason that makes a separation between the two disciplines difficult is that apologetics (a discipline of theology that is focused on a rational defense of Christian faith) deals naturally with rational (philosophical) clarifications, terms, and insights.

In 1 Peter 3:15, we read:

But in your hearts set apart Christ as Lord. Always be prepared to give an answer to everyone who asks you to give reason for the hope that you have. But do this with gentleness and respect.

For many Greeks—the philosophically trained opponents of early Christianity—believing that it is God's word because the "Scriptures said so," and believing the Scriptures because they contain what "God said" may have seemed like a tautology. Therefore from the second century, early Christian apologists substantiated the reasons of their faith using Greek (Stoic, Platonic, Pythagorean, and other) philosophical terms, thereby bringing Hellenistic philosophical thought to the young Christianity. On the other hand, philosophy was used increasingly as a tool in introducing Christianity to the Hellenistic world. Those first significant theologian and apologetic writers in the second century AD included Justin, Ignatius, Teophilus, and Meliton. A later particularly prolific apologetic writer was Augustine. From the ninth century, apologetics got a new start. From the scholastic period until our era, theologians and philosophers developed different variants of the cosmological, teleological, ontological, moral, and other arguments substantiating God's existence.

However, from the sixteenth century on, the general trend in philosophy took a different direction. The happy marriage of theology and philosophy first degenerated into mutual suspicion and estrangement. This happened mainly, according to Geisler, after Descartes, and especially Kant, who argued that since "all knowledge is formed or structured by a priori categories, we can only know things as they appear to us, not as they are in themselves."[26] As a consequence, philosophically, we no longer really know objective reality as it is, but only how our human condition allows us to perceive and grasp objective reality. Therefore, the focus of many modern philosophers (from Kant to Rahner), artists (from Courbet to Picasso), and psychologists (from Freud to Frankl) was on the human condition, which makes it possible to know and react to reality in a uniquely human way.

For others, this modern and postmodern trend has adverse consequences. While from a metaphysical philosophical perspective human thoughts are sufficiently capable of representing the world and its reality in the sense that they can recognize and acknowledge God, many postmodern philosophical systems seem to become increasingly self-defeating constructs of insecurity. Therefore, in the minds of ordinary people, speculative and metaphysical philosophy is slowly giving up its ground to the technical sciences. Thus, only that which is visible, touchable, and measurable is considered to be of real value. This trend has contributed to a bitter divorce between theology and philosophy. Unfortunately, often the philosophy preferred and used by theologians is retreating to the security of medieval scholasticism. This siege mentality of postmodern metaphysical philosophers further deepens the gap between the reasoning of theologians and that of lay professionals.

Do such estrangement tendencies imply that faith does not question reason anymore, or that we are defenseless against postmodern cynicism when reason questions faith?

In the preface to this book, we noted that since its foundation Christianity has confronted in every period of its existence a new and unique challenge. Times and challenges changed, but Christianity endured and overcame them. This question then arises: Does God, through the shift from speculative to experiential thought, challenge his people not to exchange, but to supplement classical speculative, theoretical, and metaphysical concepts of the God of philosophers with an experientially and mystically experienced Living God? Let us leave this question open for now, and hope that the answer will come to us in subsequent reflection and study.

On the other hand, as we see from the overview, no philosopher is able to give a final explanation to humankind's dilemmas. Philosophy provides a plethora of competing speculation-based explanations of God and human nature, but none of them is absolute. Therefore, in searching for a thorough explanation let us now consider biblical revelation.

Notes

1. Will Durant, *The Story of Philosophy* (New York: Washington Square Press, 1953), 20-21.

2. Mihail Jarosevski, *Istoria Psihologii* (Moskva: Izdateljstvo Misl, 1966), 64-67.

3. Durant, *Philosophy*, 56-57.

4. Jarosevski, *Istoria Psihologii*, 68.

5. F. L. Cross and E. A. Livingstone, eds., *The Oxford Dictionary of the Christian Church* (New York: Oxford University Press, 1997), 102.

6. Norman L. Geisler, *Baker Encyclopedia of Christian Apologetics* (Grand Rapids, MI: Baker Books, 2000), 60-63.

7. Jarosevski, *Istoria Psihologii*, 107-9.

8. Anton C. Pegis, *Basic Writings of Saint Thomas Aquinas* (New York: Random House, 1945), 1: 683-94.

9. René Le Trocquer, *What is Man?* (London: Burns & Oates, Hawthorn Books, 1961), 28-29.

10. Cross and Livingstone, *The Oxford Dictionary of the Christian Church*, 472.

11. Durant, *Philosophy*, 195.

12. Geisler, *Christian Apologetics*, 343.

13. Cross and Livingstone, *The Oxford Dictionary of the Christian Church*, 919.

14. Millard J. Erickson, *Christian Theology* (Grand Rapids, MI: Baker Book House, 1995), 315.

15. Bernard Rahm, *Principles of Reading the Bible-Hermeneutics* (Grand Rapids, MI: Baker Books Company, 1970), 66-67.

16. Erickson, *Christian Theology*, 43-44.

17. Etienne Gilson, Thomas Langan, and Armand A. Maurer, *Recent Philosophy: Hegel to Present*, (New York: Random House, 1966), 636-39.

18. Gilson, Langan, and Maurer, *Recent Philosophy*, 361.

19. Maurice Blondel, *L'Action—Essai d'une critique de la vie et d'une science de la pratique* (Paris: Premiers ecrits, 1950).

20. Frederick Copleston, *A History of Philosophy* (Paramus, NY: Newman Press, 1975), 9:266-68.

21. Karl Rahner, *Spirit in the World* (Montreal, QC: Palm Publishers, 1968), 142-46.

22. Erickson, *Christian Theology*, 902-03.

23. Ferenc Szabó, Az ember és világa (Roma: Self-published, 1969), 183-84.

24. C. Williams, "Conscience" in *New Catholic Encyclopedia, 2nd ed.* (Washington, DC: Thomson Gale in assoc with The Catholic University of America, 1993), 4:143-44.

25. E. R. Callahan, "Conscience" in *New Catholic Encyclopedia, 2nd ed.* (Washington, DC: Thomson Gale in assoc with The Catholic University of America, 1993), 4:140-41.

26. Geisler, *Christian Apologetics*, 402.

Chapter 14

Biblical Revelation about the Spirit, the Soul, and Conscience

Most people of faith have a fundamental intuition of biblical anthropology, solidified through their reading of the Scriptures, through catechesis or discussions, or simply through the process of Christian maturation. In this chapter, we will substantiate biblically what people of faith already implicitly or explicitly believe, feel, or assume about the interplay between the Spirit, soul, conscience, and mind.

The Bible, however, does not "think" in modern medical or psychological terms. Concepts such as mind, psyche, or psychology did not exist in biblical times. We, however, will discuss biblical ideas and terms from the perspective of modern terminology and knowledge, using them to supplement each other.

14.1. The Terminology of the Old Testament and St. Paul

If we turn to Paul for an explanation of his vocabulary, we realize that it is not always easy to follow his thought. He was a diligent student of the Pharisee Gamaliel, who made a lasting impact on his vocabulary. He was also fluent in Greek and used the Septuagint. He quoted Greek poets and used stoic vocabulary. Above all, however, he was influenced by Ampliatus, Urbanus, Andronicus, Junius, and the other Christians mentioned in Romans 16:7. Finally, what makes Paul a challenge to us is that he does not define the words he uses. The appropriate way toward a deeper understanding of the meaning of his words would be to study all of the sources that he mentions as influential. However, let us take a shortcut; let us turn to the Old Testament scriptures that formed the religious vernacular in Paul's time.

The authors of the Old Testament differentiated the idea of spirit expressed by the Hebrew "*ruah*" (or the Greek "*pneume*") from the notion of soul articulated by the Hebrew "*nefesh*" (or the Greek "*psyche*"). In contemporary usage, spirit may be defined as a "non-physical part of a person," according to the *Concise Oxford Dictionary*. The soul is also spiritual; it is as well the "moral, or emotional or intellectual nature of a person."[1]

Brian Hebblethwaite, in *The Oxford Companion to Christian Thought*, explains that

> soul includes both mind and spirit, the mental including sensation, desire, belief and reason, the spiritual including aesthetic and religious experience and many other aspects of specifically human life. Philosophers tend to equate soul and mind, religious people tend to equate soul and spirit.[2]

We conclude that spirit and soul have a non-material nature in common; in a real sense they are both "spiritual." They both serve humans' relationship with God. These common attributes justify the frequent interchangeable use of the two ideas both in the Scriptures and in everyday language. However, the Bible also differentiates between a simple view of the spirit/soul as merely the non-material part of the human personality and an understanding of spirit/soul that enables the human person to realize a relationship with God.

According to Genesis 2.7, *ruah*—or *pneume*—is God's "breath of life." We read, for example, in the Book of Job 34:14-15, "If it were his intention and he withdrew his spirit and breath, all humankind would perish together and man would return to dust." Biological life itself is an essential (but not the only) manifestation of this relationship between God and humans which *ruah* establishes. According to Fucak, *ruah* does not only enable biological life, but it establishes a basic existential relationship to God. Thus, life is the expression of a basic existential relationship to God.[3]

The attempt to understand what the Bible means by "soul" is complicated by the various metaphors used. For instance, to depict *nefesh* the Old Testament used expressions like breath, wish, appetite, life, feelings, desire, belief, reason, and aesthetic and religious experience. By adjusting these to modern vernacular, we could abstract the meaning of the term "soul" to a principle making possible a responsible encounter with God.

Let us summarize: while the spirit makes a basic human existential relationship with God possible (expressed, for example in biological life), the soul makes a conscious, free and responsible relationship with God possible (expressed, for example in believer's faith).

The Greek name for the soul, *psyche*, should not confuse us. Note that in the days of the Old Testament, the ideas of "mind" and "psyche" as we understand them today did not exist. *Psyche* at that time meant only the soul. It would therefore not be accurate to connect *nefesh* or *psyche* to the modern term "human mind" or psychology. Rather, in a biblical context, soul is a principle steering the behavioral, emotional, and intellectual facets of human beings toward a union with God.

14.2. Biblical Anthropology Revealed in Three of St. Paul's Letters

In 1 Thessalonians 5:23, we find a condensed overview of biblical anthropology relevant to our topic, where St. Paul wrote, "May God himself, the God of peace, sanctify you through and through. May your whole spirit, soul, and body be kept blameless at the coming of our Lord Jesus Christ." Thus, Paul tells us here that the human personality is composed of spirit, soul, and body. What are the similarities and differences between these three human dimensions?

In the believer's everyday experience, the spirit, the soul, and the body work together in realizing the biblical lifestyle of discipleship, in the sense that all three are unified and act as one in glorifying God. On the other hand, the spirit, the soul, and the body are very different in their regulation, functioning, and purpose. We know from Old Testament revelation that the human spirit is transcendent and not experiential. We know from the same source that the soul is transcendent, but psychologically experiential. The body in Christian understanding (in contrast to Plato's concept) has a role of paramount importance. It is the body, according to Trocquer, that allows us to take our "appropriate place in the universe in the hierarchy of created things, and to progress beyond the threshold of animal nature."[4] Biologically it is composed of visible and palpable entities that perform biological functions.

We have been discussing St. Paul's terms "spirit," "soul," and "body." However, St. Paul also used different ideas and terminology in his letters. For example, in 1 Corinthians 2:13 we find a personal testimony given by him: "This is what we speak, not in words taught us by human wisdom but in words taught by the Spirit expressing spiritual truths in spiritual words." Here St. Paul differentiates and connects three categories in his message: his speaking (a function of the body), human wisdom, (a function of the mind), and the Spirit (God). Thus, to pursue our discussion we also need to clarify the term "mind"—the resource of human wisdom, which is indeed very different from "words taught by the Spirit."

The expressions used by St. Paul are not identical to modern terminology. When contemporary persons speak about their inner psychological experiences they spontaneously use the word "mind." It is part of everyday vocabulary. But what is meant by the "mind" and how does it relate to our discussion of the "spirit" and the "soul"? For agnostics, the mind has been understood as a purely physiological product of the brain. For the believer, mind is not only the product of the brain but also a basis for the interaction between the body and the soul. A reader may ask which biblical references support this understanding?

We will get the answer to this if we first answer another question: What convinced St. Paul that he was indeed transmitting a message taught by the Spirit, rather than merely human wisdom?

To answer this question we have to turn to verses of 2 Corinthians 1:12 where Paul states:

> our conscience testifies that we have conducted ourselves in the world,
> and especially in our relationship with you, in the holiness and sincer-
> ity that are from God. We have done so not according to the worldly
> wisdom but according to God's grace.

Once again three elements are interconnected: Paul's behavior, God's sincerity and holiness, and another word Paul has added for us to consider—"conscience." Conscience is a unique psychological function and is also a typical Pauline expression. As noted, the apostle used it in some twenty-five places in his letters. What is interesting here is that the apostle involves his conscience and gives to it a prominent role in explaining the dynamics of his own personality. It is Paul's conscience that testifies and assures him that he acted according to "the holiness and sincerity that are from God."

Using this information, we can get a step closer toward understanding the interaction that took place between St. Paul's mind, conscience, and the Spirit, when the apostle justified his behavior in 2 Corinthians. We realize that St. Paul's conduct stemmed from a synchronized and hierarchical organization inside his personality, based on the interaction of three components: (1) the "holiness and sincerity that are from God," (2) Paul's conscience, which was able to offer a testimony about his conduct, and (3) his body, enabling a "relationship with you" (i.e., his disciples in Corinth).

Paul's conscience was a psychological function—a product of his brain—in modern agnostic understanding. But it was able to contact and communicate with God and to "testify." Thus, "something" had to mediate between his conscience, which was a function of Paul's mind, and the "quite other" Spirit, i.e., between the transcendental Divine and psychological human realities. This is the "missing link" we are looking for.

Using Paul's teaching we may detect such a "missing link" in the spiritual entity which the apostle talks about in 1 Thessalonians 5:23, and calls the soul. The soul, as noted, according the Old Testament Scriptures is the spiritual precondition of a conscious, free and responsible communication with God. Thus, Paul's (spiritual) soul, *nefesh*, acted in a biblical context as the "missing link" between the transcendental Godly and the apostle's person. Just how this communication between the Spirit and St. Paul's soul happened we cannot grasp or analyze psychologically. It happened in the transcendental realm.

As the next step in this transmission process Paul's soul (which according to the Scriptures is experienced psychologically) shared with his conscience the information that it received from the Spirit. This was a mysterious process on the borderline between the spiritual and psychological.

As the last step in this process, the Spirit's information, transmitted through Paul's soul and his conscience, became consciously realized by the apostle's very self. This last step was a psychological process; the apostle's conscience, was then able to "testify" about Paul's conduct to his mind, as well as to his contemporaries and to us, his latest disciples.

14.3. Is Our Hypothesis Theologically Plausible?

God's interventions and his communication with his people do not only happen in the form of dramatic and awesome miracles (such as Jesus' intervention on the road to Damascus). They also happen in everyday occurrences, in life events, and in the minds of people living in union with him. St. Paul lived in a permanent, delicate, grace-filled union with God. In fact, believers most often discern and communicate with God in this way.

How can we didactically and formally differentiate between typical miracles and a steady communication with God? Miracles are mostly short, unique interventions of God, often connected to sensory (visual or auditory) experience, happening in a particular place and time. They are almost always striking and out of the ordinary, causing dramatic turning points or insights in the believer's (and sometimes the non-believer's) life. There are no biblical hints explaining sufficiently the mystery of a miracle.

Experiencing ongoing personal communication with God is differently mysterious and awesome. It usually happens in a believer in an extensive, lasting process, marked not by sensory experience, but by introspective evidence of having received gifts from the Spirit and gifts of faith. It tends not to be connected to a space or time that could be easily identified. The biblical person's experience is more helpful in providing insights (as much as this is possible for finite humans), and in general there are more details in biblical descriptions of communication with God than in descriptions of miracles.

Let us now apply these criteria to St. Paul's verses.

1. In 1 Corinthians 2:11-13, and especially in 2 Corinthians 1:12, the apostle talks about a pattern of conduct ("that we have conducted ourselves in the world, and especially in our relationship with you"). This had to have been an extensive, long-lasting process, not a short term, dramatic miracle.
2. St. Paul does not mention that he had a sensory experience of God's intervention. On the contrary, he speaks in 1 Corinthians 2:13 and 2 Corinthians 1:12 about non-sensorial, introspective, ongoing experiences that consist of receiving gifts of the Spirit, such as talking "in spiritual words about spiritual truths" and "holiness and sincerity that are from God."
3. His communication with God did not happen in an exact place and had no beginning or end (as in a miracle). Instead, it was a continuous process, one part of which is described in 1

Corinthians 2:13—that he was "taught by the Spirit expressing spiritual truths,"—and another in 2 Corinthians 1:12—
that he conducted himself according to God's grace. Introspections like these were a permanent relationship and
communication with Jesus, rather than a one-time great
miracle.

A reader may ask:

Why do we so explicitly and vehemently insist on distinguishing
between a "miracle" and the "personal communication" models? Aren't the boundaries between dramatic miracles and steady
communication between God and his people mostly fuzzy? And
if that is true, isn't precise distinction between God's miraculous
interventions and his steady communication with believers also
less than essential?

Indeed, both kinds of God's interventions are mysterious up to a
certain point. However, there is a difference in their inexplicability. A
typical miracle is often marked with the sensorial acknowledgement of
God's call or intervention, for example, Saul's seeing the light from
heaven and hearing the voice "Saul, Saul, why do you persecute me?"
(Acts 9:3-4). God used a "meta-psychological sensorial channel" in performing this miracle, which we are unable to grasp. Moreover we are
unable to explain how Saul could see a great light and hear Jesus' voice
while his companions saw and heard nothing. God's transcendental intervention in Saul's mind and senses, as well as in Saul's conscious psychological perception of God's intervention, are both inexplicable
mysteries.

We insist on distinguishing between a miracle and a steady communication between God and his people because if the three verses of St.
Paul discussed earlier involved a miracle (rather then steady and ongoing
personal communication with Jesus) then our discussion of these verses
would be impossible, because God's actions and the subject's perception
of the miracle would be completely inexplicable psychologically.

In the case of steady communication with God, however, the situation is different; God's message is received non-sensorially. Thus, it had
to be experienced through a non-sensorial interaction between God and
St. Paul. St. Paul then psychologically became aware of the Spirit's mes-

sage through a non-sensorial "channel," enabling the apostle to utter spiritual words and perform behavior characterized by the "holiness and sincerity that are from God."

On the basis of psychological deduction from Scripture, we conclude that there is only one such biblically appointed and psychologically possible "route" or "channel" through which such steady communication can occur. It is what the Hebrews called *nefesh*, the Greeks called *psyche*, the Latin called *anima*, and we call the *soul*. From a biblical understanding, however, the "soul" was spiritual, but psychologically experienced as well.

There is also only one "place" where such communication (from a psychological perspective observed) could end. To be able to "testify" as described in St. Paul, the message had to be delivered to one place only: conscience. Thus, from the biblical perspective, the soul holds the key to communication between the Spirit and the human mind, and from the psychological perspective, conscience holds the key. The "receiver" or "microphone" in the channel was Paul's soul, and the "loudspeaker" that enabled him to realize and testify about his communication was his conscience—which we called hyperego.

From a biblical perspective, St. Paul, and we his successors, experience communication with the Spirit through the interaction between our soul and our conscience. A similar process probably occurred in Abraham in his extensive "living with God," in Moses, in Wesley, and in countless other known and unknown people communicating with God or living in union with him.

St. Paul explained much to us, but we still have many puzzling questions. For example, how does the transmission process between the Spirit and soul occur? We know that both are transcendent, but have no idea with which to compare or grasp this transmission process. Nor does Paul discuss the relation or interaction between the Hebrew (biblical) idea of the soul, and the Pauline (empirical) idea of conscience. He provides no discussion which would help us to take a stand concerning Hebblethwaite's observation: "Philosophers tend to equate soul and mind, religious people tend to equate soul and spirit." Nevertheless, we are able to partially reconstruct the channel of God's personal communication with the Apostle Paul discussed above, based on his description in 1 Thessalonians 5:23, 1 Corinthians 2:13, and 2 Corinthians 1:12.

14.4. Other Theological Considerations and Biblical Revelations

As theologian and psychologist Franz Delitzsch (according to Millard Erickson) emphasized, spirit "enables the human to perceive spiritual matters and respond to spiritual stimuli."[5] Thus, the human spirit (the soul in St. Paul's letters) is the source and instrument of human spirituality. Put even more broadly, we said with Thomas Aquinas' *Summa Theologiae* that human spirit is the "first principle" of life and thus the vehicle of biological existence. However, the soul (using Aristotle's terminology) is the "shaping force" of a person's spiritual life and communication with God.

Although the biblical authors sometimes used the terms carelessly and often interchangeably, and despite the fact that the soul and spirit are both spiritual entities and have somewhat overlapping roles, they are not synonyms. On the one hand, "spirit" is a broader reality, the "shaping force" of the whole human being in his or her relationship to God. The, "soul" is the "shaping force" of the individual, personal, and psychologically-experienced spiritual life of a person. In this context, the general and innate ability to be a human, and potentially to become a believer, stems from the human spirit. Nonetheless, the call of the Spirit for one to actually become a believer is transmitted in people of faith through their soul and is ultimately experienced psychologically (in their mind) with help of their conscience.

The Scriptures emphasize the connection between Spirit and the new lifestyle, "new birth" of the disciples. For instance, John in 6:63 explains that "the Spirit gives life; the flesh counts for nothing. The words I have spoken to you are spirit, and they are life." Romans 8:16 states, "The Spirit himself testifies with our spirit that we are God's children." In 1 Corinthians 6:17 it is written, "But he who unites himself with the Lord is one with him in spirit," and in John 3:6, "flesh gives birth to flesh, but the Spirit gives birth to spirit."

We can see from these biblical descriptions that the spirit (or, more precisely, the soul in St. Paul's terminology) of believers is "transformed" and "adopted" by, and in an intimate relationship with God's Spirit, and becomes the principle and "shaping force" of life and union with God.

However, the Spirit's "transformed" soul requires a new birth (as in John 3:3-5) or more exactly a birth from above. Such "adopted" soul requires freedom from sin and freedom from the rules and power of the world (as in John 3:8). Such soul, as the "shaping force" and the "principle of spiritual life," does require a different conscience, one enabling a new spiritual life. Such a new conscience requires faith; it entails becoming a new person, being in a new union with God (as in John 4:13). Such a new conscience requires freedom from the fear of death (as in John 5:24, and 5:29). It requires union and joy in God (as in John 6:39 and 6:55). Thus, conscience is psychologically enabling the believer's union with God and the attainment of gifts of faith as well.

Not only do spirit and soul have somewhat overlapping roles, but so do soul and conscience. Both enable us to experience the gifts of faith. While soul is the principle of the spiritual, conscience is the principle of psychological, responsible regulation of the believer's relationship to God. The difference between the two is that soul is essentially immaterial and spiritual although it is experienced psychologically, while conscience is an empirical-psychological reality that is connected to the functioning of both the physical brain and soul. The concept "soul" is fundamentally a biblical one, while the concept "conscience" has its roots in Greek philosophy. However, they are two different concepts, not merely a biblical and a Greek term for the same reality.

During the process in which the believer's soul is adopted and transformed by God, the believer plays a more or less passive role; he or she is not able to willingly "cause" or "manage" this transcendental process, but is able only to pray for it. In contrast to the believer's initial passivity, the Spirit is active in this process of "giving birth" to the believer's new soul. Next, this new soul of the believer "gives birth" to a new conscience. (Note that in biblical and in vernacular terminology, this process is often referred to as gaining a new "spirit." Using the differentiations we have made, however, it is important to note that the change occurs not only in the human spirit which is the general, impersonal basis of human life, but in the soul, the personal, responsible shaping force of the spiritual, personal life of the individual.)

Receiving a new soul means receiving a new conscience as well. Receiving a new conscience changes the situation. Being born in the Spirit becomes psychologically experienced; the believer becomes psychologically aware of being called by God to make a choice of fundamental importance. The new conscience has an active, responsible role— it "unites" itself with the Lord, and "testifies" actively as the Apostle Paul described in 2 Corinthians 1:12. Such biblical description is in harmony with everyday psychological experience: conscience is in a perma-

nent search for and has an "innate docility" towards the ultimate goodness of the Spirit. This "innate docility" (the affinity with and attraction
to God), is a unique characteristic of conscience. It is neither indoctrinated into people, nor given to them by their parents. No instinct, superego, will, attention, or thought has a comparable ability. Conscience,
and especially that which we call Christian conscience, is the active psychological reflection of the soul, transformed and adopted by the Spirit.

We began this chapter by stating that we will in fact discuss nothing
fundamentally new in it. Probably, every Christian has already "felt" or
implicitly realized the connection between the Spirit, the soul, the conscience, and the self. But now we can put those ideas more easily in
place while thinking in philosophical, psychological, theological, and
biblical terms. The other purpose of this chapter was to find a hypothetical "missing link" between the transcendental and "quite other" God and
the believer's moral conscience. From this biblical-theological vantage
point of St. Paul's letters the most probable "missing link" that enables
communication with the almighty, eternal, and ultimate love of God is
the soul. It is the soul that bridges the "transcendental gap" between the
"quite other" God and the believer's conscience.

Only one question remains: how does such biblical thought confirm
modern positivist/scientific ways of thinking and perceiving, so widely
accepted among professional and lay people alike? Probably nowhere
does faith challenge our reasoning more than in the topic we will discuss
in the next chapter: namely, how revealed truth confirms modern professional concepts applied in hospitals, universities, and research laboratories.

Notes

1. R. E. Allen, *The Concise Oxford Dictionary* (Oxford: Clarendon Press,
1990), 1162

2. Brian Hebblethwaite, *The Oxford Companion to Christian Thought,* ed.
Adrian Hastings, Alistair Mason, and Hugh Pyper (New York: Oxford University Press, 2000), 681-83.

3. Marijan Jerko Fucak, *Dogadjaj Isus Krist* (Zagreb: Institut Za Teolosku
Kulturu Laika, 1989), 31-33.

4. René Le Trocquer, *What is Man?* (London: Burns & Oates, 1961), 26.

5. Millard J. Erickson, *Christian Theology* (Grand Rapids, MI: Baker Book
House, 1995), 520.

Chapter 15

Conscience from an Experiential Perspective

As the title says, the purpose of this chapter is to provide basic insight from a practical perspective into how communication between the Spirit and people occurs. The discussion will be based mostly on psychological and neurological facts, supplemented with revealed, and even philosophical, background information. Indeed, our aim is not to review all details and implications of the interrelations between mind, conscience, soul, and Spirit, but to discuss only those principles that may be relevant to our understanding of Thomas' case, as well as the union with God of Thomas' successors: contemporary believers.

15.1. Why a New Paradigm is Urgently Needed

As noted earlier, the Greek term *psyche* meant "soul" in biblical times, not "mind," as we define it today. "Mind" is a much broader category than "soul." The soul's authority is reflected by only a part of the mind—the part that is directed by conscience. In other words, the soul in the believer's mind is expressed by and directs the psychological functions of the mind (i.e., thoughts, feelings, memories, will) that serve as a foundation for a personal, conscious, and conscientious relationship with God. In exceptional believers, this part of the mind is pervasive and powerful, directing virtually all other functions, as well as the individual's behavior. In non-believers, the soul's role and influence is sometimes virtually non-existent, and their mind serves only worldly purpose and well-being.

An agnostic neurologist, nurse, psychiatrist, brain-surgeon, or psychologist, (I was trained by them all during my residency), would have a different explanation. An agnostic professional would discover electrochemical impulses caused by the exchange of sodium and potassium ions in a nerve cell membrane, convergent or divergent transmission of impulses through neurons—heightening or lowering thresholds in synapses, arithmetically evaluating the quantity of inputs, calculating and adjusting the middle excitement levels in nerve cells and brain centers, etc. As humans experience heartbeat and breathing, they also experience the results of reflexes happening in the brain. We call these experienced brain processes "feeling," "thinking," "remembering," "attention," etc. First the Nobel Laureate Charles Scott Sherrington and countless researchers after him received the highest scientific award for researching the brain processes that enable psychological experience of brain activity and modern biochemical and pharmacological understanding of the brain and mind's functioning.

Working in a hospital as a neurologist and psychiatrist, I had the opportunity to experience daily the efficiency of this medical paradigm. I saw that by adjusting biochemical processes in the patient's brain, the ways a patient thought, felt, and behaved could be changed and improved. For my professional colleagues and me, that was an obvious, experiential fact. However, this experience had a deep religious-philosophical effect on some of my colleagues. Even for my religious colleagues, the beliefs of those who used ideas like the spirit or soul seemed like an anachronism. They took the view that the action of the Spirit, the soul, or a Christian conscience could be explained by the action of the organ of psychological life, that is, the brain and the mind. They attempted to keep their private religious life separate from professional knowledge and opinion. Slowly, for many of my colleagues, soul, spirit, or even Spirit have become irrelevant in explaining human behavior, and such "outdated" ideas have no place in their professional language.

On the other hand, the paradigms of both believers and non-believers reflect a unique education and background, a professional worldview expressed in a particular language and way of thinking. As the well-known Sapir-Whorf hypothesis states, the language believers and non-believers speak shapes their minds, ideas, even their personality and behavior. The ideas reflected through a particular language cause an almost dissociate communication "gap" between believers and agnostics sharing the same era, continent, and culture. Modern neurologists, brain surgeons, psychologists, sociologists, psychiatrists, biochemists, and biologists dominate the language (and thought) of contemporary ordinary people, while theological language becomes increasingly relegated to religious institutions.

As a consequence of this linguistic and ideological gap, Christian philosophers, theologians, as well as priests, ministers, and orthodox and biblical believers generally, have had little interest in the brain and its functioning. For their part, neither positivist nor agnostic nurses, physicians, neurologists, psychologists, mental health practitioners, or psychiatrists have been interested in *nefesh* or *ruah*. These differences in understanding who and what humans are lead to a gap between faith and reality, between thinking as a believer and thinking as a professional, even in people of faith. An urgent need obviously exists for a new paradigm to enable communication between professionals and theologians, between biblical believers and scientifically educated specialists.

If two obviously true and valid explanations (the revealed and the empirically proven) seem to be mutually exclusive in explaining the same phenomenon, then the problem is not in those valid explanations, but in their synchronization. The cause of the seemingly unsolvable contradiction between revealed and empirical models lies in our inability to connect both explanations, putting both paradigms in their proper place with the help of a "common denominator."

Promoting such a common denominator in the thinking and reasoning of theologians and professionals is not effortless. For readers it might be cumbersome, and it may seem meaningless to switch attention from a detailed discussion of biblical revelation in one chapter, to a discussion of neurological or psychological functioning of the human brain, mind, and soul in another. However, if we find a substantiated explanation for how believers actually experience their union with the invisible God, then our effort pays off. To primarily biblically oriented readers, such a discussion helps to demonstrate that we humans are, in fact, what the Bible defines us to be. To readers preferring the ideas and philosophies of Thomism and scholasticism, such a discussion will help to rephrase classical philosophical-theological ideas into an experiential/empirical paradigm needed by modern professionals. For readers accustomed to professional paradigms, such a discussion enables them to connect and harmonize empirical, professional with biblical thought. It enables them to respond as St. Peter requested (1 Peter 3:15) in situations when agnostic and positivist "reasoning questions faith," and also in cases when their own "faith questions reasoning."

15.2. Onto Whose Shoulders Can We Climb in Looking for a New Paradigm?

We have already discussed Leibniz's controversial teaching on the interaction between the immaterial spirit and the material brain. Let us now consider other teachings relevant to our discussion.

The question "Where does the idea of the untouchable and invisible God comes from?" was first asked and answered, according to Jarosevski, by Plato in the fourth century BC.[1] Plato thought that the idea of gods existed in his contemporaries' minds, despite any external experience, as a consequence of a very deeply embedded inborn idea of deity originating from the soul's experience of the time before its imprisonment in a mortal body.

The concept of "inborn ideas" that enable us to think, reason, and behave in ways typical of the human species dominated philosophical thought for almost two thousand years. As we saw, a variety of such inborn ideas, thought to be implanted by God himself, were Descartes' proof of God's existence.

In 1690 however, John Locke introduced a new concept of the human mind, based primarily on sensory experience. (As we noted, he proclaimed, "Nothing is in the intellect, that was not first in the senses.") As a consequence, the concept of inborn ideas (including an inborn idea of God) appeared out-of-date. According to Ferenc Szabo, however, Gottfried W. Leibniz, one of Locke's contemporaries, responded to Locke's statement around the year 1710 with a short phrase: *Nisi ipse intelectus* ("Except the intellect itself").[2] Leibniz's observation coincided with experience. It was already recognized that the human abilities to reason, feel, and behave differently from animals are, at least partially, inborn qualities. But was it possible to explain this phenomenon without using the now invalid notion of "inborn ideas," while simultaneously respecting Locke's proven empiricism?

According to Jarosevski, the Swiss naturalist Charles Bonnet (1720-1793) contributed a new perspective to this matter in his writings published between 1755 and 1759.[3] He described the nervous system as small machinery, patterned by its anatomical and functional characteristics, to produce particular mental experiences such as sensations, thoughts, feelings, memories. Thus, the concept of inborn ideas was replaced with the concept of an inborn neurological construct.

Modern brain research accepts both Locke's and Bonnet's approaches. The brain is composed of the brain stem and cortex. The brain cortex contains mostly learned and personally experienced behavior, while the brain stem contains only inborn reaction and behavior stereotypes. The brain cortex can be compared, according to Locke's model, to a computer, which has not yet been programmed and must first be filled with information for it to work properly. In contrast, the brain stem works according to Bonnet's model. Brain centers in it regulating emotions, instincts, and basic human inborn behavior stereotypes (as well as breathing, blood pressure, and body temperature—the "homeostasis") are "given in forward" (i.e., they are independent of any childhood or later experience or upbringing). In the computer model used above they are comparable to the hardware; the brain centers of the brain stem make possible the functional characteristics of the human brain and mind. A complex coordination of cortex and brain stem enables a subject's discernment of reality and behavior in a manner unique to humans.

The next turning point in the development of an explanation for the coordinated functioning of the brain and mind is connected to the work of the physician John H. Jackson (1836-1911). According to Srboljub Stojiljkovic, Jackson attributed mental disorders to the fragmentation of the highest, most complex brain structures, and the consequent reduction of brain (and mental) functioning on lower, less complex levels.[4] Around the middle of the twentieth century, the French psychiatrist Jean Delay set up a clinically supported approach, which he called neo-Jacksonism. According to this approach, the brain functions in hierarchically organized shifts or layers. The highest, most complex brain centers produce the most complex psychological functions. These brain centers are the newest, last established, and most vulnerable. If those newest structures are damaged, then older, better entrenched brain functions (such as instinct or affect) will take over and direct behavior on a less complex level, causing personality or mental disorders.

Frankl's *Dimensional Ontology* presents probably the latest in such hierarchical concepts, formulated in an existential-psychological paradigm.[5] He places the body, mind, and spirit not one beside the other, but "one above the other"—organized hierarchically. Freedom consists in being a spiritually directed, unique, and responsible person, able (free) to do good deeds. Frankl's Logotherapy (*Logos* translates from the Greek as "meaning") helps people to discern and fulfill objectives and values beyond and despite biological, psychological, and sociological limitations.

In our paradigm, we shall connect Delay's biological and Frankl's existential concepts with revelation. Such an approach may produce interesting insights into the interrelations among spirit, soul, mind, and body.

Let us now work out the rationales of the different argumentation needed by professionals, and establish a new paradigm encompassing biblical, theological, and professional perspectives.

15.3. Hierarchical Principles in the Functioning of the Brain and the Mind

From a biologist's, anthropologist's, or physician's perspective, the difference between living beings and inanimate objects is the intricate organization and complexity in the functioning of the former. There is a strict blueprint, a unique structure and hierarchical organization of the physical, chemical, biochemical, neurological, and elemental psychological regulation principles typical of every plant or animal. Such hierarchical organization works in the human body and mind as well. Systems with their own regulation systems (such as those listed above)—which we call "dimensions"—are organized and connected in a joint-like manner in performing their function inside the organism. Higher, more complex dimensions regulate and sustain lower, less complex dimensions, while lower dimensions contribute to and facilitate the functioning of the higher dimensions. Let us observe some well-known examples, of how such joint-like organized connections work in the human body and mind.

The diencephalon (an important anatomical structure in the brain) represents one example of how such a joint-like connection works, in this case in a neurological-biochemical link. Stress (registered neurologically) has an impact on the production of ACTH (adrenocorticotropic hormone), a biochemical substance regulating the secretion of adrenaline in the suprarenal glands. In this way two very different systems, the brain's higher, neurological processes and the less complex biochemistry of the body (e.g., production of hormones) are combined in a seamlessly unified function to respond automatically to threats by counterattacking or by fleeing.

In another example, the brain and mind perform as a psychological-neurological joint, in which neurological processes of the brain are used to facilitate psychological experiences. In this joint-like connection the objective of the brain's neurological functioning is to produce psychological processes. We can quite simply summarize the essence of the interactions occurring in the brain-mind joint in three paragraphs.

In a way similar to how we experience the functioning of some organs (heartbeat or breathing, for example), we "feel," or more exactly experience, the unfolding of physical, chemical, biochemical, and neurological processes in our brain. A subject experiences those processes as thinking, feeling, remembering, or other psychological functions. So, from an agnostic neurologist's perspective, what we call the human psyche or mind is the self-experience of the processes happening in a person's own brain. However, this is only half of the truth.

We know from experience that the brain is "trainable." By regulating its own physical-chemical-biochemical-neurological functioning it is able to learn from psychological experiences, and produce new psychological skills. This ability, is enabled by a unique characteristic of the brain called plasticity. Plasticity is demonstrated in a developing brain. In an immature brain there are billions and billions—virtually countless—workable synaptic connections. During maturation, futile, useless synaptic connections—i.e., those that do not produce a useful output—become eliminated due to their own inactivity. On the other hand, fervent use reinforces those synaptic connections which produce an appropriate output (in our case an appropriate psychological experience). Thus, a purposeful selection process is at work as dysfunctional (useless) synaptic connections disappear, while those in frequent use thrive. By such plasticity the brain can regulate its own "functional wiring," (its own physical, chemical, biochemical, and neurological functioning) on the basis of appropriate input (such as learning, maturing, and "conditioning") and producing appropriate output (appropriate thoughts, feelings or behavior). We could say that brain functions are teleologically organized to "teach themselves" and to regulate their own functions, to accomplish an ultimate purpose: the production of appropriate psychological functions.

If upbringing, education, and maturation of the brain do not achieve production of healthy mental functioning and behavior, then psychological counseling or psychiatric (e.g., pharmacological) treatment is required to help achieve the purpose and goal of brain functions: producing appropriate, healthy thoughts, feelings, or behavior. When producing mental functions, the brain and mind perform jointly in the sense that particular brain functions are united and organized to produce meaningful, healthy, psychological contents; production of healthy psychological (and other) functions is the ultimate purpose and criterion of the brain's performance.

Now we can raise the crucial question: can a similar principle—of the lower dimension's serving (or at least assisting) a higher be applied to the interrelations between soul and mind? To discuss this will be our goal in the next section.

15.4. A New Paradigm of Conscience

Based on empirical observations and biblical references, we have depicted the soul as the principal facilitator of a fundamental, conscious relationship with God. God's sincerity and holiness are reflected through the soul. Moreover, the minds of believers evidently contain ideas that are "non-empirical" (i.e., non-sensorial) and reflect not only "worldly matters," but also quite other spiritual information concerning the Spirit and the biblical soul.

Spiritual contents are evidently present in the believer's mind, but there is no such psychological function as "Spirit" or "soul." Does this fact not oblige us to question whether believers then experience the Spirit and soul's messages indirectly through some other psychological function?

From a biblical perspective, the standards of the soul that is "adopted and transformed" by the Spirit are transmitted into the believer's entire personality through the conscience. Conscience (we also called it hyperego) contains not biological standards but standards of everlasting life, connecting those standards to psychological functions (such as attention, thought, will, and feelings) regulating behavior. In contrast to the psychological-neurological joint which connects two very different dimensions, Christian conscience connects two "quite different" dimensions: the spiritual soul and the conscious functions of the mind.

Accordingly, we call the integration of the conscience and soul in one unified functioning system, a "spiritual-psychological joint." The term is an abstraction but one that expresses factual behavioral evidence. It explains why the believer's psychologically-experienced conscience is, ideally, in agreement with the biblical requirements of the soul and Spirit, (not only with the natural worldly reality, as is true of the superego).

The spiritual-psychological joint, by assimilating and transferring information from the soul, enables the subject's conscience, mind, and whole self to be receptive to the transcendent reality existing beyond the natural and its requirements. By its spiritual component, the joint enables the mind to step over the biological-sensorial barrier, to bridge the gap of transcendence, and thereby pass from a worldly psychological reality into a meta-experiential realm. This window, providing a glimpse into an awesome actuality, enables the discernment of God's kingdom, which is just as real for believers as sensory perception of the natural world is for non-believers.

An example would better explain this: The prophet Jeremiah felt God's call around 626 BC. As Louis Bouyer points out:

> He had no wife, no family. His vocation placed him not only aloof of people but in opposition to them. The God who forcefully placed dreadful words in his mouth made the effect on him of being his enemy. Jeremiah was tempted to revolt, refuse his mission and its message; but the Word was stronger. Finally, it appears to have crushed him.[6]

In that vein, we read in Jeremiah 20:7-9:

> O LORD, you deceived me, and I was deceived, you overpowered me and prevailed. I am ridiculed all day long; everyone mocks me. Whenever I speak, I cry out proclaiming violence and destruction. So the word of the LORD has brought me insult and reproach all day long. But if I say, "I will not mention him or speak any more in his name," his word is in my heart as a fire, a fire shut up in my bones.

But in verse 20:11, Jeremiah expresses a different sentiment: "The LORD is with me like a mighty warrior; so my persecutors will stumble and not prevail."

This sort of "being in the world, but not of it" behavior pattern would be impossible to explain by pragmatic, worldly psychological functions only, without taking the demands of the spiritual-psychological joint into account. Not only Jeremiah, but all people living with God, are either "suffering from a socially tolerated form of delusion" or really must possess a special "channel" of being joined to the LORD. We call this special channel the spiritual-psychological joint.

Reflecting on the examples of Abraham, Moses, Jeremiah, and Christian saints and martyrs of all ages, and on sayings such as, "A Christian is another Christ," we realize that in Christians there must be a connection between the Spirit and soul on one hand, and the conscience and the mind on the other. We called this connection the "spiritual-psychological joint."

15.5. Visualizing the Spiritual-Psychological Joint

According to an anecdote, an atheist would say, "Nothing is really understood so long as it is not mechanically explained!" But is it possible to explain mechanically everything that exists? Just as abstractions such as the super-ego, ego, or instinct in psychology and many constructs in mathematics, physics, or astronomy are impossible to touch or mechanically verify, so also the spiritual-psychological joint cannot be seen or touched. However, its effects are measurable. Although the abstraction of the mathematical formula $e = mc^2$ and the abstraction of a spiritual-psychological joint are very different, the effects of both are equally evident.

Let us, therefore, visualize the concept of the spiritual-psychological joint instead of attempting to define it mechanistically. We can illustrate the relationship between the spiritual and psychological dimensions of the soul and conscience in Figure 15-1.

Figure 15-1

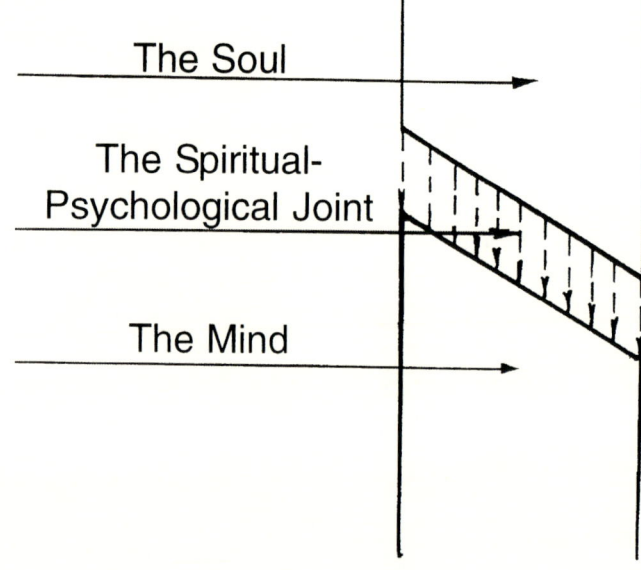

The Soul

The Spiritual-
Psychological Joint

The Mind

If we observe the figure from the top to the bottom, we see the soul first, and then the point of contact between the soul and conscience inside the abstraction of the spiritual-psychological joint. We are able to visualize this contact or transmission point by a joint-like connection, but we are unable to explain its functioning as an atheist or positivist would prefer. The soul is spiritual and transcendental, inaccessible to scientific, sensorial, or psychological reasoning.

Moral conscience, on the other hand, is a psychological entity. It does not elude our attempt to explore it. Therefore, let us observe the functioning of the spiritual-psychological joint from the psychological end (i.e., the conscience), from the bottom upward on the drawing. Let us focus on how believers, through conscience, experience the leadership of the spiritual entity we call soul. By such an approach, we avoid discussing the ineffable transcendent characteristics of the soul and instead concentrate on the believer's psychological experience of the soul's guidance, registered in and through conscience and the believer's mind.

Let us ask the difficult, centuries-old question: How can believers have a psychological experience of the spiritual soul's guidance? How can the conscience, which is experienced psychologically, know what is expected by the transcendental soul and Spirit?

In discussing the functioning of the psychological-neurological joint, we noted that production of healthy and correct mental functioning is the ultimate purpose of brain functions. The brain is constructed to regulate its own physical, chemical, biochemical and neurological functions, so that it fulfills its (psychological) purpose: producing correct thoughts, memories, perception, or behavior. We can generalize this principle of purpose-driven regulation to the functioning of the highly complex organism as a whole. In fact, it is difficult to spot any psychological activity that is not aiming to fulfill a teleological goal. Not only the brain, but also the human mind functions teleologically. Conscience is not exempt from this principle of serving a higher, teleological purpose. Its unique ultimate task and purpose is to establish communication with the Spirit and soul, so as to establish and maintain communication with God.

If we now put all the pieces of this mosaic into their places, we get the following purposefully-functioning chain: The brain is programmed to fulfill a psychological purpose (to produce appropriate thoughts, feelings, perceptions and other psychological contents). The mind is programmed to fulfill a purpose as well: to be the "master of instincts and servant of conscience," as Frankl formulated it in *The Unconscious God*.[7]

The purpose of the conscience is to reflect the soul. The soul is programmed to fulfill a purpose as well—to reflect the "holiness and sincerity that are from God" (2 Cor. 1:12).

We can visualize this complex process in Figure 15-2.

Figure 15-2

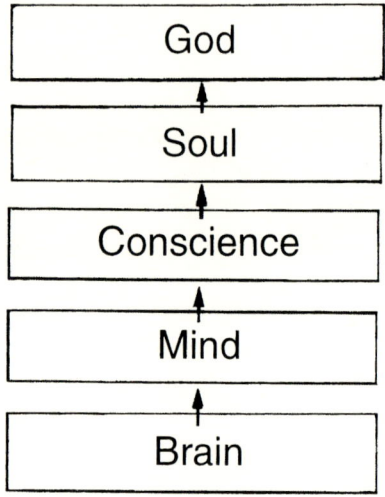

This drawing illustrates a chain of teleological regulation in humans. Therefore, the ultimate purpose of the brain is to produce a "healthy mind." The healthy mind's ultimate purpose is to serve conscience. The ultimate purpose of conscience is to serve the soul, while soul serves a responsible relationship with the triune God. This is the essence of the teleological spiritual regulation unique to and characteristic of the human species.

15.6. What is a Human Person?

First, let us frame the perspective we will use, correlating the increasing complexity of the organisms and their behavior, with the increased complexity of their regulation principles.

Biological functions in most simple living creatures (viruses or bacteria, for example) are regulated by simple physical and chemical processes—such as adhesion, cohesion, oxidation, reduction. The functioning of organisms consisting of multiple cells (for example of sponges or plants) is regulated by physical-chemical functions as well, but also by biochemical functions. The behavior of more complex animals that possess a nervous system (insects and reptiles for example) is regulated by physical-chemical, biochemical, and neurological principles. The behavior of even more complex animals (such as primates) is regulated by physical-chemical, biochemical, neurological, and additional elemental psychological functions (such as elemental feeling, remembering, and attention).

We have now come to humans. Our bodies and minds are regulated by physical and chemical functions (like oxidation processes in the lungs), by biochemical processes (for example, regulation of blood sugar by insulin), by neurological functions (reflexes, for example), and by psychological functions (like abstract thought and an emotional life deeper and more complicated than that of animals). However, what enables the typical and unique human form of being (including discipleship, faith, and Christian love) is the contribution of the soul and conscience—and thus ultimately of God—to the lower psychological, neurological, biochemical, and physical-chemical functioning in the human body and mind.

We present the correlation between more complex body functions and increasingly sophisticated regulation principles in Figure 15-3.

Figure 15-3

ORGANISMS   **REGULATION PRINCIPLES**

Organisms					
Viruses & Bacteria	Physical & Chemical				
Sponges or Plants	Physical & Chemical	Bio-chemical			
Insects or Reptiles	Physical & Chemical	Bio-chemical	Neuro-logical		
Primates	Physical & Chemical	Bio-chemical	Neuro-logical	Psycho-logical	
Humans	Physical & Chemical	Bio-chemical	Neuro-logical	Psycho-logical	Spiritual

Humans are physical, chemical, biochemical, neurological, psychological, and spiritually regulated complex organisms. This last dimension, the spiritual, is the ontological difference between humans and all
other living things that God created on earth.

In previous chapters, we observed the human mind, conscience, and
soul, and their interactions from philosophical, theological, and professional perspectives. Let us give a brief overview of our conclusions. We
concluded that if humans are indeed, in the words of Carl G. Jung, a
homo-religious species, and if humans are, in the words of Akos Pauler,
"a race searching for God," then there must be a reason for these human
behavioral characteristics. If such human qualities, so different from those
dictated and appreciated by the natural world, are not found in the brain
and mind itself, then they must exist outside of it.

Just as the "joint-like function" enables two very different regulations (psychological and neurological) to work together, the spiritual-
psychological joint connects two quite different dimensions. It connects
the spiritual and the mental through the joint of the soul and conscience,
enabling the person to act as Jesus' disciple. Just as many joint-like connections have to be taken into account to understand and explain the
functioning of the human body and mind, so a spiritual-psychological
joint has to be taken into account to understand and explain the spiritual
lifestyle and experiences of billions of believers, and, their spiritual and
ethical functioning as Jesus' disciples, which is so different from the
worldly perspective.

St. John reveals the same essential human condition concisely: "Flesh
gives birth to flesh, but the Spirit gives birth to spirit." (John 3:6) According to Rudolph Schnackenburg, the verse expresses that "man belongs, by virtue of his earthly birth, to the region of the sarx, and the
divine and heavenly world of the pneuma is beyond his reach."[8] However, despite one order being beyond reach, two quite different orders of
being are in fact connected in Christians. Both the biblical fact that Christians belong not only to this world but also to the divine and heavenly
world, and the behavioral fact that true Christians are distinguished by
their discipleship and biblical/spiritual conduct, are the consequence of a
"birth from above." Inversely, "birth from the Spirit" is not a theory
only, but is factually expressed in the Christian lifestyle and behavior
pattern. The Christian behavior pattern is impossible to understand without realizing the Spirit's active role, through the soul, conscience and

mind, in directing the behavior and conduct of true Christians in a teleological pattern.

15.7. Summary

We are unable to "know" the transcendent Spirit and the spiritual soul as we would objects. We do know, however, that believers experience in their minds the Spirit's/God's existence, presence and love. We discern also another fact: empirical facts confirm what revelation reveals, maybe not in genuine scholastic terminology, but certainly in modern scientific paradigms. We realize also that modern neurology and psychology, placed in an appropriate context, are becoming an increasingly useful tool in elucidating something that many religious philosophers intuitively felt, and what theologians from St. Paul, to Augustine, to Thomas Aquinas, to postmodern times implicitly confirm that, metaphorically, conscience is a spiritual-psychological joint.

Now we can reconstruct what a human is. As Maria Ungar formulated:

1. The body works in a causal "must" pattern.
2. The "will" pattern is a typical way the mind works.
3. Typical of the spirit and soul—acting through the conscience— is the "ought to" pattern, which sets an ethical and moral request.[9]

The Spirit's "ought to" motivates the highest and most complex human dimension—the soul—and through it the conscience, mind, and body in a goal-oriented (or more exactly God-oriented) way. Paradoxically, this "ought to" is more powerful in believers than the "will" of the mind, or the "must" of the body. In God's people, the "will" and "must" serve the "ought to." This very thing happened in Thomas' conversion. He did what he felt he "ought to," despite the rejection of his mind's "will" and his body's "must" to be of the world.

The connection between the Spirit and spirit (soul) is psychologically ineffable; it is a biblical-theological reality. The joint-like connection between soul and conscience is a theological-psychological reality. The connection between conscience and mind is a psychological reality. Finally, the joint between mind and body is a psychological-physiological reality.

The realities of soul, spirit, and Spirit are difficult to grasp because they are untouchable. For somewhat-positivists, as we all are, trained from early childhood to primarily recognize only worldly dimensions, it is hard to conceptualize the reality that we are part of another dimension as well—that we are a body, soul, and spirit, and that we are in fact living in and with God, the unimaginable yet experiential.

15.8. How Did Thomas' Soul and Mind Work Together in His Conversion?

By using Freud's ideas, we can now understand the dynamics in Thomas' mind before Jesus' intervention. His mind was virtually disconnected from God's Spirit because his conscience was virtually immobilized, and Thomas was directed by his superego, instincts, and ego.

At Jesus' second appearance, this changed. While Jesus' first sentences according to John 20:27, "Put your finger here; see my hands. Reach out your hands and put into my side," did offer sensory-psychological proof, his next sentence was a command, "Stop doubting and believe." It marked a spiritual-psychological turning point for Thomas. Those words were an appeal to his vocation, targeting the highest layer of Thomas' personality (his soul), and mobilizing his conscience.

Why do we assume this? Because every one of us could have uttered the same words or command, but without a particular spiritual context and without Jesus' Godly personality, our words would not have had the effect that they had on Thomas. Not the logical power but the spiritual connotation of the words was relevant. These words had a special effect because of a transcendent essence and spiritual meaning beyond Jesus' words; the Spirit acted in Thomas' spiritual-psychological joint. This is what enabled him to cry out, "My Lord and my God!" (John 20:28)

Because Thomas was spiritually touched, Jesus' words were all the proof he needed. They gave him as much, if not more, solid proof in his conscience than sensory-psychological proofs would satisfy a worldly person. Because of this proof, Thomas no longer required the offered visible, touchable, and measurable proof, and for this reason the Scriptures do not describe his touching Jesus.

Let us use a metaphor to visualize what went on in Thomas' soul and his spiritual-psychological joint. Thomas was touched by God similarly to the way Michelangelo depicted in *Creation*. He became a new creation, born of the Spirit. His new spiritual identity was acknowledged first by Thomas' conscience and then spread to the rest of his personality: his thinking, feeling, remembering, will, and all other mental functions. Being "touched" and spiritually transformed could explain the sudden change in Thomas, different from the discernment of the disciples on the road to Emmaus, who were touched by Jesus in a different mode.

After Jesus' intervention, Thomas' feelings, thoughts, volition, and even sensory recognition, in short his whole being, was put under a new command of God's Spirit, experienced and evidenced through his conscience/hyperego. Thomas no longer worried about possible warnings from his superego and instinct, or about the preservation of his life at all cost. His only goal now became to solidify his union with the Lord. His thoughts, feelings, and reactions had definitely changed. Thomas' psychological functioning was now under the command of a new headquarters: his conscience. Through the re-vitalization of his spiritual-psychological joint, Thomas became a new spiritual and, as St. Paul would say, a *pneumatic* person. He experienced this psychologically through a union with the invisible God, having received both gifts of the Spirit and gifts of faith.

15.9. Discussion

Let us now give an opportunity to a hypothetical devil's advocate to raise criticisms about the topic discussed in this chapter. He or she can start the discussion stating:

> The eighteenth century French materialist Pierre Cabanis proclaimed, "The brain is producing thoughts just as the liver is producing bile."[10] Later, in the nineteenth century, the Russian physician Ivan Mihalovie Sechenov described the "reflexes of the brain."[11] As Jarosevski comments, in Sechenov's teaching, the engine (the reflexes of the brain) replaces the engineer (the mind and soul).[12] Sechenov was the prophet of Pavlov's reflexology and (in some way) also of orthodox Behaviorism. All this leads us to examine how modern materialists explain the human ability to reason and think abstractly. The question arises whether Thomas' reasoning can be explained also in some way other than being influenced by Jesus' intervention—perceived through Thomas' soul and conscience.

During my residency, young physicians were trained in discussing the relationship between the brain and mind, particularly how their interaction enables logical thinking. Basic functional principles can be summed up as follows: In general, human logic imitates cause-and-effect principles in nature. Thus, from a perceived cause—the input—nerve cells of the brain's frontal lobe (connected to and acting in synchrony with other brain centers) arithmetically calculate and produce the effect (the output). Logical thinking is our psychological experience of the electrochemical activity in these nerve cells and nerve centers.

Figuratively, logical thinking can be compared to the oscillation of a pendulum. The input or cause on the left side oscillation of this pendulum has to be virtually equivalent to the output (the effect on the right side). For example, in logically correct statements such as "2 + 2 = 4," "today is a nice day," or "e = mc²;" the left oscillation ("2 + 2," "today," or "e") equals that on the right (4, "nice day," or "mc²"). The brain cells of the frontal lobe first assess the exact extent of oscillation on the left side of the logical equation (by arithmetically counting input, the average excitation level, and then by heightening or lowering thresholds in synapses, convergent or divergent transmission, and other neurological operations); they then predict the extent of the required (logically obligatory oscillation) on the right side of the logical pendulum. We can illustrate this in Figure 15-4.

Figure 15-4

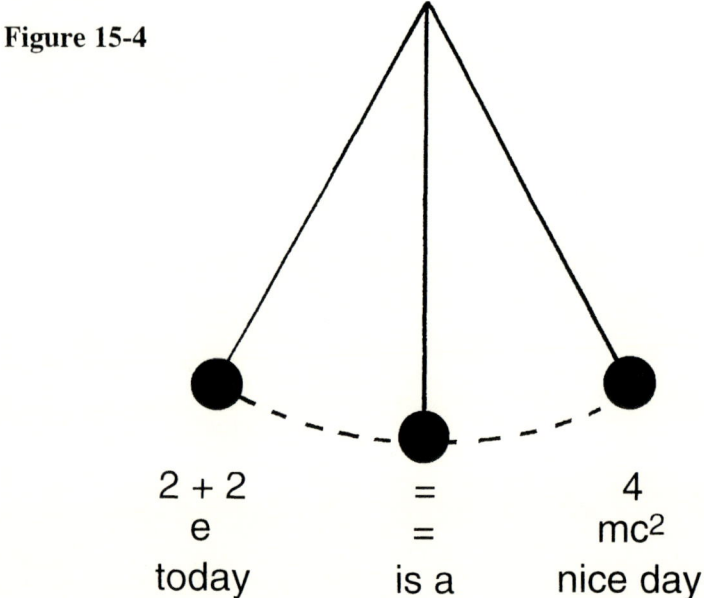

2 + 2	=	4
e	=	mc²
today	is a	nice day

The essence of logical thinking is predicting the arithmetical output required by assessing the input, all the while keeping balance and reciprocity between the two sides in the logical equation.

As human persons mature, oscillations of the metaphorical logical pendulum in abstract thinking get increasingly wider and greater. In such persons brain cells of the frontal lobe, those that make possible widening and deepening of the "swings" of the metaphorical logical pendulum, facilitate not only concrete logical operations, but also abstractions (i.e., focusing only on general and essential characteristics of the relevant ideas) such as "e" equals "mc^2."

Why is this explanation relevant to our topic?

It is relevant not only in the interest of unbiased fairness, but also, because if misinterpreted, this model seems to provide an explanation supporting the claim of our devil's advocate that the "engine has replaced the engineer," i.e., that Sechenov's "reflexes of the brain" render the soul redundant when tracing the source of logical reasoning. In this view, human thought, which the neo-Thomist Trocquer understood as a definite spiritual process, is reduced to a merely natural, physical phenomenon, almost like Cabanis' saying that "the brain is producing thoughts just as the liver is producing bile."

Let us now consider whether the input/output equation in logical thinking can provide an explanation for Thomas' reasoning that would undermine the argument that we have established, namely, that Thomas' revival was due to Jesus' intervention, perceived through Thomas' soul and conscience?

We have demonstrated that it would be impossible to explain Thomas' conversion without reference to a miraculous intervention of the resurrected Jesus, received through Thomas' soul, and psychologically perceived by his conscience. Our basis for concluding this was that we found no natural, psychological input to justify the output, his crying out "My Lord and God!" Apparently in Thomas' reasoning we have a reaction without an action; he acknowledges Jesus' resurrection without a sufficient sensorial proof (such as visual recognition of the resurrected Jesus). So what we see in Thomas is a "right oscillation" of the metaphorical logical pendulum that is not preceded by a "left oscillation." Indeed, such dynamics cannot possibly occur; a sufficient reason, (if not a sensorial then a spiritual reason), had to act in order to enable the oscillation of Thomas' logical pendulum, or his reasoning and conversion. Thus, without Jesus' intervention, registered through Thomas' soul, and psychologically through his conscience, the apostle's revival could not have occurred.

An agnostic could, however, object:

It is an empirical fact, that all psychological functions are connected to brain functions. If psychological functions (including the conscience) are connected to, or produced by neurological processes of the brain as we noted earlier, then how could such neurological processes—like "the reflexes of Thomas' brain"—be influenced by his immaterial soul?

By discussing this issue we are back at the question discussed since the time of the Enlightenment: How could the mechanically functioning brain be truly directed by a non-material spirit?

Indeed, if both the causally acting reflexes of Thomas' brain and the teleologically acting soul are real, if humans really consist of both body and spirit, then we need a paradigm where both systems are integrated. How may have such an integrated model, such a spirit-body paradigm, worked in effecting Thomas' conversion?

In the model of a logical pendulum not only does the input determine the output, but the model works in the opposite direction as well. Thus, the required output selects the number and kind of received inputs. In professional language we would express it this way: The neurons participating in logical reasoning are trained (by education and maturation) to raise or lower the thresholds of cell membranes in transmission of impulses from one nerve cell to the other. They are also trained to use convergent or divergent transmissions (and by this to concentrate and increase or dilute and decrease the input). By adjusting transmission in the synapses, neurons are also trained to regulate the quality and quantity of the received input. All this activity has a teleological purpose: that a required output (like appropriate thoughts, memory or behavior) be produced. By this process, not only does a neurological input causally determine the output, but the required psychological output (teleologically) determines the quality and quantity of received input. The interaction of the brain, mind, and the soul (participating in logical reasoning) are regulated in both a causal and a teleological way. Biblically and empirically we are simultaneously free and responsible spiritual beings, and also a causally functioning brain and body. For that reason, causal (neurological) and teleological (psychological and spiritual) principles regulate a human persons' behavior in a synchronized way.

A reader playing the role of devil's advocate may still argue:

> You have put forth mere hypothetical speculation demonstrated through the metaphor of the logical pendulum. The real question is whether we can pinpoint a real and concrete example of such a joint-like, teleological, regulation, which can achieve goal-oriented cooperation between the brain and the mind?

I admit this is a crucial question. To answer, let us use the neurology and psychology of human sight to demonstrate that such a joint-like teleologically directed connection between the functioning of the brain and mind does indeed exist.

When the world is observed, photons of light energy are transformed in the retina of the eye into electrochemical codes. These codes ("prints") of visual reality travel along the optic nerve in the form of electrochemical potentials into the primary visual area in the occipital brain. The nerve cells of the primary visual area, if inactive, as when the eyes are closed, are in a state of electrochemical balance. Newly arriving electrochemical codes of reality perceived by the eye disturb the existing electrochemical balance of the primary visual center in a unique way typical for the particular object "photographed" by the eye. Therefore cells of the primary visual area have to invest a particular energy to re-establish the previous electrochemical balance. Human subjects experience— "feel"—this effort by the nerve cells in the visual area as a sensory experience—the seeing of patches, colors, and contours. This is how neurological brain processes enable the psychological experience of the sense of sight.

Newborn babies see only colors, patches, and contours, but cannot recognize animals, things, or persons. By learning to see in perspective, to differentiate images from background, to establish logical and visual ideas of persons and things, the baby's brain learns not only to "see," but to visually distinguish and interpret the visual images in accordance with knowledge obtained in other ways, i.e., experience learning to see and recognize.

Adults see and recognize not only what their eyes "photographed," but also how this visual image should be organized and interpreted to represent a meaningful visual image. For example, we adults distinguish the car from its driver, even though the eye sees them as one. South American aboriginals, on the other hand, first perceived Spanish cavaliers as one creature. Only after establishing the rational ideas of the horse and the horseman did they see and acknowledge them separately, as two creatures. Here's yet another example. It is a well-known fact that lenses in our eye invert the visual image 180 degrees; therefore, the world is projected and seen by the retina in our eye upside down. But as we all know, we see the world upright. We can illustrate this in Figure 15-5.

Figure 15-5

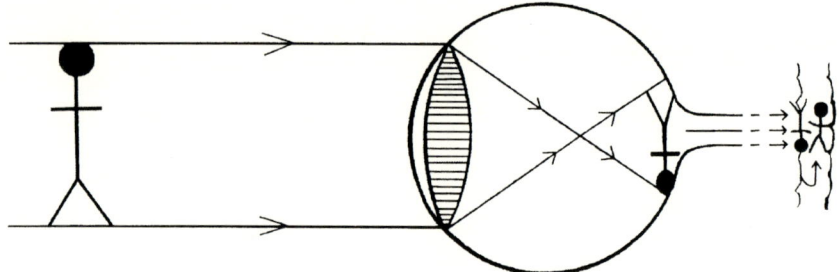

This illustration shows why the world is projected and seen by the retina in our eye upside down.

The image of the observed object is subsequently transported through the optic nerve to the visual area as upside down. However, since we have the knowledge and experience of what reality looks like upright and are trained to expect it to be upright, our brain in its secondary visual area automatically turns over the visual image 180 degrees and enables recognition that coincides with everyday experience and knowledge.

What do we realize from these examples?

Thanks to plasticity, when learning to see and recognize, the brain is trained to use and to adjust its neurological activity, regulated according to the cause-and-effect principle, to an ultimate goal: the production of meaningful visual images that match rational and experienced facts. Here we may discern the mechanism described in a previous discussion—that the neurons of the secondary visual area participating in seeing and recognizing are trained (by learning and experience) to raise or lower the thresholds of cell membranes in transmission of impulses. They are also trained to use convergent or divergent transmissions (and by this to concentrate and increase or dilute and decrease the input). By adjusting transmission in the synapses, neurons are also trained to regulate the quality and quantity of the received input. All this activity has a final purpose: that a required output (like appropriate seeing and recognition) may be produced.

In the act of recognition, the brain and mind perform jointly: the plasticity of the brain enables those adjustments to occur that enable a psychological meaningful recognition of visualized objects. Thus, the causally regulated neurological processes involved in vision are organized to serve a final psychological purpose: correct seeing and recognition. The teleological goal, the purpose of all the involved neurological processes is to ensure the psychological experience of correct seeing and recognition. This is the previously discussed principle of hierarchical organization of various dimensions in a human person. In a similar teleological way, the soul regulates conscience, Christian conscience regulates the believer's mind, and the mind regulates the body.

The next question may be, "Do feelings and instincts act in the same teleological way as the Christian conscience?"

It would be metaphorically appropriate to say that profane functions (like superego, antisocial feelings, or sexual instincts) are "compulsory-pushing," while spiritual calls are "teleological-pulling" in regard to human behavior. Thus, those functions not under the command of the soul and conscience are, in non-believers, generally not teleologically but causally regulated.

However, if feelings, thought, or volition (and even instinct) are put under the supervision of the Christian conscience, then the regulation pattern of those mental functions also contributes to the ultimate goal of holy, biblical living. Thus, they are unified under conscience's teleological regulation.

In animals, regulation of all behavior by the instincts is paramount. For civilized people, the highest control system is the superego. For people of faith, this supreme criterion is Christian conscience.

One reader may comment:

Indeed, the activity of the spiritual-psychological joint fits very well into biblical anthropological thinking. However, many professionals would consider this mere speculation that is far removed from reality. How can you prove that a spiritual-psychological joint truly exists?

Let us emphasize here that we are positing its existence not only because the Bible implies that the interaction between the Spirit and the mind enables one to speak spiritual words about spiritual truths. Neither are we re-discovering that there is mediation between the Spirit and conscience only because St. Paul implies this, or simply because the apostle's behavior and lifestyle witness this. Revelation is not the only evidence that implies that such a joint exists. Rather, we are asserting the existence of such a spiritual-psychological connection because the lifestyle of billions of true Christians, past and present, forces us to search for an explanation of a behavior pattern of "being in the world but not of it," a conduct that is very different from that of the "world" and that of the "sarx" ("flesh"). In short, the human brain and mind would not be programmed to perform such behavioral characteristics that serve a relationship with the invisible God if conscience, soul, and Spirit did not actively call for such a union.

We do explain true Christian behavior with the help of revelation, because the lifestyle of those who are called "saints" in the Acts of the Apostles cannot be explained otherwise. Revelation explains visible and touchable facts, and visible and touchable facts prove biblical revelation!

The next question from our devil's advocate can be:

Isn't it controversial to talk about the conscience's "union with God," about its "innate docility for ultimate goodness," or an ability of the conscience to "testify" enabling a "new birth" from the Spirit? In fact, conscience is arguably the most corruptible and unreliable of all human psychological functions. It is extremely biased, subjective, and arbitrary!

The conscience, when reflecting the soul's requirements, is not "unreliable," "subjective," and full of arbitrary inferences. The self, however, the part of the personality that resists hearing or acknowledging the requirements of his or her conscience is the source of all selfish differences, deceitfulness, and self-deceptive unreliability.

We can illustrate this typical characteristic of the human personality with an anecdotal example. According to one account, the Soviet leader Khrushchev and the American president Kennedy ran a race. Kennedy was younger, so he ran more rapidly and thus became the winner. The American newspapers reported this in big letters: "America first, Russia last." Soviet journalist's exercised damage control by responding in even bigger letters: "The Soviet Union second, and the U.S. second to last."

Journalists on both sides described "the truth, only the truth, and nothing but the truth." There was no lie in either report. However, the emphasis and wording made such a difference that the message was manipulated. Even more general is the manipulation of ethical requirements.

On the other hand, we may deceive others, but not ourselves. We realize in ourselves that if no true discipleship is chosen, then no true meaning, joy, peace, and freedom, and no reflection of God's love occur within. We are unable to protect ourselves from experiencing the consequences of such self-deception—evident lack of those "gifts of faith": true, biblical love, forgiveness, joy, peace, and others. Since gifts of faith are an outcome of a union with God, a lasting self-deception is difficult for a self-critical and responsible believer to maintain. In this mechanism is the reliability of the conscience anchored.

A reader may comment:

> We noted that conscience is informed about all psychological processes occurring in the self, relevant to a person's ethical choices. In other words, conscience ethically and morally "knows" a person—his or her mind, thoughts, feelings, willful behavior, problems, actions, and reactions. May not the soul have a similar "knowledge" about the moral choices, experiences, problems, feelings, and contents of the mind, and indeed of the whole person? Or, asked even more affirmatively: Does not the soul have to have full knowledge of a person in order to give a particular moral directive?

Unfortunately, we cannot answer this question based on experience because it is impossible to explore the soul or research it psychologically. However, let us turn for help to revelation. In Luke 23:43 we read Jesus' words to the repentant criminal: "I tell you the truth, today you will be with me in paradise." Another clue may be what St. Paul wrote in Philippians 1:23: "I am torn between the two: I desire to depart and be with Christ which is better by far." The apostle talks about the same issue much more in detail in 2 Corinthians 5:1-10. According to Josef Weismayer,[13] the apostle Paul speaks not about "resurrection" (which will happen at Jesus' second coming), but rather speaks explicitly about "being with Christ" after his death. However, how can a believer, whose body and mind had turned to ashes, be with Christ after death? The only possible logical answer seems to be through his or her soul. Let us see what theology teaches about this issue.

According to Weismayer, Pope John XXII (1316-1334) preferred the concept of a "waiting period" after death—meaning that the souls of the deceased believers have to wait until Jesus' second coming in order to see God "face to face." Nevertheless, on January 29, 1336, his successor, Pope Benedict XII, proclaimed in his bull *Benedictus Deus* as an infallible dogma that the souls of exemplary Christians enjoy an eternal "face to face" union with God beginning immediately after death (i.e., before Jesus' second coming and bodily resurrection). In this context, the soul represents the whole person, is judged immediately after death, and is able to have the benefit of eternal glory with God right after death.

Most Protestants also accept this formulation explicitly or implicitly. Like Catholics, they understand the soul not only as an instrument requiring a rebirth and a new way of living, but as a representation of the believer's true, immortal self, and one's personality after death. If the soul represents the person after the death of the body and mind, then personal information (for example, moral qualities) must be transmitted in an "ascendant" body-mind-conscience-soul direction, so that the soul represents one's personality in a spiritual realm. As noted, we have no empirical ways to research this ascendant transmission process or the mystery of the soul, which is on the "other side of the gap of transcendence." But we have something even more reliable than human reasoning: revelation may help us out in our quest for truth beyond the boundaries of human knowledge.

An agnostic or atheist reader may ask:

How does the Spirit concretely act through the spiritual-psychological joint? You noted that this regulation happens in a teleological way, but how we consciously feel, or experience it, remains unclear. Many people do not feel or experience teleological regulation in themselves, and neither are they aware of communication with the soul, Spirit or God.

St. Augustine in *Teacher* and *On Free Will* already realized that people do not acknowledge reality only with their actual physical eyes, but also, metaphorically speaking, with their "inner eyes." Perceiving internal reality such as biblical hope, trust or love in their deepest self with their inner eyes is, for people of strong faith, at least equally if not more important and evident than seeing worldly reality with their external eyes. For them, the same holds true for their communication with God, their experience of his spiritual gifts, the Spirit's presence in their conscience, and the messages received through their spiritual-psychological joint. The behavior of true Christians proves their communication with the invisible God.

For non-believers, the activity of the spiritual-psychological joint is less evident. Their brain/mind is an almost perfect tool of self-preservation, but they close themselves off from God's grace. This choice has not only spiritual, but also psychological, consequences. Metaphorically, the purpose for which one uses his or her brain determines its "wiring." If one's mind is used 99% of the time for serving self-preservation and successfully navigating through everyday life, it is less trained to recognize and acknowledge, as well as to observe with "inner eyes," God's active presence via one's spiritual-psychological joint.

In Andrew Murray's words:

> As long as in our worship of God we are chiefly occupied with our own thoughts and exercises we will not meet Him Who is a Spirit, the Unseen One. But to the man who withdraws himself from all that is of the world and man and waits for God alone, the Father will reveal himself.[14]

Therefore, would God's presence evidenced through the spiritual-psychological joint really remain hidden to an agnostic to the same extent if he or she spent 99% of the time actively asking for God's gift of faith? The answer to this question is self-evident.

Notes

1. Mihail Jarosevski, *Istoria Psihologii* (Moskva: Izdateljstvo Misl, 1966), 63-66.

2. Ferenc Szabo, *Az ember es vilaga* (Roma: Self-published, 1969), 81.

3. Jarosevski, *Istoria Psihologii*, 207-8.

4. Srboljub Stojiljkovic, *Psihijatrija sa Medicinskom Psihologijom* (Beograd: Medicinska Knjiga, 1975), 181-82.

5. Viktor E. Frankl, *Ärztliche Seelsorge* (Wien: Franz Deuticke, 1965), 287-89.

6. Louis Bouyer, *The Church of God* (Chicago: Franciscan Herald Press, 1982), 205.

7. Viktor E. Frankl, *The Unconscious God* (New York: Simon and Shuster, 1975), 53.

8. Rudolph Schnackenburg, *The Gospel According to St. John* (New York: Herder and Herder, 1968), 371-72.

9. Maria Ungar, *Viktor Frankl's Meaning-Oriented Approach to Counseling* (Edmonton, AB: Doctoral Dissertation. Department of Educational Psychology, 1999), 48.

10. Jarosevski, *Istoria Psihologii,* 223-25.

11. Jarosevski, *Istoria Psihologii,* 381-90.

12. Jarosevski, *Istoria Psihologii,* 390.

13. Josef Weismayer, *Dogmatik, VII Kapitel: Hoffnung Auf Vollendung* (Wien: Fernkurs Fur Theologische Bildung, 1985), 24.

14. Andrew Murray, *With Christ in the School of Prayer* (New Kensington, PA: Whitaker House, 1981), 25.

Part 3

How Does the Genuine Seeker Psychologically Experience the Reality to Which the Bible Bears Witness?

Chapter 16

An Experiential Discernment of Faith

For a hypothetical person living in only one dimension (like length), it would be difficult to understand that width also exists. For another person living in a two-dimensional world, length and width—as on a painting—it would be difficult to understand that there is another dimension, that of height. Classical physics recognized three dimensions, but since Albert Einstein's work, humans perceive reality in a four-dimensional, space-time continuum. Physicists admit the possibility that other dimensions may also exist. In our time, no one is able to imagine or experience what a hypothetical fifth dimension may be. Nevertheless, if adequately proven, even indifferent skeptics and agnostics would theoretically accept the idea of a multidimensional reality with no reservations, even if they were unable to visualize it.

However, for a person living in an agnostic-positivist paradigm, it is almost impossible to accept the notion, even if only at a theoretical level, that a spiritual dimension is present and acting in people of faith. Despite Christians' witnessing, it is almost hopeless to attempt to substantiate the existence of a Spirit, soul, or Christian conscience to a person living in only one dimension—a worldly form of being. Why do agnostics and atheists have a deeper resistance against the invisible God then an average person has against realizing the hypothetical fifth dimension? Where does this deep resistance against the invisible God come from?

It is not easy to answer this question because thus far we have only discussed the anthropological principles through which believers experience living in and with the Spirit. In order to solve the problem, we need to turn from a phenomenological analysis of what occurs when the Spirit and the believer's soul, mind, and brain interact, to an exploration of how a believer experiences those processes (i.e., exploring through which psychological processes a believer experiences faith). In the third part of the book we will discuss faith from an experiential perspective.

Hopefully, the ensuing discussion will not only answer the question we asked, but also elucidate agnostics' resistance against God and help people of faith find justification for and clarification of why their faith is not a mistake, illusion, or self-deception but the correct recognition of the invisible, almighty, eternal, and ultimately loving God.

Chapter 17

Can the Human Mind Register That Which is Scientifically Immeasurable?

Lajos Kardos illustrates orthodox behaviorist thought with a statement from the psychologist Karl S. Lashley, which could be summarized: "Everything existing can be examined scientifically; if we cannot explore a phenomenon through science, the only reason is because it does not exist at all."[1] Thus, what is essential for people of faith, such as the invisible God, is non-existent for Lashley and those who think like him. How can one take a stand concerning these questions which are of prime importance to all believers?

17.1. The Positivist Paradigm vs. the "Human Condition"

According to Frederick Copleston, the French philosopher August Comte (1798-1857), author of the *Cours de la Philosophie Positive,* described human thought as having evolved through three stages: the theological, the metaphysical, and the positive. The theological stage, according to Copleston, was "the age of the gods or God." In the metaphysical stage the concept "of supernatural and personal Deity is succeeded by the concept of all-inclusive Nature;" this transition was completed during the Enlightenment. The positive stage was characterized by the decline of interest in speculation about the supernatural. It focused instead on the visible, touchable, and scientifically-measurable world, hence positive facts only.[2] According to F. J. Thonnard, in Comte's *Positive Religion*, the personal God is replaced by the abstraction of "humanity," which becomes the criterion of progress and knowledge, right and wrong, good and evil.[3]

Comte's book reflects nineteenth-century thought. His followers in the twentieth century, "logical positivists" such as Alfred Ayer (1910-1989) and Ludwig Wittgenstein (1889-1951) avoided discussing faith. According to Geisler, "Whereas Kant had a metaphysics, Ayer did not." His belief was that "we cannot speak meaningfully of what may be beyond the empirical."[4] Thus Ayer, and especially Wittgenstein, did not explicitly deny the possibility of being in a relationship with God. However, in their opinion, since such transempirical experience cannot be discussed or even meaningfully shared with anyone who did not have the same experience, it is useless to talk about it.

Comte predicted well the attitude of his positivist followers, as well as present day trends occurring in the agnostic mental climate, such as an appreciation of science, thinking not in speculative but in positive terms, and a general interest among contemporary thinkers in touchable facts rather than in metaphysical and philosophical problems. This trend led ultimately to modern "scientific reductionism"—an understanding that everything that exists is scientifically explicable.

The theologian and philosopher Ian Barbour ascertained that, "Many people view science as objective, universal, rational and based on solid observational evidence," and that "Science starts from reproducible public data. Theories are formulated and their implications are tested against observations. Additional criteria of coherence, comprehensiveness, and fruitfulness influence choices among theories."[5] Here the author refers to positive scientific observation enabled by sensorial-scientific recognition. However, is observational scientific and positive evidence (really) reliable and factual in discerning what existing reality is truly like?

Pondering the answer to this question we may recall what we already discussed. When discussing the functioning of the brain and mind in visual recognition, we noted that a person recognizes externally what is "contained in him or her internally" in the form of visual images, ideas, and knowledge. Thus, the concept of "external reality" is a mixture which contains, not only true external perceptions, but also the projection of the person's experiences, interests, or training. For example, artists see and recognize different details than do others. Thus, the "solid observational evidence" Barbour talks about is always and unavoidably "contaminated" by the person's subjectivity. However, human ability to scientifically recognize, discern, or perceive reality is even further limited by the fact realized by Kant, that we quote according to Cross and Livingstone, as "the understanding *(Verstand)* which prescribed to nature her laws."[6]

A reader may ask: "Is this last statement only a philosopher's speculation, or an evident and proven empirical fact?"

Psychological observations do substantiate this philosophical conclusion as well. The avalanche of observations started to roll into the collective consciousness after the Gestalt psychologists described the experiment of projecting first a vertical, and then in a short time interval (less than 6/100 of a second) later a horizontal line, as "phi phenomenon." An experimental person's brain will "know" that such discernment signifies a movement, and he or she will see it as that. This is illustrated in Figure 17-1.

Figure 17-1

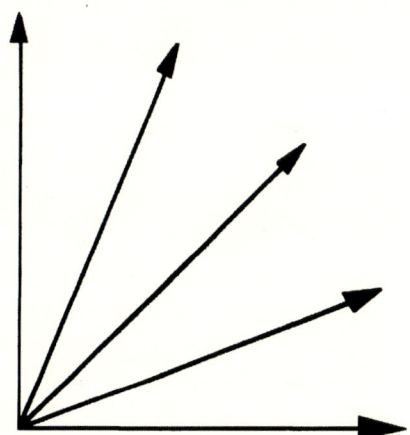

The drawing shows the subject "seeing" and recognizing a movement that in actuality never took place. As known, this "illusion," (a "false recognition") in which the brain interprets successively projected static positions as a movement, is used in the movie industry.

Another gestalt principle describes the completion of every incomplete observation into a cohesive form. Thus, an incomplete observation has a tendency to be observed as an already known, complete figure. This is shown in Figure 17-2.

Figure 17-2

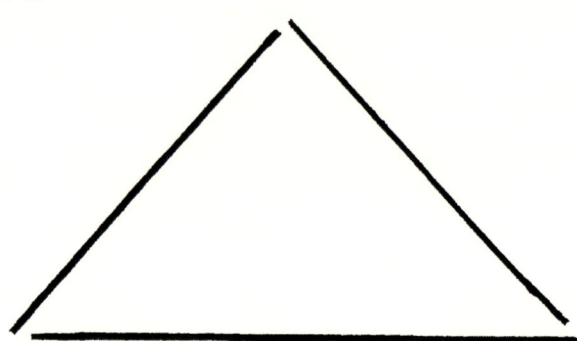

The observed figure is not a triangle, as we would like to see it, but three disconnected lines. Nevertheless, our brain seeks to create, from the visual image of three disconnected lines, the familiar image of a triangle. Perception and recognition operates according to some 114 Gestalt laws, enabling the senses and brain to create a picture of reality based on the subject's experience, training, and education.

The fact that the brain interprets sensory impressions according to its own rules and laws, creating unique images of reality, enabling us to see things not as they are, but as they seem to us, is widely known and widely used in everyday practice. For example, techniques of military disguise use these principles to disable the enemy observer's ability to distinguish an object from its background, causing the enemy not to recognize what the eyes are seeing, or enabling recognition of false images which do not exist, but which nonetheless the eyes are tricked into seeing. Skillfully manipulating that which is "known" and that which is "sensed" results in magicians' visual illusions.

What we epistemologically realize is that by sensorial or scientific recognition we do not perceive reality as it is. True reality may be very different than positive sensorial-scientific observations allow us to realize! In everyday life situations those subtle discrepancies between sensorial-scientific discernment of Kant's "thing for us" and the "thing in itself" may seem meaningless. In answering ultimate questions, however, they may be relevant.

The relevance of what we discussed is as follows: Humans see, recognize, and know the world differently from animals, cherubs, or angels; we perceive reality only from a human perspective. Discerning reality from a human perspective means that we are passionately persuaded by our experiences, which are neither "factual" nor based on impersonal, positive, or scientific observation, knowledge, or measurement. For humans, our experiences are the most persuasive elements in our lives, as they reflect our own thoughts and emotions, memories, will, conscience, and perceptions—our whole personality. As the French existentialist Saint-Exupery wrote in his *Little Prince*, as quoted by Joseph Ratzinger: "What is really important is invisible to the eye; you only see properly with your heart."[7]

However, is this really so? If even our sensorial and scientific observations exist only "as perceived from a human perspective," then is anything unconditionally true and absolute in our discernments?

Or is Jean P. Sartre's conclusion correct, (which I summarize as the message of his books *La Nausée—Nausea,* and *L'être et la Néant—Being and Nothingness*): Humans are thrown into the world without possessing a safe lighthouse to help them navigate their way through life?[8, 9]

Sartre emphasized very well the paradox of human existence: that for modern people neither the common sense experience nor instincts (like instincts do to the animals), culture, religion, family, or tradition elucidates what is unquestionably right, true, or absolute. Considering our previous discussion of the "human condition," however, this statement is not entirely true. All humans possess at least some kind of a "lighthouse"—that we all see, recognize, and know the world observed from a typical human perspective.

This means that our weakness is also our strength; that the "human condition" is the most persuasive criterion of knowledge, truth and reality. Particularly, this means that there is no human being without a fundamental need to search for joy, meaning, peace, or love. The search for bodily pleasure, psychological happiness, and spiritual joy is "programmed" into all of us. It comes from the "wiring" of the brain, the activity of the mind, and interaction with the soul and Spirit. The search for pleasure, happiness and joy is the "lighthouse" which makes it possible to know and react to reality in a uniquely human way, to navigate our way through life, and ultimately, to respond to his call and search for the absolute and quite other God.

In this context, Frankl refers to widely publicized and replicated experiments. Electrodes were implanted into the hypothalamic pleasure centers of the brains of monkeys. One monkey, who was taught to stimulate his own brain's pleasure center with electrodes, causing himself to feel a great deal of pleasure, unfortunately did not live very long. He was so preoccupied with stimulating his brain's pleasure center that he had no time to eat or drink.[10]

The brain center of pleasure in humans has a similar imperative role as well. People's use and abuse of drugs is a repetition of the mentioned experiment. Drug users try to biochemically stimulate their own pleasure centers. Indeed, a high price must be paid for such a shortcut. Nevertheless, this also proves the paramount importance of non-scientific motivators acting in humans.

Thus, humans are not thrown into the world without the aid of a lighthouse. Experiencing pleasure, happiness, and joy is our ultimate behavioral goal, an innate, natural law written upon our hearts, minds, and souls which navigates our every activity in every moment of our lives. Indeed, nothing sets us apart from others more than our own unique ways in which we imagine achieving this goal. This diversity, however, does not change the fact that the search for joy, despite being subjectively (but not positively or scientifically) experienced, is more imperative in human life than any cognitive discernment. To use a metaphor that captures the truth about the "human condition:" psychological functions in search for joy are the sailor, while sensorial and cognitive recognition functions are the boat, both of which enable navigation through life.

What is the relevance of all that we have discussed in this section to our topic? First, that humans are unable to perceive the world any more "objectively" than thinking and feeling allow. Second, that the paramount power of the human search for meaning and joy, and not sensorial-scientific knowledge, is the motor and criterion of the dynamic within the "human condition." Third, despite the fact that every believer's psychological experience of God is unique, there are also such important commonalities as discerning biblical joy and meaning. These connect God's people and enable them to talk about a shared, not empirical, but transempirical experience of God.

Ultimately, our discussion in this section raises many questions: Should those psychological dynamisms of paramount significance (the search for joy) not supplement positive recognition processes in discerning the "ultimate truth?" Are functions that are not sensorial-scientific but personal, more valuable in answering the ultimately important questions in life than empirical, rational, logical and scientific discernments? Is it possible to form a paramount, true and relevant experience of something that is neither visible nor touchable or scientifically provable?

17.2. Debunking the Prejudice: "What is Inaccessible to Science Does Not Exist at All"

In 1 Corinthians 2:13 and 2 Corinthians 1:12, St. Paul talks about non-sensorial experiences such as his receiving such gifts of the Spirit as talking "in spiritual words about spiritual truths" of the "holiness and sincerity that are from God," and about acting "not according to worldly wisdom but according to God's grace." Similarly, with the help of Jesus Christ, Thomas experiences something through his soul and conscience that cannot be examined scientifically, i.e., the resurrected Jesus. But although that resurrection was not "positively" proven, it was the most important reality for him; he experienced it, and it influenced his behavior and changed his life. Despite all of these facts, was what influenced Thomas' life so profoundly and powerfully real, or only a figment of his imagination? Could it have been an instance of self-deception, or an "illusion" as Freud labeled religion in the title of his book, *The Future of an Illusion*?[11]

Let us return for a moment to the example of the preacher Wesley. When asked how he knew that Jesus is alive, he responded "Because I talked to him for a half an hour this morning!" Obviously, communicating with Jesus was, for him, an experiential reality, despite not being a "positive" fact.

A skeptical person from the last pew or a scientist/positivist could make a video, or even an audio tape recording of Wesley communicating with Jesus, but it would show nothing. However, an EEG or Polygraph would register that Wesley was really experiencing an awesome encounter in his mind and brain. How is such experiencing of God, the Spirit, and faith possible if it is not a provable phenomenon?

Let us begin discussing this question by reviewing some simple, almost trivial facts, and discuss the importance and reliability of a typical non-sensorial—scientific experience, that of love. One cannot see, touch, or measure love in another person. We can only see (true or false) signs or expressions of love, but never love itself. Furthermore, from a scientific-psychological perspective one unbiased observer can merely register its signs but never really know what love really is. Love is an internal experience, and one cannot be familiar with it any way other than by experiencing it personally. Yet, for someone who is in love, there is nothing more important, more convincing, than the experience of his or her love. It is the most important reality for that person, even if his or her love isn't a scientific fact measurable in inches, pounds, or seconds. Even if, theoretically speaking, the experience of being in love was solely unique to that person, or everyone thought the lover a fool, for him or her nothing is more important or evident than the fact that he or she loves.

To take another example, throughout our lives each of us in his or her own way searches for meaning and purpose. It is impossible for us to take the view that, "No, my life has no purpose; it is meaningless." Only depressive or suicidal people would arrive at such a conclusion about their lives. But neither is purpose a scientifically measurable fact. Yet, people do not need scientific proof that their life has a meaning if they experience it in themselves. This internal evidence is more convincing, safe, and certain than any scientific explanation.

Viktor Frankl, in *The Unheard Cry for Meaning,* described the story of a young lady with inoperable cancer. Feeling that her future life had no purpose, she came to Freud to ask for help. Freud, however, responded thus: "O my young lady you are very mistaken: your life has never had meaning!"[12] Thus, in Freud's or another atheist's understanding, young or old, healthy or sick, rich or poor, human life has no meaning at all. However, despite the fact that hope, trust, joy, optimism, or peace is invisible and untouchable, there is in my experience as psychiatrist and psychologist nothing more evident than man's search for meaning as the title of another of Frankl's books puts it.[13]

The third example is hope. To my knowledge at least three poets, the British John Baillie, the German Friedrich Schiller, and the Hungarian Janos Pilinsky, stated in their poetry the idea that hope blossoms even on the grave. Despite the importance of hope (and not only to poets), there is no scientific evidence for hope either; it is not possible to see, touch, or measure, but only to experience it.

The same is true for depression. A patient cannot be treated simply by being told, "Forget your feeling of depression and guilt, for it is only your internal experience which nobody else can see, touch, or measure, and therefore, it does not exist in reality." The truth is that so long as the patient experiences this depression, meaninglessness, or guilt, nothing is more real for the individual than these feelings, and suicide will continue to be a very real and dangerous threat.

As we can see, joy, finding meaning, purpose, and value in life, optimism, hope, and forgiveness are not touchable or measurable scientific facts or qualities. They are impossible to scientifically prove or to disprove. Nonetheless, these non-scientific experiences and facts are substantially important in the life of every one of us. Thus, what is sensorial (visible, touchable, testable, measurable) and what is experiential are not synonymous; for non-sensorial phenomena can be very experiential indeed.

Notes

1. Lajos Kardos, *Behaviorizmus* (Budapest: Gondolat Konyvkiado, 1970), 17.
2. Frederick Copleston, *A History of Philosophy* (Paramus, NY: Newman Press, 1975), 9: 78-79.
3. F. J. Thonnard, *A Short History of Philosophy* (Paris: Publishers of the Holy Apostolic See, 1955), 769.
4. Norman L. Geisler, *Baker Encyclopedia of Christian Apologetics* (Grand Rapids, MI: Baker, 2000), 783.
5. Ian G. Barbour, *Religion in the Age of Science* (San Francisco, CA: Harper, 1990), 3.
6. F. L. Cross and E. A. Livingstone, eds., *The Oxford Dictionary of the Christian Church* (New York: Oxford University Press, 1997), 919.
7. Joseph Ratzinger, *Behold the Pierced One* (San Francisco, CA: Ignatius Press, 1986), 55.
8. Jean Paul Sartre, *La Nausée* (Paris: Gallimard, 1938).
9. Jean Paul Sartre, *L'être et le Néant* (Paris: Gallimard, 1943).
10. Viktor E. Frankl, *Antropologische Grundlagen der Psychoterapie* (Bern Stuttgart, Wien: Hans Huber, 1976), 20.
11. Sigmund Freud, *The Future of an Illusion* (London: Hogarth Press, 1922).
12. Viktor E. Frankl, *The Unheard Cry for Meaning* (New York: Pocket Books/Simon and Schuster, 1984), 30.
13. Viktor E. Frankl, *Man's Search for Meaning*, Revised and Enlarged Ed. (New York: Washington Square Press, 1984).

Chapter 18

The Concept of Transempirical Discernment

How we perceive reality has always been an important question in philosophy and, in modern and post-modern times, also in psychology, neurology, psychiatry, brain research, and other empirical sciences. It is one of the main topics of interest of this book as well. Thus, how and through which psychological functions do we experience that which is non-sensorial, scientifically inexplicable, and as Karl. S. Lashley noted, non-existent?

18.1. An Historical Overview

From a professional perspective, it is interesting to observe how the same ideas appear, disappear, and reappear through history. Let us review a history we have established earlier. In the fourth century BC, according to Jarosevski, Plato realized the impossibility of sensorial observation of geometric ideas. According to Plato, perception of these stems not from sensorial reality, nor from the physical world, but from the world of ideas.[1] Plato thus raised the problem of non-sensorial information, but without giving a plausible explanation of how we realize such information.

Some 800 years later in the fourth century AD, St. Augustine realized that "man gains knowledge of God and his soul by looking inward, not by examining the outside world" (Hyman and Walsh[2]). In *Teacher,* Augustine describes such internal dialogue as an "inner light of truth which illuminates the inner man and is inwardly enjoyed."[3] In *On Free*

Will, he says "It is also clear that the interior sense perceives not only the data passed on to it by the five senses, but also perceives the senses too."4

Sometimes an attempt is made within modern psychology to avoid the term "introspection" because it is associated with subjectivity or bias. However, it is difficult to find any practitioner who would be uninterested in precisely this human subjectivity or who would not use the internal experiences first described by Augustine, and given such various names in modern vernacular as "automatic thoughts," "irrational beliefs," "insight learning," or simply "tension," "frustration," "pain," "depression," or "suicidal risk."

Some twelve hundred years after Augustine, John Locke, in his ground-breaking *Essay Concerning Human Understanding* accomplished the next great step in the substantiation of empiricism. Locke acknowledged a point of fundamental importance: that human knowledge is based not on inborn ideas, but on experience. He concluded that the human mind is at birth a "blank slate" (*tabula rasa*). He then analyzed how the mind works. Experience itself, according to Locke, encompasses two different kinds of recognition functions: sensation and reflection.5

Geisler points out that in Locke's understanding, the senses, despite being unavoidable, do not mirror the whole truth about the reality in which we live.6 Subjects receive information about external reality not only through their senses, but from the ideas obtained and abstracted from the senses as well. To discern reality (from experienced senses and ideas) humans use reflection. Locke understood reflection as the self-experienced internal operations of the mind that help us to reconstruct reality. Reflections can be intuitive when the harmonization of particular ideas happens directly, or demonstrative when harmonization happens indirectly, with the help of other ideas. Reflections enabling us to know our own mind happen directly (intuitively), while reflections aiding our acknowledgment of God happen indirectly (i.e., by demonstration).

We will use Locke's idea of reflection, but balance his rationalism with the thoughts of another giant, who was almost Locke's contemporary—the French mystic Blaise Pascal. Pascal was originally a mathematician. He constructed an inventive precursor to the computer, experimented with the barometer, made discoveries in the mathematics of probability, and made an essential contribution to the mathematical theory of binomials. However, in 1654, his interests changed, and he turned towards philosophy. He discerned something that can be summarized from *Pensées*. In Ferenc Szabo's translation: "It is in transcending that people become fully human."[7] Through faith, "humans infinitely transcend themselves." Thus, the believer's self-transcendence is fully accomplished in his or her relationship and union with God.

Another leading idea of Pascal's theology is "the heart has reasons unknown to reasoning" (see Ratzinger's *Behold the Pierced One.*)[8] We should not belittle these proofs of the heart as emotional, subjective, arbitrary inferences. Pascal is instead talking about a reliable and immediate internal experience based on transcending oneself. This experience is a stronger and more relevant source of truth than the logical arguments of dogmatists or the doubts of skeptics. Thus, Pascal built his philosophy on the internal consensus of emotional and rational discernment of subjects, which is simultaneously passionate and rational.

Some three hundred years after Pascal, a modern existentialist, Viktor E. Frankl, founder of logotherapy, used terminology different from that of Augustine, Pascal, or Locke in his discussion of a unique phenomenon, namely, "*Man's Search for Meaning.*"[9] Frankl described human conscience as a "*Sinn Organ,*" (an "organ of purpose") enabling believers to discern ultimate purpose. In *The Doctor and the Soul,*[10] he illustrated the functioning of the "organ of purpose" with a story.

> One day I was sitting in a restaurant with an internationally famous psychoanalyst. He had just delivered a lecture, which we were discussing. He denied that such a thing as conscience existed at all, and asked me to tell him what this conscience was. I answered briefly: "Conscience is what has made you give us such a splendid lecture tonight." Whereupon he lost his temper and screamed at me: "That isn't true—I did not deliver this lecture for my conscience, but to please my narcissism!"

Thus, even in people who do not realize its power, conscience enables a self-criticism.

Frankl did not explicitly describe what we will call "functions of purpose" and "functions of existence." However, his description seems to imply that the function of conscience as an organ of purpose is distinct from other recognition functions, which we will call functions of existence and which serve worldly tasks of survival and well-being.

Finally, we arrive at the main point. In *Crossing the Threshold of Hope*, Pope John Paul II argued that even though human knowledge is primarily sensory, ". . . the limits of these 'senses' are not exclusively sensory."[11] Humans, therefore, know "extrasensory truths" or, in other words, the *transempirical*. In addition, it is not possible to affirm that when something is transempirical it ceases to be empirical." He continues,

> It is therefore possible to speak from a solid foundation about human experience, moral experience, or religious experience. And if it is possible to speak of such experiences, it is difficult to deny that, in the realm of human experience, one also finds good and evil, truth and beauty, and God.

Accordingly, here is a discernment which is experiential, real, and evident to the one who experiences it, but is non-sensorial and therefore not the same, not touchable, and not equally measurable for every observer.

A believer's relationship with God is almost always a mixture of introspective, meaning-oriented, or mystical elements and it is always a paramount transempirical experience. This is the reason that from now on we will focus on epistemological characteristics of this philosophical term and its psychological materialization in introspections, meaning, and mystical experience.

18.2. Clarification of Terminology

Unfortunately, we find considerable terminological confusion about psychological expressions that have philosophical connotations. There is even a greater confusion when we attempt to connect psychological and philosophical concepts. Thus, at first glance it may seem that the writings of Augustine, Locke, Pascal, and Frankl have few things in common, except that they all deal with a kind of non-sensorial experience.

For the purpose of comparison and in order to find commonalities, we may define "introspection" (paraphrasing the *Concise Oxford Dictionary*,) as a method of investigating mental phenomena that consists of examining one's own mental processes.[12] Introspection is a method of observing oneself with "inward-looking eyes." Introspection may become morally neutral for the subject, as in the process of taking a projective psychological test like the Rorschach, in which responses carry neither a positive nor a negative moral connotation.

"Reflections," according to the same source, may be defined as the process of reconsidering and deliberating on previously experienced introspections. Reflection represents thinking about one's own thoughts, most often with a moral connotation. Conscience eminently participates and plays a decisive role in these activities of weighing and consideration.

"Mystical experiences" are those made possible by a contemplative seeking of contact with the transcendental; and "mystics" (according to the *Concise Oxford Dictionary*) can be defined as "those who seek to obtain unity with God through contemplation and self-surrender." Therefore, in practice, mystical experiences, which are the least psychologically understandable of the four categories, are most often theocentric.

"Functions of purpose," a concept extrapolated from Frankl's teaching, organize psychological experiences in a meaningful (or, in an ultimately meaningful) context, thus enabling us to understand the experiences in their entirety from a new meaning-oriented perspective. We will most often stand on Frankl's shoulders and use his term "functions of purpose" as an eminent expression of the transempirical.

What is common in all the aforementioned, partially-overlapping, psychological descriptions is that they enable the discernment of a non-sensorial reality echoed in one's personality. These psychological functions enable believers to experience the ultimate reality who is God.

A philosopher would call these psychological descriptions a "transempirical experience." The term is a philosophical abstraction; it is an umbrella term that encompasses the psychological terms used by Augustine, Locke, Pascal, and Frankl. Inversely, the philosophical abstraction of "transempirical" may be expressed and concretized in a particular psychological activity or discernment process, like introspection, reflection, mystical, or meaning-oriented experience.

Internal reality may seem to depend only on the subject's intimate and personal discernments but it would be a mistake to view it as chosen arbitrarily. Are we really able to "choose" joy (instead of depression), trust (instead of distrust), or peace (instead of angst)? According to neuroscientists and psychodynamically-oriented psychiatrists and psychologists, our feelings, thoughts and even fantasies have a particular reason and explanation. On a Rorschach or other projective tests, responses are almost always explicable by personal dynamic.

In various forms of cognitive-behavioral therapy (like Beck, Ellis, Meichenbaum), the patient is not instructed to arbitrarily choose a way he or she "ought" to be. Rather, the intent in the therapy is to discern new or previously unappreciated reasons for one's thoughts, feelings, and behavior, enabling a patient to stop being depressed, angry, or sui-

cidal. Insights are not an arbitrary choice, but the discernment of existing, valid reasons to change thoughts, feelings, and behavior.

This is because in our internal reality we are confronted with regular
and stringent recognition and discernment processes which are not less
strict than processes involved in external, cognitive discernment. Augustine already knew this, but Freud focused explicit attention on the fact
that psychologically, in relation to the reliability of introspective discernment, the subject's ability to arbitrarily control his or her internal reality
is often limited.

18.3. Transempirical vs.
Sensorial-Scientific Recognition

According to one story, the Roman emperor Caligula was so impressed
with horses that he brought his horse into the Roman Senate and proclaimed it a Senator. But despite the emperor's proclamation, the horse
could not perform as a Senator. Caligula was unable to arbitrarily change
the visible and touchable reality, the properties of his horse. However,
after the unsuccessful attempt, he continued to love his horse even more.
His affection was based not on the horse's visible or touchable qualities
to be a Senator, but on Caligula's internal and intimate recognition of the
lovable qualities of and of his personal affection for his horse.

This example is one more demonstration that our notion of reality,
and that everything we know or experience of it, is composed of two
different recognition functions. The first is the recognition of the external reality, which is virtually the same for all of us and can be seen,
touched, measured, and explored, and which can be perceived objectively, independent of the observer. The second is "inner experience"
such as love, hope, the act of forgiving, happiness, or optimism, all of
which are personal and unique experiences for every one of us, and
which we experience inside ourselves as the deepest, most personal knowledge, feeling, or thought. Both recognition functions are substantially
important, but they are very different kinds of acknowledgments. We
can envision the difference between these two recognition functions as in
Figure 18-1. In the drawing, the discernments of both psychological functions are enabled by the functions of the brain, mind, and soul but their
focus is different.

Figure 18-1

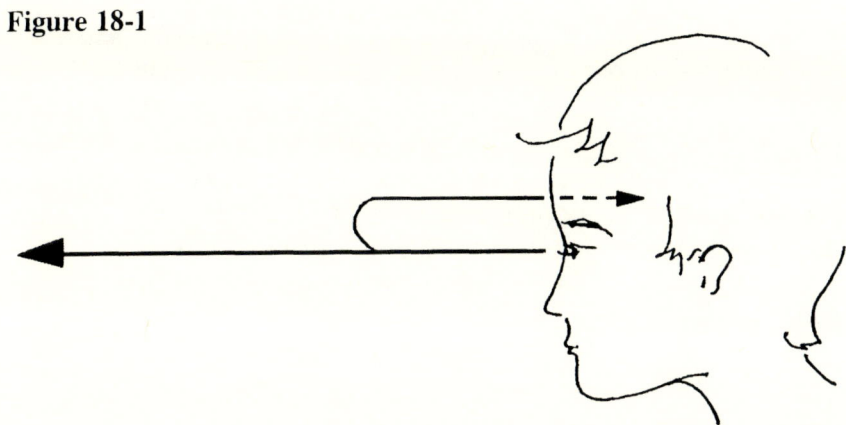

We have said that the first recognition function serves the functions of existence. As we are using this phrase, we do not mean the existentialist's idea of existence—"a form of being characterized by a responsibility to become what one ought to be." On the contrary, the sensorial-scientific, cognitive or existential recognition function encompasses solely the functions enabling worldly survival and well-being. It is used in physics, mathematics, astronomy, biology, and medicine. It enables us to answer the "how's" of our world—how to work, how to safeguard our lives, how to survive.

The second type of recognition function (transempirical recognitions) serves primarily to discern meaning, purpose, and values (the functions of purpose). This recognition function answers the "why's"—why work, why struggle, why give birth to and bring up children, why live at all? Knowledge acquired by a transempirical recognition will not give security or material well- being, but it does grant joy, value, and meaning. The more meaning we find in our lives, and the more valuable tasks we dedicate our lives to, the more we will be rewarded with strength and happiness.

In many of his works, e.g., *The Doctor and the Soul,* Frankl cites a quotation by Friedrich Nietzsche: "Whoever has a reason for living endures almost any mode of life."[13] The same quotation, from Frankl's *Ärztliche Seelsorge* in a different translation, may sound like, "He who has a why to live, can bear with almost any how."[14] In this lies the importance of the reflective realm. Without the "why," life becomes meaningless and difficult. Without a firm "why," every "how" is painful.

From the interaction and cooperation of both (sensorial-scientific and transempirical recognition functions), it is apparent that the two are not entirely different; there are transitions from one to the other. Most discernment is neither exclusively sensorial-scientific nor purely transempirical functions, but both simultaneously. Boundaries between the two recognition functions are sometimes enmeshed. However, this does not change the fact that the central focus of each is different.

If we outlined the functions and their roles in a diagram, it would look like Figure 18-2.

Figure 18-2

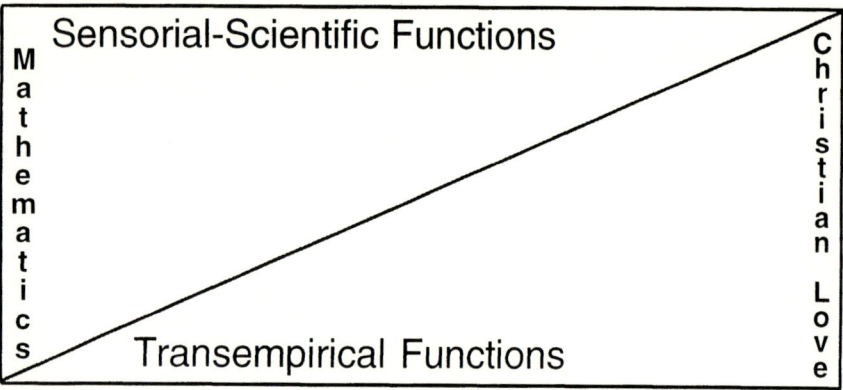

From left to right in the diagram, the importance of the sensorial-scientific functions decreases while the importance of the functions of transempirical recognition grow. Between the two extremes, almost all of our experiences and activities can be listed. In this central area, everything has lesser or greater importance in maintaining existence, and lesser or greater importance in discerning meaning.

The two psychological functions are often supplementary. For example, studying enables a student to attain skills necessary to earn money, so as to sustain his or her life. Thus, studying is a cognitive task—it is a sensorial-scientific function. However, it serves also to fulfill meaning and to attain joy. Hence, studying gives value to a student's life and therefore has an evident transempirical purpose as well.

A unique discipline encompassing and unifying both sources of human knowledge on a rational level is philosophy. Philosophers in general bring the wholeness of human experience together, integrating that which is experienced through sensorial-scientific channels with the recognition of meaning and values acquired through transempirical recognition. Scholastic and metaphysical philosophy, as we discussed, was especially concerned with connecting visible and experiential facts with those discovered through introspection, reflection and mystical experience, creating one meaningful context.

Our focus in this book is less upon connecting non-sensorial and empirical recognition; rather, it is concerned with analyzing the psychology and even "spirituality" of transempirical experience and discernment. We will use those "tools of choice" in analyzing the dynamics of faith, and we will draw repercussions relevant to our understanding of the believer's tangible experience of his or her relationship with the invisible God.

Notes

1. Mihail Jarosevski, *Istoria Psihologii* (Moskva: Izdateljstvo Misl, 1966), 63-68.

2. Arthur Hyman and James J. Walsh, *Philosophy in the Middle Ages* (New York: Harper & Row Publishers, 1967), 16.

3. St. Augustine, "Teacher," in *Philosophy in the Middle Ages*, ed. Arthur Hyman and James J. Walsh (New York: Harper & Row Publishers, 1967), 32.

4. St. Augustine, "On Free Will," in *Philosophy in the Middle Ages*, ed. Arthur Hyman, James J. Walsh (New York: Harper & Row Publishers, 1967), 35.

5. John Locke, *An Essay Concerning Human Understanding*, Complete and Unabridged, Collated and Annotated by Alexander Campbell Fraser (New York: Dover Publications, 1959), 273.

6. Norman L. Geisler, *Baker Encyclopedia of Christian Apologetics* (Grand Rapids, MI: Baker Books, 2000), 426-27.

7. Ferenc Szabo, *Az ember es vilaga* (Roma: Self-published, 1969), 14.

8. Joseph Ratzinger, *Behold the Pierced One: An Approach to Spiritual Christology* (San Francisco, CA: Ignatius, 1986), 68.

9. Viktor E. Frankl, *Man's Search for Meaning*, Revised and Enlarged (New York: Washington Square Press, 1984).

10. Viktor E. Frankl, *The Doctor and the Soul: From Psychotherapy to Logotherapy* (New York: Vintage Books, 1986), xxvi.

11. John Paul II, *Crossing the Threshold of Hope* (New York: Alfred A. Knopf, 1994), 33-34.

12. R. E. Allan, *The Concise Oxford Dictionary* (Oxford: Clarendon Press, 1990).

13. Frankl, *The Doctor and the Soul*, 54.

14. Viktor E. Frankl, *Ärztliche Seelsorge* (Vien: Franz Deuticke, 1965).

Chapter 19

The Epistemology of Faith: How Do We Know that We Have Faith?

Everything we experience psychologically happens through our sensorial-scientific and/or transempirical recognition functions. The believer's communication with God, and his or her experience of faith, do not occur without being registered by psychological (epistemological) recognition functions. (Epistemology, as the reader may recall, is a discipline analyzing the theory of knowledge). As the title of the chapter indicates, we will focus on how we experience, feel, and know that we have faith.

We live in a time that attempts to reduce almost everything, including Christian faith, to socialization, cultural tradition, or personal habit. Therefore, let us first set criteria to help identify things that do not involve the epistemology of faith.

Faith does not assure security or well-being of life. Faith will not help to make a believer richer or more successful, or his or her life more secure or comfortable. Quite the contrary is true. As we can see from the life of Christ, the lives of the saints, and others who exemplified faith throughout history, faith can bring loss of wealth, security, and even one's life. Thus, Christian faith definitely does not serve biological, economical or sociological well-being and is not experienced psychologically through a sensorial-scientific discernment or function of existence. If faith serves primarily biological, economic, or sociological gain, then it is not genuine faith!

Genuine faith, however, has provided direction, value, and meaning to the disciples (including Thomas), to the saints, and to believers past and present. This is the reason why as a member of God's kingdom, Thomas was exhilarated and hopeful when he cried out, "My Lord and my God!" This is the kind of a paramount transempirical experience—a pursuit of biblical meaning and faith. Thus, faith is transempirically known.

In logical thinking, the differences between sensorial-scientific and transempirical discernment ought to be meticulously respected, and borders not enmeshed (as in the case of the ancient dictator Caligula). Reflections or functions of purpose cannot prove sensorial-scientific facts, just as a mathematical equation cannot prove or disprove one's joy or love.

This principle is especially important in faith discernment. God's existence cannot simply be proven to everyone by overwhelming cognitive, scientific, or touchable proof, as faith is not merely scientific knowledge.

This is valid even for philosophical implications derived from proofs, such as the second principle of thermodynamics or the big bang theory. For example, Norman Geisler describes the apologetic argument derived from the second principle of thermodynamics presented by C. S. Lewis.[1] Lewis maintains:

> despite the fact that entropy by its very character assures us that it may be the universal rule in the Nature we know, it cannot be universal absolutely. If a man says, "Humpty Dumpty is falling," you see at once that this is not the complete story. The bit you have been told implies both a later chapter in which Humpty Dumpty will have reached the ground, and an earlier chapter in which he was still seated on the wall. A Nature which is "running down" cannot be a whole story. A clock can't run down unless it has been wound up.

The argument is tight and logical. However, is this evidence strong enough to prove God's existence? Yes, but only to believers!

For agnostics, the same deductions will not lead to the same conclusion. They will explain the events with an eternal and infinite model of nature, which is eternally running down, like Humpty Dumpty eternally falling down or like a yo-yo forever moving up and down. One can observe such a trend in different cosmological models of postmodern philosophical-scientific thinking. This is the pitfall in philosophical-apologetic proofs of God's existence as well: they prove their objective, but only to believers.

As we will discuss in Part 4 of the book, while non-believers (and believers as well) do need sensorial-scientific, logical evidence, they need more than this. They need to hear the introspective, mystical or reflectively experienced calls of God, enabling them to wholeheartedly accept their discipleship, as well as their roles as followers of Jesus, even in suffering, if needed. That is what makes or breaks faith.

In the pop literature of apologetics, one can find quotations by Max Planck, Albert Einstein, Werner Heisenberg, or other great scientists, witnessing to, explaining, or justifying their belief and trust in God. Their faith, however, is not acquired through sensorial perception, nor founded on scientific proof based on knowledge. Rather, the faith of the greatest astronomer, physicist, or mathematician, like that of every average person, is a response to God's personal call—experienced transempirically.

God's calls can be received through the senses (for example, hearing) cognitively and sensorial-scientifically through functions of existence. However, even in such cases a relationship with God is realized not through, but beyond, scientific or sensorial events. Recall that the disciples on the road to Emmaus received visible and touchable proof of Jesus' resurrection. Despite this they did not believe that it had actually occurred. The real proof hit them through Jesus' intervention, experienced not empirically but transempirically, enabling them to discern an ultimate significance beyond the cognitive, sensorial information. Thus, sensorial perception was necessary to see and hear Jesus, but was not sufficient to enable the disciples' faith.

Similarly, cognitively exploring the universe enables an astronomer "to see," but not to recognize, God, the Creator of the universe beyond the universe itself. Only by realizing the transcendent and "quite other" invisible God and his call beyond scientific reality, can even the greatest scientists recognize God.

On the other hand, the above seemingly trivial facts are equally relevant for those disproving God's existence cognitively and scientifically. Joseph Schwarz states:

The pathologist Schwann wrote, "I completed the autopsy but I didn't find any spirit." Similarly, the astronaut Titov, when asked by Khruschew responded, "No . . . we were upstairs but we didn't meet God." The astronomer Laplace argued similarly: "I examined the whole universe with my telescope, but I couldn't see God anywhere." For the people who search to prove or disprove God's existence in a visible, touchable, measurable way, he will always be hidden and unavailable.[2]

A reader may now object: "Everything discussed here seems self-evident. So why must we then dwell on these simple and obvious logical principles so persistently?"

The reason is that the same logical mistake is often widely communicated in our contemporary mass media. It is scientifically, suggestively, and propagandistically "demonstrated" that human birth, life, sexuality, love, and death have no meaning or significance other than those of animals or plants, or that of other natural phenomena. This happens, for example, when the Christian relationship to God (experienced only transempirically, through reflections and functions of purpose, and by being a believer) is proclaimed by non-believers who never experienced God and faith as nothing more than a "socially-conditioned belief system" or a "learned habit."

Once a blind person I was counseling told me, "To psychologically know what blindness is, one has to experience it [introspectively] and not only to be able to explain or understand it [scientifically]." The same is true concerning faith. Scientific understanding, even if it would be possible, would be unable to confirm or refute faith—the experience of faith is irreplaceable and essential to know God.

Nevertheless, for agnostics swimming with the current of our postmodern society, such "gray propaganda" functioning according to the maxim, "As long as you repeat it, they will believe it," may have a tremendous effect, despite its obvious logical incorrectness.

In summary, functions of existence, like general and impersonal astronomical, biological or physical theories, can neither efficiently prove God's existence (as some apologists have tried), nor disprove it (as some atheists have attempted). In contrast, hearing God's call—based purely on reasons for faith discerned through transempirical functions (such as experiencing God's love, joy, and peace, and accepting Christ-like suffering for the sake of others)—often validates exemplary Christian faith.

Even in day-to-day experience, profane transempirical recognitions (like the discernment of love, hope, meaning, joy, or optimism) transcend space and time as well as sensorial boundaries. They are not limited to the "here and now," or only to the recognition of visible, touchable, and measurable natural qualities. Discernments of purpose, and of mystical or reflective experiences, have an advantage over sensorial-scientific, functions of existence or cognitive recognition; they enable the recognition of the "quite other" and holy. Through transempirical recognition, believers experience the transcendental reality of God.

How does such a recognition occur? Believers experience being the objects of God's love, they experience God's affection, his care and providence, which are eminent characteristics of God's personality. Believers experience their union with God tangibly by receiving biblical joy, purpose, peace, hope, and other gifts of faith, which help them to discern what God is like. Through this transempirical recognition, God's transcendental reality becomes experiential to people of faith. Let us recall John Paul II's words, "If God is a knowable object—as both the Book of Wisdom and the letter to Romans teach—He is such on the basis of man's experience both of the visible world and of the interior world."[3] In my understanding, the experience of this "interior world," which enables communication with God, is essential. This is a transempirical experience; it facilitates the possession, feeling, and knowledge of the gifts of faith.

Let us recall that by the term "gifts of faith" we mean the special gifts of the Spirit, available only to people of faith. The Spirit blows where it will among believers and non-believers alike. When the Spirit "blows," or speaks, to believers, they experience the "gifts of faith," biblical peace, love, joy, and other gifts.

While we live in a time of the church, we simultaneously live in a "period of faith," in which no face-to-face encounters with God and no cognitive knowledge of him—save only the believer's experiential union with him experienced through functions of purpose—is possible.

When will we have full visible, touchable, and measurable cognitive knowledge of ourselves and the mystery of the Almighty, eternal, and ultimate love which we call God? According to one story, when a TV reporter asked Mitterand what he thought God's first words to him would be after his death, the French Prime Minister responded, "Probably, 'Now you know,' and maybe, 'Welcome.'"

Now we can answer the question raised in the title of this chapter. Believers experience communication with God transempirically, (or psychologically through functions of purpose, reflectively, mystically, and introspectively). In the following section, we will explore the credibility of transempirical discernment in detail.

The Mystery of Christian Faith

Notes

1. Norman L. Geisler, *Baker Encyclopedia of Christian Apologetics* (Grand Rapids, MI: Baker Books, 2000), 420.

2. Joseph Schwarz, *Argumente fur Gottes Existenz* (Eisenstadt, 1988), 4.

3. John Paul II, *Crossing the Threshold of Hope* (New York: Alfred A. Knopf, 1994), 34.

Chapter 20

The Criteria for the Accuracy of Transempirical Recognition

According to one anecdote, a man attempting suicide jumps from the tenth floor of a high-rise building. Falling down with ever-increasing speed, he reaches the level of the first floor, and then says to himself "Until now, everything is okay. . . ."

Mistakes are made in sensorial, scientific, and also in transempirical acknowledgments. Thus, there are mistakes in belief systems and faith discernments as well. In this chapter, let us discuss the criteria for correct acknowledgments in transempirical recognition and their implications to faith questions.

20.1. The Criteria of Correctness in General

Cognitively experienced visible and touchable information, acquired through sensorial—scientific functions in everyday life, is a factual reality. In general, we accept it wholeheartedly. The primary advantage of these functions, for example when building a bridge, is that the bridge can be easily and quickly tested for accuracy by weighing, testing, or measuring. If the bridge performs well, then we have no doubts that the engineering, building, or developmental efforts have been accurate.

But how reliable are discernments enabled by introspection and reflection? How do we know that we are right (or wrong) in our internal, non-sensorial discernments? How do we generally justify the reliability of value discernments that are untouchable?

We know from everyday experience that long-lasting self-deception in transempirical discernments is not possible. If such self-deception would be possible then the prodigal son would never return to his father, and nobody would be sad, depressed, suicidal, unhappy, or divorced. But a question may still be haunting us: What is the criterion for, and difference between right and wrong in transempirical discernments?

Instead of theorizing, let us analyze an example, one of the basic human transempirical recognition functions—love. Let us ask the following banal-sounding questions: How do we know the criterion for genuine love? How do people in love feel, know, and determine that their love is a correct, real, deep, and well founded?

Indeed, love is a unique and authentic experience, which is known introspectively, reflectively and through functions of purpose (i.e., transempirically). It is a sensation, but not only that. It is composed of genuine feelings, knowledge, the approval of the conscience, will, instinct, and all other mental functions that are impossible to reduce, measure, or substitute by some "parameter." Despite that, it is a fact that in conjugal, parental, Christian, or any other type of love, the people involved are happy and joyful. There is no true love without joyful experiences substantiating it. In contrast, the internal experience of losing joy often means losing mutual attachment, affection, trust, optimism, and confidence and signifies the end—the "death" of love.

The more one loves, the more happy, joyful, passionate, optimistic, hopeful, and content one's life becomes. And the more hopeful and joyful a loving person's self-experience generally becomes, the more he or she loves. The "angelic cycle" turns as follows: love causes an internal experience of trust, optimism, confidence, power, and other joyful experiences, while the joy, optimism, and trust caused by love proves, justifies, and enables giving and receiving even more love. Let us illustrate how this cyclical process occurs in transempirical discernment in Figure 20-1.

As a general rule, true love and other true and correct transempirical recognitions cause joy, while the experience of happiness, joy, value, trust and optimism, prove, justify, and corroborate love. Just as realizing a pragmatic goal proves cognitive facts, (for example, the static measurements of the engineer when building a bridge), so joyful experiences prove the correctness of the transempirical discernments.

Love (just like other non-sensorial, but introspective, transempirical discernments) may seem to be a matter of personal choice, rather than a questions of false or correct discernment. However, this is an illusion: not everyone is able simply to "choose" to love and be happy!

Figure 20-1

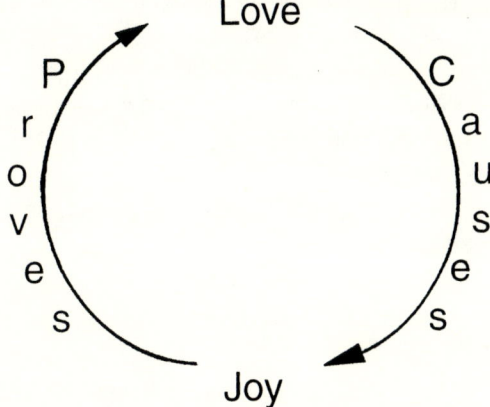

Neither spousal nor family love is a simple matter of choice. One cannot simply "choose" to love any person as a partner, but only someone who fits, who has the appropriate, needed, and cherished spiritual, personal, and physical qualities.

Not even parental love is purely a matter of choice. I have been witness to enormous suffering and feelings of guilt in the father of a child with special needs, as he cried out "I simply cannot love her!" The most painful aspect of this situation was that, in spite of his ardent desire to love his handicapped daughter, he was simply unable to "choose" love.

Why is this so? Because love is always a transempirically experienced mystery. The mysterious aspect is that love hinges on the existence of a spontaneous, conscious, and subconscious "giftedness" to recognize and "know" a particular person's unique qualities that are hidden to others. This "giftedness" resides in the highest and deepest "layers" of a loving person, in his or her soul and conscience, corroborated by thoughts, feelings, instinct, will, memory, and all other psychological functions as well. It is a complex experience, encompassing the beloved person's soul, mind, and body.

In people of faith, love contains one more important factor: in Christian love, God is always included. For believers, acts of love are always an internal proof of loving and being loved by the almighty, eternal, and ultimate love of God. Love, as well as the joy discerned in love, are attested to and proven by God's closeness. This is especially so when

Christians love even enemies, or those who do not return their affection, but it also happens within Christian conjugal, parental, and other relationships characterized by love. Christian love always originates in God's love, and joy of closeness to God strengthens its joy.

Of course, all of this does not mean that a loving person never suffers. It is a fact that love and pain often coexist. I assume this is exactly the reason Jesus mainly suffered: because he loved the most. The primary cause of Jesus' suffering, which is described in Luke 19:41 and Matthew 23:37, wasn't the physical pain of the crucifixion, nor the fear of suffering, as much as his sense of powerlessness in the face of human freedom to reject him, his inability to prevent the triumph of resistance, indifference and apathy in humankind whom Jesus loved so much. His pain was caused by the realization that despite all of his efforts, his mission was seemingly unsuccessful, because neither the world nor his disciples understood and accepted him and his teachings as he wished. Perhaps only some parents can understand the pain of such powerless and helpless love, despite their hope and confidence that good will triumph in the end.

Since love and pain are often present together, the balance between them is important. Indeed, the "happiness balance" is not a simple arithmetical equation. In true love, the total quantity of happiness, affection, empathy, and especially of hope is larger than the quantity of temporary disappointment and pain. As long as hope, trust, and confidence outweigh pain, most people are able to preserve their love and joy. This is the case when Christians forgive and love their enemies as well. God's love is that which they receive in return, and which is more important to them than revenge or hate.

20.2. Fulfillment of Meaning

In transempirical recognition, especially in functions of purpose, as their name signifies, one more function is always involved. Joy (in love and any other pursuit) is always connected to striving towards the realization of a purposeful goal. Without the fulfillment of meaning in transempirical discernment, there is no true, lasting joy, but only a more or less euphoric state of mind. Euphoria is happiness without adequate reason, that is, true fulfillment of meaning. It ends quickly with a feeling of absurdity and emptiness caused by its meaninglessness.

However, what is the meaning of the word "meaning"?

Most simply, meaning is a measurement, proportion or quotient. It measures how much any given activity contributes to the achievement of one's important, or even ultimate goal. For example, if the goal of a student is to achieve a diploma, then all of his or her hard work and studying has a meaning and purpose—it helps him or her to achieve this goal. Even enduring exhausting and draining studying can give him or her meaning, and make him or her joyful, optimistic, hopeful, and self-confident.

Thomas' life, despite all of the humiliations and suffering he had to endure, most probably seemed meaningful to him after the revival of his faith. Furthermore, he was joyful like other disciples, according to 1 Pt 4:12-13, because his life served an ultimate meaning.

How and why do striving for and fulfilling a meaning make the lives of the faithful so joyous? We may recall Frankl's clarification: "He who has a 'why' to live for can bear with almost any 'how.'" When Thomas had a "why" to live for, he could bear with almost any "how." This was one component of the disciples' joy. However, every meaningful activity is rewarded by a different quantity and type of joy. For example, true love is experienced as meaningful by a lover in the sense that it enables the lover to discern a reason "why to live," thereby giving and receiving joy, hope, trust, confidence, affection, and optimism, which in turn enable the lover to bear almost any "how" so long as he or she is in closeness with the beloved.

In a relationship, meaning (or lack thereof) is the marker that measures how close the lover and the beloved are to their permanent, lasting aim, the goal of giving and receiving lasting joy. Mutual, spousal, or family love in people of faith fulfills an important spiritual function as well. For believers, the more there is a permanent progression toward the common objective of giving and receiving biblical joy through the mutual building of a union with God in love, the more meaningful love feels.

A reader could object, saying:

However, people understand life, meaning, purpose, and values very differently. Therefore, is connecting a "right" meaning as a criterion of correct discernment a usable standard at all?

It is true that different people seek to obtain their meaning in life from different sources. However, it is even truer that disappointment and suffering due to practicing "mistaken" transemperical discernment of meaning, purpose, or values, (like pedophilia, or drug abuse), are inevitable, while biblical gifts of the Spirit such as those found in Luke 24:52 or Acts 13:52 are lasting sources of joy.

However, one may further object, and say:

> So many goals which are at first discerned as extremely meaningful end with disenchantment and disillusionment. Some promising relationships are spoiled, and love or other meaningful pursuits are later proven as great reflective mistakes. Is there any guarantee, therefore, that a discerned meaning is not false, and that it will not sooner or later turn into boredom, pain, disappointment or suffering?

Let us consider four criteria:

A. A true discerned meaning (i.e., a true love) has to be proven by lasting, time-tested joy, and not merely by temporary or short-term ecstasy or euphoria.
B. It has to be proven by a relatively growing, increasing, and deepening joy in a relatively steady and permanent progression, or at least without a regression or disillusionment.
C. The goal, value, or pursuit of meaning has to be meaningful in the sense that it contributes to the fulfillment of a higher, or an ultimate and important purpose.
D. It has to contribute not only to the subject's, but also to virtually every good and godly person's joy, wellness, and happiness.

If tested by these four criteria, then the diversity of different meanings, goals, choices, and sources of fun, joy, and happiness can be fairly reduced. Lasting, well-founded, and ever-increasing joy, as discussed in the previous chapter, cannot be achieved by numerous or very diverse means. The prodigal son and tax collectors, the Good Samaritan and Jesus' disciples, were neither equally correct nor equally happy in their meaning discernment.

True meaning fulfillment and lasting joy are connected. We deduce that the fulfillment of the right purpose causes joy, while joy in turn validates the correctness of the discerned meaning. However, as Frankl noted, no joyful person carries through with a meaning just to become happy.[1] In a genuine, loving, and meaningful relationship we do not love someone to become happy; neither do artists paint nor believers go to church to become joyful. The people in these examples do not even think of joy! In everyday practice, joy, peace, optimism, or hope are not the aims, but the byproducts of fulfilled meaning in love, prayer, or hope, while the declared goal is always the fulfillment of an important and meaningful purpose! Nevertheless, it is equally true that finding happiness is a very important byproduct. It is also true that the correlation with joy (or a positive joy balance in the long run) is the proof of correctness, and the criterion of the meaningfulness, value and purpose of any discernment of purpose.

If happiness is the explicit, proclaimed goal of a pursuit or activity, then happiness will be achieved only briefly, and such activity will consequently be experienced as meaningless. A subsequent identical or similar attempt to achieve joy by a meaningless activity will have the same result. A successful escape from such a meaningless trap will become impossible, while joy will become an ever more unachievable mirage.

In everyday life, most disappointments and disenchantments stem from a hedonistic striving or pursuit of a desire for joy—achieving joy independently of fulfilling a comprehensive meaning. This is the Achilles' trait of people striving only to achieve new and more attainable variants of fun, pleasure, happiness, and joy, independent of meaning and purposefulness. Such a life unavoidably ends in what Frankl terms an "existential vacuum."[2] In her book *Life with Meaning*, Maria Mendez explains that long-standing frustration of the Will to Meaning can lead to its repression. "This condition is called an existential vacuum." It is "characterized by a sense of meaninglessness and purposelessness. Its main symptoms are a feeling of emptiness and boredom." She further warns:

> The danger of the existential vacuum lies in attempts to fill it with activities such as pleasure, or success-oriented activities such as "workaholism," defiance of authority, the hoarding of material goods, drug use, excessive behaviors, etc. These further create distress by suppressing the will to meaning.[3]

On the other hand, it is always possible to discern many different meanings in healthy people to choose from. Moreover, by losing the possibility to accomplish one meaning in life, other meanings can be found and pursued. In this manner, life never really becomes meaningless. Rather, the question is whether the subject accepts the "replacement meaning" as sufficiently meaningful to strive for. The transempirical cycle—meaningfulness as a precondition of joy, and joy as proof of meaningfulness of an activity—sets strict natural and psychological limits to euphoric joy, and to any attempt at escaping the reality of a meaningless life.

According to Frankl, one does not "give" but only discovers the right meaning that fits one's personal characteristics, abilities, and gifts.[4] He emphasized in many of his books that not every meaning is equally "meaningful." The same is obvious in the four points we set as "prerequisites" for a meaning to be lastingly meaningful. When choosing to fulfill a less meaningful, or even a meaningless goal or value, we are condemning ourselves to be disappointed, like Caligula, Herod or the prodigal son. Often, the source of suffering in a life perceived as meaningless, stems from the giving up of striving for the highest achievable value in life, and replacing it with a less meaningful surrogate.

What is the highest joyful internal experience that we can choose, one that is available in every possible situation, circumstance, and condition, and which enables us to reflect on attainable ultimate joy?

The answer for people of faith is clear and self-explanatory. There is only one such "ultimate meaning" which is almost permanently available, and which cannot be lost or taken away—an experiential union with God. Without living in such a relationship, we may rephrase the well-known saying of Saint Augustine: Restless is our heart without you, O Lord.

In the next section, we will discuss why this is so—why human hearts are restless without God.

20.3. Pleasure, Happiness, and Joy

According to one anecdotal story, Alexander the Great on his deathbed was asked how much conquest would make him happy. His response was: Always one territory more.

This story illustrates the principle that true, lasting happiness, pleasure, and joy are never permanent states of mind, to be attained once and retained forever. New and better reasons for joy are always required. Without such change and improvement, the previous reasons for happiness, pleasure, or joy would become stale, or even boring. Without new reasons for delight, life becomes monotonous or meaningless.

Let us observe how such an explanation works in practice.

For didactical reasons, we can simplify things as follows: All types of delight spring from one of three sources.

1. The idea that happiness comes from power and possessions, from the accumulation of wealth and respect, from being affluent and influential, from living in luxury and pomp. This idea almost always proves false because, as noted, the greatest enemy of happiness is the status quo. Therefore, permanent improvements in finances, lifestyle, or prestige, are needed to overstep the customary level, and discern new reasons for being happy. Paradoxically, the more wealth or power one already has, the less possible a proportional (in percentage) change in the previous balance and increase of wealth, (and consequent happiness), becomes.

For example, purchasing a humble car for an underprivileged driver is a greater improvement in previous "balance," as well as a greater reason of happiness, than the eleventh Rolls-Royce for a tycoon.

Lasting and permanent improvement in happiness becomes a mirage. We suggest the dynamics of happiness in Figure 20-2.

Figure 20-2

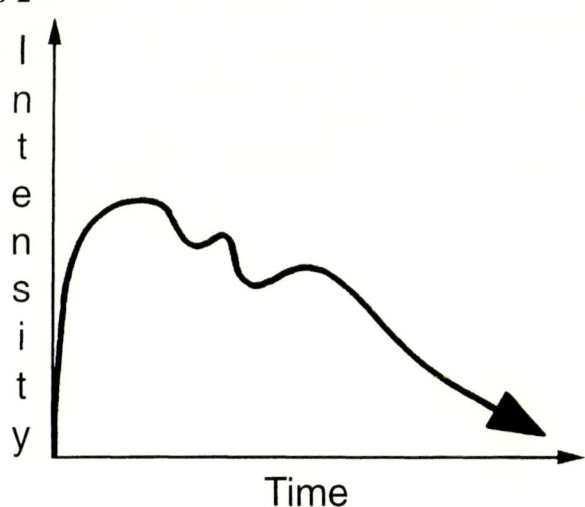

2. Pleasure stemming from the enjoyment of life's delights, such as leisure activities, or living by the maxim "Let's eat, drink, and be merry." There are psychological boundaries of pleasure which cannot be overstepped. Fullness will limit the pleasure of overeating, drunkenness, of drinking, satiation (even disgust), of sex, while boredom signals the "natural boundary" of enjoyment of leisure. However, through abstinence or hard work, change and improvement in the balance of life becomes possible once more, and the same quality and quantity of food, sex, and leisure can again be pleasurable. A daily, weekly, and yearly rhythm of holidays and work, and the rotation of abstinence and indulgence have maintained balanced living for millennia. We offer a diagram of the dynamics of pleasure in Figure 20-3.

Figure 20-3

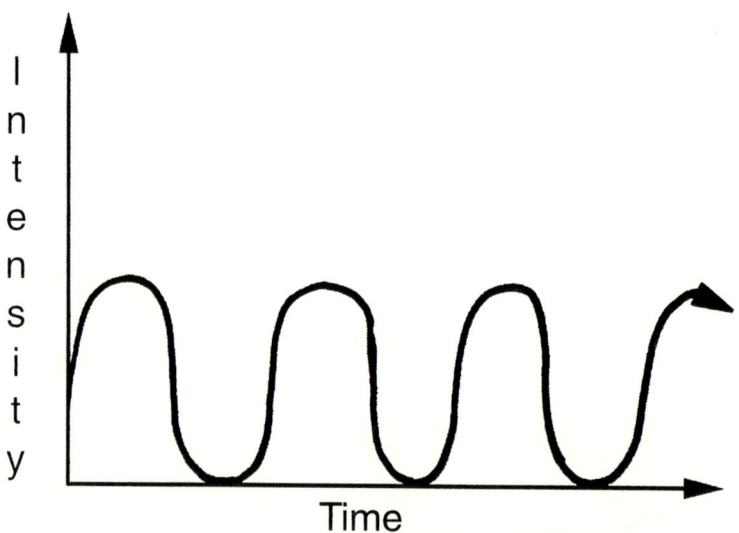

3. The Christian experience of joy stemming from living in and with God, experienced through the soul and Christian conscience. This third possible source of joy we may define as "the reverberation of the almighty, eternal and ultimate love of God within the believer's conscience." Such joy is then

echoed by the whole personality and behavior, and is witnessed to whole world. In such joy there is always a possibility for progression, "change and improvement," and new, "quite different," unexpected depths and heights of biblical joy can be experienced. We suggest the dynamics of such joy in Figure 20-4.

Figure 20-4

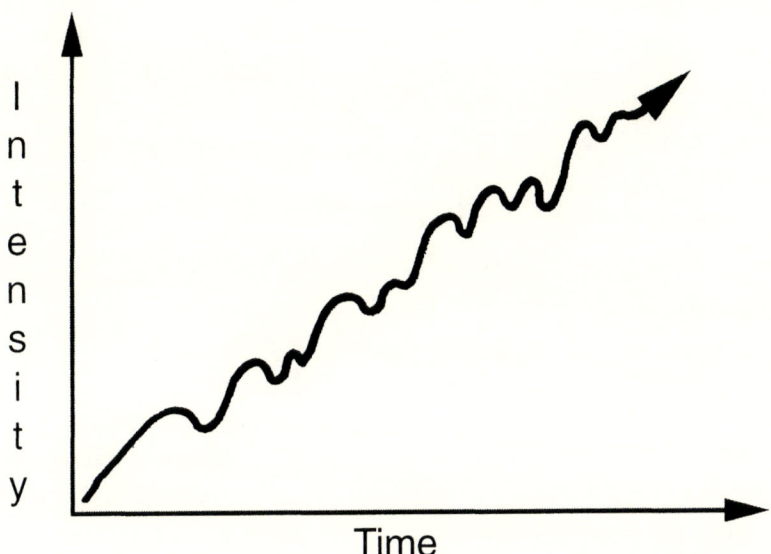

Now we may understand why the human heart is restless without God!

In practice, in the life of everyone a mixture of all three—happiness, pleasure, and joy—is present. However, people of faith always respect priority and hierarchy among them. They respect St. Paul's words in Heb. 11:26 and regard ". . . disgrace for the sake of Christ as of greater value than the treasures of Egypt."

Accordingly, in this book the term "joy" primarily means a biblical joy: the joy of appreciating the almighty, eternal, and ultimate love of God. biblical joy is the fullness of joy that a human being is able to realize. Indeed, nothing can be greater, more satisfying and rewarding than "resonation of the almighty, eternal and ultimate love of God within the believer's conscience" and his or her whole person.

However, a devil's advocate may object here:

Let's be realistic. Is the expansiveness of biblical joy able to replace the intensity of true pleasure and happiness, even in exemplary Christians? Are exemplary Christians in fact not looking for the same pleasure and happiness as their agnostic, worldly or atheist counterparts, and does everyday life not prove this?

By asking such a question, it becomes obvious that it is important to realize one more distinction—the difference between the Christian and non-Christian understandings, not only of joy, but also of pleasure and happiness. There is an essential qualitative difference! To discuss it will be our next topic.

20.4. The Christian Understanding of Pleasure and Happiness

In Section 17.1, discussing the "Human Condition," we concluded that humans are not thrown into the world without a lighthouse, as Jean P. Sartre put it. But the activation of the brain centers enabling the experience of pleasure, happiness, or joy is the ultimate behavioral goal—the given and innate "natural law" written in our heart, mind and soul, navigating every human being's activity in every moment of life.

The human brain and mind, conscience and soul, are so constructed that no one is able to avoid a personal commitment to principles directed by the search for pleasure, happiness or joy. Believers and non-believers are alike in this respect. We are all directed by the same fundamental biological-psychological-spiritual program: the search for happiness, pleasure and joy. This is how we are, and we cannot be otherwise.

The Scriptures, Hebrew, and Christian tradition, and the lifestyles of people of faith since the earliest times of our tradition, fully respected, promoted and asserted the requirements stemming from the mentioned "human condition."

Abundance of biblical joy is the characteristic of the believer's current life, according to Psalm 16:11, Ps. 9:2, Rom. 14:17, and Rom 15:13. Is, however, biblical expectation regarding abundance of happiness and pleasure in the believer's life indeed possible to realize, if we take into account what we discussed previously—the unavoidable and natural limits that are imposed on the satisfaction of the human need for pleasure and happiness?

Furthermore, since Jesus himself, and his disciples, did not demonstrate such a happiness-filled and pleasant lifestyle for us, his later disciples, is the biblical ideal not directly opposed to that of the happiness-and-pleasure-seeking world?

On first glance, it may seem that the life of Jesus was full of godly joy, but lacking in worldly enjoyment and happiness. Thus, the lives of God's people have a positive "joy balance," but a negative "happiness and pleasure balance." But is such an interpretation realistic, or was the Jewish rabbi correct who, according to J. I. Packer, ". . . suggested that on judgment day God would take account of us for neglecting pleasures that he provided."?[5]

When discussing questions of biblical happiness and pleasure, let us keep in mind that what Christians search for is radically different from Freud's "Pleasure Principle," which, according to Fenichel, is directed by "the need for immediate discharge."[6] Christian pleasure and happiness is also different than the hedonist's search for "happiness" as the ultimate goodness. For Christians, happiness and pleasure are not ethically or morally indifferent or irrelevant goals, and neither are they self-serving or self-centered ultimate purposes.

Instead, for Christians, happiness and pleasure are never independent of one's relationship with God, but originate from a grateful acceptance of God's gifts, causing, above all, biblical joy. Such biblical joy is what substantiates and justifies the Christian's happiness and pleasure, giving a very different meaning to both from that which the world gives. According to Packer, Christian pleasure and happiness always provide an opportunity for joyfully glorifying God. And inversely, glorifying God is in Christians actualized and concretized through biblical pleasure or happiness. Note that Christians are not so much happy or pleased with the event causing happiness or pleasure itself, as with the opportunity of glorifying God through the gracefully-granted reasons causing them happiness or pleasure. Paradoxically, but very truly, the opportunity of glorifying God beyond the events causing happiness or pleasure is the real reason behind the Christian's pleasure and happiness.

What does "glorifying God" mean in Christian practice?

According to Packer, God's "Glory means deity in manifestation."[7] Thus, glorifying God means discerning the manifestation of his deity—his almighty, eternal, and ultimate love, discerned beyond visible or touchable reasons for happiness and pleasure. Glorifying God means discerning God's providence, omnipotence, wisdom, love, help, grace—in short, his quite other goodness—beyond worldly health, wealth, prestige, or other reasons for happiness. What gives real meaning to Christian happiness is not that one succeeds, performs, or achieves, but rather that one experiences God's presence, deity, and "quite other"-ness, beyond the worldly events evoking happiness! Thus, happiness becomes synchronized with and conformed to biblical joy, as in Jesus' Sabbath healing (Mk. 3:1-6) which we discussed earlier. In it, the happiness of the healed man is only an opportunity to glorify God beyond the event—his healing.

The same is true for pleasure: Christian teaching is not an enemy of eating, drinking, sex, or leisure, if the purpose of these is to glorify God's deity. The purpose of seeking pleasure is to make God's presence, love, help, care, and providence manifest! The pleasurable event in fact enables the manifestation, feeling, knowing, experiencing of God's deity, his closeness. The wedding in Cana, described in John 2:1-10, illustrates this; the wedding itself is only an opportunity to glorify God.

From all this, we draw the conclusion that God, his requirements, revelation, and faith, as well as the experience of living in a tangible union with him, are not opposed to human happiness or pleasure. On the contrary, sin, the process of human estrangement from God, is the greatest enemy of our enjoying seasons of pleasure and happiness by joyfully glorifying God; rather, it reduces such God-given opportunities to meaningless, euphoric "fun." Despite the inflation of a pleasure-and-happiness-seeking attitude, which always characterized the "world," in our time its deflation is unavoidable if, and because, God is not joyfully glorified as the true reason and source of happiness and pleasure. Psychologically, estrangement from God (sin), is the real reason for the postmodern addiction to such pleasure-seeking thrills, as "living on the edge," "street-racing," and "living life to the (so-called) fullest." Nevertheless, no quantity of meaningless joy, pleasure, and happiness can replace the missing quality!

The most remarkable truth from a Christian understanding is that pleasure and happiness are justified by biblical joy. Joy is not dependant on any sensorial-scientific experience. The cause of genuine joy is not a visible, touchable, or measurable source, quality, or reason. It is, as noted earlier, the reverberation of God's love within the believer's entire being and spirit. It is a genuine experience of God—internally experienced evidence of belonging to the Almighty, Eternal, and Ultimate Love. No externally imposed pain, suffering, or disappointment can take away such a believer's joyful self-experience. Therefore, as Packer noted:

"There can be no greater glory for man than to glorify God." Moreover, even a life without worldly reasons can, for Christians, be full of happiness and pleasure, through their glorification of God. True Christians discern spiritual reasons for joyful and godly happiness and pleasure.

20.5 Correcting a Misconception

Does the joy we are discussing here represent affect or mood regulation? Are not biblical joy, peace, and love primarily feelings?

By asking such a question we are lured onto thin ice, since the next question may be: "Are then biblical joy and other 'gifts of faith,' and the believer's relationship with God, based only on unreliable, changeable and often irrational emotions?"

Such an incorrectly asked question would presume an incorrect answer. Namely, that only in cases of mood disorders such as mania or depression, are human personality and behavior explicitly emotionally directed phenomena. In fact, faith is primarily not a feeling at all. As Frankl defined it, faith is an "ultimate meaning."[8] The by-product of such "ultimate meaning" fulfillment, which we call joy—and especially biblical joy—is neither an affect, a quality of mood, nor a feeling only! Joy, and especially biblical joy, is the "end result," the summary of all psychological experiences of a person. It is the end result of the integration of all psychological functions that are involved in the reverberation of God's love in the mind of genuine believers.

The previous fact has an important practical implication. Since biblical joy is not purely an emotion or affect but an experience of God's closeness, it is possible to remain in, or come into contact with the almighty, eternal, and ultimately loving God, despite mood swings. Thus, for example a depression does not psychologically exclude a relationship with God, but is sometimes an acid test of faith. Faith is not a "medicine"—it will not heal somatic or psychological symptoms of a major ("endogenous") depression. However, believers of strong faith will mobilize their knowledge of biblical joy, meaning, optimism, power, and hope—despite such emotions as feeling depressed. The biblical believer's experience is expressed through a saying: "God is most close to you when you feel most miserable"—this is because a depressed believer can have the feeling of going under in everything: yet not lose the knowledge of a relationship with God!

Paradoxically, suffering may become "Christ-like"—ultimately mean-ingful, because the believer knows that he or she feels suffering that ultimately serves God's glory, if accepted with faith. In the long run, attention, knowledge, and willpower, and ultimately conscience, soul, and Spirit, can and will modify and overcome the power of feelings through the recognition function of faith.

The same is true in controlling ecstatic euphoria, hyperemotional fanaticism, or irrational religious enthusiasm. As Jesus demonstrated to his disciples during his earthly life, biblical faith is not an affective state of mind, a trance, ecstasy, or an uncontrolled, affectively-directed act-ing out. Even less is Jesus' and his disciples' faith like a "euphoric kin-dergarten," where believers "ascend" into an objectless religious fan-tasy world through music, manipulation, or a self-induced narcissistic regression. (This was rather the practice of Gnostics.) Faith never facili-tates euphoria, and euphoria excludes biblical faith. Biblical joy is more often caused by rational reasons than by pleasure or happiness. It is ultimately substantiated by the "witnessing," of the conscience; biblical joy is always primarily the joy of conscience, or it does not exist at all.

The essential factor in experiencing biblical joy and in its power to overcome mood swings, is the message of the Spirit transmitted through the soul and experienced through conscience. In this process, the triune God, the soul, and conscience gain more importance and power in regu-lating one's "joy balance" than feelings or other-worldly experiences and facts. The knowledge, will, attention, and other psychological func-tions, together with feelings, all participate in the same echo in a strong believer: the Spirit's spiritual message, transmitted through the soul and its "loudspeaker," the conscience. This is the strong believer's powerful weapon in fighting against unreliable and changeable emotions.

We discern this pattern when we analyze the biblical joy in the de-scription of the "beloved disciple" as he "started to believe," or through the story of Mary Magdalene, of Thomas and of the disciples on the road to Emmaus, and indeed throughout the Scriptures. None of the protago-nists experienced biblical joy merely as a result of their cognition and feelings. Joy was always an experience of a disciple's whole personality, enabled by the knowledge of the resurrected Jesus (God), and experi-enced through his intervention in the soul, conscience, and mind.

Indeed, the Scriptures do not always focus on biblical and godly joy. However, we may be certain that throughout the Scriptures, from Adam and Eve's appearance to The Revelation, the soul and conscience do enable the resonation of God's almighty, eternal, and ultimate love. This is the model of biblical joy.

20.6. A Living Faith Must Lead to Joy

According to one story, the Greek mathematician Archimedes, upon discovering the principle that submerged bodies lose as much weight as the amount of water they displace, was so joyful, that he jumped out of his bathtub and, running naked through the streets of his hometown, Syracuse, shouted "Eureka! Eureka!"

By and through his discovery, Archimedes fulfilled a unique meaning in his life, which granted him enormous joy. The search for, and fulfillment of, a meaning that grants joy does shape the lifestyle of every individual. The rich tax collectors, the prodigal son, the Good Samaritan and Jesus' disciples, the false and the true prophets, all followed very different paths in their lives, striving to fulfill different meanings and ideals—or idols—in their pursuit of joy.

Let us first focus on "false prophets." In Mt. 7:15-20, Jesus talks about false prophets, promoting a false purpose, idols instead of ideals, and he compares them to bad trees and their fruit. Bad trees' bear bad fruit—a promise of joy which cannot be fulfilled, or which can only be enjoyed for a brief time and which inevitably leads to disappointment, dissatisfaction, or feelings of guilt, because of unavoidable estrangement from God.

In contrast to false prophets, an even more intense and lasting joy than that of Archimedes upon his discovery is granted to those living the "Full truth." The phrase "Full truth" in biblical terminology means Jesus. Living the "Fullness of truth"—Jesus—is associated with a "Fullness of joy." From a biblical perspective, joy, love, and peace of mind, which come from the "Fullness of truth," are reflected, witnessed, and embodied by people of faith. Joy, despite suffering, is what sets them apart from others.

Here is how Daniel W. Hardy in his article "Joy" describes the correlation between joy and closeness to Jesus: "In the history of the Jews, those who steadfastly rely on God and his 'path of life' find the fullness of joy (Ps 5:11, 17:15)."[9] With Jesus' revelation of God's personality, and proclamation of his kingdom, this concept changed in the sense that "relying on God and his path" also meant accepting suffering for the sake of others as an essential characteristic of being Christ-like.

Although discipleship did not, as Hardy puts it, "elicit a quick response of joy," in God's kingdom, "Joy is found through the incorporation of humanity in Jesus' suffering, dying, and being raised by God." Those who live in the resurrected Jesus are "filled with joy and with the Holy Spirit."

In short, according to Hardy, the joy of the disciples comes from living a life fulfilled with the Spirit, a foretaste of real life, of life to come!

But what is this "real life" which Christians get a foretaste of? In Gen. 2:16-17 we read as follows:

> And the LORD God commanded the man, "You are free to eat from any tree in the garden; but you must not eat from the tree of the knowledge of good and evil, for when you eat of it you will surely die."

Adam and Eve ate of the tree, but did they die as the Lord predicted? They continued to live biologically for many years, but spiritually they were dead. They were distant from God, and no longer in a close relationship with him. They lost real life.

To appreciate the difference between biological and spiritual death, we have to keep in mind that the original texts of the Bible were transferred to us from the Greek. The Greek translators used two words for, and had two different notions of "life." They used the words *bios* and *zoe*. The *Bios* meant the biological aspect of life, which medicine is interested in. *Zoe* also meant life, but a "holy" and "everlasting" life, one lived in union with God. This is the ultimate and eternal echo of God's love within us. Christians already experience a foretaste of it through faith.

Thus, the two kinds of life—biological and everlasting/spiritual—are in a peculiar relationship. In Mk 8:34-35, we read Jesus' statement regarding this very matter:

> If anyone would come after me, he must deny himself and take up his cross and follow me. For whoever wants to save his life will lose it, but whoever loses his life for me and the gospel will save it.

How did Jesus' disciples visualize and experience their new form of existence, not only through *bios* but also, and much more importantly, through *zoe*?

According to Fucak, perhaps we should consider that Christ's disciples were not afraid (as people would normally be) of having to suffer, of being humiliated, or dispossessed.[10] Everything we have internalized as healthy, normal fear of servitude, poverty, injustice, suffering, sickness, and death was somehow missing from these people. Moreover, as unbelievable as this may seem, they even forged virtue from these experiences!

Isaiah attests to this: "But he was pierced for our transgressions, he was crushed for our iniquities; the punishment that brought us peace was upon him, and by his wounds we are healed." (Is. 53:5) In the Gospel according to Mark, we get a similar idea: "For even the Son of Man did not come to be served, but to serve, and to give his life as ransom for many." (Mk. 10:45) But how exhilarating were such new experiences of the reality of life for the disciples?

Peter's words speak for themselves:

> Dear friends, do not be surprised at the painful trial you are suffering, as though something strange were happening to you. But rejoice that you participate in the sufferings of Christ, so that you may be overjoyed when his glory is revealed. (1 Pt. 4:12-13)

The early church and its members saw clearly that the kingdom of God began its victorious reign on earth with the birth of Christ, and his subsequent teaching, preaching and healing, glory and triumph. However, the greatest and most startling proof was Christ's death and resurrection. Thus, the final stage in the fulfillment of his great work involved his bearing the cross and his crucifixion. But the greatest victory over the powers of evil was his resurrection, and this was the disciples' "gate to *zoe*," to real life, to union with the "almighty, eternal, and ultimate love" that is God. The effect of the resurrection is sustained through the factual experience of being in union with the "almighty, eternal, and ultimate love," already but not yet completely fulfilled. Through the sacraments and a personal union with God, one anticipates the fullness of joy in a complete, face-to-face union. During their earthly lives, believers experience only its foreshadowing.

Can we now answer the question whether biblical joy is one of the criteria of correct discernment in faith problems, and of the believer's relationship with God?

There are external, "objective" (visible) criteria of living in union with God, (like belonging to his church, praying, or receiving sacraments). However, an increasing and shared balance of biblical gifts of faith is an important internal, transempirical (introspective, reflective, and meaning-oriented) criterion measuring and informing believers about their closeness to God. For them, the biblical joy, peace, love, hope, and power that correlate with living in Jesus, are important (although not the only) internal criteria, whose importance in the modern world of "faith chaos" is paramount.

Fullness of biblical joy and meaning always remains an ideal that can never be completely achieved. But neither is mature faith a stationary process. It does not evolve from the constant repetition of life's ups and down; nor does it remain on a lasting status quo level. People of faith are distinguished by their effort and striving towards progress in their relationship with God. With God's help, such unwavering progress in faith, verified by the steady increase of biblical joy, is achievable.

20.7. Testing Our Hypothesis in Practice

A hypothetical devil's advocate could object, saying:

> Your description of joy, love, peace, and fulfillment of meaning, all of which serve as criteria of correctness in all transempirical discernments is nice, but how well does it pass the test of reality? The true criterion is how consistent and unchangeable is the discernment of purpose that we have learned. Is it perpetual, or is it transitory, like the lover's "certainty" of the beloved that so often ends in disillusionment? At present, more than one third (almost half) of marriages end in divorce! How reliable, then, are the functions of purpose by which a value-discerning believer experiences God's presence in his or her life— and, is the believer's faith as unreliable as his or her love? If so, then the correlation between faith, union with God, and biblical joy is negligible!

In responding to this objection, let us reverse the situation. Indeed, couples want their love to be happy, and imagine it to be so. If the success of love depended solely on human will, then all marriages would be successful. Since they are not, that is a circumstance in which we would have to doubt the validity of transempirical knowledge. We would justifiably call it uncertain, unreliable, and arbitrary, as it would have no objective reality except being purely self-induced. Paradoxically then, compulsory disappointment in a mere mistaken wish for love proves the reliability of a lasting, correct experience of love! It further proves that no lasting deception is possible. Disappointments in love are numerous, not because discernments of love are unreliable, but because many people try the impossible: to deceive themselves and their partners, thereby inferring true love where it is not even present. Theoretically, the same is valid in faith discernments.

Biblically, the Christian witnessing of many believers, supported by the examples of the disciples, prophets, and saints, proves that life can be very hard, and that one can be disappointed in almost everything, except in a biblical God. If one is disappointed in God, then his or her faith is like mistakenly-perceived love that ended in disillusionment. It was not anchored in a true biblical God, but in an arbitrarily inferred or created god. In contrast, faith is psychologically as authentic, genuine, and biblical as there is biblical love, peace, and joy reflected in it. Because of this, arbitrary self-invented faith neither enables the experiencing of biblical gifts of faith, nor is it enforced by a union with the living God. This may seem like an overstatement to those modern agnostics who proclaim that "all belief systems are equal." But can we substantiate such reasoning?

As noted, the precondition of experiencing the almighty, eternal, and ultimate love of God and living in union with him, is to be his disciple. Discipleship also means accepting suffering for others, because of others, or in witnessing to others. John 15:20 gives a principle of suffering for others: ". . . 'No servant is greater than his master.' If they persecuted me, they will persecute you also."

It was always difficult even for the disciples to accept and identify themselves with the dichotomy of suffering and a glorious Messiah. However, without discipleship, even in suffering one cannot gain a real union with God. The discovery, through suffering, of meaning and value in being a Christian, is paradoxically the strongest possible proof of belonging to God, of being one with Jesus in his victory, as is asserted in Acts 5:41. In contrast, if one does not discern one's role and significance in suffering as a disciple of Christ, then suffering very often kills hope, trust and faith in an almighty, eternal, and ultimately loving God. Suffering that is deemed meaningless and hopeless is perhaps the most common reason for disappointment, not in God, but in god.

From a biblical, but also from an experiential perspective, the following could be the motto of this book: There is no other way of receiving the fullness of the Father's love than through the Spirit's grace; in union with the suffering and glorious Jesus, joy and suffering for others is one inseparable cycle. This is also the response to the question often asked by struggling, suffering believers: "Why do I feel nothing of the biblical joy that we are here talking about?"

Paradoxically, the biblical gift of faith is impossible to gain or experience without accepting discipleship, especially identifying with Jesus in suffering. Avoiding identification with the suffering Redeemer is also one of the common causes of losing communication with what one may come to conclude as a "dead," or "nonexistent God." It is difficult to maintain union with the triumphal, glorious, Almighty God without first being his true disciple in suffering as well. Nowhere is the already mentioned Latin saying "Christians alter Christus" ("A Christian is another Christ") more valid than in the disciple's identification with Jesus in suffering. Let us answer the present question directly: By first living as "another Christ," biblical joy will surely follow!

How does such an explanation prove itself in biblical examples? Before Jesus' crucifixion, Thomas was already Jesus' disciple. His discipleship and faith were, however, not yet perfect. They were merely modified Jewish expectations of the Messiah. Indeed, he hid his attraction to the Jewish idea of the wish-fulfilling, triumphal Messiah leading his people in a triumphant march over the corpses of defeated enemies. But this was not Jesus' teaching! Disappointment in such a faith was inevitable. Sooner or later, without discerning the meaning and worth of Christ-like suffering, disappointment would kill Thomas' faith. Indeed, a strong enough temptation kills self-created faith, whereas it strengthens true faith.

For Thomas, the former occurred when Jesus was crucified, and the latter when the resurrected Lord restored that apostle's faith.

However, let us stop for a moment and consider the following: What would the right reaction of Thomas have been when confronted with Jesus' death, and in addition, the probability of his sharing a similar destiny?

Let us answer using an example. The writer Janos Erdody described the sixteenth century Florentine Dominican priest Girolamo Savonarola's walking through the streets of Florence, when suddenly he saw a painting in a window.[11] The painting presented the Virgin Mary crying under the cross. Savonarola rushed into the shop and told the artist something like this: Correct this painting at once! Yes, the Virgin Marry stood under the cross, but she did not cry. On the contrary, she was joyful in her heart. Although she was in enormous pain, she felt triumphant as well. Jesus' glory was finally achieved through his suffering. She was grateful to participate in and witness the fulfillment of God's redemptive plan.

Indeed, we can agree or disagree with Savonarola's interpretation and message. However, if we apply this example to Thomas' case, then we discern not only that Jesus predicted Peter's denial, but he also knew about the disappointment of Thomas and other disciples. This is because the type of Messiah that Thomas and other disciples previously naïvely imagined—a Messiah who grants victory, but who neither requests nor gives what the biblical Messiah gives: biblical meaning and joy even in suffering.

We can now substantiate the truth: that correct recognition is possible only where mistakes can also happen, that the impossibility of self-deception, misunderstanding, or a lasting mistake proves the opposite—the possibility of correct faith discernment.

If the success of, and reasons and justifications for, the personal faith of believers depended on their will or imagination, then all belief systems would be ultimately perfect, and nobody would be estranged from God (or gods). If such self-deception were possible, then faith in a self-made, "wish-fulfilling god" would be equally possible as trust in a jealous and demanding biblical, almighty, eternal, and ultimately loving God. Under those circumstances, we would have to doubt the validity of a believer's experience of faith and God. We would then justifiably call Christian faith uncertain and deceitful, having no factual background but being purely self-induced and arbitrary. Note that, paradoxically, the disappointment of believers in a mistaken wish for faith, or in a "wish-fulfilling god," proves the reliability and correctness of the experience of genuine faith, and of the true biblical God! Another paradox is that disappointments, estrangement, indifference, or losing faith prove that where it is possible to be mistaken, there true recognition is also possible, and lasting self-deception is impossible.

When I first heard this statement, it seemed controversial to me. But after pondering it for a while, I could substantiate in myself why and how the possibility of being mistaken in faith, as well as the possibility of losing it, proves the impossibility of lasting self-deception. Paradoxically, (and for believers very painfully), one person's disappointment proves the possibility of accurate faith discernment for another.

As mentioned, transempirical experiences are never unchangeable facts, but an ever-evolving process. Similar dynamics are valid also for faith. Faith involves not just a single acknowledgment, or the knowing of mere facts, such as in sensorial-scientific recognition. Rather, faith is a slowly evolving process of growth, development, and progression despite all temptations, setbacks, and even estrangement from God. The maturing of one's faith can sometimes take unpredictable directions. Under God's guidance, even estrangement from God, or an attempt at self-deception in faith, as well as suffering as Thomas' story proves, may be used for the growth of our faith. In this context, following the thoughts of O'Hear in discussing how God could allow suffering and evil, we may paraphrase Augustine and say: The absolutely good God would not allow any evil to afflict his people unless something good would come out of it. Discerning a good coming out of suffering and evil is most often the acid test of believer's faith.[12]

To expand the deductions drafted above with additional principles of transempirical recognition will be our further objective. However, let us first discuss possible objections.

20.8. Discussion

A reader may open the discussion asking:

> After the tragedy of September 11, 2001, when terrorists destroyed the towers of the World Trade Center, some, as shown on TV, celebrated, and joyfully cried out "God is great!" This joy was different from Christian joy; nonetheless, how such self-deception was possible if transempirical discernment is reliable?

Before we answer, let us take a step back, and observe, from a distance, the psychological climate brewing within such individuals as those who participated in this horrific act. The fundamental motive in acts of kamikaze, suicide bombers, and terrorists, is hate, more exactly a special kind of hate termed in psychology as "helpless rage." What is "helpless rage?"

Let me illustrate this in a hypothetical example. If a perpetrator slaps someone's face, his or her action would unquestionably cause pain, humiliation, or anger in the victim. If the hypothetical victim would return the slap, then in some form justice would be served. Formally at least, the insult and revenge would be evenly leveled. What happens, however, if the victim is unable to avenge the insult? The victim's frustration, humiliation, and anger would then persist.

Now, what would happen if the same superior and sadistic perpetrator would slap the helpless and defenseless victim's face again and again? Even then a Christian would try to forgive, just like Jesus did. In contrast, inside of those unwilling to search for forgiveness or peace, ever-increasing hatred, anger, and frustration would slowly consume them, resulting in helpless rage. Helpless rage creates such an unbearable tension in the humiliated person that he or she is unable to endure it. The tension must be released somehow; one feels that: "I will go mad if I don't react!"

Organized manipulation, indoctrination and brain washing evidently contribute to the choice of becoming a kamikaze or suicide bomber. However, the main motivator of such choice and behavior is that in the minds of kamikazes, terrorists, and suicide bombers, their people are humiliated and, to use the above metaphor, repeatedly "slapped on the face." Humans can endure many frustrations, but not helpless rage. It is the most destructive, unbearable feeling that needs to "explode"! If the "explosion" cannot harm the untouchable perpetrator, then the rage will turn against the person in question (by suicide), or against innocent victims (by suicide bombers and terrorists).

In suicide, the message is "You see, I am killing myself. But you are responsible for my death, and you will never be able to forgive yourself; so you will suffer until the end of your life!" Using a moral stick in slapping back gives the powerless suicidal person an opportunity for revenge, or even a taste of some sort of paradoxical self-destructive triumph. In the case of a terrorist's punishment of innocent victims, the perceived aggressor is punished. The revenge turns the unbearable tension and frustration into a moment of triumphal euphoria caused by the perceived punishment of the superior and untouchable enemy. The greater, more unbearable the frustration, tension and rage was, the sweeter revenge feels. Such vengeful "joy," however, is very different from a lasting, increasing, and unselfish biblical, godly joy! The short-term joy of revenge must already be "prepaid" by helpless rage, and will exact even more suffering from innocent victims afterwards. Such joy, despite expressing itself through cries of "God is great," is in no way comparable to the lasting, increasing, and well-substantiated joy of living in union with God, and sharing this joy with everyone else as Christians ought to do. The relevance to our topic of self-destructive behavior is in its demonstration of how complex the human mind is, and how perplexing and destructive, for both the individual and society, is putting false "meaning" into practice.

Indeed, the struggle against suicide and suicide bombers can be won only in the souls, consciences, and minds of all engaged in examining the reasons for and consequences of such revengeful suicides. It is also a question of whether we Christians are guiltier for the atheism of suicide bombers, as well as their rejection of God's love, than they themselves are.

The next question may be: "Earlier we mentioned Wesley's case, who one morning "talked to God for half an hour." If we are unable to make a person's transempirical reflections visible and measurable, how can we then discern their correctness? Concretely, can we assess if Wesley's communication with God really occurred, or was it only "in his head," an illusion, a hallucination, or a delusion?

It is possible to externally assess or validate the correctness, merits, or mistakes of one's reflections, mystical experience, and functions of purpose. Beyond unhealthy behavior patterns, we often discern unhealthy ("neurotic") introspection, or ("psychotic") delusions. They disturb the person's well-being not only in one, but many areas of mental functioning.

Thus, if Wesley's behavior had been directed by mistaken introspections, perceptive or thought disorders, then clearly his relationship to reality would have been jeopardized or disordered in many other areas as well. Inversely, the absence of personal, family, professional, and social dysfunction in his life would indicate the absence of psychopathology.

Even more effectively than by the exclusion of psychopathology, the experiences of people of faith, like Wesley's "talking to God for half an hour," can be authenticated by their consequences, and by the abundance of spiritual gifts of faith that result from his talking to Jesus. Consequences arising from one's introspection, such as biblical gifts of faith, prove that communication with God has taken place. According to John 15:11: "I have told you this so that my joy may be in you and that your joy may be complete." Accordingly, "My joy" proves one's closeness to

Jesus, and the credibility of a mystical faith experience in Wesley's case, as well as those of other believers.

Another reader may ask a similar question:

In the introduction to this book, you told the story of a psychiatrist who compared a "fear of God" with fear of an "attacking tiger" experienced by a psychotic individual. How can we delineate the difference between a kind of mental disorder and genuine faith?

Let us answer this first question from a psychiatrist's perspective. If we were to apply the deductions extracted from Wesley's example, it would be easy to draw a differential diagnosis between mental problems and faith. We may generalize and say "the fear of a tiger" caused by a mental disorder compromises a person's peace, trust, confidence, optimism, and other reflections, while trust in God increases them. A mental disorder compromises one's personal, social, and professional functioning, while trust in God increases them. A mental disorder compromises one's general "well standing" in the social environment, while trust in God increases socialization, and (Christian) cooperation inside the societal matrix.

Second, the sensorial recognition of an "attacking tiger" must be equally visible for everyone, or be nonexistent—a mere hallucination. However because faith is the necessary "recognition function of God," God must be invisible to everyone and be transempirically experienced by people of faith only.

Third, the logical consequences of a sensory hallucination can be easily disproved (though only to people with intact reasoning), e.g., by acknowledging the absence of damage, a wound, or a victim. Recognition that, "Even though I see the tiger, I know that my perception of a tiger simply cannot be accurate," would indicate a perceptive confusion, but exclude a psychotic disorder. A transempirical communication with God, on the other hand, is verifiable by its effects. The "quite other" (than worldly) gifts of faith, such as biblical love, peace, and joy witnessed by Christians, paradoxically prove the reality of the encounter with the "absolutely different" God.

It is interesting to note that even in communist countries there did not exist a diagnostic category that would explicitly or implicitly cover "symptoms of faith." However, people of faith (dissidents or political opponents) were sometimes diagnosed by Soviet psychiatrists as suffering from "Sluggish Schizophrenia." The diagnosis signified a "peculiar" and "different than normal pattern of thought," an unconventional lifestyle characterized by not participating in the zealous building of the euphoric playschool-like (communist) society, in its grandiose steps toward a bright future.

The next question posed by our devil's advocate is this:

> False belief systems have existed throughout history, and they persist today. They are often enforced and justified by "gifts of faith." This is as equally valid for Christianity as for non-Christian belief systems, and even for religions based on animism or magic. So, how would such lasting mistakes in faith survive if lasting self-deception were not possible?

As noted, the degree to which faith is psychologically authentic, genuine and biblical, depends directly on how much biblical love, peace, joy, and union with God is reflected through it. The reverse is also true: only a biblical relationship with God enables authentic faith and receiving biblical gifts of faith. Thus, non-biblical belief systems provide "gifts of faith" only in proportion to how close they are to the biblical God. We can observe this, for example, in Stone Age beliefs. They are a response to God's call as well. In his introduction to Heschel's *Between God and Man*, Fritz Rotschild supports this view.

> Even the most ludicrous and perverse idols created by primitive tribes are not simply the products of delusion that stand for "nothing," but are genuine reactions to the objective mystery that challenged and addressed them. Their error consisted in relating the transcendent to conventional needs, by making the temporal ultimate. . . .13

At that time, humanity was spiritually, psychologically, and socially simply too underdeveloped to understand highly demanding ethical teachings and discipleship. People of the Stone Age were unable to respond more appropriately to God's calls. Theoretically, the closer to biblical faith such magic and animistic religions came, the more "gifts of faith" they granted. (Indeed, in practice, worship of Stone Age idols was not "proven" or justified by the biblical gifts of faith, but by superstitious attempts to bribe and appease gods in the hope that they would be benign and helpful.)

Something comparable is true for modern non-Christian religions: they enable their believers to receive biblical gifts of faith only to the extent that they offer closeness to the biblical God.

But then, how and why do deception and mistakes in revealed Christian faith survive? Why do we have an abundance of mutually competitive Christian denominations?

Let us, for the moment, not discuss this question in detail. Instead, in a subsequent section, we will discuss in detail the psychology of fanaticism and agnosticism, as well as the phenomenon of religious plurality within Christianity. Let us note in advance that one's commitment to non-biblical belief systems is never fully or solely "put into effect" either by biblical gifts or by a "quite other" biblical joy, but mostly by worldly and psychologically understandable reasons. In other words; it is not the believer's search for the Spirit, biblical joy or holiness that substantiate lasting mistakes in faith questions between Christians, but selfishness, will to power or uncritical self-confidence, that contain a promise of worldly pleasure, supremacy, or entitlement.

Our devil's advocate appears once more:

> Previously, we noted that faith enables successful personal and social functioning, and promotes unselfishness, peace, and love, advantageous modes of functioning for all of society. Can we now recognize the opposite: Namely, that faith does not help to preserve life, or to make it more successful or prosperous?

There is a saying implying that if someone is abundantly criticized, then the question should be asked: "What have you done that is so good?"

Christians were always distinguished by "having done something too good." In the early Christian centuries, builders of God's kingdom were easy to recognize. Their "Way" was always required to fulfill a characteristic moral quest of honesty, peace, love, fidelity, being the "slaves of righteousness." Also in their personal, family, and social life the "Christian journey" meant a transformation, and becoming an honest, industrious, hard-working, and unselfish person.

Nevertheless, true Christians were never loved by worldly establishments. They almost always remained set apart from the world and its values, thereby challenging it. The world never liked the moral difference and superiority of true Christians. As a consequence of this hatred, Jesus, his disciples, and Christian martyrs and saints did not lose their lives because of criminal or political rebellion or for being outspoken. They were persecuted because of their contemporary culture's resistance against "being in the world, but not of it," a principle discussed in John 17:16 and 17:11.

This explains the paradoxical contradiction that the Christian lifestyle on the one hand contributes to personal, familial, and societal functioning in all facets of life, and, on the other hand, Christians are always in opposition to the world. Building God's kingdom, or serving a world founded on natural selection and survival of the fittest, are incompatible. True Christians were, as an old song says, "Strangers in the world," for a similar reason. Even Jesus Christ was characterized in John's Prologue as follows:

The true light that gives light to every man was coming into the world. He was in the world, and though the world was made through him, the world did not recognize him. He came to that which was his own, but his own did not receive him. Yet to all who received him, to those who believed in his name, he gave the right to become children of God— children born not of natural descent, nor of human decision or a husband's will, but born of God. (John 1: 9-13)

The next question from our skeptic in this chapter can be formulated as follows:

We discussed three different sources of human satisfaction: pleasure, happiness, and joy. Happiness and pleasure are temporary experiences. They have definite natural limits, and are not characterized by a permanent, steady progression. However, is the same not valid for joy stemming from a steady relationship with God? Faith, too, does not develop in a pattern of steady growth, a "crescendo of joy," but is rather a "roller-coaster" of ups and downs.

This is a very thoughtful question, one that deserves a just-as-thoughtful answer. What, indeed, is the reason for this "roller-coaster-like" relationship with God? Is the reason found in Jesus himself, or within a particular believer?

According to his own self-revelation, God is faithful, unchangeable, and cannot be manipulated. Therefore, God's nature cannot be the reason for this roller-coaster-like relationship with him in us believers. Is the reason instead found in our own self-assessment and self-esteem?

Our emotions, including those generated by religious experience, oscillate and change. Indeed, a state of mind closer to depression generates a different experience of God than what is typical. However, note that the relationship with God is neither a mere emotion and feeling, nor a hedonistic, "sacral ecstasy." In addition, faith involves a willful choice, attention, memory, behavior, knowledge, and awareness—all of these are present in the psychological experience of faith. Knowledge and will, choice and struggle, persistence and endurance are parts of the relationship with Jesus. I dare say that the intellectual processes of rational knowledge and personal choice are even more essential than only feelings and emotions in faith dynamics!

And so, in our journey through a roller-coaster-like faith experience, may we adhere to the advice one mystic gave: When God is silent, intentionally do everything as though he is (loudly) speaking to you, and sooner rather than later, you will hear his response . . . this is how He coaches your growth in faith.

The last question in this chapter is this: "Does setting joy as the criterion of living faith mean that believers are in the end (Christian) happiness, pleasure, or joy-seeking hedonists?"

Christians reject the egocentric hedonism of the world, and shift towards a God-centeredness. In practice, this means that not only joy is experienced by Christians inside a biblical context, but pleasure and happiness, as well. In Christians, happiness and pleasure are, according to Packer: ". . . divinely designed to raise our sense of God's goodness, deepen our gratitude to him, and strengthen our hope of richer pleasures to come in the next world."[14]

Biblical joy is in this context the criterion and parameter of closeness to God. This means that joy is not a goal at all, but only the by-product and the consequence of the faith and living in a tangible union with the invisible God.

Thus, the essential difference between hedonism and Christian understanding is that for believers joy is not a goal, but the consequence and by product of closeness to the ultimate goal—God. On the contrary, for hedonists there is no ultimate goal other than achieving elusive pleasure and happiness.

Notes

1. Viktor E. Frankl, *Ärztliche Seelsorge* (Wien: Franz Deuticke, 1965), 49.

2. Viktor E. Frankl, *Ärztliche*, 18.

3. Maria Mendez, *Life with Meaning, Guide to the Fundamental Principles of Viktor Frankl's Logotherapy* (Victoria, BC: Trafford, 2004), 65.

4. Viktor E. Frankl, *Ärztliche*, 57.

5. J. I. Packer, *God's Plans for You* (Wheaton, IL: Crossway Books, 2001), 54.

6. Otto Fenichel, *The Psychoanalytic Theory of Neuroses* (New York: Norton & Co., 1972), 39.

7. J. I. Packer, *God's Plans*, 31.

8. Viktor E. Frankl, *Antropologische Grundlagen der Psychotherapie* (Bern, Stuttgart, Wien: Hans Huber, 1976), 307.

9. Daniel W. Hardy, "Joy." in *The Oxford Companion to Christian Thought*, ed. Adrian Hastings, Alistair Mason and Hugh Pyper (New York: Oxford University Press, 2000), 354.

10. Marijan Jerko Fucak, *Dogadjaj Isus Krist* (Zagreb: Institut Za Teolosku Kulturu Laika, Unpublished Presentations, 1986).

11. Janos Erdody, *Requiem Firenceert* (Budapest: Szepmuveszeti Kiado, 1977), 13-14.

12. Anthony O'Hear, *Experience, Explanation, and Faith: An Introduction to the Philosophy of Religion* (London: Routledge & Kegan, 1984), 202-234.

13. Abraham J. Heschel, *Between God and Man* (New York: The Free Press, A Division of Simon & Shuster, 1959), 15.

14. J. I. Packer, *God's Plans*, 54.

Chapter 21

Transempirical Recognition of the Truth and Values

It is a commonly accepted view that positive facts and truth, discerned by sensorial functions, are objective; what we can see or touch exists independently of us, and without the presence of an observer.

But what about internal discernment—does what we experience in a transempirical way within ourselves also exist independently? Do invisible, untouchable, and unmeasurable discernments exist in reality, also independent of the subject, or only in the subject's mind?

21.1. Value Discernment and Value Blindness

Let us begin by discussing a transempirical experience quite close and meaningful to all of us, one to which we will repeatedly turn to in our discussion: Love. We recognize love in ourselves—it is an essentially important and evident introspective experience for the one who is in love. Is love, however, only the lover's own affection? Does he or she recognize in the beloved objective reasons for love that really and truly exist, independent of the loving person—or is the recognition of reasons for love only present in and experienced by the subject in the form of unreliable, transempirical reflections? Let us formulate an even more challenging question: Do we truly love husbands, children, or parents because of their true characteristics—or are their beloved lovable characteristics only our own wish-fulfilling fantasies which nobody else can substantiate?

Frankl asserts that love is not an imaginary phenomenon, nor an instance of self-deception.[1] Love is always value-discerning (*vertsichtig* in German). Only the one who loves can see and experience in the be- loved the concealed, but existing, experienced values. To someone who does not love in the same way, these values will remain concealed. Val- ues in the beloved person do exist independent of the observer and his or her observation, but not in the same way for everyone. An indifferent observer is unable to observe the beloved's qualities, so acutely noticed and cherished by the lover; hence, only the loving person will be a value- observer.

Such a conclusion makes Comte's positivist reasoning (so deeply entrenched in post-modern people's agnostic world-view) open to dis- cussion. Sometimes, what is invisible or untouchable is not always so as a consequence of being nonexistent, but of value-blindness to its recog- nition! What is invisible to the value-blind can be an experiential reality for the value-discerning.

A similar value-observing attitude is operative in joy. Only a value- observing person can see the existing value and is able to recognize it and experience happiness because of it. It will not bring joy to someone who cannot see particular value in the same way. The value, however, exists independently of both observers.

In love, the arts, hobbies, and other similar recognition processes, value discernments make recognition of truly existing qualities possible. True recognition functions discern that which exists in us, and also that which exists objectively, independent of the subject. That means that reasons for biblical love, joy, peace, or hope, truly exist, even though they remain hidden to value-blind individuals.

To live, teach, and witness to a value-discerning attitude—to develop the ability to recognize the real reasons for rejoicing in a particular per- son, to embody peace and love—is the paramount task of every human being. It is the precondition and prerequisite of being able to live a life worth living.

Probably nowhere is faith more a prerequisite of mental health than in enabling not only a value-discerning, but an *ultimate* value-discerning attitude. And, inversely, the widespread "suffering of a meaningless life," as Frankl calls it—correlated to a lack of love, joy, and peace, and to consequent depression, aggression, and suicide—is the most serious re- sult of value-blindness to biblical values.[2]

In this context, it is important to remember that in transempirical recognitions, value discernments make the discernment of factually-ex- isting qualities possible. Thus, a real reason for love, joy, peace, or hope truly exists, but is recognizable only to a value-observing person. Note, however, the inverse implication of that principle: reasons for depression, hate, sadness, pain, suffering, or hopelessness also truly exist for a value-blind person. Consequently, reasons for depression, sadness, or hopelessness exist really, almost "objectively," also for the subject who is unable to recognize and remedy what is causing his or her suffering. Thus, value discernment or value blindness makes the difference between joy, hope, and optimism and apathy, disappointment, and despair!

A biblical viewpoint observes the transitory and finite qualities of human earthly reality from an infinite, godly perspective. From a biblical perspective, the worldly is transitional, while the infinite is the decisive reality. Christian, i.e., a Jesus-like, suffering is, from such a worldview, the certain gateway to biblical glory. Thus, while a biblical viewpoint and faith are unable to prevent or take away suffering, they abundantly compensate for it by granting biblical gifts of the Spirit! Note that this is no longer merely a "belief," but an evident and real experience for exemplary believers!

We read in Philippians 4:4-7, what St. Paul wrote while waiting in prison:

> Rejoice in the Lord always. I will say again: Rejoice! Let your gentleness be evident to all. The Lord is near. Do not be anxious about anything, but in everything, by prayer and petition, with thanksgiving, present your requests to God.

In my professional encounters, I have witnessed many times that a true Christian attitude enables a value-discerning attitude of perceiving God's presence beyond, and despite, suffering, as described in Paul's letter. Even suffering is perceived as meaningful to someone who has a strong faith and is able to discern a Christ-like vocation. Such a person accepts suffering so that others do not have to suffer.

21.2. Love and Faith as a Value Discernment

We noted that faith is God's gift. However, God does not simply "give faith" like he gives life. If it were so, then all humans would be God's people. The Spirit only invites all people, and enables and aids a value-discerning attitude to recognize God. It is, however, the responsibility and decision of the invited subject to either accept or reject such a call and to participate in a relationship with God.

It is not accidental that Isaiah referred to the coming Messiah as the one "who opens the eyes of the blind." In other words, the Messiah brings value discernment to his people. The Holy Spirit has a similar role for "those who have not seen and yet believe." (John 20:29). It grants believers value discernment and the desire, ability, and strength to strive for ultimate value: God.

We may say that love is faith in a human being, and faith is love of an ultimate being. Both love and faith are experienced by different, specialized value discernments. Let us briefly compare the similarities and differences between the experience of love and faith, focusing on how value discernment helps believers experience God's closeness.

We have affirmed that the human person is constituted of a body, mind, and soul. Unlike the body, the mind and soul are non-sensorial, untouchable, and immeasurable, but despite that fact, they still provide knowledge for a person who loves. In fact, love is enabled by the value-discerning knowledge not only of the visible (the body) but even more importantly of the invisible traits (the qualities of mind and soul) of a beloved person. For the love to be true and authentic, the invisible parts of a person (like fidelity, devotion, or unselfishness), existing beyond the body, are more important than the visible ones.

Like love, faith is a trusting relationship with God. Just as loving persons recognize the invisible mind and soul of the beloved person, value-discerning believers recognize the personality of the invisible God.

However, here an agnostic reader could object:

> You say that a loving person communicates with the invisible mind of the beloved person through his or her body, words, gestures, and behavior. This is true in every kind of love; in parental, spousal or children's love there is always a close, touchable and visible bodily appearance and communication between people who love each other. A lasting, platonic loving relationship with complete bodily unavailability (i.e., existing only in thoughts, ideas, and fantasies but without the real visible and touchable existence of a person) is barely possible. However, God has no body! The greatest difficulty for post-modern people that hinders their trust and faith in God is the fact that God is solely spiritual in his partnership with people. It is difficult to appreciate the platonic love with an invisible person that Christianity promotes. Unavoidably, we suspect that such an invisible

person is the product of our fantasy. How can value discernment help believers overcome this difficulty?

Let me first answer this question with a literary example. According to Kohan's description, the medieval poet Dante was deeply in love with the young and beautiful Lady Beatrice.[3] She was the embodiment of an ideal spiritual beauty; her true home was not on earth but in heaven, and angels begged God to bring her to heaven as soon as possible. When Beatrice died, the young Dante continued to love and, in some way, even communicate with her. According to Kohan, helped by the flame of Christian love that Beatrice's memory lit in his heart, Dante forgave all the injustices, pain, suffering, and insults he had endured. By her death, Beatrice's being did not become invalid or non-existent; it could not be blotted out of the world's history. She existed for Dante in a way that was very different from the fantasy of a person who never existed—she was spiritually present to a value-discerning Dante, continually helping his conscience to empower his self-esteem, optimism, and Christian ideals.

Sometimes I have observed a similar process in widowed spouses; the deceased person has continued to act in the life of the value-discerning survivor. It seems that the difference between "is" and "is not" is not always a black and white matter in the human way of experiencing reality!

Let us apply this discussion to faith. Faith is not a platonic relationship with God that exists only in dreams and the imagination. Through the meaning that is present beyond the deeds of God, recognized through value discernment, the invisible God becomes visible. This value discernment happens in different ways.

On one hand, despite the fact that God has no visible and touchable "body," the whole created world is the expression of His love. In this lies the essence of the believer's value discernment, and the essence of the mystery of Christian faith: to know the personality of the invisible Creator from visible creation. On the other hand, the authentic, biblical church (expressing the personality, ideas and teaching of its high priest, Jesus) is the true "body of Christ" for value-discerning believers. Through the sacraments of the church, (for example, the Eucharist), believers experience God's "bodily presence." For Christians, the sacraments are a union with the invisible God—indeed "quite other," but still in some aspects comparable to closeness with the beloved person.

A further commonality in the two value discernments of love and faith is that both enable the recognition of factually existing attributes.

Just as joy has real and existing reasons for a person who loves, the real reasons for biblical love, joy, peace, and hope truly exist—in God's person. The extent to which human love is alive depends on the mutual giving and receiving of joy. Analogously, the extent to which union with God is experiential and tangible depends upon how evident the experience of biblical gifts of faith and the gifts of the Spirit are in the believer's life. From being disciples of the ultimate truth, believers gain an ultimate joy; the ultimate joy of Jesus' discipleship proves its ultimate truth.

Value discernment makes the invisible God visible to the transempirical inner eyes, thereby making all the difference in a believer's life. This is the reason that, for believers, the grace of faith is the most eminent expression of God's love. It enables value discernment (seeing the invisible reality of God) to those disciples "who have not seen and yet believe."

21.3. Reasons for Value Blindness in Non-Believers

Faith, as noted, makes the invisible God "visible" only to value-discerning people. For example, in the first part of the book we noted that Jesus' resurrection was a meta-historical event. Many Jewish and Roman observers witnessed the resurrection, but did not acknowledge it. By witnessing and participating in the events, they were called by and to Jesus. But most did not want to recognize the meaning of Jesus' resurrection and its relevance to their personal lives; they therefore chose to remain value-blind. They only became value-discerning people, able to recognize the true meaning of the resurrection, with Jesus' and the Spirit's help, albeit after the fact.

Why did most Roman and Jewish witnesses to the resurrection choose to reject Christian value discernments? More importantly for us today, why do modern agnostics do so? Because value discernment is not always a problem-free or a euphoric experience. On the contrary, to accept responsibility for value discernments regarding faith questions is almost always an excruciating and precarious mission. It is almost never simple enough for people to agree upon, as in Amos' observation: "The Sovereign Lord has spoken; who can but prophesy?" (Amos 3:8) More often than not, as in Jeremiah 1:6, it is an extremely strenuous, sometimes frustrating task, even though it may be ultimately rewarding, as illustrated in Isaiah 49:4. "I have labored to no purpose; I have spent my strength in vain and for nothing. Yet what is due me is in the Lord's hand, and my reward is with my Lord."

Thomas' resistance and his request for safe, touchable proof stems from a similar source: fear. Thomas was afraid of accepting the responsibility that accompanies a value discernment because it could have cost his life. Accepting responsibility for one's value discernment often entails "witnessing;" it entails the determination to take a stand, and courage and persistence in making a difference in the non-sensorial discernment of others.

Let us keep one more fact in mind. The reciprocal process of faith's enabling value discernment and value discernment's enabling faith, always involves two factors: God's gift and the particular subject's conscious, positive response to God's call. This interrelation is, however, not always connected to Jesus' dramatic interventions, as in the cases of Thomas and of the disciples traveling to Emmaus. It is often a seemingly quite natural or subtle evaluative process, not forced, but helped by the Spirit, of recognizing connections between revelation and everyday life, between the witness of the church and events in which one willingly or unwillingly participates. It understands "the signs of the time," recognizing, interpreting, putting into context the most important things, with one's heart. A value-discerning attitude, which is made possible by functions of purpose, requires journeying through life self-critically, as well as being critical towards societal standards and expectations. It requires eyes open to God's calls, and above all, it demands courage.

Accepting personal responsibility in hearing God's call has always been characteristic of people of faith. Almost all the great prophets, teachers, apostles, and martyrs of the Old and New Testaments are distinguished by their willingness and readiness to see, understand, and thereby be able to explain that to which others were value-blind. It may be surprising to acknowledge that God's gifts and calls are abundantly available to all of us in western culture, while a personal value discernment and the courage to accept and witness to one's discipleship make almost all the difference between receiving and losing one's relationship with the living God.

Notes

1. Viktor E. Frankl, *Ärztliche Seelsorge* (Wien: Franz Deuticke, 1965), 132.

2. Frankl, *Ärztliche Seelsorge*, 18.

3. P. S. Kohan, *Istorija Zapadnoevropske Knjizevnosti* (Sarajevo: Veselin Maslesa, 1967), 48-51.

Chapter 22

Plurality in Discernment, Its Relevance to Faith Questions, and a New Chance for Ecumenism

In our postmodern time, two paradoxical and painful phenomena run together. On one hand, widespread religious indifference and apathy, on the other, the painful denominational fragmentation of Jesus' body. Is the fragmentation of the church the consequence of losing a biblical respect for and union with the living God, and compromising it with a human-made religious chaos? Can our commonalities in transempirically experiencing a tangible union with the invisible God help us find an approach to denominational plurality that is biblically, theologically, and pastorally constructive?

22.1. Defining the Problem

Although everyone knows and agrees with simple sensorial and cognitive truths, such as two times two equals four, quite the opposite is true for even the simplest of internally acquired discernments. Personal taste, hobbies, or interests in sports, are unique for everyone. Truths that one discerns by introspection, reflection, mystical experience, or functions of purpose, are not generally held values because they are not the same for each person, and bias is unavoidable. However, at the same time, in a psychologist's, psychiatrist's, or physician's office, what the patient experiences internally has paramount value!

The phenomenon of religious plurality is especially relevant to the question of how a genuine believer experiences the reality to which the

Bible bears witness. Sometimes plurality substantiates an unjustified rela-tivism that often goes to extremes. As the saying goes, "Where there are many truths, there is no truth." Doesn't such a statement most accurately characterize the mental and spiritual attitude of many religiously indif-ferent, undecided, and/or skeptical people toward faith?

Historically, agnosticism, and subsequently atheism, emerged in the time of the Roman philosopher Lucretius (96-55 BC). At that time the Roman Empire incorporated the cultures of almost all surrounding Medi-terranean people, including their religions and gods. Suddenly the Ro-mans started wondering:

> We have our gods; the Greeks, Egyptians, and Persians have their own. Can it be possible that all of these gods are true and authentic? Perhaps none of them is true, because gods may merely be the inven-tion of particular cultures.

In our time, a similar relativism reappeared with a vengeance. Our culture is deeply divided.

For religious people there is nothing more convincing than that Jesus Christ is with us, and that nothing and no one is closer to us than God himself. By contrast, for non-believers like the philosopher Bertrand Russell (see his *Why I am not a Christian*), just the opposite is true.[1] Indeed, it is thought that both positions have the same right to be re-spected, and that it is not reasonable to give more credibility to the believer's experience than to that of the non-believer. The consequence of such relativism is that for one person God does exist, and for another he does not. This solution, logical or not, is how our culture deals with this controversy—mutually exclusive concepts and explanations are ac-cepted as equally sustainable.

The problem of plurality, relativism, and egalitarianism may be seen as one of the greatest challenges confronting both believers and the church. It may be seen as questioning the trustworthiness of the whole system of religious discernment, and of all human discernments that are not based on positivistic, scientific facts. However, does plurality in non-sensorial discernment really mean unreliability?

22.2. Does Plurality Mean Unreliability?

The reason for plurality in our everyday introspections, reflections, and other non-sensorial discernments lies in the fact that just as we are all different in our outward appearance, so are we also different in our inner, psychological make-up. All in all, every person's inner profile is relatively different and unique. Everyone has relatively distinct psychological characteristics, natural endowments, potentials, experiences, and obligations. Consequently, the manifestations and embodiments of internally experienced reality are different. This difference is the reason that everyone finds relatively distinct meaning and values in life. It would be quite difficult to prove that only one way is the right way, as is done in physics experiments and in mathematical calculations. A person with different gifts, experiences, and goals is allowed to have different discernments, in which his or her unique personal characteristics are best utilized.

However, this does not mean an absence of a basic common denominator valid for all people, nor does it imply an unreliability of discernments in reflections, in functions of purpose, or in transempirical discernment in general.

This last statement may seem controversial. How can we reconcile plurality and reliability in discernment, if plurality means difference, while reliability means dependability and uniformity?

Let us follow Frankl's thoughts regarding this very topic.[2] The values, meaning, and purpose one pursues in one's life are subjective inasmuch as a different, relative truth is present in every person. However, they are objective only insofar as they can be found by the factors that are active in the person not able to be deluded, those not arbitrarily inferred, or directed by others. The purpose will be experienced as a correct one if it is in harmony with the subject's internal (however reliable) principles of non-sensorial, transempirical acknowledgment.

To visualize this, let us take an analogy from sensorial-scientific knowledge. Let us suppose my sedimentation rate is 4/8, another person's is 6/10, and a third person's is 8/12. Everybody's rate is different or subjective. But the way it develops is objective, not by will, mood, or arbitrary choices. Quite similar is the reliability and objectivity of introspective, reflective, mystical, and other transempirical discernments.

Note that we are not talking about objectivity in the philosophical sense. We are using the term *objectivity* to mean inner experience without the possibility of being dominated by one's desires or by lasting self-deceit or self-delusion. There are rules and regulations that determine what is meaningful, valuable, and important in a person's life with his or her potentials and natural endowments.

Since different and unique personal characteristics and distinctive-
ness are active in every person, conclusions, too, often need to be different. Note, that such plurality does not include any relativism, and it is
justified only where individual characteristics are different and unique.

From our discussion, it becomes obvious that plurality in the discernment of transempirical recognition is necessary and justified in some
circumstances. However, where are its limits? Is it possible that a justified difference in such discernment is the reason that one will accept
faith and the experience of living in union with God, while another will
reject them?

To answer these questions, let us keep in mind that human
transempirical experiences can be truly different, but only where psychological and spiritual make-up, and therefore also meaning, tasks, and
goals differ. Indeed, we differ in many things, but not in everything!

The most essential facts in the lives of all of us, independent of our
unique gifts, endowments, and abilities, are the same. Because our human make-up is similar concerning fundamental questions of human life
(such as the search for ultimate meaning, love, joy, and peace), since we
are all created in God's image and likeness, our attitudes towards God
cannot be completely different, and regardless of all differences, equally
correct. Thus, no relativism and egalitarianism such as those proposed
by Russell are justified. However, we must ask ourselves this: Where
are the limits and boundaries of diversity and plurality, and above all,
where and how ought we take a stand to heal the existing faith chaos
caused by millennia-old wounds in Christ's body?

22.3. Addressing Denominational Plurality

I grew up in an eastern European country ruled by communists, where
atheist ideology was presented as the only possible worldview and pen-
etrated all of society. But as a youngster traveling by train, I once saw
written on a wall of a big train station these words: "Marxism proclaimed
that 'God is dead'—God proclaimed that 'Marxism is dead.'" The writing on the wall predicted for me, and for many others, a quite improbable event—the collapse of communism. As unlikely as it had seemed at
the time, it occurred right before my very eyes!

But what came after the collapse of communism? Two competing
processes are evident in countries of the previous Communist bloc. First,

in countries where fifteen years ago there existed only an atheistic religion, people are in great numbers returning to Jesus' church.

Others, perhaps the majority, are confronted by a consumerism of beliefs, religions, ideologies, teachings, and worldviews imported from the western and eastern countries, in which a devastating spiritual vacuum seems even more prominent now than it was under communist rule. Thus, in the ex-illusory communist East almost the same trends are occurring as in the ex-illusory Christian West.

That people living without God's self-revelation are all very different in their self-created, or socially indoctrinated belief systems, is understandable. But such extreme, unprecedented plurality in belief systems, even among Christians who nominally belong to one and the same flock, is often counterproductive and detrimental.

Although perhaps no Christian is happy with this fact, unfortunately denominational tensions exist as they have existed for almost a thousand years. Christians have been trying to resolve these differences for the same period of time. They formally all agree that there is only one criterion that all Christians should really worry about—how God views things and what his opinion is. In the past, church leaders and theologians held countless unionist and ecumenical discussions to discern God's one, unquestionable, revealed truth and to re-establish the unity of his church on the basis of this truth. However, as practice shows, it is difficult even today to find a Christian consensus regarding God's unquestionable revealed truth. This is so, partly because different denominations sometimes interpret the same Scriptures in relation to the relevant questions of the foundation of their faith very differently.

The church is supposed to be the authentic interpreter of Scriptures and of Jesus' teaching and commands. But even for the church it was and is impossible to demonstrate to all Christians God's ultimate truth or the true meaning of Scriptural messages, by conventional theological reasoning, debates, and discussions. Therefore, we will here go down a different path in search of a solution to the unjustified plurality problem.

We can draft our rationale as follows: Since the problem lies not in Jesus' revelation, but in the human inability (or unwillingness) to understand his message, we will, in the following, focus not on the theology of the revelation, on exegesis, or hermeneutics, or on God's message itself nor on its interpretation. Specialists, exegetes, apologists, and theologians have tried this many times throughout the centuries and have not succeeded because the complex factors influencing discourse are not hermeneutical or exegetical, but historical, personal, and above all, psychological. Thus, our focus is not on logical, exegetical, or theological demonstrations that discern the limits of religious plurality, or the common essentials among different theological interpretations. Nor is it on demonstrating which theological stance best represents God's unquestionable revelation.

Our focus will be on the theology, mind, and psychology of the subject, the interpreter and respondent and the particular cleric or lay believer who must take a stand in religious plurality for him or herself. We will analyze and discern criteria that may aid every believer in making necessary, fundamental, responsible choices, such as how to interpret Scripture, or how to choose the right denomination for him or herself. These criteria may also help people to accept (or reject) a theological teaching. We will also explore how to help a genuine seeker (supplementing classical theological approaches) discern and experience the Ultimate Reality to which the Bible, the Spirit, and the church's teachings and traditions bear witness.

Thus, in short, our focus will be not on the message of God's unquestionable teaching, but on how to discern the message and unquestionable truth when confronted with problems of religious plurality.

How would such an approach work in practice? During my residency training I was often warned by my teachers to respect the advice which a famous physician used to give his students when confronting a difficult problem in treatment. Paraphrased it sounds like this: Forget your therapeutic eagerness. First try to understand what is really happening in your patient's mind, and the therapy will follow by itself.

We will follow a similar path. First, we will discuss what Jesus' church is. Second, we will get an overview of how and why Christianity became fragmented. After those preliminary considerations, we may hope that new, transempirically-focused insights and solutions will come almost by themselves, with help from the eternally almighty and wise God.

22.4. The Mystery of the Church: A Dichotomy between the Sacred and the Worldly

Jesus' ministry represented the greatest turning point in human history. By establishing a new covenant with his disciples (which was, according to Martin Reardon, aimed at reconciling "a sinful and divided world into unity with God") and by establishing his church, Jesus gave a new direction and purpose to human history. According to the same author, "The church was thought of as a sign, instrument, and foretaste which would be completed in the Kingdom of God."[3]

The Dogmatic Constitution of the Church promulgated by Vatican Council II, (see: Austin Flannery, *Vatican Council II: The Conciliar and Post-Conciliar Documents*) talks about church as a mystery, and then describes it as "people brought into unity from the unity of the Father, Son, and the Holy Spirit." In addition, it states, "The Church is in Christ as a sacrament sign and instrument of intimate union with God. . . ."[4]

From this definition it is obvious that Jesus' church mysteriously integrates two inseparable aspects of his intent for it. One is for the church to be in the world as a sign and instrument of people's union with God, and the other to be a foretaste (to borrow Reardon's term) of what it will be like meeting God face-to-face in heaven. These two inseparable aspects of the church truly illustrate and embody the words of John 17:11 and 17:16—being in the world, but not of it. The integration of both, the church being in the world and simultaneously holy (not of the world but of the "quite other" God), is an awesome task! But the triune God slowly and mysteriously guides the church and promotes this mystery. Paradoxically, this is especially so in our time.

The true biblical church's function is primarily the expression of God's grace, but also a manifestation of the faith of believers, as well as of their responsibility and fidelity to Jesus. God and his people, who are enabled by the Spirit's grace, act in a dialogical relationship that continuously perpetuates the mystery of the virtual dualism of the church. This interaction between God and his people is enabled by the High Priest's permanent presence with his church, sustaining the commitment of the faithful to be a "sign and instrument" of the union with the "quite other" God. Communication with the high priest (Jesus) is experiential to his people, who in turn respond to his call. At the same time, however, he respects the freedom of those who exclude themselves from a union with the life-giving God, who choose not to be members of "the body of Christ."

From a biblical perspective, Jesus' church is like a "sheepfold," a mysterious, unique, and necessary "gateway" to Jesus, according to John 10:1-10. Accordingly, the church has an evident Christological dimension. It is the visible sign of an invisible, godly, and spiritual essence. The commitment of God's people also plays a role in realizing its task. The role of the faithful is, according to Matthew 9:37 and Luke 10:1-11, to spread God's kingdom throughout the world. This role, if fulfilled, makes Jesus' church "the pillar and foundation of the truth" (1 Tim. 3:15) and the visible sign of the "fullness of truth," namely, Jesus. From this perspective, the church is a visible institution that is guided by the invisible, transcendental "Spirit of truth" into "all truth" (according to John 16:13). The church fulfills its God-given task by being a "gateway" to holiness.

From a third perspective, the church is a sacrament. Sacraments are, as the reader may recall, the visible signs established by Jesus of an invisible reality. The church is a visible, material body that expresses an invisible holy essence. Its invisible component is its high priest Jesus Christ, and its invisible but experiential qualities are the aforementioned biblical attributes, such as the "sheepfold," the "fullness of truth," and the mystical "gateway to Jesus." Its touchable and visible component is the institution, "constituted and organized as a society in the present world," according the Tridentine Profession of Faith.[5] All other sacraments, like Baptism, the Eucharist, and Marriage, originate from the church; therefore, it is the primordial sacrament—it serves to deliver all other sacraments. Despite the dichotomy between fallible members and holy essence, the institution ought to serve the invisible Spirit's purpose as a catalyst promoting God's kingdom and salvation to all people.

The two-fold nature of the church has an especially important aspect, which becomes relevant when we observe the mystery we call "church" from a fourth, pastoral perspective. It is painful for all Christians to acknowledge that the visible aspects of the church, that is, its institutionalized manifestation, are not yet synonymous with the biblical faith and church. There still remains a gap between them. God's people sometimes underestimate these differences, while opponents of the church tend to overestimate them. Hence, while living under a communist regime I was often confronted by accusations put forth by atheists. They passionately told me that believers have committed many scandalous sins (such as the crusades, the inquisition, and sexual abuse) in the name of institutionalized religion, and therefore neither religious institutions nor institutional religion are sacred at all. Furthermore, they contended that religious institutions are not of God, but an instrument of worldly exploitation, an "opium for the masses"—as Marx proclaimed in his well-known phrase.

Confronted with such challenges, I readily admitted that yes, the religious institutions are sometimes represented by humans who are flawed and imperfect, and certainly not without sin; however, note that this sinful, greedy, power-hungry, and abusive image, even if there is some truth in it, is not what the church is and represents. This image, fraught with blemishes, is not the essence of the biblical church, established by Jesus as his own holy body. If we keep in mind that the church is, according to the Scriptures, the "pillar and foundation of the truth," and a "sheepfold" and "gateway" to the "fullness of truth," (Jesus), then sinners, though welcomed into the church in the true spirit of Christ, do not, by their sins, constitute, represent, or define the church.

If the church is not of the world, but holy, then all that contradicts holiness and does not serve the "fullness of truth," is not what the church really is. Thus, true churchly qualities in the visible religious institutions encompass only that which reflects the biblical church and the Spirit's holiness in it, but not what contradicts Jesus' teachings even if and when it occurs within a religious institution itself.

Relying to the greatest extent on church leaders, the responsibility of God's people may be, with the Spirit's help, to critically and—above all—self-critically, discern and perfect the institution of the church, so that it becomes more and more the "pillar and foundation of truth," as well as a "gateway to Jesus." By this, the institutional church may come ever closer to the "fullness of truth" that Christ is. By such a process, the biblical ideal and the institutional church become increasingly synonymous and closer to completion in God's kingdom.

22.5. The Fragmentation of Christianity: An Historical Overview

According to Franzen, in the first Christian centuries, "As diverse local churches spread through the Roman empire, it was judged necessary to establish norms of identity and visible bonds of unity between them."[6] Apostolic sources and succession were deemed necessary because they guaranteed the preservation of Christ's original teachings. (Note that we are discussing a time before the canon of the New Testament was established.) Thus, the respect of a particular congregation was determined by its apostolic founder who guaranteed the authenticity of the beliefs and teachings accepted and practiced by it. Since Peter was always accepted as the founder of the Roman diocese, at first nobody contested the bishop of Rome's primacy, just as nobody contested Peter's primacy among the apostles.

On the other hand, Peter's successor, the bishop of Rome, was situated in a megapolis (the capital of the Roman Empire) where the church, despite persecution, was rapidly growing. Thus, it substantiated the influence, theology, and prestige of the bishop of Rome; this was documented in many contemporary documents, both sacred and secular.

In AD 330, however, the emperor Constantine moved his capital, and the capital of the administrative center of the world, to Constantinople, which then rapidly grew in ecclesiastic, political, and cultural importance as the "New Rome."

While the Western church called Constantine "emperor," Eastern bishops gave him the title "Isapostolos" ("Equal to the Apostles"). Indeed, for a person "equal to the apostles" to transforming his ecclesiastic capital from the "Old Rome" to the "New Rome" seemed to most Eastern theologians justifiable and right.

The "New Rome" soon became so valuable in discussing and defining of theological questions and solving disputes that many Eastern theologians believed it should replace the "Old Rome" as the capital of the church.

Even though the same teachings of Jesus were accepted everywhere, the question of primacy among the bishops already caused tension between the "old" and "new" Romes in the great ecumenical synod in Nicea in 325, and twenty years later in the synod in Sardica. In the midst of the fighting concerning the Arian heresies, the Western members of the synod excommunicated the Eastern, and vice versa.

This crisis did not last. However, according to Franzen,[7] the tension between East and West unfortunately continued to grow. Consequently, when Pope Leo the Great requested the Emperor Marcian to arrange the fourth ecumenical synod of Chalcedon in 451, a new confrontation loomed. Despite Pope Leo's protest, Canon 28 of that greatest of all ecumenical synods, granted rights to the patriarch in Constantinople similar to those of the primate of the Western Church. This added fuel to the already-raging fire!

To clarify what the controversial canon really meant, we must keep in mind that the person of the pope served three interconnected functions. First, he was and is the bishop of Rome. Second, he was the primate of the Western church—a title no longer in use. Third, he was and is the shepherd of the whole of Christianity. Indeed, Canon 28 of Chalcedon did not promote a complete equality between the patriarch of Constantinople and the pope in his function as the shepherd of the whole of Christianity, which was and is the essence of the Roman Catholic understanding of the pope's position.

Despite the fact that Jesus prayed that his disciples might be one as he was one with the Father, so that "the world may believe" (John 17:21), the process of confrontation between Peter's successor in Rome and the patriarch in the New Rome was just the beginning of a continuing pattern of competition, disputes, schisms, and eventually bloody extermination of opponents in religious wars in and outside of Europe. In the ensuing sixteen centuries, not every particular church teaching was adjusted to biblical teachings, (especially St. Paul's hymn of love in 1 Cor. 13:4-7); rather, the interpretations of biblical and the Holy Spirit's teachings were sometimes adjusted to secular needs—a process we call "political theology." What we deem non-churchly behavior patterns sometimes existed alongside those exhibiting holiness and realizing the church's role as the gateway to Jesus.

As a consequence of estrangement between Western and Eastern theology, after the year 1054, two Christian belief systems officially existed. Just 500 years later, there existed the Catholic, Orthodox, Lutheran, Calvinist, and Anabaptist denominations. Again, some 500 years henceforth (in our time) one can find in the telephone book of every city a great abundance of registered Christian denominations. I learned during my theology studies that, according to a UN report, some twenty thousand Christian denominations exist.

For the most part, they share elements of Church-hood and respect the same Holy Trinity, the same traditions and Scriptures, but interpret and understand the same verses in the Bible very differently at times. In practice, believers more or less identify themselves with the teachings of their denominations. However, despite their loyalty, modern believers cannot avoid the painful and tormenting question, "Which is the right interpretation of the Scriptures, and does the Christian denomination that I have adopted as my own accurately promote Jesus' teachings?"

Christians must take a stand on different and mutually exclusive interpretations of verses such as the following: Matthew 16:18 and 19: "And I tell you that you are Peter, and on this rock I will build my church," and, "I will give you the keys of the kingdom of heaven; whatever you bind on earth will be bound in heaven, and whatever you loose on earth will be loosed in heaven," and John 21:15-17, in which Jesus orders Peter, "Feed my sheep."

A personal and responsible stand on these and similar verses that polarize Christians had become almost a Rorschach test on which one's whole understanding of faith hinged. One atheist thinker commented on the continued fragmentation of Jesus' one church, speculating that in the future, perhaps every believer would belong to his or her own denomination.

The fragmentation of Christianity has been a progressive process. It continues in our time, most probably not directed—to use the metaphor of the theatre—by the conscious malicious intentions of the protagonists, but rather, as in a Greek tragedy, by the subconscious self, id, and superego. In the next section, let us analyze why Christianity is suffering such a divisive fate.

22.6. Why Did Christianity Become Fragmented?

In theory, the responses of believers to faith questions are determined by the universal, general, and particular criteria of their conscience. The universal standards of Christian faith include the Ten Commandments, the Scriptures, and the teachings of ecumenical synods. They include the church's authoritative teachings, creeds, and the special roles that the sacraments occupy within the church. They are virtually the exclusive and identical foundation of a relationship with God for most mainstream Christians and are deemed objective, in the sense of being valid beyond and independent of the particular believer's appreciation.

The Spirit, acting through the believer's conscience, as well as through his or her personal experience of biblical joy, love, meaning, and intimate communication with God, is the believer's personal criterion in discerning answers to faith questions and pursuing biblical discipleship.

History proves that God's people were often in a dilemma as to how to choose between the two: universal criteria and those unique to their own conscience. Let us next discuss the implications of this dilemma.

Biblically, the Father's intent, Jesus' teachings, and the Spirit's leadership serve the same purpose, but sometimes use different didactical means. God the Father and God the Son generally proclaim laws valid to every believer, whereas the Spirit instructs believers how to apply general principles of law to particular life situations. Since every situation is unique, and every believer possesses different spiritual gifts and gifts of faith, he or she will sometimes have distinctive tasks in the one goal of realizing God's kingdom. The Spirit's leadership enables the specification of where, when, how, and which universal principles revealed by Jesus ought to be used in the building of a relationship with God. The leadership of the Spirit, soul, and conscience enables a free and responsible personal discernment, as well as the application of the general laws of God's kingdom. To enable such discernment and application in oneself, one's personality ought first to introject the universal standards of Christian faith, and then use freedom and responsibility to apply them according to his or her conscience. As Saint Augustine (according to Szabo) taught, "Be a disciple, and then do what you will."[8]

Listening to the Spirit's acting through the conscience of Christians was, and is, not without risk of making mistakes in good faith. Even more risky is excluding the Spirit's leadership and avoiding personal responsibility by relying on the security of obedience to laws, as did the Temple and Pharisees. The law of love is essential in God's kingdom: Law should be fulfilled promoting love.

But what if love and law, conscience and institutional practice conflict?

According to Hastings, the scholar Peter Lombard thought that if conscience and ecclesiastic teaching conflict, then universal teaching should always be obeyed. However, Thomas Aquinas thought, "It is better to die excommunicated than to violate one's conscience." He insisted (according to Hastings), "that the moral duty to follow one's conscience allows no exceptions." However such obedience does not exclude "the duty to ensure that one's conscience is well informed."[9]

A similar importance of the freedom of conscience is confirmed by the Declaration on Religious Liberty of Vatican II which, according to Hastings, emphasizes that it is through his conscience that man sees and recognizes the demands of divine law. He is bound to follow his conscience faithfully in all his activity.[10]

On the other hand, conscience and revelation have the same source. Thus, the teachings of the Spirit and conscience versus those of the Father, Jesus, and the church, if correctly understood and applied, should never be in contradiction. However, the requirements of the Spirit and conscience as opposed to those of Scripture and of Jesus' teachings can be misinterpreted by one's self, id, and superego—by one's personality.

Thus, the division in practice between the requirements of conscience and of general standards of faith occurs if the interpreter reads arbitrary lines into the biblical lines, thereby misinterpreting the criteria of either or of both. The choice of a responsible conscience in such a situation ought to be assessed according to adherence to universal standards of faith. At the same time, interpretation of universal standards of faith ought to be evaluated and validated according to a well-informed conscience. Both conscience and universal standards of faith may be assessed according to the criteria of the law of love, peace, biblical joy, forgiveness, and humility, which enables mutual synchronization, if we paraphrase the words used by a recent pope in a different context, like two lungs breathing the same air.

Biblically, there was a difference between the attitudes of Jesus, his disciples, and his followers towards the universal standards of faith and those who abused those standards—some Pharisees, the Temple, and other religious establishments. In fact, Jesus himself vigorously respected the Old Testament Scriptures. He quoted and used Scripture in his apology, even against his one and only enemy, Satan. Note that Jesus criticized the Temple not because of obedience to the universal and general standards of faith (such as the law, liturgy, and piety), but because of disobedience to them! From a psychological observation, Jesus fought not against the conscience of the Pharisees, but against their id, ego, and superego's use of the law for worldly purposes.

On the other hand, although Jesus was a Jew, blind obedience to general, universal laws and religious principles was practiced neither by him nor by the disciples. Healing on the Sabbath was one of the reasons that he was condemned by law-abiding Jews.

The relevance of this to the history of Christianity's fragmentation can be expressed by the following three suggestions.

1. On the surface, the fragmentation of Christianity was almost always declaratively justified by fidelity to Spirit, soul, conscience, the Scriptures, and/or other universal standards of faith. In truth, however, this fragmentation was directed by some of the protagonists' instinct, ego and superego.
2. Unjustified denominational plurality sometimes stemmed from, and at other times was exacerbated by, disrespect and neglect of the law of love and by adherence to worldly interests, logic, and rules.
3. The fragmentation of Christ's body is fueled by disregard for the rules and laws of God's kingdom and by adherence to "political" theology and worldly, loveless prudence.

Thus, the fragmentation of Christianity occurred not because of visible, touchable, and measurable reasons (like the decline of the West and the rise of the East, Constantine's decision to move his capital to Constantinople, or the sale of indulgences for money that prompted Luther's reformation). Rather, it happened then and happens today because of psychological choices and dynamics (like interpreting the Spirit, conscience, the Scriptures, and all that we have been calling universal standards of faith by a worldly instinct, ego and superego, instead of a spiritual hyperego). The real reasons for the fragmentation of Christianity are found not in historical, cultural, or even political events, but in the progressive mutual estrangement caused by the unloving, impatient, boastful, envious (according to Paul's words in 1 Cor. 13:4-7) record-keeping attitude on the part of at least some of the key players in the process of fragmentation. These psychological reasons and attitudes were those essential causes of fragmentation, that were often expressed and became visible through unessential, visible, touchable, and measurable phenomena (e.g., countless social, cultural, political, economical, theological, liturgical, exegetical, and doctrinal differences and reasons). Stating this, we are not promoting a kind of egalitarianism (e.g., "All protagonists were equally guilty") or favoring a finger-pointing attitude (e.g., "Certain protagonists bear most guilt"). Our purpose is to discern a new solution to the old psychological reasons for fragmentation.

22.7. A Transempirical Rationale in Ecumenical Reasoning

It is now the right time to apply transempirical recognition principles. In the following discussion, let us apply our theoretical concepts to the complex practical issue of religious plurality and the denominational fragmentation of Christ's body.

In biblical times, receiving the gift of faith and discerning the "fullness of truth" were almost always marked by changes such as new biblical behavior; renewed spirituality; an awakened appreciation of biblical meaning, joy, and trust; and direct experience of God's love. Note that spiritual, behavioral, and psychological changes were always interconnected. Biblically, receiving gifts of the Spirit was always connected to psychologically experienced meaning, joy, peace, love, and other psychological-behavioral gifts. Those value discernments enabled the disciples to recognize the resurrected Jesus—the "fullness of truth," who brought (according to Xavier Léon-Dufour) the "fullness of joy" (John 7:13).[11] This is in agreement with our conclusions stated in section 20.6, that a living faith must lead to a biblical joy.

The essence of what we shall call "transempirical rationale" in ecumenical reasoning aims to apply the above drafted biblical logic—paramount in the reasoning of the disciples in communicating spiritual truth by spiritual words—into the modern theological and faith vernacular and practice. Simply formulated, the purpose of such rationale in theological reasoning is to supplement classical (mostly theological, logical, and rational) reasoning with biblical, introspective, reflective, and meaning-oriented categories and criteria.

How would such a rationale work in practice? For the purpose of demonstration, first let us ask:

Could we turn around the above-drafted logic (that the "fullness of truth" positively correlates with the "fullness of joy") and could we then recognize the "good trees" from their "good fruits?" If we accept that living and teaching "fullness of truth" correlates with "fullness of joy," could we, from the biblical joy, peace, and love that true believers experience, discern our own theological correctness in interpreting God's revelation, or even know if we belong to the right denomination? Could we correlate from experiencing the "fullness of joy" our closeness to the "fullness of Truth—Jesus?"

Such validation in fact already occurs in everyday practice, consciously or subconsciously, and is externally and internally assessed. It occurs externally by what Robert Barnes describes in this way: "Look at the theorist first, to see if he knows how to live."[12] From one's whole lifestyle, spontaneous behavior patterns, words, and deeds, one's entire "project of life" is visible—whether he or she "knows how to live." Enabling others to experience biblical spiritual gifts, proves the correctness of one's "theological theory"—the correctness of one's biblical interpretation, adherence to the teachings of the church and the Spirit, and general closeness to Jesus. Jesus himself proved that he possessed the right theory by "knowing how to live." If we, people of faith, really are the "salt of the earth" (Luke 14:34) and the "light of the world" (Mark 4:21-24), then our lifestyle is the best evidence that we correctly understand the message of Scripture.

Internally, the correlation between awakened faith and the consequent experience of joy, peace, love and other gifts is even more evident in the subject's transempirical recognition. The behavior, as well as self-disclosures, of biblical and historical exemplary Christians demonstrate that these Christians did painfully or joyfully experience the difference between that which separates us and that which brings us closer to the ultimate meaning of human life: God. Such a pattern could be abstracted from the works of the classics like the *Confessions* of St. Augustine,[13] *The Interior Castle* by Teresa of Avila,[14] *Ascent of Mount Carmel*[15] and *Dark Night of the Soul* by John of the Cross,[16] and in the writings and lives of more contemporary mystics like Don Bosco, Maximilian Kolbe, or Vincent de Paul. Progress in our closeness with God is always corroborated by gifts of the Spirit, while spiritual gifts (and especially gifts of faith) confirm and strengthen the union with God; that is how this cycle of transempirical logic turns in correct recognitions.

Our primary tool in our sensorial-scientific and cognitive functioning is logic. Our confidence in the reliability of logic is so great that in everyday life what is non-logical is immediately rejected as false. Transempirical logic in faith discernment functions similarly reliable and trustworthy to scientific logic. That which is not corroborated by the resonating of the almighty, eternal, and ultimate love of God within the believer's conscience, and that which is not substantiated by biblical joy, optimism, power, or peace, is consciously or subconsciously rejected in faith discernment as dissonant, insecure, or mistaken. Inversely, biblical and spiritual gifts corroborate faith and are among the essential criteria of a correct relationship with God.

How reliable or trustworthy can such discernment be in theology?

We noted that true biblical joy cannot be faked. The criterion of true transempirical recognition is the reflection of God's almighty, eternal, and ultimate love within a believer's conscience. This criterion has true validity. The term "validity" in this context means that biblical joy truly measures what it is intended to measure: the believer's experience of his or her closeness to God. Everyday experience proves that giving up discipleship inevitably leads to loss of union with God. Nevertheless, as we noted previously, where it is possible to be mistaken, there true recognition is also possible. Thus, if it is inevitable to be painfully estranged from God due to a mistake in faith, then accurate recognition of God is also possible by being his disciple, and a lasting self-deception is impossible.

But how would transempirical reasoning work in practice when attempting to take a new look at historical conflicts between various Christian denominations?

As history and contemporary life prove, sometimes even God's people can be deceived or mistaken in the wisdom of knowing how to live biblically. Such deception can sometimes temporarily succeed. However, what can never succeed is lasting self-deception. The reflection of peace, joy, forgiveness, benevolence, or Christ-like love cannot be internally faked. Thus, the purpose of this rationale is not to judge others, but oneself. This is the reason that it is emphasized that the rationale is introspective. Even though we all have a conscious or subconscious impression about the correctness of the theology of others, or knowledge of how to live, the purpose of this rationale is to assess oneself—how close one is to the "fullness of truth"—by introspectively and reflectively (i.e., transempirically) assessing one's own progress towards a "fullness of joy."

Based on the above discussion, we can summarize our answers to questions like: Which is the correct interpretation of Scripture, the true denomination, or the right theology among the many that every believer is confronted with in our time?

According to the transempirical, introspective/reflective theological criteria proposed here, the right theology, correct interpretation of Scripture, or the true denomination are confirmed by the receiving and experiencing of biblical gifts of faith.

Thus, those believers whose conscious and subconscious theological logic and way of thinking selects, confirms, and corroborates the interpretation of Scripture or theological teaching that promotes discipleship and a real, lasting, and increasing experiential union with the invisible God as authentic, are able to demonstrate "knowing how to live biblically."

As noted, biblical joy, peace, and love as criteria of closeness to God, if correctly understood and applied, can never be in contradiction to the requirements of the Scriptures, church teaching, and what we called the universal standards of Christian faith! Rather we may imagine both inside an "angelic circle," where adherence to universal standards of faith enables biblical joy, peace, and love, while the experience of biblical joy, peace, and love confirms the correctness of the understanding of the universal standards of Christian faith. Through this process, the previously discussed transempirical rationale is one important criterion, but not the only criterion of adhering to Christ's teaching! Personal theological discernments focused on experiencing and helping others to experience biblical peace, love, joy, meaning, and ultimate meaning may help to avoid the main handicap of spiritless logic and legalism. Unfortunately, replacing the law of love with legalism is the most efficient "God killer" in his people. The main task of the rationale we are discussing is to avoid this hazard.

Such a rationale in theology may help avoid the pitfall of the Pharisees and answer the needs of postmodern society submerged in a chaos of faiths. It may help focus on the essence of Christ's teaching: adherence to the biblical law of love.

22.8. Respecting the "Human Condition" in Ecumenical Practice

At the start of my studies in theology, an introductory presentation was given to students, affirming that theology is not a "religious free association course," (meaning that we could not pass exams merely by echoing back religious buzz-words and clichés instead of demonstrating true knowledge). Thus, theology is a science, using known historical, ethnological, archeological, hermeneutical, philosophical, biblical, and other facts in gathering knowledge about God.

A good example of such logical theology is the example of St. Anselm. The theologian Walter Kasper wrote the following about him:

> Anselm of Canterbury (1033-1109), the father of Medieval Scholasticism, defined God as *id quo maius cogitari nequit*. God is "that than which nothing greater can be thought," and indeed that which is greater than anything that can be thought.[17]

According to Cross and Livingstone, Anselm's purpose

> was to establish the being of God solely on rational grounds. Ontological proof implied that one can prove God's existence to everyone by using overwhelming theoretical proofs independent of all previous experiences and superior to all other knowledge.[18]

Let us now observe St. Anselm's work from a different perspective.

St. Anselm wrote his *Proslogion* (in which he discussed his ontological proof) between 1078 and 1079. At the time of this work's publication, he was already deeply committed to Jesus. Thus, his trust in logic, philosophy, or the power of human thought did not convince him of God's existence and neither did the power of his ontological proof. Anselm's ontological proof is a post-factual justification, a philosophical, logical, and verbal substantiation of his previously experienced call by God and of his response to it. His experience of his call occurred by functions of purpose and was experienced mystically, reflectively, introspectively. He responded to it accepting discipleship and faith. Logical-scientific theology is essential for believers to clarify their own faith and theological stance, but it does not cause or substantiate faith independent of a transempirical rationale. Faith is always enabled by God's call (experienced internally) and by the believer's response to it.

Logical-scientific theology has many irreplaceable advantages but is not particularly useful in ecumenical theological disputes. It shifts one's attention from subjective reasons of mutual estrangement (the real problem) to exegetical, hermeneutical, practical, logical-theological problems. These latter seem unsolvable because of the real, underlying root of the problem: discourse expressed with an unloving, impatient, boastful, envious, etc., record-keeping attitude that causes a counterfeit interpretation of one's own conscience and of universal standards of faith.

An example of this occurred in 1054. The formal reason for the Great Eastern Schism that has divided Orthodox and Catholic Christians for almost a thousand years was the addition of one word—"Filioque" ("by the Son")—to the Nicene-Constantinopolitan Creed. The addition of "Filioque" addressed the crucial question of whether the Holy Spirit precedes the Father or the Father and the Son. However, according to the church historian August Franzen, "The dispute around the Filioque was not the essential question that caused the schism at all." The real reason lay in a deep competition and animosity between Rome and Constantinople that was "logified" in a cognitive-logical-theological dispute with an outcome that likely made only the devil happy. The disagreement was "unsolvable" and theological discussions were futile because the real problem was in a transempirical area that was logically and theologically "justified" by raising the Filioque dispute.[19]

Theology since the Middle Ages has become more scientifically, cognitively/logically oriented, eager to rationally substantiate, dispute, and overwhelm. As a consequence, even modern theologians often think, search, and talk in terms of "overwhelming proof," rather than engage in a mutual search for union with God. As history proves, such discursive theology is hardly able to deal with psychologically-caused ecumenical problems.

What may be the solution to these differences, stemming from and expressed in emotional, competitive, unloving attitudes?

The answer is a radical return to the roots! The reasoning of Saints Peter, Paul, or John, and other early disciples of Jesus was different from using such overwhelming rational/logical or exegetical proofs. Biblical authors did not care to "prove" God logically. Their strength, which came from a real moral power born from their union with God, inspired them to proclaim Jesus' teachings and to help their audience discern the natural law of the "almighty, eternal, and ultimate love" of God already written in their hearts and souls. The apostles verbalized the knowledge which is imprinted into every human being by the Spirit and justified and proven by biblical joy, peace, love, hope, and other spiritual gifts. The apostles' rationale enabled biblical peace, love, forgiveness, and above all, the joy of belonging to one common "sheepfold." Because of this, even two thousand years later, such biblical logic and argumentation has a genuine introspectively experienced power, as it corroborates the apostles' spiritual words with the spiritual truths that reside deep within every person. Among other things, the modern world needs a similar biblical joy-centered witnessing, whose purpose would not be to logically prove the opponents' mistakes, but that recognizes that ". . . whoever is not against us is for us." (Mark 9:38-40) This is especially valid if the real problem is an unloving, record-keeping attitude that spoils the interpretations of the conscience or applications of universal faith standards.

As the already-mentioned Decree on Ecumenism of the Vatican II Council emphasized, modern ecumenism requires adherence to St. Paul's recommendation in Romans 12:10: "Let us all love one another with brotherly affection, outdoing one another in showing honor," focusing not only on that which cognitively, historically, theologically, or exegetically divides, but that which unites as well. The love that St. Paul describes in 1 Corinthians 13:4-7 is the "panacea" (the Middle-Age concept of medicine that heals every ailment in every patient) for ecumenical problems. Accordingly, a future hierarchically-initiated grassroot movement in ecumenical theology will probably be based on a more inclusive transempirical theology. Cognitive/logical, theological, dogmatic, exegetic, or canon-law consensus will easily follow after a breakthrough, resulting in the promotion of common gifts of the Spirit, a tangible union with the invisible God psychologically justified by biblical joy, peace, forgiveness, and love of living in a common "sheepfold."

However, let us emphasize that all this does not mean introducing some arbitrary, self-made, hyperemotional theology to substitute for classical theological reasoning. Quite the opposite! The relationship between a classical and a transempirical theological rationale could be expressed by paraphrasing Frankl's analogy (used in a different context in *Ärztliche Seelsorge*). Theology can be seen as an orchestra, composed of many instruments. All the instruments have a particular place and role in playing a symphony. It would be a grave mistake if any instrument would attempt to replace others. But the role of every musician and instrument is to play only their own part.[20]

The role of transempirical theology ought to be seen similarly inside the "theological orchestra" which consists of exegesis, fundamental, moral theology, and other disciplines. Its purpose is not to replace but to supplement classical theology through the previously described "angelic circle." Thus, transempirical discernments like biblical hope, peace, and joy are made possible by a correct exegesis, fundamental, and moral theology, while biblical gifts confirm the correctness of exegesis, fundamental, or moral theology.

The new ecumenical trend toward re-integration may be the response to the critic who says, "Where there are many truths there is no truth." In topics in which ecumenical consensus already exists, Christian believers are like a mosaic: they are witnessing through the plurality of theologies to the same "fullness of truth." Biblically formulated, if "they drive out demons" in Jesus' name (Mark 9:38-40), and if—and the more—they share common elements of church-hood (as Vatican II formulated) and strive for the same kingdom of God, then in areas where ecumenical commonality is already established, there the entire "Christian mosaic" proclaims the message of the same high priest: Jesus Christ.

Today Christians cannot yet claim that they have achieved the unity that Jesus prayed for; however, with the Spirit's help we are already well on our way!

22.9. "The One Faith and the Plurality of Theologies" Document

As history books tell us, the thirty-year religious war in Europe between Catholics and Protestants ended in 1648 with a treaty in Westphalia that proclaimed a well-known and infamous solution: *Quius teritorium huius religio* ("Whose territory prevails, that person's religion prevails.") The ruler's faith denomination determined that of his people, and the religious map of Europe has become like the leopard's skin, divided into different denominations.

To dictate or indoctrinate one's denomination and faith to others was barely possible in 1648 and is even less possible today. In postmodern times it has become a fact of life to respect the responsibility of every believer to decide for him/herself how to respond to God's calls. As a result, a hypothetical "leopard skin-like" religious map would today be even more fragmented. Christians divided by justified or unjustified plurality represent a mosaic-like structure. The institution of Christianity is composed of different believers with different theological viewpoints and interpretations. Nonetheless they are united in common essential elements. Thus, every Christian is called to answer this question: how far can justified plurality go in interpreting Jesus' teachings?

The Protestant and Orthodox denominations embraced, from the very beginning, a relatively far-reaching diversity and plurality, while among Catholics a progressive development in this direction is observable.

According to Peter Nemeshegyi:

> It seemed natural in ancient and Middle-Age Christianity that inside the one faith of the church there existed different theological schools. Only from the end of the 19th until the middle of the 20th century was church leadership dominated by the concept that not only faith, but also theological teachings should be monistic (i.e., unified).[21]

Scholastic-Thomist theology was by and large accepted as the blueprint of such unification.

A shift pointing to the trend of the unification and centralization of theologies marked the Vatican II Council. According to Nemeshegyi, the new approach is paramount in the conclusions of the International Theological Council in 1972, published as *The One Faith and Plurality of Theologies* (*L' Unitë de la Foi et le Pluralisme Thëologique*). The subscribers to this document were, at that time, almost all of the best-known Catholic theologians, like Hans Urs von Balthasar, Yves Congar, Bernard Lonergan, Henri de Lubac, Karl Rahner, and Rudolph Schnackenburg, while the president of the council preparing the document was Joseph Ratzinger, who would later become Pope Benedict the Sixteenth.

Here are some points and conclusions from this document (in my own free translation) which are relevant to our topic. The unity and plurality in faith questions are based on the mystery of Christ that surpasses the ability of complete expression in any historical period. The truthfulness-orthodoxy of faith is connected to its historical journey, first from Abraham to Christ, and then from Christ to his second coming. Consequently, orthodoxy does not accept any particular system of thought but participates in the pilgrimage of faith and thereby partakes in the "self" of the church as well. The criterion for differentiating justified from unjustified plurality is the faith of the church, while the fundamental measuring instruments are Scripture and dogmatic definitions, especially those proclaimed by the synods of ancient times. While it is true that the current situation in the church encourages plurality, limits are set on plurality by the absolute truth that became approachable for us through Christ's ministry.

Can we now, in one sentence, define how far justified theological plurality may go?

Formulated in one sentence, justified plurality may continue as long as it promotes a true biblical discipleship and an increasing tangible union with the invisible God. From our transempirical, psychological-theological perspective, plurality may continue so long as it promotes the same principle, established by Jesus, of true discipleship, which is experienced through biblical joy, peace, and love, even despite Christ-like suffering.

Let us conclude with the words of the Pope John Paul II[22] writing about denominational plurality. He asks whether denominational divisions have been a "path continually leading the Church to discover the untold wealth contained in Christ's Gospel and in redemption accomplished by Christ?" He continues:

> It is necessary for humanity to achieve unity through plurality, to learn to come together in the one Church, even while presenting a plurality of ways of thinking and acting, of cultures and civilizations. Wouldn't such a way of looking at things be, in a certain sense, more consonant with the wisdom of God, with His goodness and providence?

22.10. Discussion

A reader could open this discussion asking: "What is the relationship between the concepts of faith and religion? Does religious and faith plurality jeopardize salvation?" Regarding the first question, Cardinal Joseph Ratzinger distinguished three possible positions: exclusivism, inclusivism, and personalism.[23] Exclusivism signifies the position "that Christian faith alone saves people and that other religions do not lead to salvation." Such a position was promoted by the famous Swiss reformed theologian Karl Barth. For Barth, religion "is the opposite of faith. For him religion is a network of human attitudes by which man tries to climb up to God; in contrast to that, faith is a gift from God." However, "it is not our activity that saves us but God's kindly power alone." Therefore, "Everything in Christianity that is 'religion' falls under Barth's condemnation." Also some great Catholic theologians, (like Romano Guardini), emphasized a radical difference between faith and religion.

Inclusivism was represented by Karl Rahner's teaching. According to Ratzinger, in Rahner's understanding:

> Christianity is present in all religions, or (putting it another way) all religions, without knowing this, are moving toward Christianity. It is from this inner direction that they derive their power to save: they lead to salvation insofar as they carry the mystery of Christ hidden within them.

Personalism promotes the idea that salvation does not come from Christ alone, but all religions are approved by God as unique ways to a person's salvation.

Is it possible to harmonize the three different positions?

In our understanding, a biblical faith of the people of God is the only and eminent gateway that leads to ultimate truth and union with the triune God. Religion is a broader and sometimes partially overlapping term. While faith is a relationship with the biblical God facilitated by the Spirit, soul, and conscience, religion signifies a fundamental human relationship with the revealed God, the unknown (not revealed) God or gods. Thus, every human relationship with God or gods is a religion. According to Ratzinger, a "Christianity without religion is contradictory and illusory." [24] On the other hand, all religions (revealed or not) are primarily a response to God's call. For example, for our ancestors who lived before revelation occurred, there was no other or better way of living in union with God and salvation than primitive beliefs, worship, and obedience to conscience, i.e., a religious reverence. Nevertheless, despite our belief that Jesus is the only way to salvation, He took up the cross for the sake of all humans; Old Testament (and probably also prehistoric) people are not excluded—if they adhered to their best, God-given way of salvation written in their hearts.

During the times that preceded God's self-revelation, plurality was "normal." However, after the faiths jeopardize people's relationship with the revealed God, though not so much in the case of responsible and well-informed individuals (who resist social indoctrination) as in the case of those who are easy to manipulate. The gradual losing of the relationship with the living God in these people happens in an "evil circle." On the one hand, insecurity in the area of religious and faith-related questions are the consequences of missing a tangible relationship with God. On the other hand, missing such a relationship causes and justifies the buzzword "Where there are many truths, there is no truth." This situation promotes a willful refusal to search for the demanding ultimate truth— Jesus Christ. It would be quite difficult to determine which came first: "the egg or the chicken." Either way, unjustified plurality in religions and faiths contributes to the erosion of a tangible union with the invisible God, and in turn, losing this relationship undermines one's knowledge of how to live in a genuine biblical relationship . . . and thus the evil cycle continues to turn.

However, let us also mention here that there is a chance that something positive may result from this sad situation. As the saying goes: "Ignorance will give way to truth more readily than will false knowledge." Plurality in religions and faiths inevitably leads to options and competition. Competition between denominations, paradoxically, may foster a religious revival, a "revival of right choice." It may revive the choice to return to a biblical church and lifestyle justified by gifts of faith in a way that has not been seen since biblical times.

The next question may be:

> In everyday language the term "church" is used in at least two different meanings: as the institutional church and as the biblical body of Christ. Which is the "true church" the visible and touchable, really existing institutional church or the ideal biblical one?

Let us first discuss this highly charged, prejudicial, "either-or" question from a theoretical perspective. Christian religious institutions exist with a purpose: to fulfill the ideal of Scriptural holiness promoting God's kingdom. Such a biblical/spiritual ideal influences the being and functioning of the institutional church more prominently than its blueprint or statute influences the functioning of any other institution or organization in the world. It is not worldly, biological, psychological, sociological, or economical principles, or a simple, Freudian pleasure principle, that determines what the institutional church stands for and teaches; rather, it is led by its goal of promoting God's kingdom/holiness. In fact, any religious institution is a true church to the extent that it mirrors its invisible essence as Jesus Christ's body. Even though it is invisible, the biblical church ideal is valid and real—spiritually and institutionally.

In practice, there may be a gap between the church's being a religious institution—"constituted and organized as a society in the present world"—and its ideal purpose: to be the mysterious "pillar and the foundation of truth" (1 Tim. 3:15) as well as the "gateway to Jesus" (John 10:1-10). However, if such a gap exists, then the problem is not with the reality of the ideal, but with the ideality of the institutional reality!

Let us now discuss the question from a practical perspective.

The visible and touchable religious institution is churchly to the degree that it expresses the church's tradition (established by Jesus, the Bible, synods, documents, other authoritative and authentic teachings), declared essence, and aforementioned purpose. Inversely, the church is not present (even if called "the church" in everyday language) in that which does not reflect and witness to Jesus' teachings, or in what contradicts biblical and declared principles of "church-hood."

For example, the writer Janos Erdody[25] described the murder that was committed in the Santa Maria del Fiore Cathedral in Florence, Italy on March 25th, 1478. The plan for the assassination of the rulers of Florence, Giuliano and Lorenzo Medici, was agreed upon in advance, and the signal to enact this plan was given by Cardinal Raffaello Riario by lifting Jesus' body in the ritual of transubstantiation during the holy mass.

The point is that the murder happened in the institution but not in the church itself.

Thus, the true church is what would remain if we subtracted the unchurchly and un-Christian elements from the institution, removing from it all behavior patterns that are alien to Jesus' teaching. By such an imagined experiment, we would come to the true visible and touchable essence: biblical faith and union with Jesus expressed through his body, the biblical church. This essence is like a "sheepfold" and "gateway" to Jesus. Paradoxically, even though invisible and untouchable, the ideal is real; it serves as a standard and ultimate model for religious institutions.

A step resembling the above-mentioned imagined experiment was undertaken by the American Catholic Bishops when priests who were perpetrators of child sexual molestation were released from the priesthood. By such a step, the institution became a step closer to Jesus, the "Fullness of truth."

Indeed, the debauched sinners released from the priesthood remain welcome and equally appreciated members of the church (which is a "holy institution of sinners"). Their membership in the church, however, is not enabled by their sin (estrangement of God), but on the one hand by Jesus' grace and mercy, and on the other hand by their faith and repentance.

We could compare the institution with an organism, or even better, with a personality. A human personality, despite being composed hierarchically of mutually (sometimes) competing structures (such as instincts and conscience), functions as an indivisible union: the person. As the human personality consists of indivisible sinful and holy constituents, so the church as an institution consists of churchly and unchurchly elements. Both are real; nevertheless, the task of the members of Christ's body is to ensure and enable the transformation of the institution ever more into the biblical church. The holy remainder in the above imagined experiment—the "body of Christ," the "sheepfold," and "gateway" to Jesus—should reach fulfillment in the entire institution.

A reader may next ask:

> If everything is happening according to God's plan, but modern "faith cacophony" is not his will, how, then, did such fragmentation of the body of Christ happen in the first place?

Not only God's will, but also that which he allows to happen occurs in the world. For example, God allows sin to happen, despite that it is not his will. Thus, despite the fact that unjustified religious plurality is not God's desire but mostly a consequence of humanity's sinful nature, God obviously allowed it to happen.

The next question may be:

> May I recall a true historical example that illustrates well the unreliability of personal discernment based on one's "free conscience," and even more of "introspective discernment" in faith questions?

According to Franzen, the so-called Anabaptists in the sixteenth century were labeled as enthusiasts because of their passionate zeal which was labeled irrationalism. They demanded, among other things, complete financial equality and the freedom to share their wealth amongst themselves. Led by Thomas Munzer and others, they conquered the city of Münster in Germany, and there established their community called the "New Zion." In 1534-35, troops opposing their ideas laid siege to the city.[26]

Munzer was convinced that God would protect the "New Zion" by making him invincible and by enabling him to catch artillery shells fired against the city walls. In the end, after heavy warfare the city was conquered and the Anabaptists were hanged around the church steeples to show everyone, even those visiting the city from great distances, that "true faith" was victorious in the city of Münster.

Obviously, the Anabaptists as well as their opponents discerned a strong spiritual meaning, fought for religious values, had optimism, power, zeal, hope, and trust, and were confident in God's approval. Most probably, many of them, whether conquerors or defenders of the city, felt even a "Godly joy." However, were the proponents really close to Jesus? If so, how was it that their Godly joy caused and confirmed un-Godly mistakes?

Note that not every meaning, and not every joy, is an expression of living in or building on God's kingdom. Practicing a completely worldly goal does not prevent the experiencing of joy. Probably Hitler, Mao, and Stalin also strove (in their reflections) for meaning and had joyful moments when fulfilling their objectives. Their joy was granted by their instinct or superego but explicitly not by the hyperego, soul, or Spirit. Everyone, even the greatest atheists and those intentionally or unintentionally destroying Jesus' church, find meaning, triumphal moments, and fun, but not biblical joy—not a resonation of the almighty, eternal, and ultimate love of God, within the believer's conscience as experienced by Christian believers!

The essence of Christian responsibility is not confusing biblical and profane joy (as happens in religious fanaticism) and being aware that "no servant can serve two masters" (Luke 16:13). It seems that participants in the above recounted story tried to do just that. However, the joy, peace, and "love" that Mammon gives—that euphoric feeling of victory and resistance or of almost omnipotent elation and grandiosity—which the protagonists in the above example probably enjoyed—cannot replace or be mistaken for God's biblical joy, stemming from genuine and lasting peace, love, forgiveness, and humility.

A reader could now ask:

Isn't self-assessment and self-validation of the believer's conscience, of his or her progression in faith, measured by received "biblical gifts of faith," the most unreliable, partial, and self-deceptive of all possible criteria of closeness to God?

Indeed, a self-deception or misinterpretation is possible in any kind of discernment. Even Saul or apostles like Peter and Thomas were free to attempt to deceive themselves. No human being and no believer is free of mistakes, transgressions, and sin. However, at the same time nobody is free to avoid the consequences of a mistake, sin, or self-deception. We are free to make choices but not to choose the consequences of our choices! In practice, this means that every believer can estrange him or herself from God. However, no one can avoid experiencing the adverse consequences of losing the living union with God. In the long run, the fullness of biblical joy, love, and peace will not confirm a mistake, sin, or self-deception in faith.

A relativistic and populist watered-down interpretation of Jesus' teachings, along with slavery to the world and Freud's pleasure principle, inevitably cause the loss of the believer's behavioral connection to God and the loss of the experienced biblical joy of living in union with him.

The next question could be: "Are Christians belonging to different, or even strange denominations, able to experience biblical love, peace, and joy as I am?"

For the most part, biblical joy does not follow an "everything or nothing" path. Believers of different, even very different, theological viewpoints can experience biblical joy, but they are not all equally joyful and equally close to God! There is a difference in the quality, extent, and intensity of biblical joy present in believers, which depends on how close they are to the biblical God.

The real pitfall and danger lies in self-deception, to which every one of us is prone. If we believers seriously scrutinize the dynamics and balance of received "gifts of faith," we realize the difference between progress and regression in our relationship with God. We learn to notice the difference between how our relationship with God ought to be and what it ought to feel like, and what a less ideal closeness to him is. Regular self-examination and soul-searching may show us the direction in which we ought to grow. Again, however, the purpose of such a self-assessment process is not to assess others' but one's own progress or regression in one's union with God.

The next question could be: "What are the implications of the 'transempirical theology' to everyday practice for every Christian?"

Let us illustrate the answer by summarizing the play, *Nathan the Wise*, written by the controversial writer Gotthold E. Lessing. According to P. S. Kohan, the story goes that the ship belonging to the Jewish merchant Nathan was captured by the fleet of the Muslim ruler Saladin.[27] Nathan was brought to Saladin to be interrogated. The Muslim ruler asked a highly-charged political question: Which religion is the true one— Judaism, Christianity, or Islam?

To avoid taking a stand, the non-Christian but worldly-pragmatic Nathan told a story. In one family, it was customary for the father to give a ring to the son who was most loved by both him and God. Thus, the ring traveled from generation to generation. One father, however, had three sons, and he could not choose the best among them. Therefore, he ordered two additional identical rings from a goldsmith and secretly gave all three of his sons a ring.

After his death the sons discovered what had happened. They took the rings to a goldsmith to find out which one of them had the original. But the rings were so similar that no determination could be made. The sons then took their rings to a wise rabbi asking the same question: "Whose ring is the original?"

After a while, he responded: "It is impossible to determine which is the original ring. But the one among you who, by his lifestyle, honesty, and unselfishness proves that he is the best, that one has the original ring."

What is the message that we should take from this story?

It is not to advocate egalitarianism among religions (as Lessing proposed) because religions in fact are theologically not equal. No other faith besides Christianity contains ideals like Jesus' blessings in Matthew 5:1-12. No other faith demands forgiveness and love even towards one's enemies. No founder or leader of a religion ever sacrificed his or her life for the spiritual well-being of others as Christ did. No other founder of a religious community rose from the dead, and no other religion on our planet demands an attitude and behavior similar to that which Christianity requires of its believers. In short, the Christian faith is unique indeed, "quite other" than any other belief system. Therefore, true Christians ought to be "quite other" than those belonging to other religions as well.

The message of *Nathan the Wise* is, we emphasize, that a particular Christian should prove that he or she possesses the "original ring"—the correct theology, the correct interpretation of Scripture, and true discipleship. He or she should do so not only theologically—through words—by using logical, exegetical, doctrinal proof, but also by living biblical discipleship, making real a Christ-like meaning, joy, and love, as well as by living in genuine union with Jesus. It is not only the case that the right theology enables the receiving of gifts of faith; the reverse is also true: possessing many gifts of faith proves the correctness of a theology.

The last question can be:

Does not proclaiming the subject's conscience as reliable in questions of faith open a Pandora's box for all kinds of self-created interpretations and deceptions which would then be proclaimed as "legitimate expressions of faith" if they are justified by biblical meaning, joy or hope?

We can reply by reversing the question as follows: "Can biblical meaning and joy justify and verify a self-created, arbitrary, or mistaken interpretation of conscience?" Every one of us probably senses that the most likely and sensible answer is no, but let us substantiate why.

Let us illustrate the correlation between true discipleship and the receiving of biblical gifts by a profane example.

Perhaps the treatment of alcohol and drug addiction is the most difficult task in psychotherapy. The best results I ever saw were achieved in an almost military setting. As a precondition of receiving the treatment, it was required that patients run a distance akin to a marathon. On the first day, nobody was able to run more than a few hundred yards, but with the help of strong motivation, everyday training, coaching, and singing "No pain, no gain . . . no pain, no gain," the patients were trained to prove that the impossible is indeed achievable. The "gain" could not be achieved by some self-deception, imagination, or indoctrination but only by "discipleship"—overcoming resistance against achieving "gain by pain," which was then psychologically rewarded by "gifts" like self-confidence, power, courage, determination, increased self-esteem, and a feeling of competence needed for later healing. Note that without really working out, or by deceiving or faking it, one cannot gain fitness, strength, endurance, determination, or self-confidence.

Something similar, but also quite different, occurs in the dynamics of faith.

Although God's gifts are offered to everyone, only people at least ready to hear God will realize them. The gifts of faith are connected to biblical discipleship, in the sense that only true faith enables true gifts of faith such as true biblical love, peace, joy, and others. Thus, if true biblical gifts of faith are received, then true biblical discipleship is present as well!

Let us now focus on the essential difference between attaining profane gain, and receiving biblical joy, peace, and love as God's gifts: Spiritual gifts are always the sovereign and free gifts of God. Thus, faith is not a give-and-get relationship; biblical "gains" are not an achievement or causal consequence like the gain in the previous profane example. However, much more important to the Father than the result is the effort one puts into becoming his disciple. According to Andrew Murray, "The master judges by the result, but our Father judges by the effort," and even failure in one's effort to become a disciple of Christ "does not always mean fault."[28]

On the other hand, if one does not accept and enter into a self-denying biblical discipleship, then communicating with God and receiving his gifts are impossible. Discipleship may be demanding, but, as Matthew 11:30 reminds us, Jesus said "For my yoke is easy, and my burden is light."

Notes

1. Bertrand Russell, *Why I am Not a Christian and Other Essays on Religion and Related Subjects* (New York: Simon and Shuster, 1967), 12.

2. Viktor E. Frankl, *Ärztliche Seelsorge* (Wien: Franz Deuticke, 1965), 18, 59.

3. Martin Reardon, "Unity," in *The Oxford Companion to Christian Thought*, ed. Adrian Hastings, Alistair Mason, and Hugh Pyper (New York: Oxford University Press, 2000), 732-33.

4. Austin Flannery, *Vatican Collection Volume I; Vatican Council II: The Conciliar and Post-Conciliar Documents* (Northport, NY: Costello Publishing Company, 1992), 799-812.

5. Austin Flannery, *Vatican Council II Documents*, 357.

6. August Franzen, *Kleine Kirchengeschichte* (Freiburg: Herder Bücherei, 1968), 5.

7. August Franzen, *Kleine Kirchengeschichte*, 69.

8. Ferenc Szabo, *Az Ember es Vilaga* (Roma: Self-published, 1969), 175.

9. Adrian Hastings, "Schism." in *The Oxford Companion to Christian Thought*, ed. Adrian Hastings, Alistair Mason, and Hugh Pyper (New York: Oxford University Press, 2000), 643.

10. Adrian Hastings, "Schism." 643.

11. Xavier Léon-Dufour, *Rjecnik Biblijske Teologije,* ed. Josip Turcinovic (Zagreb: Krscanska Sadasnjost, 1988), 343.

12. Robert Barnes, *Theories in Counseling* (Abilene, TX: Department of Counseling and Human Development, Hardin-Simmons University, 1994), 2.

13. Augustine, *The Confessions of Saint Augustine* (Grand Rapids, MI: Christian Classics Ethereal Library, 1999).

14. Teresa of Avila, *The Collected Works of St. Teresa of Avila* (Washington, DC: Institute of Carmelite Studies Publication, 1976).

15. John of the Cross, *Ascent of Mount Carmel* (Grand Rapids, MI: Christian Classics Ethereal Library, 2000).

16. John of the Cross, *Dark Night of the Soul* (Grand Rapids, MI: Christian Classics Ethereal Library, 2000).

17. Walter Kasper, *The God of Jesus Christ* (New York: Crossroad, 1992), 4.

18. F. L. Cross and E. A. Livingstone, *The Oxford Dictionary of the Christian Church* (New York: Oxford University Press, 1997), 1035-37.

19. August Franzen, *Kleine Kirchengeschihte*, 151-53.

20. Viktor E. Frankl, *Ärztliche Seelsorge* (Wien: Franz Deuticke, 1965), 26.

21. Peter Nemeshegyi, *Egy Hit, Sokfele Teologia* (Budapest: Magyar Papi Egység, A Tavlatok Melleklete, June 1998), 2-9.

22. John Paul II. *Crossing the Threshold of Hope* (New York: Alfred A. Knopf, 1994), 153.

23. Joseph Ratzinger, *Truth and Tolerance: Christian Belief and World Religions* (San Francisco: Ignatius Press, 2004), 49-52.

24. Joseph Ratzinger, *Truth and Tolerance*, 49-52.

25. Janos Erdody, *Requiem Firenceert* (Budapest: Szepirodalmi Kiado, 1980), 63-64.

26. August Franzen, *Kleine Kirchengeschichte*, 232-34.

27. P. S. Kohan, Istorija Zapadnoevropske Knjizevnosti (Sarajevo: Veselin Maslesa, 1967), 285-90.

28. Andrew Murray, *With Christ in the School of Prayer* (New Kensington, PA: Whitaker House, 1981), 52.

Chapter 23

The Transempirical and Faith Dynamics in Religious Fanatics

23.1. Defining the Problem

In the Old Testament, one finds examples of when God was "silent," or even when he turned his back on religious people. To a religious Jew, God's "silence" caused an experience of great pain and suffering. We assume that such was also the experience of the disciples after Jesus' death. For them, in their disappointment and "adjustment disorder with depressed mood" (as a modern psychiatrist would classify their experience), not only Jesus, but also God, was "dead" in the sense that they did not feel his love, consolation, or hope. They had lost everything.

Medieval mystics described a very different silence on the part of God. They explained the experience as one in which a believer is unable to experience Jesus' closeness. Such inability caused real desperation in the one suffering such a feeling of abandonment. But this experience (of the dark night of the soul) extends far beyond the Middle Ages. One recent saint complained that praying may sometimes feel like talking to a brick wall. In fact, we all may sometimes have the feeling that God is distant and detached from us, excluding us from living in union in and with him.

Is God really distant and silent at times?

We can already hint at the fact that God, as the ideally loving Father, is never silent. However, when we only hear God's seeming silence, then as Andrew Murray noted,

> We should not look for the answer in our feelings. All spiritual bless-
> ings must be received, that is accepted, or taken, in faith. Believe that
> the Father gives the Holy Spirit to His praying child. Even while I
> pray, I must say in faith: "I have what I ask, and the fullness of the
> Spirit is mine."[1]

Through faith, believers, even when not hearing or feeling God's responding, know that God is not silent. As noted, such knowledge is often more important, substantial, and evident to believers than the feeling of God's absence.

In fact, God is never really silent. What really is the case is that we are not always willing to hear him, or would like to hear a different response. Mostly, in the following sets of circumstances, God may be perceived as silent:

1. Perhaps every one of us has experienced this—God's virtual silence has an educative purpose when by his perceived silence, God edifies his disciples teaching them about himself—what he is like. We will discuss this topic in more detail in the fourth part of this book.
2. God's calls are not heard by those who consciously and willingly exclude themselves from God's love, such as agnostics or atheists, whose transempirical recognition processes we will discuss later.
3. God may be silent to religious fanatics as well. Their common characteristic is a very intense pursuit of worldly goals, masked by fervent quasi-religious activity. Consciously, and much more so subconsciously, they falsify God's biblical image and consequently suffer from his "warning silence."

The religious fanaticism that we are now discussing is often combined with at least some schizoid, sadomasochistic, or obsessive personality traits and is, phenomenologically, often an extreme form of unjustified religious plurality. In the case study that will follow, we will be able to test in practice the theoretical concept that we discussed in the previous chapter, namely, that trust in the Ultimate truth (Jesus) is the precondition of ultimate joy.

23.2. A Case Study: Ivan the "Terrible"

Let us begin our discussion with this question: "If the religious fanatic does not reveal it, then how do we know that God is "silent" in his relationship with that fanatical person?"

To better visualize the problem of denial and deafness to God's warning silence, first let us visualize, and after that analyze, an historical example of fanaticism, or mistaken faith.

According to historical data, the Russian emperor Ivan Vasiljevich (1530-1584) made territorial gains on the western borders by defeating the German knights and the united Swedish, Danish, and Polish armies, and then began conquering Siberia. By his internal policy, he modernized Russia, importing German and Italian scientists, artists, and craftsmen, and promoted trade with England.

According to Vladimir Stanojevic,[2] the emperor's castle was in Aleksandroskij kvart near Moskva. Ivan followed a strict daily schedule: a morning mass before dawn, a mass again at 8 a.m., then Bible and meditation after the worship. After breakfast, his daily routine continued in the torturing hall. Ivan tortured and killed with his bare hands. His victims included the entire noble Adashev family. First, the mother witnessed the execution of her husband and five sons, then she herself was tortured and executed by Ivan. Another time, while Ivan rang the church bells, approximately 12,000 people were kept in frigid temperatures until they froze to death. In punishing the city of Novgorod for separatism, he ordered his troops to kill, rape, and loot the town for five weeks. About 60,000 men were killed, and their wives and children drawn below the ice of the nearby river.

Ivan's lifestyle was in some aspects deeply, but certainly falsely, religious. He may have mistakenly understood his holy duty before God, the state, and his people to be one of exterminating the enemies of Russia. The Soviet movie producer S. Eisenstein celebrated him as a visionary patriot, almost a holy man, a suffering martyr fighting for the highest ethical purpose: the greatness of Russia. However, his own people gave him the nickname "Grozni"—(meaning "thundering" or "terrible"). He is known in history as "Ivan the Terrible."

23.3. Can Self-Deception Excuse Evil?

There is a saying: "The one who is screaming is the one whose house is burning." Thus, the "terrible" person is one who is suffering from fear, anger, aggressive impulsivity, and who feels threatened and hated. However, could it be possible that Ivan did not discern that he was becoming infamous for practicing a non-biblical lifestyle and that he was convinced that he was doing his best despite causing streams of blood to flow all around him?

As history, and even the example of the apostles proves, it was and is always possible for individuals to be mistaken in their faith. It is possible that Ivan or other religious fanatics misunderstood the Bible, that they misunderstood the requirements of their Spiritual-psychological joint, or even that they misunderstood God's call. Ivan the Terrible and the disciples such as Thomas and Peter—just as every modern man or woman—could and did make mistakes in what they believed.

However, as we concluded in the previous chapter, it is not possible that any of those who were mistaken in faith misconceived their own internal experience, thereby missing out on a truly close union with God, as well as biblical gifts of the Spirit and gifts of faith. There is no way (even for a religious fanatic) to imagine or experience by some self-deception biblical forgiving, love, peace, or joy, if one is revengeful, bloodthirsty, hateful, and suffering from paranoid fear.

Ivan the Terrible could have made mistakes in his faith discernments. But he could not have experienced, by means of any mistake, actual communication with God in the form of lasting biblical hope, trust, peace, love of his enemies, forgiveness, or steadily-increasing biblical joy. Psychologically, if Ivan could find and enjoy biblical peace, love, forgiveness, or other gifts of faith then his bloodthirsty personality would probably have been better controlled and he would not be remembered by his nickname "Grozni." God's silence towards Ivan (actually God's withholding of spiritual gifts and gifts of faith), perceived by Ivan consciously or subconsciously, was a consequence of his value-deafness. Unfortunately for him and his victims, he did not understand why God appeared silent to him.

Receiving (or not receiving) God's gifts of joy, peace, and love is what prevents one's moral discernment from making mistakes such as those of Ivan the Terrible. However, as Ivan's example proves, these conditions are not absolute safeguards, but are effective only if one is self-critical enough, and ready to truly appreciate God's messages. Such attitude is, however, often lacking in fanatics. Contrary to healthy self-criticism, fanatics are caught in a vicious circle. Ivan's behavior was a reaction to a perceived silence on God's side, in the sense that because of not having perceived peace, love, and forgiveness, Ivan became "Terrible," and, because he was "Terrible," God was virtually silent in the sense that Ivan did not realize that God was speaking to him through his silence.

What is the safeguard against possible religious fanaticism, irrationalism, and misunderstanding of God's communications?

The problems of religious fanatics, contrary to popular opinion, are never caused by too much faith or too much respect for God, for their soul or for their conscience. On the contrary, they are caused by their disrespect of these realities!

Ivan the Terrible respected his superego, but neglected his hyperego. His horrific deeds were motivated by fear, fueled by lust for power and an ambition to exterminate his enemies and make Russia a great power, not by a desire to build God's kingdom or to search for *zoe* through union with God. Fanaticism always sours by replacing obedience to the hyperego with conscious or subconscious obedience to the superego. This happened in Ivan's case.

What is the main conclusion, valid for every one of us, that we can draw from our discussion of religious fanaticism?

For me, it is one awesome insight. Small cognitive mistakes in sensorial-scientific discernments in our everyday or professional lives can cause grave and lasting consequences (like a traffic accident). We are aware of this and take great care. However, we may have the impression that in relationship to God—almost everything is permitted without consequences. From the discussed example, and also the case studies in the next chapter, we discern that such irresponsible freedom is a dangerous illusion. Ethical self-deceptions which may appear to us as insignificant and trivial can have detrimental consequences in our relationship with ourselves, others, and with God.

Notes

1. Andrew Murray, *With Christ in the School of Prayer* (New Kensington, PA: Whitaker House, 1981), 57.

2. Vladimir Stanojevic, *Tragedija Genija* (Beograd: Nolit, 1976), 85-95.

Chapter 24

Are Non-Religious People Really Less Happy Than People of Faith?

We have discussed many examples of how biblical joy correlates with true faith. Let us now test the opposite: are non-believers unhappier and do they live more meaningless lives than people of faith?

24.1. Suffering from an "Acute Loss of God"

If we wanted to analyze the feelings, self-experience, and mood swings of Thomas or the disciples on the road to Emmaus in the period after Jesus' death, we would find little biblical information.

The Apostle John does not provide a detailed psychological profile of Thomas before the revival of his faith; nevertheless, we discern an apathetic caution beyond his skeptical outburst, by now very familiar to us: "Unless I see the nail marks in his hands . . . I will not believe it" (John 20:25).

Although the Bible does not give an account of what the disciples went through psychologically before their meeting with the resurrected Jesus, we can, with a little empathy, imagine how they must have felt. They probably felt similar to how we would feel if suddenly we lost God. Let's try for a moment to position ourselves in a situation in which, almost in an instant, we would lose our loving and supporting Lord. With that, our faith would be gone as well. We call this all-devastating, almost annihilating experience "suffering from an acute loss of God." In this situation everything would collapse in the blink of an eye.

This condition of acute loss of God was what the apostle Thomas likely suffered as well. His value-blindness and suspicious resistance against the news that could have given him new hope was the source of his suffering. Furthermore, his firm refusal even to explore the possibility that the report of Jesus' resurrection might be correct was probably the consequence of his mind's preparedness to defend him from any new pain which the unrealistic hope of seeing Jesus again would cause.

If Jesus had not worked his miracle on Thomas, or on the disciples on the road to Emmaus, such a state of mind would not have lasted forever. Sooner or later, depending on the strength of his personality and the future events in his life, Thomas would acquire a new meaning to live for and perhaps his personality would, at least outwardly, return to the way it had been prior to Jesus' crucifixion. Most probably he would eventually come to terms with his new reality and would therefore be able to accept the loss of his old purpose, values, hopes, ideals, and faith.

In this stage of recuperation, he would probably be able to deal with concrete problems in his life. He would find new goals and establish a new existence. In the stage of full recovery, he would even appear to be a happy man. He would smile, joke, and laugh. He would enjoy friendships, celebrations, love, and work.

However, if Thomas had made all of these strides, but had not regained his faith, he would have permanently lost his previous markers of being special and worthy: having a unique meaning, mission, and value in life, the warm feeling of being accepted and loved by God, and his own union with Jesus Christ.

24.2. Transempirical Dynamics in People Transitioning From "Naïve" Belief to Atheism

William J. Hague, in *Evolving Spirituality*, cites Alfred. N. Whitehead's three levels of estrangement from God.[1] Whitehead's first stage, "God the void," is similar to that which we call "naïve belief."

"God the void," a phrase describing immature or naïve faith, signifies a belief system where sensorial-scientific or cognitive proofs are used to justify faith. This kind of belief is also characterized by an expectation of personal and cognitive gain: "If I am good, you will reward me." One's success, wealth, health, and longevity are seen as proof of God's love. In their personal lives, naïvely religious people wage a war on two fronts. They fight against losing their relationship with the (cognitively) non-existent God and are often engaged in a fervent search for proof—miraculous signs and mysterious healings—as both testament to God's existence and justification of their faith.

Moreover, naïve believers defend themselves against meeting the biblical God who requests discipleship and rewards faith with spiritual (but not always with lucrative or worldly) gains and rewards. In practice, naïve belief is often an uphill battle to defend or preserve a compromise between the two mutually exclusive images of God and god in one self-created, non-biblical framework.

Paradoxically, a slow estrangement from, or a quick disappointment with, the naïvely-imagined god often makes or breaks the relationship with the true God as well. It will make the relationship if one is learning from one's disappointments and maturing in one's faith. However, if disappointment with God breaks not only one's naïve faith but causes deafness to God's calls and makes one lose one's interest and longing for God in general, then the whole dynamic takes a different direction, evolving from naïve belief to agnosticism. Such estrangement from God by many millions of ex-naïve believers is probably the greatest challenge confronting Christianity in the twenty-first century.

Norman Geisler quotes Jean P. Sartre as follows:

> My family had been affected by the slow movement of de-christianisation that started among the Voltaire-ian upper bourgeoisie and took a century to spread to all levels. [So] I was taught . . . the Gospel and catechism without being given the means for believing.[2]

As Geisler notes, "Outwardly he continued to believe, but he thought of God less and less."

Sartre's last sentence is significant. Naïve believers are, as was Sartre, according to his self-revelation at an early stage of their journey, in a relationship with God but one who seems to them impersonal, indifferent, or even absent. Nevertheless, at this early stage God is still ambivalently respected as the "almighty creator and sustainer of heaven and earth," an ultimate, dreadful, and magical unknown power. The respect for such an almighty, silent, and distant God is primarily a kind of awe, a mystical fear, a mixture of uncertainty, and angst expressed in the compulsion to perform rituals. Such a person procrastinates in making his or her ultimate choice against God. A peculiar hesitation and status quo is kept. However, because such a person lacks experience of God's love and perceives God as "silent," he or she becomes increasingly apathetic, frustrated, and unhappy because of God's "absence." Slowly, the need to contact the biblical God decreases, while the anger against the "silent God" intensifies.

In the next stage of this seamless transition, by those already estranged from the church but still in some way religious, God may be imagined as a Higher Power to whom in situations of despair and disappointment they can more or less turn for help and hope. This relationship, however, is not permanent and does not involve a true commitment. It is characterized more by a magical and mystical fear than by trust; what trust there is lasts only as long as the need for hope and help exists.

For those who have not only lost faith, but are estranged from any kind of religion, the biblical God worshipped and experienced by Christians has only one prominent weakness: "He does not exist."

"By killing God," according to Ferenc Szabo, the agnostic "murders something in him or herself as well."[3] The more the modern agnostic is alone and lives in this world apart from God's kingdom, the more he or she loses evidence of biblical meaningfulness, joy, ideals, hope, love, confidence, and other gifts of faith. The agnostic lives without the reflection of God's almighty, eternal, and ultimate love within his or her conscience, mind, and heart. This is how the demonic cycle begins, trapping the non-believer. With the loss of biblical happiness, affection, and optimism—evidence of being loved by God—life becomes devoid of ultimate meaning, and this experience causes more estrangement from God. This in turn causes renewed suffering and bitterness and again deepens the feeling of estrangement, absurdity, and angst. Thus, the demonic cycle continues in every internal, non-sensorial experience of the agnostic (and atheist). Such meaninglessness confirms to those experiencing it that a caring God, the ultimate meaning, does not exist at all.

Let us illustrate this process in Figure 24-1.

Such a dynamic is often the beginning of the third step in becoming estranged from God: atheism.

We can summarize the transempirical dynamic in the atheist's mind as follows. There is nothing more painful than the experience of feeling left out and unable to gain admittance into God's kingdom. Often this unbearable feeling is the motivator behind the turn towards militant atheism, which is really an attempt by the subject to convince him or herself

Figure 24-1

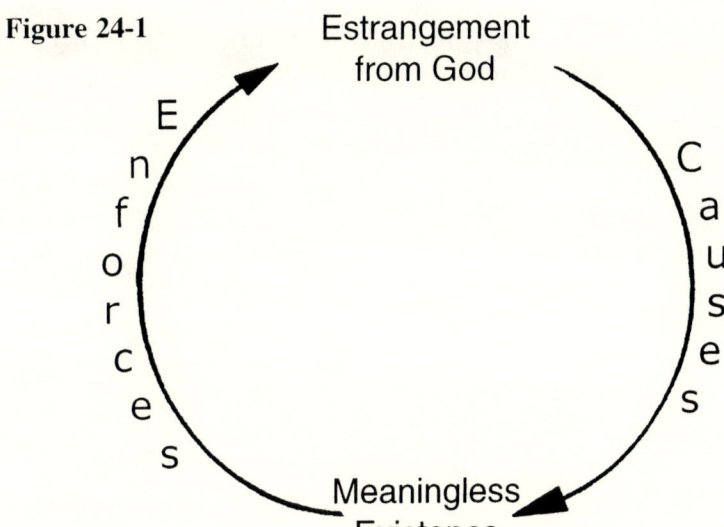

that: "if I don't experience God's goodness, then you (the believer) can-not possibly experience it, and neither you nor I lives with God in God's kingdom."

Faith in God, the church, and the faithful in general, all become enemies for the militant atheist, because the former have something that the latter would like to have as well. As a final consequence, the image of God evolves into what, according to Hague, Whitehead called "God the enemy."

John Stuart Mill's rationale portrays well the psychology of such an atheist:

> In everyday life I know what to call right or wrong, because I can plainly see its rightness or wrongness. Now if a god requires that what I ordinarily call wrong I must call right because he so calls it, even though I do not see the point of it and by refusing to do so he can sentence me to hell, to hell I will gladly go. (Quoted by M. Peterson, W. Hasker, B. Reichenbach, and D. Basinger[4])

Mill was a sophisticated liberal thinker. He was not an atheist but a proponent of god. His god, an intelligent person, gave nature its laws, but is uninterested in humankind and does not care for our well-being, because if he were God, he would not allow evil and suffering. Mill was in some aspects similar to those whom the apostle Paul characterized in 1 Corinthians 2:14: "The man without the Spirit does not accept the things that come from the Spirit of God, for they are foolishness to him. . . ." People like Mill shut themselves off and are therefore deaf to the requirements of the soul, as well as value-blind to "things that come from the Spirit of God." As a highly-intelligent person, Mill had to be aware of his own ultimately meaningless existence, fundamental powerlessness, and personal fundamental worthlessness—of being only part of nature without God. This utterance of his came from being ultimately unloved, from surviving without ideals and fundamental optimism, from feeling abandoned in a cool, indifferent, God-less world.

Such suffering from a meaningless life, without a union with the almighty, eternal and ultimate love, we may call suffering from a chronic loss of God. This has nothing to do with a diagnosis or with the approach of some mental disorder. In fact, it is worse than that. Its main symptom is a deep philosophical, existential, and religious denial, a special kind of apathy tinged often with an overly self confident euphoria which has the task of masking the suffering.

The suffering of atheists fuels their suspicion of those who have what they would like to enjoy: namely, union with the almighty God. This is, in our time, an anti-Christian attitude almost equal to that of Saul's before his conversion.

24.3. "Suffering from a Chronic Loss of God" as a Social Problem

At one psychiatrists' conference, a referent characterized our time precisely, while simultaneously taking a little poetic liberty. He said that in our country in the past hundred years, depression has doubled, juvenile suicide has tripled, divorce quadrupled, single parent families quintupled, drug abuse in children sextupled, . . . and so on.

These behavior patterns, comparable to acting out, are triggered by genuine suffering and are not only connected to poverty, joblessness, or neglect, or limited to what were once classic problem cases. They are present among the affluent and successful young who, while blinded by a mirage of omnipotence and invincibility, live in a perpetual race for more fun and demonstrate an over-reactive interest in increasingly deviant and bizarre sexual activity, living "on the edge," street-racing, extreme sports, and drugs, all of which they attempt to use as defenses against suffering from a lack of ultimate meaning. They choose an idol—a thrill—to live for, instead of an ideal that could fill their need for ultimate meaning. It may seem that such suffering is not expressed equally in every stratum of society and by identical "acting-out" patterns. However, although the problem may manifest itself differently in various social strata, it is factually present in every cell of our societal matrix.

What is causing this trend of general meaninglessness in our culture? The World Health Organization defined the idea of mental health, as quoted by Stojiljkovic as "a state of complete physical, psychical, and social well-being, and not merely an absence of sickness or ailment."[5] Accordingly, healthy people need more than the absence of mental disorders as categorized by the DSM IV; they need internal evidence of psychological well-being that does not depend solely on social circumstances or financial success.

On what does internal evidence of well-being depend?

Fritz Rotschild wrote that "man knows God because God knows man, and man's purpose is to live in such a way that he may be worthy of being known to God."[6] Indeed, in a biblical understanding, every human being is worthy to be known by God. The problem is rather that atheists and agnostics consider God unworthy to be known. Is the reason for this phenomenon a psychological one that agnostics and atheists, like Adam and Eve after eating the fruit of the forbidden tree, live in such way that they feel unworthy to be known by God?

Being human is based on a fundamental relationship to God. Complete psychic and social well-being cannot be achieved without having a satisfactory communication with God. A lack of such relationship does not signify a sickness, but something that has a worse spiritual prognosis than do delusions, illusions, hallucinations, or other psychiatric disorders. It signifies a threat of losing life—real, biblical life in and with God.

On the other hand, paradoxically, only the hope of everlasting life can give meaning to biological life. If such meaningful hope and hope of ultimate meaningfulness of one's existence are lacking, then the quality of biological and psychological well-being becomes reduced as well. The rise in acting-out behavior, depression, and divorce rates is only the tip of the iceberg.

In my experience, the real culprit that causes people to suffer from a meaningless life lies in reductionism; people see themselves as nothing more than "human animals" rather than spiritual beings created in God's image and likeness. The loss of a vital connection with the Almighty, the sense of being unworthy of being known to God, bring with it painful feelings of powerlessness, despair, and worthlessness, as well as feelings of having been abandoned and being unloved and unlovable: a feeling similar to that of Adam and Eve after their estrangement from God.

It may seem that the lives of believers and non-believers are equally pleasant, joyful, and happy in everyday life situations. However, the balance of joy we are concerned about here is something other than enacting a euphoric mood. It entails having a courageous, peaceful, and optimistic attitude; discerning value in life despite suffering; overcoming unavoidable pain; defeating disappointments by faith; and accepting suffering for others and Jesus joyfully, as described in 1 Peter 4:12-13. Therefore, at the end, the "joy balance" of a believer who lives in an ultimately meaningful way is more positive than even that of an euphoric non-believer whose life is ultimately meaningless.

In everyday life situations, agnostics and even atheists do not joke, smile, or laugh any less than do people of faith. They are not less joyous, cheerful, or euphoric than are believers. They enjoy earning and managing wealth and take pleasure in luxuries and holidays and in food, drink, and merriment, just as much as some believers do. They, however, do not enjoy the lasting joy of living in union with the almighty, eternal, and ultimate love of God experienced by believers; they live and accept only that life which the Greek translators of the Bible called *bios* but have no *zoe*.

But if the introspections of non-believers are so sad, and if they really suffer meaningless lives, how then is it possible for them to preserve and maintain an image of abundant joy so successfully? On the one hand, the suffering caused by a meaningless existence manifests itself in the widespread proliferation of what we could call "as if" happiness and joy.

The Austrian philosopher Leo Vaihinger published a book titled *The Philosophy Of As If* in 1911.[7] We may summarize his ideas:

> In modern societies we are friendly with each other "as if" we genuinely loved; we work "as if" we were committed to our job, bear children "as if" life had a purpose, and many people go to church "as if" they had faith. On the surface, they are "as if" joyful.

In extreme cases, the "as if" joy takes a grotesque expression. One of the symptoms of a florid tetanus infection is a peculiar, painful smile on the patient's face, caused by spasms of the facial muscles. This smile was named after the Greek mythical hero Sardonicus, who smiled before he was executed. It is commonly known as the Sardonic smile. I feel that something similar is occurring in affluent Western societies, within some individuals suffering from a meaningless life but demonstratively enacting excessive fun, pleasure, and joy.

There is another peculiar phenomenon which is abundantly socially present. One can openly ask most agnostics and atheists many questions about the most intimate and private details of their lives, except one: God. Their religious indifference, or more exactly their religious apathy/resistance against seriously confronting God, is part of a defense mechanism that enables one to experience a seemingly carefree and joyous mood and lifestyle. Religiously apathetic people defend themselves against that which they ultimately and urgently need—closeness to the living God—by two widespread defense and defiance mechanisms: repression and denial.

Repression is the refusal to acknowledge consciously particularly painful, tormenting facts. It is a type of selective forgetting that happens mostly unconsciously. By means of repression, such unpleasant contents are not erased, but exist and threaten the self (ego) from the subconscious mind. Denial entails the suppression of the troubling contents of the mind from consciousness into the subconscious mind as well. However, such suppression occurs more or less consciously, as in the statement: "I know, remember, and feel that, but let us drop the issue."

On first glance, it may seem that repression and denial are almost perfect, impenetrable defense mechanisms. Nevertheless, they are classified in psychiatry as unsuccessful or unsatisfactory. The unavoidable fear and angst of approaching aging, slowing down, sickness, and being confronted with dying and death, often change the way of thinking and feeling of even a hard-core atheist. Angst surrounding unavoidable death (which is a taboo in our society) seems to melt even the armor of denial and repression. It is a strong call to God, that small talk, fun, vanity, and euphoric joy—all of which are encompassed in a lifestyle mimicking TV advertisements—cannot answer or solve. On the contrary, angst and fear signal the approach of death, the last opportunity to break out of denial caused by suffering from a chronic loss of God.

According to one story, a desperate mother of a boy who committed suicide weeps, "My son, my son, what have you done? God will not forgive you for this!" However, a minister responds to her as follows:

"Oh, rest assured; for he repented a thousand times during his fall from the bridge into the river."

According to Ferenc Szabo, this "moment of total freedom and total conscientiousness" as Rahner describes it, though situated at the very end of life, holds, according to Boros, a "central position in life."[8] When nothing of the world is any longer important, one can experience God's love in an encounter of the most pristine nature. Moreover, in this moment, truly unlike any other, one may make the ultimate choice: Christ. Hopefully this is the last earthly experience for agnostics and atheists and for religiously indifferent and apathetic people.

How urgently do we need the Spirit's help in causing a religious, spiritual, and mental revival today? At a psychiatrists' meeting I once attended, someone in an informal conversation told the joke, "There is an urgent need to redefine the criteria of mental health as soon as possible, no later than 2019 in fact."

"Why so soon?"

"Because after that time there will be no normal people left."

I assume that we all feel justified in making a prophetic conclusion to this anecdote: This will be so unless humankind turns to living in union with the living God and regains the self-experience of being "worthy of God's love!"

24.4. Case Studies

Let us discuss a few examples to illustrate the mentality and behavior pattern of people suffering from chronic loss of God.

In 1974 after completing my medical studies, I started to work as a young physician in the hospital of my hometown. One of my first patients was a young man who had attempted suicide. He was lying unconscious. I fought hard to save his life. After two or three hours, he finally opened his eyes. I expected him to say, "Thank you for saving my life." However, he surprised me with the questions, "Why did you save me? Why must I live?" I was astonished. I did not know how to respond to such questions. My medical education taught me how to preserve human life but nothing about the purpose of human life. I realized that for my patient this was paramount.

The patient was admitted to the psychiatric ward but was discharged after a short time because he was not depressed. Shortly after his discharge from the hospital, he made a second suicide attempt. This time, he succeeded. I was consumed by the puzzle of how I should have answered his startling questions.

I realized that he was not just an important medical case study, but also a philosophical, and even more so, a pastoral/theological one. According to medical criteria, my patient was not depressed—he was not sad, was not functioning more slowly than usual, did not lose his interests and activities, had no guilt feelings, and had no weight loss or sleep problems. Nor was he suffering from any psychiatric disorder. He needed something that neither medicine nor psychology could provide. Only faith could have helped him to discern an ultimate meaning worth living for. Without at least some faith, at least some relationship with the Ultimate, without some purpose in life, he did not have the tools that would motivate him to endure. He was not unsuccessful, poor, or humiliated. He was not suffering from catastrophic pain or disappointment, but the element that was missing from his life was a tangible, mystical, sacred union with the almighty, eternal, and ultimate love. If he had had this, he would have had everything.

We will examine also the case of an 18-year old girl, sexually abused, abandoned by her parents, and brought up in foster care. She was referred to my office because of sexually intrusive attacks using sexualized language, touching and fondling. These were performed against boys and girls indiscriminately, as well as teachers and the police. When asked about the reasons for her behavior, she bluntly explained that she wanted to become a "popular girl" at her school. When asked what this meant, she explained that popular girls are intentionally mean. For them "good is bad, and "bad is good." Being popular means a "free," daring, aggressive, and sexualized lifestyle.

In therapy, the young patient came to understand that she is free in choosing her behavior, but not the consequences of it. She understood and agreed that because of her challenging behavior, she would be ostracized by society. However, despite describing herself as a very spiritual person, she could not agree with one interpretation: that she was suffering because of attempting to live in such way that she would remain unworthy of being known by God and that therefore a forgiving and loving God seemed unworthy to be known by her. She almost succeeded in turning her life into a disastrous self-fulfilling prophecy.

Finally, there is an example I consider extraordinary. It is an accepted fact in medical and psychiatric literature that not every suicidal person is mentally disordered. In this context Stojiljkovic quotes the known example of the Lafargue couple.[9] Paul Lafargue, the son-in-law of Karl Marx committed suicide in 1911, leaving behind an interesting explanation of his actions. It may be translated as follows:

> Healthy in mind and body, I am killing myself so that inevitable aging does not take from me, one by one, all of the joys and pleasures of life, so that it does not paralyze my energy, so that it does not restrict my will, or make me live without physical and mental abilities. Many years ago we promised each other that we would not survive the age of seventy. . . . And I have prepared the right device: an ampoule of cyanide.

Was this a mentally disordered person? Probably not. Was he a trusting, hopeful, satisfied, and mentally fit person? No, that he likely wasn't.

He suffered from something that medicine cannot treat and that the DSM IV does not classify as a sickness: namely, frustration and angst at the slow but unavoidable loss of everything he was living for—his integrity, health, wealth, and the love and support of his wife, friends, and his referent group. He was probably even more frightened of the meaninglessness and hopelessness of imminent death. He was suffering, as Frankl would call it, a meaningless life.

However, would the transempirical discernment of true biblical gifts of faith and of communication with God in general, be of sufficient help to prevent suicide?

Being both a psychiatrist and a psychologist, I can ascertain that it indeed is the most eminent and sufficient preventive factor; there exists nothing stronger.

Notes

1. William J. Hague, *Evolving Spirituality* (Edmonton: University of Alberta, Department of Educational Psychology, 1995), 69-79.

2. Norman L. Geisler, *Baker Encyclopedia of Christian Apologetics* (Grand Rapids, MI: Baker Books, 2000), 235.

3. Ferenc Szabo, *Az Ember es Vilaga* (Roma: Self-published, 1969), 57.

4. M. Peterson, W. Hasker, B. Reichenbach, and D. Basinger, *Reason and Religious Belief: An Introduction to Philosophy of Religion* (New York, Oxford: Oxford University Press, 1991), 105.

5. Srboljub Stojiljkovic, *Psihijatrija sa Medicinskom Psihologijom* (Beograd: Medicinska Knjiga, 1975), 160.

6. Abraham J. Heschel, *Between God and Man* (New York: The Free Press, 1959), 16.

7. Hans Vaihinger, *Die Philosophy Des Als Ob* (Berlin: Reuther & Reichard, 1911).

8. Ferenc Szabo, *Az Ember es Vilaga*, 183-84.

9. Srboljub Stojiljkovic, *Psihijatrija*, 122.

Chapter 25

Revisiting Thomas' Conversion

We began the second part of our book by trying to analyze the apostle Thomas' return to faith based on the biblical description of the events according to John 20:24-29. Let us now use our psychological and theological knowledge to once again weigh Thomas' behavior.

1. Before the crucifixion and death of Jesus Christ, the apostles' belief was limited to a mixture of sensorial and non-sensorial knowledge—they could see, touch, and communicate with Jesus. The disciples witnessed Jesus' miracles, success, greatness, and divine power. It is possible that Jesus met the expectations engendered by Micah's and Zechariah's descriptions of a miraculous, almighty, invincible Messiah. As long as the Messiah's presence was visible and touchable, Thomas had no evident problems with his faith, as well as with his conception of the Messiah.
2. Then came the big disappointment. Jesus Christ was humiliated, tortured, and killed. From that point on, Thomas could only rely on his transempirical, non-sensorial knowledge just as we do today. However, his spiritual evidence and certainty were weak. As fear and disappointment grew, it became harder to accept that this is how things are in God's kingdom. Comfort, optimism and a solution did not come easily, and a crisis began in Thomas. He suffered from what we called an ". . . acute loss of God."
3. A new cycle made its first turn inside of Thomas. The disappointment, fears, and lack of success began drawing Tho-

mas away from God. This would have resulted in his suffering a meaningless existence, which would in turn have sped
his drawing farther away from God. Then the whole thing
would rotate again, faster and faster, irresistibly. It would
probably end in what we called "suffering chronic loss of
God."

4. This is the time when Thomas got the news about Jesus'
    resurrection, but made the mistake, understandable from our
    perspective, of wanting to see and touch Jesus. Thomas was
    looking for cognitive proofs and probably gains, in justifica-
    tion of his "conditional belief." By requesting proofs regis-
    tered by his functions of existence, Thomas presented him-
    self as a "naïve" believer.

5. The second time Jesus Christ came, he offered Thomas the
    proofs he sought. But, would Thomas have believed if he
    had to put his hands on Jesus' scars? Probably not. Can we
    substantiate our assumption?

Faith and experience of God are strengthened not by sensory information, but by internal evidence: biblical love and happiness that come
from finding and fulfilling the ultimate meaning and value in one's life.
Despite seeing and touching, Thomas would probably not have believed
what he saw and touched, firmly rejecting as "impossible" what his senses
registered.

Thomas was disturbed by false "knowledge"; he was missing the
inner certainty that Christ really was raised from the dead. It was impossible for him to believe without this inner certainty, because seeing becomes merely a "sensation" in such circumstances and not a "perception." The problem was that Thomas was value-blind.

We may suppose that psychologically or more exactly "experientially," something comparable might have happened to Thomas as did to
me during a visit to Paris. I was living in Canada while my daughter was
a university student in Texas. She visited Paris on a holiday trip. During
her visit, as a guest at a professional convention, I also stayed for a
period in Paris. My daughter Julia called home before her trip to Paris
and found out about my presence in the city, but I did not know about her
trip. This is how our peculiar, and for me quite unexpected, meeting
happened: I was talking to some colleagues at the reception hall at the
convention when suddenly, about 80 or 100 yards from me, a young girl

caught my attention, as she was waving to me. At first I didn't care about it, but when she started to walk and run towards me with big swings of her arms, I didn't know how to behave. "What is she doing? What is going to happen here? Is she really waving to me?" I thought to myself, and I was just about to turn away when, in a split second, I recognized my daughter Julia!

Obviously, I had seen my daughter Julia, but in spite of seeing her I only saw her without perceiving and recognizing her as my daughter. Why not? Because I "knew" that my daughter was on the other side of the world, thousands of miles from me. Consequently, my false knowledge—that it could not be Julia—made it impossible for me to recognize her. Only when she was very close to me did I correct my false knowledge and admit, "This is really Julia!"

6. Jesus' intervention occurs at this point, which will give faith back to Thomas by a mysterious inner awakening that will let Thomas see joy, and new meaning and value in his life. As we concluded earlier, Jesus' intervention (Thomas' personal communication with Jesus) occurred through Thomas' soul. From there, Jesus' message was discerned through Thomas' conscience, influencing his whole personality. Thomas' soul, touched, and empowered by Jesus' intervention, was not merely part of Thomas' mind creating, together with the rest of Thomas' mind, his personality. After his conversion, Thomas' soul (acting through his conscience) became the essential motivator of his personality and of his behavior. Thomas became a pneumatic, spiritual person.

How did Thomas experience this change in his personality? Jesus' intervention in Thomas' soul created in him a "new soul and conscience." Through the reactivated spiritual-psychological joint working in him, Thomas experienced Jesus' intervention in his conscience and mind as a new challenge, goal, and an ultimate purpose. As a consequence of the discernment of his soul and conscience, Thomas recognized freely and responsibly what "I ought to do." All of Thomas' psychological functions (his thinking, feeling, remembering, will, attention) were unified in this internal experience of recognition. Then, Thomas freely and responsibly did what he "ought to do": he revived his union with Jesus and in so doing, he became a pneumatic, spiritual person.

Clearly it was God who reached Thomas through Jesus' intervention. But what he had done to Thomas' soul, and how he had done it, remain a mystery that cannot be explained or conceived psychologically. This is the grace of God. Psychology can register the transformation in Thomas' behavior, it can speculate as to which of his mental functions Thomas experienced Jesus' intervention, but it is incapable of understanding, explaining, or imitating what Jesus did and what caused such profound change in Thomas.

John's account of Thomas' conversion is significant in one more way. The biblical story described by John and other gospel writers did not happen only once in history. The dynamic of faith described in Thomas' story continues to repeat itself, like many other biblical examples, in every generation of believers. In every man and woman of faith, a similar process is repeated, involving God's call or intervention in some form and the believer's response to it. The human response to God's call, which we call faith, is always the consequence of such Godly calls and interventions.

We modern believers are Thomas' successors. Our faith is the consequence of God's call and intervention in our own lives. There is, however, one difference between Thomas and us.

John 20:29 reads, "Because you have seen me, you have believed; blessed are those who have not seen and yet have believed." We have never seen or touched or spoken to Jesus and were not his disciples like Thomas was. We are those who believe without seeing Jesus. We have to realize God's presence solely through our non-sensorial and transempirical functions. The crucial question for us now is whether our discernment of purpose is powerful enough—whether we have the same compelling and clear mystical and empirical evidence that Jesus' disciples had.

Let us postpone answering this question until after we discuss how modern people experientially communicate with the cognitively invisible God. This will be our task in the fourth part of the book.

Part 4

Living in a Tangible Union with the Invisible God

Chapter 26

The Need for New Apologetics

For thousands of years the main pillar of knowledge about God, for the Hebrews, was the Scriptures. They did not try to explain God's self-revelation philosophically; rather, fidelity to the Scriptures and Temple was the paramount criterion of orthodoxy.

With the appearance of Christianity, a new need arose. Vittorio Messori noted in John Paul II's *Crossing the Threshold of Hope*, "Faith certainly is a gift, a divine grace. But another divine gift is reason." Thus, a Christian "believes in order to understand"; but he or she is also called "to understand in order to believe."[1] Encouraged by the need that this exhortation expressed, early Christianity introduced first Greek, then later Christian philosophical teaching into theology. Logical argumentation became utilized in understanding, in explaining, and especially in defending revelation and faith.

But how efficient is philosophical reasoning in modern and postmodern practice?

26.1. The Power and Powerlessness of a Speculative Apologetic in a Postmodern Mental Climate

As we discussed earlier, St. Anselm attempted, by one universally logical, irrefutable argument to prove the existence of God once and for all, independently of all previous human knowledge, information or subjective bias.

Is Anselm's proof rationally correct?

Yes, it is.

Is Anselm's proof convincing to most modern people?

No. That it is not.

The problem is that lay people are neither aware of, nor interested in St. Anselm's proof, nor are they touched by its logic.

A similar weakness is also present in philosophical approaches to the matter of God's person. Kasper writes,

> Various modern definitions attempt to combine the abstract philosophical and the concrete existential dimensions. According to Paul Tillich, God is "what concerns us ultimately." According to Rudolph Bultmann he is "the reality determining all else." Gustav Ebeling calls God "the mystery of reality," and, as noted, Karl Rahner speaks of God as "the holy mystery."[2]

All of these definitions are accurate. All of them pinpoint some important characteristics of God. Are, therefore, the insights of philosophers really what postmodern lay people need to hear to be able to establish a relationship with God?

Actually, modern people and society disregard speculative thought and adhere to positivism in areas where sensorial-scientific methods are not only powerless but even incompetent. In this context Pope John Paul II talks about positivism as a "modern school of suspicion" and states, "If we put ourselves in the positivist perspective, concepts such as God or the soul simply lose meaning. In terms of sensory experience, in fact, nothing corresponds to God or the soul."[3]

In our time, not only does "faith search reason" as in Anselm's saying, but even more, agnostic and positivist "reason challenges faith." The thoughts of philosophers are correct and their arguments sound, but postmodern people's thoughts are influenced by "schools of insecurity and relativism" much more than by Scholastic philosophers.

In relation to this let us ask if God's existence can be proven philosophically to people brought up in schools of relativism and agnosticism?

Before we answer this question with a "yes" or "no," let us consider a few examples illustrating the futile pattern of how proofs and counterproofs are exchanged in apologetic and philosophical discussions. According to Ferenc Szabo,[4] the German existentialist Martin Heidegger asked why extant things exist, or for that matter, why anything exists at all. Szabo's answer to this is that if there would ever be a time when nothing existed, then no thing would ever exist. Since something exists now, something always has had to exist. Thus, existence or being has an absolute reason. As noted earlier the term "absolute" in this context, is that which in no way depends on the existence of any thing other than itself—and God is such a Being. Thus, if something exists now, then the Absolute Being, God, always had to exist.

Logically, this seems a perfectly summarized substantiation of God's existence. However, agnostics will then come up with counter arguments, such as the idea of "Eternal Matter." The philosophy course I had to study while living in my communist native country was titled *The Eternal Matter*, suggesting that the Absolute is not God, but the uncreated, ever-existing, and ever-transforming infinite matter, able by its own laws of functioning to increase or decrease its own complexity and produce the universe, earth, life, animals, plants, and philosophically-thinking humans. God obviously has no place in this concept of eternal matter.

But a Christian apologist might ask: Is it philosophically possible for matter to be eternal in time? Is it not absurd and impossible to imagine time as eternal?

If we imagine the history of the created universe and life on earth, as well as human history, as regulated only by natural cause-and-effect principles, then nothing could be shortened or set aside in a chain process in which every previous event necessarily and unavoidably causes the next effect. In that case, time would then be like the mileage on the odometers of our cars. Unavoidably, after having come one mile, we would come two, three . . . one-thousand miles. An observer may ask "Why does my odometer show the total mileage that I've traveled right now, for example 2007 miles?" The reason is that independently of how quickly or slowly you drive, you had to start driving sometime, and you reached the particular mileage (of 2007) right now. Thus, the time it took to reach the point of "now" had to begin sometime. If the time, (the "big bang") had begun a thousand human years earlier, then our "mileage" (i.e., history) would be one-thousand years greater. Or if the time would have begun a thousand years later, then we would now live in the year 1007. Thus, philosophically, it is impossible to imagine time without a beginning.

Does such logic defuse the idea of eternal matter? Does it prove that a creation from nothing, at the beginning of time, had to happen, that God the creator has to exist?

The answer is again "yes" for believers, and "no" for non-believers.

Was then Sigmund Freud right, when he, (according to Wilhelm Bitter) proclaimed that "religion is impossible to prove or disprove"?5

Does this mean that we ought to abandon philosophy or philosophical reasoning in theology?

Faith is not a mere irrational feeling. Believers also need knowledge, as well as logical and rational reasons to trust God. Since science is specialized in researching only particular aspects of the natural world (like physics, biology or astronomy), it is unable to answer ultimate questions of human life, such as the mystery of being, the universe, epistemology, mind, soul, death, suffering, freedom, responsibility and many others. In order to address these mysteries, we need to adopt a perspective that considers the entirety of human knowledge and revelation. Thus, only a "God of philosophers" answers the ultimate questions of human existence in a rational language.

Consequently, the answer to the question of whether we should abandon philosophical thinking is categorical; we can not and need not abandon philosophical reasoning which St. Paul has already introduced into the Christian tradition, but we need to supplement it. What does classical apologetic philosophy need to be supplemented with? First, let us consider what is missing from classical philosophical arguments.

When searching for the God of philosophers, a positivist is in a sense like a small child. For instance, a ten-year-old child can be very smart, very intelligent, and very well informed about the sexual problems of grown-ups, and he or she can know a lot about relevant literature and theory. But is that child really able to understand what he or she is talking about? No, not at all, until the time when he or she is grown and mature enough to experience sexuality for him or herself. Knowing something theoretically, from books or second-hand information, is different from experiencing it firsthand.

This example emphasizes the insufficiency and impossibility of a solely speculative knowledge of the living God. The lives of every one of us are shaped not just by logic, scientific or psychological insights, but also by personal experiences. Without experiencing him, we are unable to really "know" God. "Knowing God" means living in an experienced, tangible union with him. Living in such a union, however, has some unavoidable prerequisites: discipleship, experiential closeness, and openness to his non-sensorial experience—not only cognitive proofs that philosophers and apologists offer. This applies also to the greatest minds that humankind has ever produced.

For example, as translated by Wilhelm Bitter, Freud described himself as a "completely Godless Jew, rejecting religion in every solution and dilution."[6] In addition, Paul Vitz notes one more relevant observation: "Nowhere did Freud publish a psychoanalysis of the belief in God based on clinical evidence provided by a believing patient."[7] It is impossible to understand or know introspective discernments (like love) without experiencing them. But even more impossible is it for one who has never experienced union with God to know him. Thus, agnostic, atheist, or positivist professionals, despite all their knowledge are unable to feel, know, or experientially recognize the value of what faith or God really is. Freud was no exception.

In contrast, believers, theologians and apologists fight the same problem with the opposite approach when trying to logically explain or prove God's existence to agnostics and atheists, without being able to first allow them to experience God's calls for themselves. The philosophical proofs provided by ancient scholastics, and by modern thought from thinkers such as Karl Rahner, Bernard Lonergan, or Paul Tillich, seem coherent, logical, and rational enough, but they are convincing to, and known only by, believers.

We are not the first to recognize this problem. According to Ferenc Szabo, Blaise Pascal already realized the weakness and limits of purely rational philosophical reasoning that is disconnected from "reasons of the heart."[8] After God's existence is logically proven, as in Heidegger's argument, many agnostics, even when compelled to agree with such logical proof, will sooner or later have the feeling that somehow they were misled. Their resistance and doubt will reemerge, and their previous unbelief will be restored.

According to Pascal, something other than mere logical reasoning determines one's faith convictions. A spontaneous experiencing or feeling of God's presence, much more convincing than a merely rational way of thinking, must be substantiated beyond rational, philosophical argument. An experienced relationship, an irreplaceable personal communication, is what makes or breaks faith.

At the aforementioned *Eternal Matter* course, the lecturer proclaimed that the idea of eternal matter explains and can do everything that God the Creator allegedly did. On first glance, I was speechless. However, one student of strong faith and intellectual prowess had the courage and brightness to respond, "Yes, eternal matter can do everything that God can, except be a loving person."

He hit the nail right on the head. To communicate and live in dialogue and union with Eternal Matter is impossible. To be a loving, empathetic, helpful, forgiving, merciful person; to give peace, joy, hope, meaning, and other gifts of the Spirit "quite other" than worldly gains and more powerful than worldly suffering, would be impossible for Eternal Matter.

From similar experiences, we realize that post-modern people need not only a scientific/logical/philosophical apologetic. They also need an apologetic of a genuine, tangible, personal communication with the living God. The main disadvantage of the "God" that philosophers talk about is that it is similar to the rational, impersonal, scientific "Eternal Matter" that materialists espouse. In truth, God is not merely a logical fact as demonstrated by St. Anselm, but a person, a friend whom the people of today may need to feel and experience!

If we would like to avoid the pitfall of a classical apologetic, which evokes in people the feeling that Pascal described, then our new apologetic should be based not solely on functions of existence, logic, or philosophical thought.

26.2. How to Feed on the Experience of Believers

Let us now return to square one. How can one be made to experience things like a believer if one has no communication with God at all?

We mentioned previously that according to Millard Erickson, the Austrian theologian Karl Rahner described the idea which we can rephrase here as "anonymous Christians."[9] We would here borrow his idea, to encourage the impossible: non-believers to "borrow faith." Thus, we who are believers encourage religiously indifferent readers to at least provisionally be unbiased and attempt to think, feel, listen, and discern their own conscience and soul as do Christians in their search for absolute standards of joy, unselfishness, morality, and the ultimate meaning of human existence. We encourage agnostic readers to have empathy and to be open to ideas and experiences of the absolute, the almighty, eternal, and ultimate love—which is who God is from a Christian understanding. We invite atheist readers to be open to the absolute, and the standards of natural revelation—which are already somewhat familiar to them—and to be, for the purpose of this discussion, a "provisional Christian." This attempt may enable the provisional borrowing of the believer's experiences and faith, as well as the discernment of a transcendent, ultimate and absolute attractiveness to faith, and, ultimately, to God himself.

On the other hand, as stated, we will not focus only on speculation or on a "God of the philosophers," but will research the mystery of how the "quite other," invisible, and transcendental God becomes experienced and present to people of faith. However, here we are again confronted with a difficulty: Two or three billion Christians have two or three billion different relationships with God, and different faith dynamics.

We can express the variety and uniqueness of faith in every believer by adapting an old medical saying and paraphrasing it. Originally the saying was "If you treat two patients with anxiety disorder in an identical way, with at least one of them you made a mistake." Let's paraphrase this to fit our topic as follows: "If you describe the same dynamics of faith in two people, then you were mistaken about at least one of them." Every one of us is unique. God's calls addressed to one person, and that person's ensuing responses, are unique as well. There is no general description of faith that is valid for everyone.

Thus, a critic could object that the relationship to God we are discussing here is only one kind, possibility, or variant of belief, but not the only one. That critic would be right. Despite that, the dynamics of faith in believers are comparable at least in the following three characteristics.

1. That faith in and union with God are not perceived sensorial or scientifically, but always have a transempirical-experienced component.
2. That God always makes the first call to humans, and faith is the human response to God's call.
3. That union with God enables a reflection, which always grants biblical love, hope, joy, peace, and/or other gifts of the Spirit.

If we define the common denominator we will focus on so broadly, then the spiritual-psychologically-experienced dynamic of faith we are going to discuss here will not be one of many possible religious experiences, but the one with which (at least to some extent) every Christian belief is commensurable.

Our next task is to clarify the discernment of God's calls, so that prospective believers may search for, respond to, and be known by him.

Notes

1. John Paul II, *Crossing the Threshold of Hope* (New York: Alfred A. Knopf, 1994), 28.
2. Walter Kasper, *The God of Jesus Christ* (New York: Crossroad, 1992), 5.
3. John Paul II, *Crossing the Threshold*, 33.
4. Ferenc Szabo, *Az Ember es Vilaga* (Roma: Self-published, 1969), 78.
5. Wilhelm Bitter, *Psychoterapie und Religioese Erfahrung* (Stuttgart: Ernst Klett, 1965), 63.
6. Wilhelm Bitter, *Psychoterapie*, 54.
7. Paul C. Vitz, *Faith of the Fatherless: The Psychology of Atheism* (Dallas, TX: Spence Publishing Company, 1999), 8.
8. Ferenc Szabo, *Az Ember es Vilaga*, 97.
9. Millard J. Erickson, *Christian Theology* (Grand Rapids, MI: Baker Book House, 1995), 310.

Chapter 27

What Might We Understand by God's Call?

As theology students, we learned about the German philosopher Ludwig Feuerbach. We could summarize in two sentences the message of his book *Das Wesen des Christentums* (*The Essence of Christianity*), thus: God did not create humankind in his own image. On the contrary, humankind created God in its image and placed him in the heavens.[1]

Nowadays, it seems that Feuerbach is rarely read or quoted, but his famous (or rather infamous) proposition has remained alive. To a great many modern agnostics, it seems that it is entirely up to us to seek God or to reject him, to decide whether to become religious or not. Therefore, in the agnostic's mind, religion is a matter of personal choice, or a question of social, cultural, or personal preference, learning, or conditioning.

The difference between people of faith and non-religious people begins at this point. According to the biblical texts that we discussed in previous chapters, we are not the ones who must initiate the search for God; rather, God is the first to seek us and call us to him and constantly puts thoughts of him into our minds. Faith is, in fact, the believer's acknowledgement of and response to God's call. However, what are God's calls and how are they addressed to humans?

27.1. Ultimate Philosophical Questions Connected with God's Personal Calls

Already at the very beginning of the Old Testament Scriptures, in the book of Genesis, we find two names for God which correspond to two, to some degree, distinct descriptions of his personality. God is sometimes called Yahweh, (in a tradition called accordingly "Yahwist ") and sometimes Elohim (in a tradition called "Elohist"). The Elohist tradition describes God as an ultimately powerful and glorious, a transcendental and "Quite other" Deity who cannot be compared to anything we can know or imagine. Opposite to this, the Yahwist tradition presents a more empathetic, warm, and caring Deity. He is a God of his people and the Hebrews belong to Him. We might compare the Elohist description with a more rational understanding, (e.g., with the God of the philosophers) while the Yahwist description we may say is a more personally experienced God. These two distinct ways of understanding and experiencing the Deity are to some degree reflected in the entire later history of humankind's theological reasoning. (Thomas Aquinas' theology, for example, was more rational than that of Teresa of Avila.) However, as the inspired authors of the Scriptures amalgamated the Yahwist and Elohist traditions into a single biblical image of God's person, something comparable happens in the everyday life of believers. Let us observe how this merger happens.

The God of the philosophers calls not only particular people but the whole of humankind, by asking the same questions (and perhaps waiting for the same answers). God is calling all people through our immanent human need to find answers to the ultimate questions of the universe, the meaning, purpose and value of human life and existence. Everyone has to give his or her answer to those ultimate questions on his or her level and from his or her perspective. This call for answers to life's ultimate questions is one of the means by which the ultimate reality, whom believers call *God*, challenges all of us, offering us union with Him as the solution to those questions. Accurate interpretation of the causes underlying the questions that most plague us aids us in discovering God standing by and addressing challenging calls common to almost every individual.

However, God's call of His people through ultimate philosophical questions is not an impersonal process. God's general philosophical calls are always personally addressed to particular and concrete persons. Even when confronting his people with the most general philosophical questions, God is sending a personal call and is establishing a very personal psychological communication.

Making correct philosophical discernments is not a stress-free speculation. It needs logical reasoning but above all, humility. According to

Xavier Léon-Dufour "turning around one's heart" helps, as does becoming like a small child (Mark 18:3).[2] It helps to acknowledge our sins and need of God's redemption (Luke 18:13). It helps believers make their personal choice—an experience like that of the prodigal son (Luke 15:11-32)—and fosters the awareness that God's biblical forgiveness, peace, love, hope and other gifts which are part of Jesus' redemptive program can only be experienced by remorseful Christians (as described in Matt. 5:3-12). Such reflections are formulated mostly in terms of a unique personal experience and are only the first step in the long spiritual growth process that ends with mature faith. These calls initiate a delicate philosophical and personal communication with a "quite other," supportive, caring, and empathetic God, concerned about the intimate problems of believers. Therefore, by changing the viewpoint and perspective of the value discernment of the believer and by connecting rational with emotional components, an image of God emerges different from the God of philosophers. Through personal communication, believers factually encounter both the transcendent God of philosophers and also a living God.

27.2. Is it Really From God? Theological and Psychological Criteria for Discerning God's Call

As the next point, let us agree how and where we will draw the line between that which undoubtedly is God's call and that which may instead reflect worldly causes, events and sources.

The importance of such a distinction is in the following: Believers live in a miraculous world. For them, everything, the whole of reality, is a theophany. They discern God's hand in and behind everything that exists and happens. Thus everything that IS, exists and happens with a purpose and is teleologically regulated. Postmodern scientific reductionism, on the other hand, recognizes only blind and impersonal natural forces behind these same realities. In an agnostic understanding, all things and events are regulated merely by causal factors, without a goal or purpose; there is nothing teleological in nature or in the world. From the perspective of agnostics, the imperative need to raise and wrestle with ultimate philosophical questions is seen as an inborn, almost endogenous drive, as though it originated from the wiring of the human brain and from the human way of experiencing reality. The need to ask ultimate questions may be seen as coming from the dignity of being a *homo sapiens*. An agnostic would ask, "If asking philosophical questions is the characteristic of every human being and if it is almost an 'endogenous drive,' then why are we saying that they represent God's call?"

The answer is, on the one hand, that raising, discussing and answering those questions is useless for sustaining the everyday life of a hypothetical average believer. Wrestling with ultimate philosophical questions does not directly contribute to the wealth, health, prosperity, or security of their life, and is not caused by biological, psychological or sociological necessity. Despite this, we are programmed to discuss those "useless" questions. Obviously, they reflect a different need and a "quite other" Questioner than everyday natural reality. On the other hand, unanswered and unsolved, these challenges cause uneasiness, disquietude and angst, which persist until satisfactory answers found. These ultimate philosophical questions, however, must remain unanswered without God. Thus the reality that is forcing us to ask and answer these ultimate questions is the one Christians call *God*. This is the reason we are saying that they represent God's call.

To avoid misunderstandings and to counter these agnostic concepts, let us in formulate the criteria for what we understand as God's call especially stringently. Let us define the idea of God's call as something that cannot be reduced to and explained away as nothing more than a natural event or phenomenon.

Based on the above perspective, this internally-experienced purpose (experienced as a challenge, motivation, inspiration, or driving force) which we cannot explain as natural because it is quite different from biological, psychological, or sociological (worldly) laws—we will define as a potential call of God. Thus, an explicit call of God can be actualized in many different ways, but it has an essential characteristic. Invariably, God's call involves the bequeathing of a "quite other" biblical meaning, love, hope, forgiveness, strength, peace, knowledge, and joy, encouraging one to follow God in faith. This could not be produced by natural causes. Receiving these gifts is conditioned by a believer's answer to God's call with faith.

Let us illustrate our definition with an example.

While living in an Eastern European communist country, I pursued studies in theology while simultaneously teaching psychiatry at the Faculty of Medicine. Though I kept a low profile, the communist medical management found out about my "suspicious connections and church activities." And so I was subjected to a scrutiny of whether I was fit, given my interest in theology, to keep my tenure as a professor.

At that time, the communist party still had immense power and they could crush, suspend, humiliate, or fire anyone in any way they wanted. Furthermore, my predicament was compounded by the fact that I had seven children to take care of. Thus, as I went to this meeting, my horror, heartbeat, and perspiration intensified. To delay my arrival, I took the stairs to the seventh floor instead of the elevator. When I got to the second floor I thought:

> Yes, the communists can crush, humiliate, or fire the most respected psychiatrist, or even drive him mad. However, their position of power does not alter the fact that I am right! I am pursuing the right thing, and God is on my side. With his help I will prevail, and ultimately win, if not here and now, then in eternity!

Paradoxically, I felt overjoyed in this moment and my fear disappeared. I therefore had the courage to be humble, not to overreact, and to present myself with dignity and with a feeling of security because "God is on my side." The examiners turned out to be benevolent. They gave me only a few pieces of advice, and then, with a big smile and in a friendly manner, they released me.

Was this dramatic turn in my feelings, thoughts, and attitude towards the situation the consequence of God's call and intervention?

For an indifferent observer, it may seem that nothing of significance really occurred. However, I experienced within my being an almost "quite other" courage, peace, and ability to forgive and transcend, which I could not attribute to some natural, biological, psychological, or social, cognitive, or behavioral theory or skill. I had every reason to be terrified and to flee, but instead I experienced an almost otherworldly peace. I cannot explain such transempirical joy, detachment from worldly reality, and the sense of "being in the world but not of it," in any way other than as a gift of God. Neither can I explain this knowledge of God and feeling of being overjoyed in my suffering in any way other than by communicating with a "quite other" Divine reality. Nor can I attribute biblical peace to anything other than to my communication with the almighty, eternal, and ultimate love, who God in fact is.

I am certain that every one of us has had experiences similar to mine. On the other hand, God's call does not always seem particularly striking to an outside observer. The call's extraordinary qualities are experienced only by value-discerning believers who are subjected to the Spirit's dramatic call from within. And inversely, even beyond cognitively witnessed, or otherwise realized awesome events, one will not experience God's call except internally, mystically, introspectively, and reflectively, discerning a purpose or meaning. However, for someone who is subjected to such a dramatic purpose that acts within the deepest layers of his or her personality, conscience, and soul, nothing is more real, convincing and overwhelming than such a factual reflection of God's love. The reality of such a "quite other" internal communication is not only transempirical but externally and behaviorally visible and measurable.

Continuing our attempt to define God's call so that it cannot be explained away as simply a natural, psychologically or socially learned behavior, let us narrow what we may deem God's calls even further.

27.3. Behavioral Criteria
for Discerning God's Call

A reader can object, at this point:

> The introspective criteria are convincing and impressive only for the subject who experiences them, but not for indifferent observers. Can what constitutes God's call not be determined more narrowly, or even more positively?

Let us, then, make our definition even more stringent. Instead of focusing on introspections, let us discuss that which is obvious and touchable. On the other hand, let us not accept behavior that expresses natural, psychologically explicable reflections but rather that which reflects gifts of faith and the Spirit as God's call.

Accordingly, let us define God's call as a measurable behavior caused by a purpose that has nothing to do with worldly reasons, laws, and necessities, but rather is a response to that which is quite different, whom we call God. A positive response to such a call must be always verified by the gifts of the Spirit. Let us first discuss the biblical rationale of such a definition.

Luke notes Jesus' words, "You will be betrayed even by parents, brothers, relatives and friends, and they will put some of you to death. All men will hate you because of me. But not a hair of your head will perish." (Luke 21:16-18) In Mark 8:31 we read, "He then began to teach them that the Son of Man must suffer many things and be rejected by the elders, chief priests, and teachers of the law, and that He must be killed and after three days, rise again." Then in Mark 8:34 we find, "If anyone would come after me, he must deny himself and take up his cross and follow Me." In addition we read in 1 Peter 4:13-14, "But rejoice that you participate in the sufferings of Christ, so that you may be over-joyed when his glory is revealed. If you are insulted because of the name of Christ, you are blessed, for the Spirit of glory and of God rests on you."

What common denominator can we deduce from these biblical quotations? The common theme is that God's call and the resulting behavior pattern, if it is indeed a response to God's call, must be quite other than natural biological, psychological or sociological requirements. They must reflect not worldly principles and expectations but God's.

A similar lifestyle is also true of contemporary Christians. By living a biblical lifestyle, and not participating in the race for more success, money, and fun, Christians choose to obey a restraint in contradiction to all biological, psychological, and sociological agendas, and to all rational, emotional, or instinctual motives. Obviously, such a choice is not accidental. By willingly choosing to exemplify Christian love, unselfishness, or even self-sacrifice, which are the universal laws of living in union with God, Christians reflect the requirements not of the world or of biological existence (*bios*), but of everlasting life (*zoe*).

(We noted earlier that the Greek translators of the Scriptures used two different words for what we call life. They used the word "bios" to signify the profane, worldly, and biological aspect of life, while the word "zoe" meant a holy and everlasting life, one lived in union with God.)

With the above biblical terms at our disposal, we can now easily define what we will take to mean God's call: God's call is what visibly and behaviorally replaces respect for *bios* with a conscious search for *zoe*. Let us now test our new definition as an instrument of measurement according to biblical standards.

A typical example of God's call, as defined above, was the intervention of the resurrected Jesus in John 20:24-29. After losing his faith, Thomas was on his way towards solely respecting the rules of *bios*.

His stubborn declaration, "Unless I see the nail marks in his hands, and put my finger where the nails were, and put my hands into his side, I will not believe it," represents such an approach. The only reality he intended to respect was the sensorial, positive, cognitively experienced one.

A firm call to Thomas was needed to fundamentally transform his attitude and to make him discern a reality quite different from the worldly. Jesus provided this call, which made Thomas cry out, "My Lord and my God!"

The respect for *bios* in Thomas was, as in his fellow disciples, replaced with a search for *zoe*, a search for holiness. Neither the world nor its psychology could cause such a displacement of priorities. Thomas' exemplary Christian behavior, his acceptance of suffering, poverty, humiliation, even death, with forgiveness, love, and even biblical joy, is impossible to explain by, or reduce to, natural biological, psychological, or social motives. Something (or more exactly someone) "quite other" had to be the reason of such fidelity to Jesus in witnessing and in embodying *zoe*. He who instigates the shift of focusing from *bios* to *zoe* is the one whom believers call God.

Using a stringent behavioral definition of God's call has here a didactic purpose. It serves to bypass the possibility of denying God's call for what it is and explaining it instead as the byproduct of some natural phenomenon.

In the next chapter, we will discuss those calls of God which are addressed not only to every believer, but also to every human being, including agnostics, atheists, and religiously indifferent and apathetic positivists. Indeed, these general calls of God are in practice always individualized and personal and they eminently require replacing the search for *bios* with that for *zoe*. Over six billion people will interpret the call to *zoe* in over six billion personal ways.

Notes

1. Ludwig Feuerbach, *Das Wesen des Christentums* (Stuttgart: Samtliche Werke, 1903).

2. Xavier Léon-Dufour, Rjecnik Biblijske Teologija, ed. Josip Turcinovic (Zagreb: Krscanska Sadasnjost, 1988), 908-909.

Chapter 28

God's Most Paradoxical Calls: Angst and Suffering

28.1. Defining the Problem

In Abraham J. Heschel's book, *Between God and Man*, Fritz Rotschild defines religion as an "answer to man's ultimate questions."[1] Humans do not ask such ultimate questions without a strong reason. They "arise under the impact of the elemental forces of reality confronting man." Rotschild goes on to say, ". . . as an answer, religion becomes not only false but meaningless and irrelevant as soon as that by which it is evoked no longer reflects challenge."

Is humankind still challenged by ultimate questions to which the only rational, satisfactory, and appropriate answer is faith and trust in God? That challenge remains very real. During the past century the incidence of depression, juvenile suicide, divorce, drug abuse, and the single-parent family have skyrocketed—illustrating, as never before, postmodern society's need for meaning in life.

Yes, the elemental forces of reality confronting humankind in the form of a transempirical challenge to discern a meaning and ultimate meaning to live for are still active. The search for answers to the ultimate questions of human life has not become inappropriate or irrelevant. The answer that faith gives remains, in the twenty-first century, a real "to be or not to be" issue for our contemporaries and our culture.

The unquestionable importance of the answers that faith gives to such ultimate questions confirms that in the lives of believers there is an empirical negative correlation between the described challenge and one's ability to give an optimal response to it. Stronger faith, however, correlates with a decrease in the suffering of a meaningless life.

28.2. Why Humans Suffer from Fear and Angst: The Theological Explanation

One ancient poet wrote, "First God created fear." Today we know that fear was not the first creation of God; nonetheless, fear is one of his very important creations, which serves to protect human biological life. However, fear—or more exactly a derivative of fear, angst—is most often connected with feelings of guilt and the dread of unavoidable punishment inflicted by God or with fright at the prospect of even meeting God. Why do people experience angst at the prospect of meeting the person who least justifies it?

The Scriptures do not indicate that our ancestors, Adam and Eve, suffered either fear or angst before committing original sin. We are left with the impression that they respectfully but freely communicated with their Creator and Sustainer.

However, very different was Adam and Eve's relationship with, and attitude toward, God after being expelled from God's nearness. Their legacy has had an impact on all subsequent human generations: ". . . sin entered the world through one man, and death through sin, and in this way death came to all men, because all sinned . . ." (Rom. 5:12). ". . . by the trespass of one man, death reigned through that one man . . ." (Rom 5:17). The trespass of one man caused condemnation of all humankind (Rom. 5:18). Thus, according to the Scriptures, the real existence and full effect of original sin make us all anxious about meeting God. Consequently, original sin is not some personal imperfection or limitation, and still less some mere abstraction. Rather, it results in a fearful state of mind every bit as distressing as fear of death.

We may stop at this point, and ask: "How can the guilt of one very distant ancestor, whom we do not even personally know, so influence the relationship to God of his successors? Moreover, what kind of justice is this anyway, that it permits such injustice?"

We can correctly understand the message of the biblical authors (writing around 500 BC) only if we adjust our Western way of thinking to the ancient Hebrew perspective. According to Tomic,

We think individualistically. For us Adam is a particular human—an individual, our ancestor, and an arch-sinner. For us the connection with Adam is only physical and genetic, insofar as we are his successors. For the biblical authors Adam is a person in a general sense, representing the whole of humankind. The name Adam appears in Scripture some 500 times. In most cases it signifies humans in general—humankind.[2]

In this context, Rebic states that Adam is not only a person, but a corporate personality representing the whole of humankind. Therefore, what he suffers or personifies are the psychological reactions and behavior patterns of all of humanity.[3] Genesis 3:1-24 reveals the characteristic psychodynamics of everyman's (and everywoman's) committing sin. And inversely, in every individual, and in every sin of every human being, the sinful nature of all of humanity becomes actualized; that is, we are all trying in our acts of sin to become omnipotent—not truly Godly, but god-like—but are instead becoming Adam/Eve-like.

We are living in an individualistic culture, and this makes it difficult for us to understand the meaning of Adam's sin. However, since each of us plays a personal role in the un-Christian behavior patterns of all of humanity (tolerating, or even enhancing poverty and abuse for example), each of us ought to accept appropriate and justly-established responsibility for all human sin. As the English poet John Donne wrote, "No man is an island."[4]

To summarize the biblical perspective: it is sin which causes anguish, insecurity, uneasiness, tension, disquietude, and other attributes of angst. Let us now discuss some contemporary professional explanations of angst.

28.3. Why Humans Suffer from Fear and Angst: The Psychiatric Explanation

In the *Diagnostic and Statistical Manual of Mental Disorders-IV* published by the American Psychiatric Association in 1994, the Anxiety Disorders section discusses panic, phobic, obsessive-compulsive, and other disorders whose main characteristics are fear, horror, panic, or anxiety.[5] However, the angst we are going to discuss is different from disorders like these. Actually, since angst is a normal psychological characteristic in humans, one would require a psychiatrist's attention if he or she were absolutely free of it. Absolute freedom from angst happens only in psychoses. However, in most personality disorders and sometimes in psychoses, symptoms of the disorder include certain defense mechanisms against angst and fear.

According to Eric, angst has characteristics in common with fear but at the same time there is an amazing difference and uniqueness in these unpleasant feelings of sorrow, threat, insecurity or uneasiness.[6] The easiest way to grasp the essence of it would be to compare it to similar experiences such as fear or panic that we all know and can easily define.

1. Alertness is a healthy psychological and physiological reaction to a potentially challenging or dangerous situation that is controllable, for example, a dangerous situation that may occur when driving a car. Alertness is characterized by increased and focused attention, emotional and intellectual readiness to act, and mobilization of one's mental and somatic potential for a possible action. It is an experience of competence and optimism, which have a positive role in mobilizing the person for appropriate action. However, fear will develop if alertness is aware of an unmanageable threat, where perceived personal mastery is insufficient to adequately respond to the challenge. Anticipatory anxiety signals such a possibility of converting alertness into fear when a person is confronted by a possible no-win situation.

2. Fear in psychiatry is defined as the unpleasant tension caused by a threat to life. That threat can have very different internal or external causes, but in every case fear is of something concrete that we can pinpoint and usually defend ourselves against. The more imminent and dangerous the threat, the greater the fear. On the other hand, fear always has a beginning and an end; it lasts only as long as the threat is not properly responded to or resolved. Fear is a necessary experience in the protection of biological life. Its purpose is to mobilize the defense system in the face of a perceived threat. Without healthy fear and its activation of appropriate defense functions (such as the fight-or-flight response), the chances of preserving life would be radically reduced.

3. Horror is the experience of extreme fear. Extreme fear is not useful for self-preservation. It produces no rational, purposeful, defense reaction. The emotions in this case are so strong that any meaningful defensive reaction is made impossible. Horror can be expressed as a general inhibition and inaction or as a "storm of useless movements." The person is paralyzed or overreacts and is thereby incapable of appropriate defensive reactions.

4. Panic can be a personal or a collective experience (collective horror). The cry "Fire!" in a tone of horror in a dark movie theater has a much more terrifying effect than observing the actual fire. The most important internal effect here is the experience of personal powerlessness, of being lost in a crowd of others who are trying to escape the danger without regard to hurting anyone in their way.

5. Angst, or anguish. So we arrive at our most interesting, and indeed, the most important topic in our discussion. While we have shown that fear and panic are caused by concrete, visible, and touchable threats to existence, angst or anguish represents a threat from an abstract, invisible, and untouchable threat. It is an unpleasant tension in reaction to a threat not in the here and now, but in the future, a threat not yet confronted but nonetheless clearly unavoidable. For example, we all know that, independent of all other variables, human life eventually ends. This realization causes in the background of the human mind an unfolding of life-long experience, an undefined awareness, and an untouchable and unavoidable feeling of threat, insecurity, and uneasiness; this is the angst of death. Unlike the horror and fear of death that are provoked by a particular (visible, touchable, and avoidable) threat and mobilize a defense against this threat, the angst of death evokes an unpleasant awareness, insecurity and sorrow concerning the unavoidable end against which no defense is possible. Thus, angst is a reaction to death—a future event that is inevitable and unavoidable. A defensive reaction in the present would be too early, and when we meet death face to face it will be too late. It seems we can do nothing against

this tormenting but unavoidable future threat, that is in fact non-existent in the here and now.

Eric states that Robert Burton, who was a contemporary of Francis Bacon, was the first to describe angst in *The Anatomy of Melancholy*. Burton described angst, sorrow, anguish, uneasiness, and other such synonyms as "fear without reason," containing two components: fear and sorrow.[7]

According to Eric, the Danish philosopher Søren Kierkegaard made the next important contribution to the understanding of angst.[8] We noted that according to Millard J. Erickson, the essence of Kierkegaard's teaching was a revolt against a philosophy in which a subject's individuality had no role. For him truth always existed in one's personal experience. Angst for Kierkegaard is the consequence of a typical human condition: freedom of choice (and consequent responsibility for undertaking action), and the continual possibility that a mistake not visible now but revealed in the future will be made by present action. The threat of such a mistake and responsibility for failures it may cause are sources of permanent, unpleasant worry and uncertainty.

Here the famous nineteenth-century philosopher is in agreement with modern existentialist thinkers. Existentialists like Jean P. Sartre expanded on Kierkegaard's thought. Sartre, as you may recall, proposed that humans are thrown into the world as raw material, without a firm lighthouse marking the way through life. The individual encountering freedom has the task to actively fulfill his or her life project. Freedom, however, is never completely achieved; it is always "in the making." Accordingly, we humans are not only being in the world, like plants or animals, but also existing in it, creating what we ought to be; this is the essence of human responsibility. Ambiguity and uncertainty always exist in this process and are the source of human uneasiness and angst. Therefore, as Eric points out: ". . . human existence itself is angst."[9] Life causes a permanent experience of absurdity, anguish, and estrangement, which Sartre poetically described in his book *L'être et le Néant* (*Being and Nothingness*).[10]

The psychiatrist Viktor E. Frankl does not explicitly describe angst, but he does discuss an essential component of it. According to *The Doctor and the Soul*,[11] unlike previous generations that were told by their religion and traditions exactly what was good and bad or what the correct fundamental options in life were, many of our contemporaries have lost those traditional support systems and are consequently challenged by their own freedom of choice and their responsibility to find and fulfill their life meanings. This task causes enduring tension because there is a permanent gap between that which one is and that which one ought to be. One of the essential human tasks is to transcend one's personal status quo and its limitations, to step over human boundaries so as to become what one ought to be, and in so doing, to fulfill a unique life meaning. The need to transcend causes one more kind of tension; namely, humans are constantly tested by life with new situations and tasks and by the challenge to discern and fulfill the particular meanings of those particular situations. Despite our best efforts in doing so, there remains a permanent gap between the realization of a particular meaning and its complete fulfillment. Until their last breath, argues Frankl, humans cannot be absolutely sure that they are accomplishing the correct purpose in life. Moreover, as Gordon Allport noted, "We can be at one and the same time half-sure and whole-hearted."[12] Such ambiguity is the reason for much tension, frustration, and the "Existential vacuum," of our time.

Despite the fact that people have various ideas and interpretations of fear and angst, and despite the fact that these two concepts partially overlap, there are essential differences between them. Differences are especially prominent and substantial in faith questions and discernments. Angst observed from this perspective is, in many aspects, the opposite of fear. For example, fear mirrors a worldly reality and threat, while anguish in religious experience mirrors a reality untouchable, invisible, and transcendental in the present, as well as the threat of the compulsory confrontation with one's true self without lies and self-deception. Fear contributes to self-preservation in the natural world, while anguish serves the search for God-self-preservation in everlasting life. One can resolve fear by avoiding danger, whereas only faith can resolve angst. God is transcendental, but he is experiential through angst—his call, and through the antidote to angst—faith. Last but not least, in this contrast of fear and angst, it is interesting to note that Jesus suffered fear, but he did not, according to biblical descriptions, ever suffer angst.

28.4. A Synthesis: Angst as God's Call

The relationship between depression and the inability to express feelings is well known to psychiatry. Depressed patients are sad, worried, and unhappy. They realize that they are unable to perform as they ought to, feel unworthy, and are often deliberating suicide. However, what is peculiar is that truly depressed patients seldom cry. They are unable to express their sadness as they ought to, by crying; instead, they express it by symptoms of depression.

We find a similar relationship between being unable to fear God and the suffering of angst. The one who cannot rely on, and have faith in, God (i.e., one who is unable to fear God), will suffer that which Jean P. Sartre described as anguish, absurdity, and estrangement.

In contrast to this, we can observe in countless biblical examples how faith works as a remedy for fear, horror, or angst. Jesus' disciples and exemplary Christians, even when confronted with the fact that they would share the same destiny as their Lord, were joyful. Note Acts 5:41 in which the apostles, instead of being afraid or anxious, rejoiced in being found true disciples, worthy of suffering as their master did. We can find many similar biblical examples, for example 1 Peter 1:3-9, Hebrews 10:34, Philippians 2:17, and James 1:2. It is obvious from the Bible that the disciples were aware of the unavoidable future threat and had all reasons to react with angst. However, their faith helped them to overcome anguish. Without strong faith, their conduct would have been different.

Indeed, everyday experience confirms Nietzsche's saying that he who has "a why to live for" can bear with almost any how (quoted earlier from Frankl's *Ärztliche Seelsorge*). Only the one who has a "why to live for" is able to overcome his or her angst in everyday life. We have noted that the philosopher Pauler characterized humans as a race searching for God. We may suppose the Homo became a Sapiens when it was able to discern faith as the right response to angst and fear.

A reader could now ask a question, which at first glance is difficult to answer:

> How can we be sure that in the human mind's reaction to unavoidable threats like aging, sickness, suffering, or death, God himself is active beyond angst? To put it more clearly, how can we substantiate that a lack of relationship with God is acting beyond angst, and that the normal and natural human reaction to insecurity, frustration, sickness or death is not the source of angst?

Let us first visualize the answer to this question in a theological example and then discuss it from a psychological perspective.

One of the questions I had to discuss in my final theology exam was: How would the earthly life of Adam and Eve have ended if our first ancestors had not fallen into sin?

My answer was that after the end of their biological life cycle Adam and Eve would probably have biologically died but not as they ended up dying. Their transition into eternal life would have been a conscious, joyful, glorious termination and a transformation of the body into the glory of Godly life and everlasting blessedness. Psychologically, they would not have suffered angst caused by their fear of irreversible annihilation of their biological existence and of losing the security of the world, as well as by the tormenting question: "What may I expect on the other side—does God really exist, or is there only nothingness?"

Perhaps more importantly, if not estranged from God, Adam and Eve would have experienced that biological dying does not mean a radical separation between them and their beloved—which is probably the most painful experience in death. Rather, death would have meant a new kind of experienced spiritual union between biologically deceased but spiritually alive people and those believers still on their way towards their spiritual existence.

On the other hand, as a consequence of Jesus' redemption, a strong biblical faith is already able to bridge that total gap of death which seems so absolute and definite to non-believers. Furthermore, faith is able to establish a commonality between all present and past members of the church. By this, the visible (alive), and invisible (deceased) members—by faith—experientially are parts of the one church.

With the aid of the above insights, we can now answer the previous question. If Adam (and humankind, which represents Adam's collective personality) had lived in God's complete grace and had an absolute and wholehearted biblical relationship with God (such as before original sin), then the fact of death would not have caused angst, but, rather, joyful hope. Fear of death would then be unknown to humankind.

Let us not forget that Christ redeemed not only his close disciples, but God's postmodern people as well. Thus, we may through faith possess the same courage, trust, hope, and joy which the disciples, according to James', Paul's, and Peter's letters, experienced while confronting unavoidable suffering and death. Indeed, having or not having a wholehearted trust in God makes the difference between the optimism, courage, and peace of exemplary biblical disciples, and the angst, fear, and horror of death of modern non-religious and apathetic people. Thus,

angst is the consequence of God's call unanswered biblically; the reason
for and solution to angst points towards God. This justifies thinking of
angst as God's call.

After exploring angst biblically, let us now explore the reasons, dynamics, and implications of this tormenting experience from a pastoral-
psychiatric perspective. We could summarize our rationale in three points:

1. Value-discerning believers recognize God's acting and call
    beyond their awareness of unavoidable aging, sickness, suf-
    fering, and death. In contrast, value-blind agnostics only
    observe natural events without seeing or detecting the invis-
    ible God acting beyond those events.
2. Because sick, aging, or dying believers react to angst in ways
    different from agnostics, angst is not caused by the genuine
    facts of suffering, but by the type and quality of response to
    these threats. Thus, different attitudes and responses will cause
    different experiences. While believers react to threats by
    deepening their union with Jesus, non-believers react by ac-
    knowledging the absurdity and estrangement from life that
    angst causes them to feel, because they are without a vital
    union with God.
3. As a consequence of these differences in people's approaches,
    believers are able to use their tangible union with the invis-
    ible God to defeat angst, while angst defeats non-believers.

Even a superficial reading of the Bible makes it obvious that the
information God gave us about himself is not like a medical diagnosis or
blueprint, and nowhere can we find an explanation or a description of his
personality that would satisfy our logical reasoning. God reveals himself
in comparisons, parables and metaphors, i.e., he communicates with us
in a transempirical language. The language of the Scriptures is primarily
a transempirical language. The same is true in God's personal calls. His
calls are seldom concrete instructions (like those found in an owner's
manual, or a cookbook). Much more often believers experience God's
calls abstractly, like an appeal to discern an ultimate meaning or fulfill a
spiritual purpose in life. Therefore, sometimes it is not easy to recognize
God's calls, and it may be even more difficult to recognize the connection between lack of trust in God and angst. For example, students may
suffer the angst connected to passing exams, adults may complain of

angst regarding job or financial insecurity, and retired people, regarding aging. Non-believers, who demand a medical diagnosis or blueprint-like instruction, instead of God's transempirical revelation and calls, will not recognize quickly and easily that passing exams, job or financial insecurity, and aging are only the triggers, while the real cause of every kind of anxiety, anguish, disquietude and tension is living without sufficient confidence in Jesus' providence. The basic insecurity caused by distrust in God is often expressed in and masked by concrete triggers of angst.

On the other hand, strong faith defeats triggers of angst. The same holds true in discerning the solution to angst. To strengthen one's union with God so as to overcome angst is not a conscious, completely rational cognitive choice (like taking a medicine). It is rather an implicit and pre-conscious generational experience and behavior pattern unique to believers and deeply embedded in the human conscience and mind, which enables them to strengthen their union with God, particularly in times of despair. That is, in general, how subtle is the psychological experience of God's challenges and calls.

Thus, we have the freedom to either react in a value-blind way or to realize the meaning of angst as God's call. We have, however, no freedom in choosing the consequences of our value discernments, namely, that with faith we defeat angst, without faith we are defeated by it.

Observed from this perspective, we realize that Burton likely did not accidentally discover and describe the phenomenon of angst in the middle of the Zeitgeist of the Enlightenment. In the mental climate of the Enlightenment, when loss of a firm connection to God occurred on a massive scale for the first time, the growth of agnosticism and atheism in the mental and cultural climate enabled angst, which at that time in human history grew into a widespread and real problem.

Unfortunately, the discernment of the real and appropriate solution—a return to God's kingdom and dominion—has not yet occurred as massively as has the angst that warns of the need for such a faith revival. Obviously, the angst has to worsen in the future before it triggers a new religious awakening. The only question is, how much does it have to worsen?

The possibility of such a religious revival may seem, to many contemporaries, remote and improbable. However, some twenty-five years ago I and many others believed that in the next few hundred years a global progression of communism would inevitably be unstoppable. As we have seen, history took a very different turn. Let us hope that, like communism, the angst so prevalent today is soon replaced by a global spiritual awakening.

28.5. Unavoidable Suffering as God's Call

I still remember vividly when in a TV interview an East German communist psychiatrist and party ideologist expressed his view that superstition and religion are impossible to erase from the human mind as long as despair, fear, and suffering exist.

An ideologist's propaganda attempted to make superstition and faith one and the same. Nonetheless, let us not argue against him here, but try to understand his true message. His underlying message may be that only in a world without pain, suffering, or death, (or in a mental state completely denying these), would humans perhaps be interested in God more than would animals. Now we realize why all dictatorships throughout history have tried to create a climate that denies suffering and promotes a euphoric hope for a terrific future under the guidance of the idol—the wise and adored leader.

On hearing the communist ideologist's comment, I also realized that angst and suffering are, as stated in Rotschild's description quoted previously, some of the "elemental forces of reality confronting man" which help us to look for a solution and turn to God. Both angst and suffering are interconnected. The main common denominator of both is that angst is unpleasant because it is a precursor of suffering, or inversely, suffering is the fulfillment of that which angst warns of. There is, however, also a difference between the two. While in practice angst often motivates the human search for God, suffering is a two-edged sword which is, on the one hand, possible to overcome only by faith, but on the other hand difficult to reconcile with the image of the almighty and eternal God. In many cases it breaks faith.

The faith of the apostles was also tested by Jesus' prediction that he would suffer, and they probably asked themselves a similar question: "If he is God, why must he suffer?"

Also Pope John Paul II wondered if the suffering and death of Jesus was really necessary for the redemption of God's people? He responded:

> God who, besides being Omnipotence, is Wisdom and—to repeat once more—Love, desires to justify Himself to humankind. He is not the Absolute that remains outside of the world, indifferent to human suf-

fering. He is Emmanuel, God-with-us, a God who shares man's lot
and participates in his destiny. . . . Even contemporary critics of Christianity are in agreement on this point. Even they see that the crucified
Christ is proof of God's solidarity with man in his suffering.[13]

By revealing the image of an unselfishly-loving God who, because of
his tender love, accepted suffering, Jesus personified one of the essential
differences between the revealed God, and gods produced by human
wishful thinking who promised enjoyment and fun without accepting, or
discerning a meaning in, suffering. Jesus' requiring the same attitude of
his disciples towards suffering excludes the possibility of a human invention of the revealed God.

Suffering was not foreign to the disciples. Paul's letters present a
good illustration of this, as in 2 Corinthians 6:10 and 2 Corinthians 12:10,
or in Hebrews 12:2 and 11:26. However, obviously, the suffering of
Jesus' disciples was very different in its reasons, symptoms, and out-
comes from that of modern agnostics living meaningless lives. Discipleship makes the difference between horror and dignified suffering for the
sake of God's kingdom.

Let us stop here and clarify this last statement.

Agnostics suffer not only, or primarily, because of pain or disappointments, but because of the meaninglessness of those experiences.
Frankl quoted Nietzsche's words, which we could translate as, "What
worried him most was not that he had to suffer, but that he did not know
why." Most of us suffer for the same reason; its perceived meaninglessness causes the worst possible pain in human suffering![14]

The worst part of suffering for non-believers is that it takes away
from life the feelings of meaning, value, and purpose. This is perhaps
the strongest discrepancy between a worldly and a biblical perspective:
Jesus gave an ultimate meaning stronger than the pain caused by suffering.

In my medical experience, helping patients who were requesting as-
sistance to discern a God-given ultimate meaning was like a panacea that
healed all kinds of suffering. Perhaps the disciples experienced such
God-given ultimate meaning in the events described in 1 Peter 1:3-9,
where Peter calls Christians to rejoice when participating in suffering
because of Christ. Rejoicing in suffering is something very different
from the meaningless suffering experienced by agnostics.

The right behavior when confronting pain is to search for the real
reason of suffering. This will often help one recognize one's estrange-

ment from, or at least lukewarm identification with, the biblical suffering and glorious God. Estrangement from and loss of trust in God, as
well as the question "Why me?" are most often the real reasons for the
most destructive nuances of pain.

I know from my psychotherapy experience that, though it seems
hard (or impossible) to believe, there is no suffering which faith cannot
help a person to endure. However, let us not forget that God's comfort is
not immediate and swift like a cognitive or sensorial recognition process.
Comfort given by God to the sufferer will follow the circular path characteristic of transempirical discernment processes—a series of events
experienced in gradual progression for which we must struggle. It is a
process that often takes time, sometimes a very long time, to be tested
and proven.

We already indirectly mentioned it when discussing angst, but let us
stop here for a moment and discuss one amazing experiential fact. The
turning point in the psychotherapy of suffering people is often marked by
the insight similar to the evidence of the disciples described in Acts, of
being worthy. "The apostles left the Sanhedrin, rejoicing because they
had been counted worthy of suffering disgrace for the Name" (Acts 5:41).

What could be the meaning of the phrase "worthy of suffering" in
this verse?

In his post-Galilean period, Jesus warned of the suffering that would
befall the Son of Man. His disciples became hesitant, disappointed, or
skeptical, and probably thought to themselves, "This is not the Messiah
we expected." At that time, the disciples were unworthy of suffering
because they were not fully identified with Jesus in both his glory and his
suffering.

In contrast to the understanding of the disciples at that time, suffering with Jesus is different. I often heard from patients receiving strong
painkillers (like morphine) that they literally take away pain. These patients would say, "I feel the pain, but it does not hurt me." Their attitude
towards the pain had changed—they felt it, but it did not hurt. Christ's
disciples feel pain, and it hurts them, but quite differently from the way
in which meaningless suffering hurts. Christ's ultimate meaning enables
happiness and suffering, joy and pain to be experienced together. It enables the discernment of meaning in suffering.

With his suffering Jesus did not take away suffering from us, but he
gave us a possibility of being worthy of suffering. Being worthy of suffering means maintaining optimism, trust, and happiness despite suffer-

ing and thereby using suffering to work to strengthen the believer's faith. The more a believer has trust and internal evidence that a Christ-like suffering is also the precondition of his or her glory and union with Jesus, the more meaning and biblical happiness that person will find to overcome suffering. This is the internal proof that such a person is worthy of his or her suffering! Such a person then proves the ability to understand and respond to God's most paradoxical programs, and such a person has reason to rejoice as St. Peter recommended. In such cases, suffering does not break, but rather makes, faith!

At this point the reader may ask this: "But how does unavoidable suffering 'make' faith?"

For believers, suffering has a powerful purpose: to glorify God. Earlier we defined God's glory, with the help of J. I. Packer, as "Deity in manifestation." Thus, glorifying God means discerning his deity. It means discerning his almighty, eternal, and ultimate love, his providence, omnipotence, wisdom, help, and grace. It also means appreciating his "quite other" consolation. Suffering helps to discern and accept God's deity, his "quite other"-ness, and his never-ending ultimate power to console. According to Packer, "Felt weakness deepens dependence on Christ for strength each day. The weaker we feel, the harder we lean. And the harder we lean, the stronger we grow spiritually, even while our bodies waste away."[15] Thus, a compulsory confrontation with our powerlessness enables us to experientially discern, and then to glorify, God. Perhaps, at least unwillingly and subconsciously, the East German ideologist realized this connection.

On the other hand, suffering—carrying one's cross despite fear or pain—is the most powerful witness to God's glory. Healing pains and disappointments through union with God is the most powerful tool in building God's kingdom.

28.6. Discussion

An agnostic devil's advocate could open the discussion by noting,

> "There are many other explanations of angst that use a very different paradigm." For example, according to Fenichel in Freud's model of mental functioning, instinctual impulses tend to lower one's level of excitation by their discharge. If instinctual discharge does not occur due to the ego or superego's veto,

then tension inside the personality increases to threatening levels. This tension is experienced as angst, phobia, or fear. The situation is then further complicated by the involvement of subconscious motives.[16]

Other psychotherapy schools offer different paradigms of angst. An Adlerian therapist will connect angst to frustrated will to power, a Jungian therapist to a lack of individuation. Karen Horney would connect it to basic insecurity caused by the feeling of helplessness, abandonment, and insecurity in the animus world. A behavioral therapist would discover a learned or socially conditioned reaction underlying angst, and so on. Not only every school of psychotherapy, but also every therapist has his or her own concept of angst. However, what is common in all these scientific concepts is that they do not make any connection between angst and God's call! We may then echo Pilate and ask, "What is truth?"

In medicine there are two kinds of treatment: etiological (focusing on the reason for the ailment) and symptomatic (focusing on the symptoms of the sickness). Etiological treatment of diabetes, for example, would involve healing the pancreas and enabling it to produce insulin, while the symptomatic treatment involves injections of insulin. According to this distinction, faith is an etiological solution to angst, because it clarifies and heals the basic reason behind angst, whereas all psychotherapeutic methods represent a symptomatic approach, focused on healing particular symptoms.

The underlying problem of all angst is the lack of interior resonance with God's almighty, eternal, and ultimate love. Lack of a tangible union with the invisible God is the reason behind phobic, jealous, or other such oedipal problems in Freud's theory, behind inadequate will to power in Adler's theory, behind lack of individuation in Jung's model, or behind suffering from basic insecurity in Horney's model. Lack of union with God is the reason behind feelings of helplessness and hopelessness and behind the appropriation of inappropriate social conditioning in cognitive behavioral models. Since faith is God's gift, which professionals cannot give, they focus on treating only the symptoms of angst.

On the other hand, often there is a personal reason, which we may call a personality disorder, lurking in the background of neurotic or dysfunctional behavior. In neurotic behavior or in behavior directed by will to power or by basic insecurity, the patient is unable to rely on God due to disordered personality dynamics. So, faith, trust, biblical joy, peace, love, and experienced union with God are often prevented in areas of personal conflict or disorder. Paradoxically, not only a believer who is a qualified therapist, but sometimes also a non-religious therapist even if unaware of his or her role, may help a patient's return to God's kingdom by facilitating a forgiving, loving, and understanding attitude.

We could summarize with ideas expressed by Frankl: The direct goal of faith is to deepen union with God, but indirectly it contributes to mental health. The direct goal of psychotherapy and counseling is mental healing—but indirectly they contribute to union with God.[17]

The next question may be: "What are the consequences of not resolving angst—how far will angst escalate?"

I worked as a psychiatrist for a few years at a cancer clinic, where I frequently had to deal with people who were helped to accept the reality of having an inoperable cancer. Sometimes wealthy, successful, well-known people came to our clinic. Even though the doctors who worked there let the patients know as delicately as they could about their cancer, in those few moments of being confronted with the reality, those people's entire lives were shattered, their scale of values in shreds, their success, material wealth, and prestige—everything they had thought important, everything they had fought so hard to attain—suddenly dissolved into thin air. What had seemed important up until the diagnosis became meaningless, and what seemed unimportant suddenly became essential. Their whole world and everything in it had been turned upside down.

The long-lasting anguish of these people threatened to turn into horror. My task was to help them regain the courage and will to fight the cancer. Often the challenge for me was that many of the patients I met in the cancer clinic at first defended themselves by refusing to acknowledge and admit the truth. Tormenting sequences of denial, aggressive bargaining with God, depression, then finally acceptance (as described by Elizabeth Kubler-Ross) followed initial denial.[18]

These patients' peace of mind depended on their ability or inability to make the most important ultimate choice: for or against God. The longer one postponed the final choice of deciding to accept the reality of dying, the more painful his/her experience of angst—threatening again and again to turn into horror of dying without God.

Thus, angst can represent a life-long warning and call to establish a relationship with God. If neglected, it turns into horror of dying without God.

I will never forget the case of a fifty-two-year-old Orthodox priest, who was tested and examined for many weeks. Finally, one of the physicians, an atheist by his own claim, told him with scarcely-concealed malicious joy:

> Well, well, my dear Father, you are in big trouble. At first we thought you only had a peptic ulcer in your stomach, but it turns out to be a widely-spread cancer; you have six months to live.

> The priest answered, "That is not a very big problem. At least for six months in my life I will live like a real saint."

Obviously, this man of faith had a grasp not only of the best response, but also of the power which only a union with God can give. His reply was the consequence of his having found a correct response to his anguish much earlier and this helped him to preserve his optimism when confronted with a situation that often brings fear and horror. I believe that the only explanation for his behavior is that he has received the gifts of living in union with the one whom we call God.

The next question posed by our devil's advocate may be: "Do believers suffer less angst than non-believers?"

The answer can be kept short: This is one of the criteria of being a true Christian: that the believer is able to defeat angst by trust in, obedience to, and reliance on God. Angst and belonging to Christ are in fact mutually exclusive: the more faith, the less angst, and vice versa.

Nevertheless, one more fact should be recalled in the context of the relation between angst and faith: no human possesses perfect faith. Yes, we are redeemed from original sin but still, no human being is without Adam and Eve's legacy of imperfection. Thus, no human being is free of angst. It is a call, warning, and reason to permanently grow in faith. Angst is a barometer which cautions that during earthly existence even the best believers never reach their objective of complete union with Jesus. We are permanently "on our way."

The next question may be:

Isn't it possible that Stone Age and modern Christian religious beliefs alike are simply the consequence of the fear and angst of unavoidable suffering and death? In that case, faith is only the product of angst and a wishful defense and phantasm that has nothing to do with a truly existing God.

Let us discuss the first part of the question: is faith the consequence of angst? There is a widespread agnostic and atheist prejudice that fear of pain, suffering, and death is the reason religious beliefs flourish. In fact, however, angst is not the cause of faith, but is a challenge, a call—God's call—to which faith is the right response.

If faith were the consequence of angst, as atheists maintain, then increasing angst should entail an increase in faith (i.e., there ought to be a positive correlation between angst and faith). However, previously, in biblical and everyday examples, we discerned just the converse: an increase of faith is related to a decrease of angst. Angst is actually negatively correlated to faith! Thus despite the fact that angst and faith show a relationship, angst cannot be the cause of faith and faith cannot be the consequence of angst. Nevertheless, since sometimes it is difficult to distinguish cause from consequence in such a complex and abstract correlation, let me illustrate the dynamic with an example.

Insulin and blood glucose levels have a direct relationship in diabetic patients. The correlation is negative: increased insulin causes lower blood sugar levels. Thus, insulin is not the cause of diabetes (high blood sugar levels); neither is diabetes the consequence of insulin shots. In a similar way, angst is not the reason for or cause of faith, nor is faith the consequence of angst "shots." To summarize, it is not angst that causes faith, but rather the lack of faith that causes angst.

Let us now focus on the second part of the question: isn't it possible that faith is a mistaken, self-invented, fantasized answer to angst?

The difference between a true and a false response always lies in answering (or not) the challenge or call. Administering insulin is not a false or arbitrarily invented fantasy, exactly because it responds to and solves the problem of hyperglycemia in diabetes. In every science, we differentiate right from wrong discernment by the criterion of whether the proposed response solves the problem, or answers the question. If this is the case, why would we make an exception when assessing the correctness of responding to God's call? Why would we proclaim that a solution that answers the problem of angst, pain, and suffering is a human invention, fantasy or self-deception?

Indeed, if faith is the right answer to the challenge that causes angst, then trust in God (just like insulin in our example) cannot be a mere fantasy, a figment of human imagination, or self-deception. It has to be the right response to the test of the almighty, eternal, and ultimately loving questioner, who is God.

Howevewr, the devil's advocate may continue to object, "Let me formulate the question even more explicitly than the previous debater: Can we classify angst not as God's call but as a natural psychological phenomenon?"

Angst itself (defined as "fear without reason") is useless for the preservation of human life or worldly well being. If the phenomenon of angst had merely a natural cause, then from an evolutionary standpoint, it would have disappeared from the human mind and behavior by now because it is physically, chemically, biologically, psychologically or sociologically useless. However, as we all know, it did not and does not disappear! It has no natural reason or justification but stems from a particular other, or more exactly "quite other" reality. This reality, to whom the essential things are those that are unessential for self-preservation, who is not a natural, biological, psychological or sociological necessity, who is not interested so much in *bios* (biological life) but *zoe* (everlasting life), Christians call God. This is why we classify angst as God's most general call to humans, one that can be correctly answered only by faith.

However, let us answer the question using a different rationale. The well-known Russian researcher Ivan Pavlov carried out a famous experiment. He projected images of a circle followed immediately by an ellipse to his dogs. The dogs were rewarded for discriminating between the two shapes. Soon, however, the projected ellipse became more and more similar to the circle. Discriminating between the two became increasingly difficult for the dogs. They were nevertheless forced to choose and were punished for mistakes with electric shocks. Soon the dogs suffered a nervous breakdown. Pavlov tried, by this experiment, to explain the dynamics of human neuroses.

Now let us consider an imaginary experiment. If Pavlov's dogs could ask the question, "Since this task is useless for dogs (just as angst is for humans) why do we then have to make the choice between the circle and ellipse at all?" They would conclude: "Because a human scientist (Pavlov) is forcing us to take a stand in this matter quite peculiar to us dogs." The dogs, if they could think, would recognize the programmer beyond this situation, which from the dogs' perspective is an unnatural program that has no purpose in sustaining life.

Believers also recognize the *quite other* programmer who places us in a situation in which we must choose between an attractive appeal of the natural world and the biologically, psychologically, and sociologically counterproductive faith and trust in God. For agnostics the attractiveness of the world increases, while that of faith decreases. Those who make a bad choice, whose faith is not strong enough, are warned about their fundamentally erroneous choice by angst—comparable to the way Pavlov's dogs were warned by their master.

Human life is like a test situation where humans are called to choose faith by an ultimately loving programmer. If our response is incorrect and we are on the way to excluding ourselves from God's closeness, then angst will overcome us, but if our response is correct, then the gifts of faith will overcome angst.

Could the programmer—God—be a sheer human invention, only a fantasy?

No human being is able to avoid making the choice between the world and God. Being metaphorically and literally tested by God is not our choice at all, thus God cannot be a human invention only. He is the ultimate and unavoidable reality of human existence.

A reader may comment:

Earlier, we were talking about humans in search of God, as being species *homo religious*, and now we are talking about God as the unavoidable reality in human existence.[18] True, there was and is an idea of gods or God present in almost every historical period and culture, but always without a deity's corroborating that idea; nobody has ever seen God! Thus, is God a truly existing reality, or was his idea implanted in the human brain and mind during the Stone Age, some 50,000 years ago like an archetype, as a consolation against pain, suffering and angst?

Let us answer this question with Frankl's words discussing a similar question. Frankl states:

I asked my questioner whether there was such a thing as a four-archetype. He did not understand immediately, and so I said "Look here, all people discover independently that two and two make four. Perhaps we do not need an archetype for an explanation; perhaps two and two really do make four. And perhaps we do not need a divine archetype to explain human religion either. Perhaps God really does exist!"[19]

The last question may be: "Is this God, who forces us to search for him by threatening us with angst, really loving?"

The torment of angst and suffering is not literally God's call. Rather, angst is essentially a result of one's rejecting his call with consequent estrangement from God.

On the other hand, note that the here-drafted model of overcoming angst and suffering by faith is an ideal. God's people are always "on the way!" In practice, we must humbly acknowledge that the faith of everyone, even of the best Christians, is not without problems and times of estrangement from God. Rather, faith ideals show the right direction we must take, which is not always easy to approach, and even less easy to accomplish. Despite the fact that even the apostles' relationship with God seemed at times like a roller-coaster ride, the general trend in a true believer's faith dynamic should steadily progress towards the realization of a permanently deepening union with the invisible God.

Notes

1. Abraham J. Heschel, *Between God and Man* (New York: The Free Press, 1959), 9-10.

2. Celestin Tomic, *Prapovijest Spasenja* (Zagreb: Provincijalat Hrvatskih Franjevaca Konventualaca, 1977), 120-58.

3. Adalbert Rebic, *Biblijska Prapovijest* (Zagreb: Krscanska Sadasnjost, 1972), 74-76.

4. John Donne, *The Complete Poetry and Selected Prose of John Donne,* ed. Charles M. Coffin (New York: Modern Library Classis, 2001), 454.

5. American Psychiatric Association, *Quick Reference to the Diagnostic Criteria from Diagnostic and Statistical Manual of Mental Disorders, IV* (Washington, DC: The American Psychiatric Association, 1994), 199-219.

6. Ljubomir Eric, *Strah, Anksioznost i Anksiozna Stanja* (Beograd: Institut Za Strucno Usavrsavanje I Specijalizaciju Zdravstvenih Radnika, 1972), 10.

7. Eric, *Strah, Anksioznost i Anksiozna Stanja,* 15.

8. Eric, *Strah, Anksioznost i Anksiozna Stanja,* 11.

9. Eric, *Strah, Anksioznost i Anksiozna Stanja,* 50.

10. Jean P. Sartre, *L'Être et le Néant* (Paris: Gallimard, 1943).
11. Viktor E. Frankl, *Ärztliche Seelsorge* (Wien: Franz Deuticke, 1965), 45.
12. Frankl, *Ärztliche Seelsorge*, 58.
13. John Paul II, *Crossing the Threshold of Hope* (New York: Alfred A. Knopf, 1994), 62.
14. Viktor E. Frankl, *Antropologische Grundlagen der Psychoterapie* (Bern, Stuttgart, Wien: Hans Huber, 1976), 243.
15. J. I. Packer, *God's Plans for You* (Wheaton, IL: Crossway Books, 2001), 154.
16. Otto Fenichel, *The Psychoanalytic Theory of Neuroses* (New York: W. W. Norton & Co., 1972), 11.
17. Frankl, *Ärztliche Seelsorge*, 222.
18. Elizabeth Kubler-Ross, *On Death and Dying* (New York: Macmillan, 1969), 265.
19. Viktor E. Frankl: *The Doctor and the Soul: From Psychotherapy to Logotherapy* (New York: Vintage Books, 1968), xvii.

Chapter 29

A Paradoxical Pattern in the Personal Calls of Our Lord

Not only in matters of art, science, medicine, or technology, but also in faith questions, ordinary people, like most of us, often stand on the shoulders of giants who for us bear witness to the life, behavior patterns, characteristics of people in God's kingdom. Intentionally or not, knowingly or not, we watch them; we watch all of their moves, their words, and gestures. Standing on the shoulders of these people, these giants whom we so admire and want to emulate, we seek an answer to one question: Who? Who is the one reflected in their actions? Who makes it possible for their behavior to become an example for us? They have a special something that we would like to possess—their calmness, possibly their enthusiasm, optimism, logical reasoning, lifestyle, love, family, peace, selflessness, or other exemplary characteristics. When we try to analyze why we were drawn to them, we find what we are looking for: God's presence expressed through their behavior. God's gifts always appear and appeal to us through truly Christian behavior.

From this description it may seem that Christian witnessing is an idyllic and enviable demonstration of one's superiority in achieving closeness with God. It may also seem that Christian witnessing is a revered function distinguishing one who witnesses as an honored and respected spiritual super-model whose life is a pure and a permanent celebration, full of the admiration of disciples, and characterized by God's appreciation, support, and power, as well as human admiration of the Almighty-and-me relationship. However, nothing is further from reality than such images.

To illustrate this, let us discuss the well-known example of St. Paul, as described in Acts 9:1-2 and 26:12-18. Upon analyzing the biblical description, we conclude that psychologically, the cause of Paul's conversion while on the road to Damascus is an inexplicable, sudden, miraculous case of divine intervention. But the story of Paul's conversion includes not only this!

Saul's keen interest in theology and his studies at the feet of the celebrated Pharisee Gamaliel were not accidental. Still less accidental was his violent anti-Christian behavior. According to Acts 9:1, ". . . Saul was still breathing out murderous threats against the Lord's disciples." Analyzing this psychologically, we realize that he was fighting against Christians precisely because his attention was drawn consciously or unconsciously to Jesus Christ's lived example and teachings, both of which attracted him and drove him to be a Christian. He was probably ambivalent towards Christianity and its followers. He consciously demonstrated his dislike, but the more he consciously hated, the more he was subconsciously attracted to the very people that he persecuted. The example of Christians disturbed his religious peace of mind—they had done what he was tempted to do, and this was one of the strongest and most important drives behind his zealous anti-Christian sentiment and behavior. From his behavior, we assume that God had called him and had worked on Saul's soul, his mind, his way of thinking, his senses, and even the experiences of the future saint long before he realized what was happening to him.

For Saul, this period was successful from a worldly perspective, but spiritually tormenting. We may feel bewildered, wondering what caused the spiritual uneasiness and disquietude in the revered and respected Pharisee's life.

We all try to convince ourselves that others cannot have what we do not have; others cannot live in union with God, while we are unsuccessful in our own attempts to do so. Learning of others' virtues is never easy, especially not when those others are citizens of God's kingdom as we ourselves are called to be, while we in our inmost hearts reject the role of humble and self-denying discipleship. The mostly repressed ambivalent attraction to Christians in Saul's subconscious mind made not only the lives of those he disliked miserable, but perhaps it made Saul himself even more so.

God used a unique personal call suited especially to Saul's character. He called Saul the Jew to be Paul the Apostle through paradoxical but genuinely Christian examples as he stood on the shoulders of the giants whom he had so determinedly persecuted. Isn't this a paradoxical, inverse relationship?

Yes, it is. However, let us note that Saul's story, persecuting the giants on whose shoulders he climbed, is one of the countless repetitions of the same paradoxical pattern that has continued to be the essence of Christian witness since Jesus Christ's ministry. In the persecuted Christians, Jesus' extreme humility, modesty, and love, which are interconnected to his ultimate glory, splendor, and omnipotence, are paradoxically replicated. This is how true giants who have been ". . . counted worthy of suffering disgrace for the Name," according to Acts. 5:41, have behaved since Jesus' incarnation.

Undoubtedly, the central life event that enabled Saul's turnaround and his acceptance of Christianity was this event on the road to Damascus. From this same source stemmed also his later fervent activity in spreading Jesus' legacy, his indestructible optimism and zeal, his unparalleled joy and love despite all of his calamities, and his enviable, unshaken certainty of living in and with Jesus. These events occurred only a few years after Jesus' ascension, around the years 34-35. It is impossible for us to grasp or explain the convincing power of Jesus' call, experienced by Saul not only introspectively but also sensorially. It was a true miracle, altering Saul's mind forever. Its effect enabled Saul to change from a persecutor of Christians into Paul, a persecuted Christian. What a mystical paradoxical evolution, observed from the perspective of normal human psychology!

St. Paul spent the rest of his life under the influence of this miraculous meeting, as we can reconstruct from his letters, filled with joy of being in union with Jesus despite all previous mishaps on his journey. However, even after his transformation Paul experienced many calamities and difficulties, and his life did not become an idyllically-painted pastoral scene. In contrast to Paul's life before his conversion, this period of his life was tormented from a worldly perspective, but remarkable from a spiritual viewpoint.

What we know from the Bible is that on his first trip (between 45 and 49) he raised some money to help the Judean church, but after his return, at the synod in Jerusalem, he was sharply opposed by Jews who had been converted to Christianity and preferred to remain faithful to their Jewish traditions. Nevertheless, this rejection of him by the Judaists initiated Paul's interest in missionary work with gentiles. Soon thereafter, on his second trip, he established a new Macedonian church. But his troubles were not over. Shortly afterwards, he had to run for his life, finding refuge this time in Antioch. His third trip led him to Ephesus; however, he evoked anger among his audience, and again only a quick escape saved his life. Between 57 and 58 he was arrested again, this time in Jerusalem. With the help of his Roman citizenship he traveled to Rome, but his ship capsized in Malta. After doing some missionary work in Malta and Rome, Paul fled yet again. The Scriptures do not reveal detailed information about his activities, but he probably visited some of the churches he himself had established, and perhaps even traveled to Spain. In any case, around the year 67 he was executed in Rome. Because of his Roman citizenship, his mission was ended not on a cross, but St. Paul was martyred by beheading.

St. Paul's faith, life, and glory, even though he often suffered worldly misery, remains an extraordinary example for us all. We may have the feeling that our contribution to building God's kingdom is insignificant in comparison to his. We may think that our testimony, feeble as it may be, is in vain, or that it will not be noticed or remembered by others. The Christians persecuted by Saul likely had similar questions plaguing them.

Nevertheless, the more a truly biblical witness to God's kingdom seems impossible, and the more bearing of Christ's cross seems paradoxical to the world, the more it is biblically genuine and sound. The more one's lifestyle and biblical love seem paradoxical, the more one resembles the anonymous Christian giants on whose shoulders Saul climbed, and the more authentically Jesus Christ's paradoxical example is given witness.

Saul is not alone. Many Christians receive God's "quite other" paradoxical calls. Being perhaps unaware of their own role of being giants, these Christians inconspicuously and humbly witness to God's kingdom. However, God's criteria, the ways he makes his kingdom grow, are different from those of the world. Saul's call, and Paul's life story, eloquently demonstrate God's paradoxical logic.

Even though inconspicuous, the testimony we have borne can never be erased from history, just as no one can destroy the contribution of the masses of unknown Christians on whose shoulders Saul climbed to God's kingdom! It will last forever. Our responsibility is great. While we stand on the shoulders of other Christians, and, others in turn stand on ours, a unique message is delivered through us. We are all tools in God's hands. May we always keep this in mind!

Elizabeth Lukas expressed this idea in the following way. I paraphrase: A man walked down the road. He noticed a little girl, shivering with cold, standing at the roadside. She had no place to go, and nothing to eat. The man cried out in despair to God: "How can you let this happen to her? Why don't you do something?" For a while, God said nothing, according the story. Then one night He replied: "I already did something about it. I created and sent you."[1]

Note

1. Elizabeth Lukas, "What is Special about Logotherapy?" *A Presentation of Casuistic Elements with Case Studies* (Paper read at the Tenth World Congress on Logotherapy, Dallas, TX: July 1995).

Chapter 30

The Human Response to God's Call: When Does Mature Faith Begin?

Faith is a gift which helps us to recognize, communicate with, and experience God's personality. Having faith is the acknowledgment of being the recipient of God's love, which enables believers to know and respond with confidence to God and to bear witness to the world. God's knowledge of a particular person, which is manifest in his gifts, allows humans to know God and have faith. Let us in this chapter focus on such pressing matters as when mature faith begins and when we can be sure that we have at least touched upon it.

30.1. Defining the Problem

Before we start our discussion, let us first clarify what the expression "maturity of faith" means. How can we determine or measure the maturity of one's response to God's call?

Note that maturity of faith, in a psychological-theological context, means neither an ethical, pious, or godly quality, nor a sort of theological merit, for who among us could competently judge these qualities? Rather, it means having an established, authentic faith in which one need not be disappointed. Immature, naïve faith signifies the opposite, the kind of faith in which one will inevitably be disappointed. The naïve believer is bound to be disappointed in faith and God, because naïve faith is not built based on the biblical image of God, but on self-created images of a god. The reason for disappointment in such a self-created god lies in one's inability to establish true and lasting communication with this god, to hear this god's word, to experience being the object and recipient of this god's love.

As Xavier Léon-Dufour noted, "the topic of God's word is not a topic of abstract speculation"; rather, "it is above all an experiential fact."[1] Naïve believers will try to be subjects exploring God. However, if one is trying to explore God or to objectify his existence, the feeling, experience, and evidence of being a recipient of his gifts will often be missing. Communication with God is always personal and real, and it takes the form of a discipleship pattern. But what are the practical characteristics of the sort of faith in which one will not be disappointed?

30.2. From Naïve to Mature Faith

As noted, immature or naïve faith signifies a belief system where sensorial or cognitive proofs are used to justify faith. In the mental climate of the Middle Ages, or even as recently as three- to four hundred years ago, such a naïve belief system, focused on the visible and touchable presence of God, was easy to maintain. The miracle of life, the outbreak or cessation of a smallpox epidemic, or the movement of the clouds in the sky were understood as obvious signs of God's presence and of his visible and touchable involvement. However, in modern times, after Galileo, Darwin, and Freud, in this time of bioengineering, cloning, and human manipulation of life, such an image of God is increasingly difficult to preserve. Regardless, modern naïve believers are still looking for obvious proofs of God, such as miraculous healings, inexplicable lucrative divine intervention, and mysterious events in nature, just as Thomas did two thousand years ago. God undoubtedly performs miraculous and inexplicable signs in our time too, but not on demand, not to everyone, and not as in a circus show, as naïve believers would prefer.

Before discussing how God enables the maturation of such faith, let us first visualize the psychological dynamics within immature believers.

When I was a young scout, our chaplain told us an anecdotal story that seemed childish but nonetheless gave me reason enough to rethink my relationship with Jesus. According to the story, one small boy prayed,

Dear Lord, please let two times two equal five. You know I gave this solution in my mathematics test, and I'm afraid it will be marked wrong, so please let two times two equal five.

Then our chaplain asked us whether we thought this prayer reflected genuine faith.

Despite its naïveté, does the story not have some relevance to everyone's life and faith at least at some time and on some level? Do we ourselves at times not re-enact the boy's example, asking for things in our prayers, perhaps overemphasizing the importance of lucrative gain? These are characteristics of naïve faith.

Theologically, by biblically communicating with God in spirit, especially in prayer, mature believers receive a sign and foretaste of *zoe*, of union with God, when we will see him face-to-face. On the other hand, immature believers prefer *bios* (such as the success or pride of the world) over *zoe*. Such naive expectations are typical when one requires God to be a wish-fulfilling, servant-idol—in other words, to be *a god*. God's response in the form of silence is inevitable, not because Jesus is not responding, but because the immature believer is not interested in hearing God's response. It is not a sign of naïve faith to present to God one's personal and even financial or business problems, needs, and hopes in prayer, but it is naïve to expect God to play the role of a wish-fulfilling god, providing prompt, abundant, visible, and measurable proof of his existence.

Psychologically, the maturation of faith is a steady process of learning and training to recognize and appreciate biblical gifts above worldly gains. It is a process of being coached to appreciate, acknowledge, and validate as genuine needs, and as reality and fact, the personal experience of biblical meaning, joy, trust, hope, and other spiritual gifts and gifts of faith, as well as to see them as more important than visible, pragmatic, cognitive worldly gains.

Andrew Murray describes this process as follows.

There is a faith that sees the promise and embraces it, but does not receive it. (Hebrews 11:13,39) When the answer to prayer does not come and the promise we most firmly trust appears to be fruitless—the promise that whatever believers pray for will be received—then the real test of faith, more precious than gold, takes place. It is during this test that the faith that has embraced the promise is purified, strengthened, and prepared for personal, holy fellowship with the living God, for the sight of his glory. It takes and holds the promise until it has received the fulfillment in living truth of what it had requested from the unseen but living God.[2]

Let us apply this to our example. We can assume that while the boy's childish belief is nice, he will surely experience dissatisfaction. He will likely be disappointed with the God who appears to him deaf, uninterested in his problem, or even dead. However, this productive disappointment has a purpose: it brings him closer to the watershed—the divider.

The watershed that makes the essential difference between a maturing believer and a rebellious semi-agnostic whose faith is stagnant, is that the believer self-critically understands the reason for God's silence. Meanwhile religious fanatics are trying to force God to talk, agnostics are becoming doubtful and turning away, and atheists are becoming enemies of the dead God.

How would God by his silence help the maturing faith of the boy in question? God would not change the rules of multiplication for him, but he would give the boy spiritually-experienced gifts. It might be a God-given discernment of a new meaning to study industriously, or renewed determination, courage, or endurance in his efforts to improve his math. Perhaps God would give him consolation, trust, or hope, despite his failure. Maybe God would give him the capacity to exercise useful self-criticism, or a new insight, a chance to grow and overcome his naïve beliefs so that they can ripen into mature faith. Or perhaps, Jesus would help him to sense security in his maturing faith, which cannot be achieved even with the most excellent knowledge of mathematics. He probably would help the young boy to experience his failure and powerlessness, and then by leading the boy to glorify and discern the true deity of God, he would enable new growth in the boy's union with the almighty, eternal, and ultimate love.

Let us also observe the dynamics of mature faith. In Matthew 21:22, Jesus promised believers that whatever they pray for will be received. The same promise is even more explicitly formulated in Matthew 7:7-8: "Ask and it will be given to you; seek and you will find; knock and the door will be opened to you. For everyone who asks receives; he who seeks finds; and to him who knocks, the door will be opened."

Note that "asking," "seeking," "knocking,"—in other words, being a true disciple first—is the prerequisite to prayers' being fulfilled. Mature believers ask for spiritual gifts such as faith, hope, love, self-control, and constructive and fair self-criticism, and their prayers will almost always be answered, just as they ask. Psychologically, the more mature a believer's faith is, the more he or she asks for gifts of the Spirit that God almost always fulfills.

A believer more close to the ideal level of maturity prays more like Jesus in the garden of Gethsemane, surrendering his own will and accepting the Father's, as described in Luke 22:42. Also, from a psychological and theological standpoint, such Christ-like prayer marks the process we described in the above subtitle. There is the moment when mature faith begins, and such prayer marks it.

30.3. A Case Study

Frankl describes a person of mature faith in a case study of one of his patients, a young man with an inoperable spinal tumor. As his illness progressed, he became quadriplegic, unable to move his arms or legs and in need of permanent palliative care. Totally immobile, the sick but spiritually powerful young man unexpectedly found new value in his life. He got into long conversations with other patients, encouraged them, comforted them, and did his best to give them strength. From then on, that became his mission, adding new value and meaning to his life. As time went on, however, he was unable to do even that. No longer able to read or listen to his radio, alive, but almost completely cut off from the world, he found still more meaning and value in his life. On the day he died, a day he somehow knew of in advance, the doctor on duty was supposed to give him an injection of morphine at midnight. During his afternoon visit, however, this patient asked the doctor to give him the injection immediately, so the doctor wouldn't have to get up at midnight just for him. Those were his last words, as noted in his case record. [3]

Isn't this uncommon care for the needs of others amazing? I assume that this man of mature faith, anonymous to us but intimately known by God, did pray for that which God granted him: peace, love, optimism, and a meaningful life and death. His deeds, not empty words or public demonstrations of his faith, were proof of his mature relationship with God. This is how a mature, value-discerning believer responds to God's calls. This is how a mature believer lives and dies. Such silent, inconspicuous behavior is a more efficient way of witnessing to God's kingdom and being a giant on whose shoulders others may climb, than any glamorous worldly demonstrations.

I have observed from time to time in my practice that, in one's re-examination of the qualities and merit of one's life, what matters most is not worldly praise. In one's dying moments, when re-evaluating the merits or demerits of one's life from God's perspective becomes unavoidable, paradoxically what is most respectable in the eyes of the world becomes least important, and what is unimportant in the eyes of the world commands greatest respect.

Notes

1. Xavier Léon-Dufour, *Rjecnik Biblijske Teologija*, ed. Josip Turcinovic (Zagreb: Krscanska Sadasnjost, 1988), 1104.

2. Andrew Murray, *With Christ in the School of Prayer* (New Kensington, PA: Whitaker House, 1981), 64-65.

3. Viktor E. Frankl, *Ärztliche Seelsorge* (Wien: Franz Deuticke, 1965), 65.

Chapter 31

The Transempirically Experienced Presence of God in Mature Belief

Since we are approaching topics that are scientifically or psychologically inexplicable, we have to be a bit mystical to discuss them. Communication with God is the most personal experience for every believer, and such experiences are ineffable. For this reason, let us discuss God's role in the communication and faith of someone whom we all know from biblical description and who can represent every mature believer.

31.1. A "Psychological Autopsy" of Abraham's Faith

Let us, living millennia after his exemplary example, reconstruct and undertake a "psychological autopsy" of Abraham's experience of faith and communication with God.

When Abraham (Abram) appears, in the twelfth chapter of Genesis, a new period in human history begins. Why? What is the real importance of his appearance? To answer this, let us first review what we know about Abraham. Abraham and his father Terah lived east of the Euphrates River, and they worshipped other gods (see Josh. 24:2). The Lord called Abraham, "Leave your country, your people, and your father's household and go to the land I will show you." (Gen. 12:1-2)

Approximately 3800 years ago, when this was taking place, civilization was limited to Mesopotamia, which is where Abraham lived. He came from a rich and respected family. We may assume that the call he received to leave his people and to move towards the west must have seemed absurd to him. Whether it did or not, Abraham obeyed. He left the abundance, civilization, well-being, and certainty of his country of origin, and with his possessions and followers crossed a parched, unfriendly, and dangerous desert in the hope that he would find the land Yahweh promised. Abraham's journey must have seemed as foolish to some of his contemporaries as we would deem a modern-day visionary emigrating from North America or Western Europe to the North Pole in hopes of finding the Promised Land.

How could Abraham have believed such an absurd promise? There were religious people before Abraham. Nearly everyone in the eighteenth century before Christ was convinced that a god or gods existed. There were no atheists at that time, but most people were naïve believers. These people obeyed, served, and worshipped their gods to gain personal advantage. But somehow, the faith of the Father of Belief was qualitatively different. "Abram believed God." (Gen. 15:6) He did not only worship or use God to gain lucrative advantage, but he trusted and believed that Yahweh was a good God and that he could have complete trust and confidence in him. Although it seemed that Yahweh was asking him to do something impossible or irrational, "Against all hope, Abraham in hope believed and so became the father of many nations . . ." (Rom. 4:18).

Belief and trust that God is good and that what he requires will work out in the end is the main characteristic of Abraham's faith.

Abraham's trust was often tested, as when Yahweh promised that his wife Sara would be pregnant when this seemed hopeless because, at the time, Sara was 90 and Abraham 99. His trust in God was tested even more when God requested him to sacrifice his son Isaac. Indeed, it is extremely difficult, if not impossible, for us to accept such a request as a genuine and justifiable demand from a compassionate God. But, it didn't seem impossible or absurd to Abraham. He had an unconditional trust in God's benevolence and providence.

According to Bouyer, "Knowledge of God in Judaism, from the beginning, supposes a union—not some union of man with god to which man could raise himself, but a union with man which God has willed from all eternity."[1] The precondition of such union is God's gift—faith. Thus, Yahweh made himself known to Abraham as the almighty, eternal, and ultimate love in whom he could have total trust and absolute, unconditional faith. Such faith may seem puzzling to us. What substantiated his reasons psychologically and experientially? We know from the biblical description in Genesis 12:1 that Abraham did not receive visible, touchable, or measurable proofs. Then what caused such a degree of faith in him?

The Bible describes Abraham's communication with God in the form of a vision, a reflective-mystical, a paramount transempirical experience.

Abraham's communication with God was—as are love, trust, and faith—composed of two parts: God's intervention (Yahweh's call), and Abraham's response. This double-sided communication between God and Abraham was the most important difference between Abraham's mature belief and the naïve belief of his neighbors. They lived mostly in a monologue with their gods. They worshipped their gods, and prayed for nice weather and good health, for military victories and a good harvest (note all the cognitive aspects), and we may safely assume that their prayers were not always fulfilled.

A person of mature faith like Abraham, had a different sort of communication with God. In the Bible, we can find numerous accounts of God visiting Abraham, of God talking to him, even of God telling him exactly what to do. In turn, Abraham could talk freely and spontaneously to Yahweh. As noted, he lived in a transempirical (to use a philosophical term), and a mystical, reflective, or introspectively experienced (to use psychological terms) unity with God. Genesis 18:1-15 describes how Abraham hosted God, how he ate and drank with God. We contemporaries may think that if we could do the same, if we could talk and eat with God, then we would believe and trust as strongly as Abraham did. But our experiences are very different from Abraham's.

Was God more tangibly present in Abraham's life than in our own? No; the difference lies in something else. We should not forget that Abraham still had only God's promise, while we today have the fulfillment of God's kingdom. The difference is not in God's presence, as God is not less present in our lives. The difference is in our unwillingness to see and acknowledge him. Why are we unwilling to acknowledge God in our everyday search for meaning and ultimate meaning?

We are, by our sensorial-scientific functions of existence, cognitively-anchored people. We rely more on visible, touchable, and positive facts than on non-sensorial evidence. Abraham's attitude was different; consequently, so was his experience. His personal communion with God was, for him, more realistic and evident than sensorial, scientifically or cognitively experienced facts. His dialogue with the reality we call God was much more important to him than communicating through cognitively-experienced worldly phenomena which he could see, touch, or measure.

Indeed, then, the peace and joy that God gave him—the providence and trustworthiness God offered him—were more evident to Abraham than to modern agnostics, who live only in the mundane dimension of the everyday world. This made Abraham a value-discerning person, while the agnostics who live only in the reality of the sensorial and cognitively experienced world remain value-blind. For people of faith like Abraham, God is, de facto, experientially present. This gave Abraham the best and most important gift: unbroken unity with God, accompanied by strong meaning, joy, power, persistence, and other gifts.

This, essentially, is also the gist of the response from my theology professor to a student who asked him if it is really true that Abraham hosted, ate, and drank with God. Paraphrased, his reply was, "If you believe like Abraham did, you yourself could eat and drink with God every day of your life." Beyond eating and drinking, beyond hosting, Abraham lived in a real union with God, and this is what gave him power to accomplish his mission. This is the reason we honor him as the Father of Belief.

Let us now discuss Abraham's faith from a different perspective. Psychologically, the feeling of affection and the depth of a relationship are connected. So it is in a relationship with God as well. Faith grants the experiencing of God's love, while it grows by the experiencing of God's affection. This circle turns ever more rapidly and more decisively for mature believers. Abraham's trust in God enabled his faith, and by experiencing the gifts of his faith, he became able to talk, host, eat with, and live with God in a permanent relationship.

We are not doubtful of the existence of the reality of the world we live in. But Abraham's even stronger certainty of God's existence gained him the gift and privilege of factually living with God. Just as we inhale and then exhale air, he was continuously giving himself to God while receiving God's spiritual gifts. We can illustrate this process in Figure 31-1.

We know that such communication was taking place between God and Abraham, not only because the Bible describes it, but for psychological reasons. Abraham would not have undertaken the venture he did without a firm and convincing reason. He had courage to rely on his transempirical reflections. They were paramount for Abraham.

The transcendent reality of God with whom he reflectively communicated has been the most important reality for people of mature faith

Figure 31-1

God's Call
to Abraham

Abraham's
Response
to God

ever since Abraham's time. By his faith almost four-thousand years ago, Abraham opened humankind's eyes for experiential discernment in faith questions.

31.2. The Significance of Abraham's Example in Our Age of Relativism

Abraham's communicating and trusting the invisible, but experientially-present God, gave him and his followers determination, power, and courage in their struggle to accomplish their mission. Such purpose and meaning in life is also what young and old, rich and poor, cleric and lay, healthy and sick people of our time need just as much as did Abraham's contemporaries.

Missing such Abraham-like unshakeable trust in God, we may observe the opposite trend. For example, Abraham's Jewish followers in the next eighteen hundred years were more focused on ritualistic, cultic, palpable, demonstrative, and formal adherence to law, king, and Temple, while the genuine love of God, expressed by many, became neglected (see John 5:42-44). Parallel to this tendency, greed, selfishness and hunger for power, assassinations, betrayal, and social injustice increased. Human-made desperation, suffering, and pain on one hand, and estrangement from God on the other, were directly correlated. Something similar also happened in the history of Christianity. From Peter's denial of knowing Jesus, to the most recent problems confronting the church (such as sexual abuse scandals), for every human-made torment throughout history, there is a common reason (or at least a common trigger), namely, distrust in God.

Joseph Ratzinger in *Behold the Pierced One* wrote,

> We must acknowledge, however, that faith is seriously weakened and threatened within the Church. Even we in the Church have lost courage. We feel it to be arrogance or triumphalism to assume that the Christian faith tells us the truth.

> We have picked up the idea that all religions are the product of history, some developing this way and others that, and that every person is as he is because of the accident of birth. Such a view reduces religion from the level of truth to the level of habit. It becomes an empty flux of inherited tradition which no longer has any significance.[2]

But if God really is the ultimate goodness, if he really is the almighty, eternal, and ultimate love, what causes in our culture the phenomenon described above, and the irrational trend of collective indifference towards him, the source of hope, courage, and power much stronger than all suffering?

The widespread suffering of meaningless and ultimately meaninglessness life started almost naturally and inconspicuously with the universal doubt in the post-scholastic period. First, it became questionable if anything discerned by the senses has an absolute or real validity. This epistemological insecurity slowly evolved into general insecurity and uncertainty, characteristic of Western culture which is steeped in Descartes' well-known motto *Omnes dubitandum est*—Everything is doubtful.

This relativism then led to an even greater skepticism, especially in the areas of morality and religion. This enabled the next step in the development of a widespread chronic loss of God: if everything is relative, if an absolute moral standard does not exist, if everything is equally morally sound, then God becomes just a god, and Christianity merely one religion among many other equally good (or bad) belief systems. However, without true, wholehearted commitment and discipleship to the absolute, Jesus' teachings as well as the gifts of faith become merely relative, and a genuine and paramount relationship with God becomes merely an "as if" reality.

As a consequence, in Kant's time metaphysical security was lost to all but a few philosophers. Today, 200 years later, humans seems to be the measure of everything, and nothing seems to be absolutely certain for many of our postmodern contemporaries. Is, however, all human knowledge, from ethics to physics, indeed uncertain and doubtful?

First, the limits and relativity of human knowledge do not exclude the existence of an absolute, beyond the relativity of our acknowledgment. On the contrary, if everything is relative, then the reliability of relative conclusions is also relative! So what is an absolute especially in relation to the discernment-of-faith questions?

Theologically, the Scriptures, Jesus, the biblical teachings of the church, church traditions, and the teachings of the Spirit, soul, and conscience constitute the absolute.

A devil's advocate might say:

Yes, but history proves that these criteria for discerning the absolute were often misinterpreted and misused because of psychological, political, cultural, or economic reasons. So, what then, if anything, is absolute?

Let us recall our discussion of the human condition. We concluded that no human is better able to perceive, understand, and grasp reality than the talented subject who obeys the Spirit and who feels and thinks with his or her brain, mind, conscience, and soul. For every subject, the absolute is—as Augustine in the fourth century, Pascal in the eighteenth, and Frankl in the twentieth, all described it—one's own (truthful) proofs of the heart. What we experience as evident in introspections, reflections, mystical experiences or meaning-discernments is undoubtedly relevant for every human being. The human search for meaning and joy, and the desire to avoid pain and suffering is the absolute for every human being. The same is true of believers' search for union with God—the almighty, eternal and ultimate love. Lasting and steadily increasing peace, love, joy, optimism, courage, and trust in the believer are the criteria of the correctness of faith. For the faithful, the evidence of being the object of God's love is the absolute experience, verified by spiritual gifts. They prove a union with the living God beyond a reasonable doubt; that is the absolute.

Such self-assessment is not arbitrary. Everyone is free to make a choice, but nobody is free to make a choice and avoid its consequence.

Thus, transempirical consequences of our choices, and the experiences caused by them, are certain, absolute, and unavoidable.

What Abraham relied on was the absolute for humans, his experiential communication with God and life in union with him. For a believer of strong and mature faith, the unconditional giving of oneself to God in discipleship and receiving gifts of faith as his response are certain experiences! In practice, the more gifts of faith one receives, the more his or her union with God becomes closer to an absolute certainty.

This answers questions about Abraham asked early in this chapter. It also answers the question of what is reliable and absolute in thinking and feeling via the brain, mind, soul, and conscience of the believer who has been blessed and enriched by the Spirit. As love, discerned meaning, or granting forgiveness can be absolutely certain to a loving, meaningfully living or a wholeheartedly forgiving person, so to postmodern believers their experiential, personal communication with the living God is absolute in the same way that it was to Abraham!

Today we live in a situation similar to Abraham's when he received and responded to God's call. We, too, have only transempirical proof, as he did. Later, with the appearance of Christ, Abraham's faith was also cognitively proven. Now, while we live our earthly life, we also have only internal evidence of living in God's kingdom. We trust, as Abraham did, that God's kingdom will cognitively, obviously, visibly and touchably be proven by the second coming of our Lord Jesus Christ. Until then, however, we have no way of experiencing the Lord other than through mystical experiences, functions of purpose, introspection, and reflections.

Notes

1. Louis Bouyer, *The Church of God* (Chicago, IL: Franciscan Herald Press, 1982), 223.

2. Joseph Ratzinger, *Behold the Pierced One: An Approach to Spiritual Christology* (San Francisco, CA: Ignatius Press, 1986), 12.

Chapter 32

God's Personal Characteristics: His Love

Michael Durrant examined the claim that the name "God" has no meaning that we can exactly define and determine. In his opinion, "It is not possible to offer a coherent account of the logical status of 'God' as an item of Christian language as a whole, since 'God' exhibits differing and indeed incompatible status." The nature of God is inexpressible because God is quite different or absolutely different from any human being, indeed different from anything that we can understand or imagine.[1]

This may be so for a rational scientist or philosopher who prefers logical-scientific discernments, but not for God's people. In the experience of believers, nothing is closer than God, and nothing is more strongly experienced than he. We are in a paradoxical situation: God is transcendent—we are unable even to exactly define, describe or grasp him, but believers are at the same time able to experience the personality of the revealed God more closely than anything else. According to the Scriptures, as noted in 1 John 4:8, "Whoever does not love does not know God, because God is love." His personal love is one of God's essential characteristics. Thus, we can conclude that the one who knows God's love knows his personality.

"But," a devil's advocate might object, "We read in 1 John 4:12 that: 'No one has ever seen God.' So how, then, do believers experience the love of a God who is invisible, untouchable, and therefore impossible to communicate with?"

We could reply: Human love is also invisible, but it is an experience that is always connected to a visible and touchable loving person, to HIS OR HER BODY, and to visible and touchable acts (signs) that prove the love or affection of that person. The personality of a beloved, despite being invisible, becomes so intimately known to a loving spouse, child, or parent, that a saying was created: "It is easier to know a loved one's personality than your own." Similarly, as one shows him or herself (beyond bodily expression) through behavior, actions, reactions, loyalty, as well as through communication, just so do people of faith experience God's personality.

How does this occur? We defined Biblical Joy as "the reverberation of the almighty, eternal, and ultimate love of God within the believer's conscience" and his or her whole person. A similar echoing and reflection enables value discernment of other spiritual gifts as well: biblical meaning, encouragement, optimism, persistence, peace, forgiveness, strength, and hope. Believers register those gifts of faith introspectively and reflectively—through discerning a meaning and ultimate meaning beyond happenings in their lives. This is the mosaic: When believers discern echoing biblical optimism, courage, peace, and joy (and other gifts of faith) beyond particular occurrences in their lives, then these value-discerning people of faith are aware that they are communicating with the transcendent God and that they are receiving and experiencing His love.

Because a concrete example is always more understandable than an abstract discussion, consider this example by a person with the pseudonym "Paul Richardson," who gave the following description of an encounter he had with God. In his medical studies, the hardest test for him was in anatomy. The young Richardson had a lot of trouble with it and, although he studied hard, he could never feel certain that his knowledge was sufficient to get him through his exams. The day before his finals he studied all night, he could not go to sleep out of fear, and by early morning he was back to his books. Finally, the time came to leave home for the exam. With every step he took toward the university his fear grew; he felt he would not survive this crisis and was on the verge of panic. Then, as Richardson described it (I summarize and paraphrase his confession): "Suddenly I remembered: I am a man of faith. I believe in God and I trust him. I live in God's kingdom. Therefore, shouldn't I be ashamed of this fear of something which is not important to my salvation at all?" Thinking this, completely banished his fear. Calmly, trusting in God, he went in to take his exam.

Later, reflecting on this incident, Richardson said:

> It became clear to me that God had undoubtedly helped me on that occasion. He gave me strength to face what I feared and to defeat my fear. By my turning to God and thinking of him, I was able to see that my fear was about a thing of no consequence to God's kingdom. That I succeeded in my exam, as I look back now, was not God's most gracious gift to me, and not even that God helped me to overcome the fear that tormented me, but that he gave me peace, hope, trust, optimism, and even joy . . . that he strengthened my faith, that He was present for me!

Every one of us may have had, at one time or another, a similar experience or encounter, but we may have questioned ourselves about it: "Was it really God's presence? Has God really helped me or have I just been carried away by my imagination, deceiving myself about the whole thing?"

These questions also arose in Richardson's mind after the exam was over and he thought about his encounter with God.

Let me summarize his lengthy answer: The fact is that he was very anxious and gripped by fear. He could not sleep, stay up, or study. No matter what he did and how much he wanted to calm down, he could not. If, in this situation, he had taken a tranquilizer pill and it had calmed him down, he would never have doubted the pill's benefit and effectiveness. Why? Because it would in fact, have been effective.

Thus, if Richardson could not achieve calmness by any imagination, autosuggestion, or willful choice, but all of a sudden it happened by confronting God, why would he doubt that he had really received help, and furthermore, that he had received it from the existing reality who is God? The effect proves its cause; biblical peace, hope, and trust echo God's love.

Richardson's value discernment helped him to recognize the "You" who communicates and answers prayers, not like a pill but as an individual, a personality. Believers call this Personality GOD.

Pondering this, one playing the role of devil's advocate could say:

All this does not prove that Richardson was really communicating with God. He could have experienced some tranquil thoughts, feelings, or insights. Imagination or a self-deception, illusion, or delusion also could have contributed. As long as one does not realize their deceitfulness, they can give consolation or make one happy.

If such self-deception were possible, who among us would not deceive him or herself?

We do not call it a mistake or self-deception when an experience rewards by steadily-increasing meaning, peace and joy in a believer. Logic calls such "self-deception" as that of Richardson correct discernment or truth. Communication, and the bestowal of gifts like peace, acceptance, courage, joy, are ways God reveals himself, ways he communicates with his people. In turn, receiving spiritual gifts is the way in which people of faith experience their communication with the invisible God.

A devil's advocate could persist with his or her argument:

> But we can also get consolation, power, and the joy you speak of from many other sources: music, hobbies, sports, the fine arts, just to name a few. It is not only God who gives us these benefits. Belief in God is only one of the ways we can get consolation, nothing more.

Of course, discovering happiness, consolation, or pleasure in music, hobbies, sports, or art should not be mistaken for self-deception. It is the discovery of a sensorial registered truth by a value-observing person. Note also, then, that neither are the biblical joy, optimism, or power that God gives, self-deceptions; rather, they are discoveries of a truth by a value-discerning believer!

On the other hand, living with God gives us what the world's sports or hobbies cannot give. God is the absolute. He is the absolute value, love, goodness, and meaning. He is, using Kierkegaard's phrase, the "Quite Other," separate from the world. He abundantly and eternally gives "quite other" gifts that amount to much more and are different from those the world can ever give. Instead of possessing only *bios*, God also gives *zoe* as seen in Richardson's case.

People of faith often cannot describe or express in words and concepts this absolute. They have nothing other than language, as limited as it is, to describe how the person of faith will come to know God, the "Quite Other." Of course, even then it can only be a best attempt; there are no words to describe the ineffable. The person of faith, however, will experience it and thereby acknowledge it. When all is said and done, God is still awesome and transcendental, but at the same time close and present.

Although God is transcendent, untouchable, immeasurable, he is intimately involved in our lives despite our being unaware of his presence, and unable to comprehend that fact until we experience it for ourselves again and again through receiving his spiritual gifts, and gifts of faith.

The theologian Ferenc Szabo provides a quotation from the Nobel Prize winning poet and novelist François Mauriac: "It is surprising to think that nothing is closer to man than God, and nothing is more strange to man than living in a godless world."[2] We discussed earlier how strange life is when God is silent, or, for the agnostic and atheist, without God. However, in God's kingdom, God is closer to believers than anything or anyone else. His paradoxical being, hidden and very close at the same time, may be one of the principal characteristics of God and his personality, as observed from a human psychological perspective.

Notes

1. Michael Durrant, *The Logical Status of "God" and the Function of Theological Sentences* (Edinburgh: Macmillan, St. Martin's Press, 1973), 3.

2. Ferenc Szabo, *Az Ember es Vilaga* (Roma: Self-published, 1969), 11.

Chapter 33

God's Personal Characteristics: "The Almighty, Eternal and Ultimate"

In previous chapters we have discussed God's relation to his people. We concluded that God communicates with the faithful, enabling them to come into contact with his transcendent personality, as well as to experience his love, joy and spiritual gifts beyond particular life events. Examples include the cases of Richardson and Abraham. Thus, despite no human's ever having seen God, believers discern God's personality through transempirical discernments (i.e., functions of purpose, beyond visible, touchable, and measurable "natural" phenomena, even beyond inexplicable, miraculous phenomena.)

However, if people of faith are really able to reliably, dependably, and credibly discern God's presence not only beyond miracles, but also beyond natural occurrences, in personal life or social events, then surely God must be able to direct all of those occurrences, and truly be present beyond them.

But let us now observe the world through the eyes of an agnostic, and ask: Does God have power over nature and its phenomena? Does he really determine and regulate events in our lives? Does the Almighty unmistakably and experientially direct astronomical events, stock market trends, or even the functioning of our car engines? Or, do we observe only the existence of indifferent astronomical, biological, economical, physical, sociological, and technical laws and principles beyond all natural events? Let's find out!

33.1. The Human Body as an Expression of the Soul

According to Le Trocquer:

> Existential unity clearly reveals the significance and nobility of the body. We can envisage the body only against the background of the soul and in its relation to the spirit, from which, by sharing its existence, the body derives all its nobility. Consequently, in speaking of the body we are speaking of that "companion" of the soul without which the soul could neither fulfill itself nor give itself in knowledge and love. Is this only an outdated Aristotelian-Aquinian concept, or is this a tangible, and almost touchable truth?[1]

Let's suppose that I just hugged my wife. How might this be explained by a bystander—say a rigorous agnostic and positivist neurologist, biochemist, or psychiatrist?

Asked to explain how the action came about, a positivist, accepting only what is cognitively visible, palpable, and measurable, might posit that certain physical, chemical, biochemical, or neurological processes in my brain, nerves, and muscles made my action happen. And he would be correct, up to a point. This hypothetical positivist could describe phenomenologically the unfolding of physical/chemical/biochemical processes in my brain and body, which were responsible for my hugging my beloved wife.

Hearing such an explanation, I (the subject), analyzing my own behavior introspectively, would have to ask: Doesn't the real reason for the event of hugging a beloved person lie in something other than the processes registered by phenomenological, scientific analysis, but in those registered solely by me, the subject, the loving husband?

Indeed, love (as in "I love my wife"), the introspective, reflective, meaning-centered and transempirical experience of love, was the real reason behind all that occurred in my nerves and muscles while executing the act of hugging my wife. To express love was the ultimate purpose and goal of all of the processes in my senses, brain, nerves, and behavior. However, to discern the real cause of the entire visible act, which was directed by one's personality and mind—namely, love—would be possible only for a value-observing person.

But what happened that was the real cause of my behavior, when my body and behavior served as tools to express pure Biblical love? Indeed, a value-discerning person of faith then recognizes the spiritual reason, set by the Spirit, and soul that directs all subordinated processes in my mind, brain, and body.

Let us apply this example to our topic, and ask: Is the way love motivates me to hug my wife, or how Spirit and soul direct Christian behavior, comparable to the relationship between God and nature? Is the relationship between one's personality (mind) and one's body at least in some aspect comparable to the way the Almighty directs all events occurring in nature for his purpose?

33.2. The "Natural World" as an Expression of God's Love

During the following discussion, let us be aware that the relation between the almighty God and nature is quite different from the interrelations between the human soul, mind and body. To avoid the deistic belief (that God created the world, but exists in himself, outside of and indifferent to his creation) or the pantheistic interpretation (that God is "nature" or even "above nature," but not a "person"), let us emphasize here that God is quite differently almighty from the way we would have to be almighty to direct nature as we direct our bodies.

Nevertheless, let us now concentrate not on the difference, but on the analogy between these two propositions, and explore if we can compare in some aspects God's reign over the natural world with the "reign" of personality over body. For this purpose, as in previous examples, first let us think like a rigorous materialist would, and after that let us analyze the same from a believer's perspective.

To present the materialistic viewpoint, let us compare natural occurrences in the world to those in a row of books. If one book in the row tips over, the "domino effect" will be observed. The books will fall, one after another, entirely determined by natural laws, totally regulated by the cause-and-effect principle. As rigorous materialist physicists, astronomers, biologists, or sociologists conceive it, all natural occurrences are guided by such cause-and-effect rules, from the big bang right up until today. All organisms, including humans, are nothing more than a complex organization of self-sustaining "living" physical, chemical, biochemical, neurological and psychological processes which imitate the aimless and meaningless domino effect in nature. This is shown in Figure 33-1.

Figure 33-1

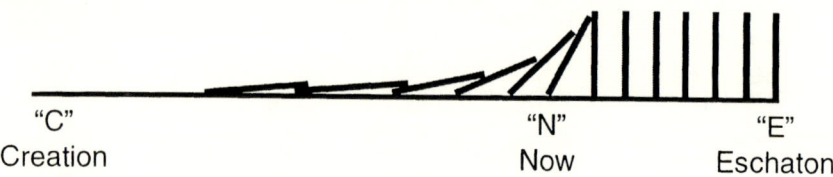

"C"	"N"	"E"
Creation	Now	Eschaton

Let us observe now the same process from a believer's perspective.

A believer would change nothing in the description of the observable facts of experiential reality, but his or her interpretation would be very different. A believer would put the whole process in a meaningful context. Thus, the overturning of the first book, "C," symbolizes in this model, the Creation. That of book "N" ("Now") represents this moment, the act of reading this sentence. Tipping over the last book "E" represents the "End," the Eschaton, the "Fulfillment of Time"—Jesus' second coming.

Can we now discern a similar interaction also in nature, such as between the human body and mind, when expressing love via bodily movements and gestures? Is it possible that all of the books starting from "C" (Creation) had to fall in order to get the last book "E" (symbolizing Jesus' second coming) to tumble over? Or, more accurately, is it possible that events regulated by cause and effect have occurred, do, and will occur in nature, in order to fulfill an ultimate purpose—God's purpose—the "fulfillment of time" of which the Bible speaks?

Everything in this model is regulated by natural laws, and the natural occurrences all serve three ultimate aims: to express God's love, to fulfill God's redemptive plan, and to bring God's kingdom into fruition.

When analyzing vision and recognition, we discerned that all physical, chemical, biochemical and neurological processes enabling recognition were purposefully organized in the brain, to enable meaningful psychological experiences of recognition. A similar process of organizing "subordinated" dimensions to fulfill a purpose we recognized in the example of my hugging my wife. Note that never were the natural, (physical-chemical-biochemical-neurological) processes blotted out, set aside, or disobeyed, but were used in a meaningful sequence to achieve an ultimate purpose: recognition, or to express love.

Now we turn to the question of whether a comparable (in some aspects at least) process can occur between God and nature.

Few of us witness great Biblical miracles. But we permanently discern all around us the unfolding of natural laws in the world. Nevertheless, if our hypothesis is correct, then, observed from the above-stated perspective, we recognize that everything that happens in this world, even what seems to be the most innocuous, trivial thing, does not happen needlessly, or by chance. It has an importance, a meaning in God's redemptive plan, in the accomplishment of God's ultimate love in the development of his kingdom, even if oftentimes we do not realize this.

If we are able to substantiate such a hypothesis, then the indifferent and impersonal natural world that we sensorially and positively observe around us would in fact be the "tool" in the hand of a personal and loving, experiential God, who uses natural occurrences to achieve his goal of establishing a "kingdom of his love." Similarly, the body, and all causal and deterministic processes in it, were, in the example of the hug, merely tools by which to express love.

33.3. God's Hand in Natural Laws and Occurrences

According to my Old Testament teacher Adalbert Rebic's book, the first pages of the Old Testament, starting from Gen. 1:1, use a poetic, solemn language that conveys in short, affirmative sentences only the most essential dogmatic facts of Judeo-Christian belief.[2] From a Biblical understanding, God is the almighty, eternal and ultimate, the creator of everything in existence, as well as of the natural laws and principles by which everything that is functions and is governed. All things serve the purpose determined by him, and the meaning he had planned for them from the first moment of Creation, especially his unique "project"—God's kingdom. This is a short summation of the Scripture's message, relevant to our current topic.

Can we experientially substantiate this concept of Creation?

Suppose that a particular person of faith is a value-discerning physicist, mathematician, or astronomer. His or her fundamental dilemma when analyzing creation is whether all cosmological processes occurred and still occur without any purpose or meaning, or whether the cosmic incidents created at the "beginning" (the Genesis), effectively and purposefully worked together so that our universe, galaxy, solar system and earth could be "born," and a step toward God's ultimate plan on this planet (or in the whole universe) be achieved? If our answer to this last question is affirmative, then we live in a world full of God's works, deeds, and management.

If the person of faith is a value-discerning biologist or physiologist, then his or her question might well be whether the reason for the billions of known and unknown influences that have concentrated on earth was a purposeful "creation" process, aiming to make possible the appearance of life, as described in Genesis in a few short and lapidary sentences. Did all of these countless billions of cosmic effects on earth, directed by God's hand—everything from the first living cell that came into being to the first animals inhabiting the air and oceans—prepare the way for the subsequent appearance of humankind? If the answer to this is affirmative, then the universe we see and can explore, is regulated primarily by natural principles, but organized to express God's personality, especially his love.

If this person is a religious physician, anthropologist, or historian, he or she might ask when testing the reliability of the Bible's creation account, whether the aim, goal, and purpose for all events in the universe, from creation onwards, could possibly be for humankind to come into existence. He or she would inquire whether God focused billions and billions of known and unknown cosmic influences on the planet earth, to move, one step at a time, closer to his purpose: to create humankind, thereby setting in motion human development and history?

If the person of faith happens to be a value-discerning theologian, a psychologist, or a sociologist, then he or she might ask a different question: Is everything that has occurred in the world up to now directed strictly causally but aimed and organized purposefully, lovingly set up in such a way that, as we progress through the twenty-first century, we may witness God's love, and live in a tangibly-experienced union with him?

If we can conform to these Biblical deductions in a value-discerning way, despite that we almost always and everywhere discern natural events (except in miracles), then we are undoubtedly the eminent objects of God's love; then God regulates events of human life purposefully, and out of love for us, the objects of his salvation. If we, however, are unable to prove God's love further, then plausibly the meaningless and purposeless evolution of eternal, infinite matter is the reason beyond the same process. Let us, in this next section, test our hypothesis from a value-discerning perspective!

A philosopher would say that a correct explanation has to fulfill three criteria: 1) not to be contradictory in itself, 2) not to contradict other known facts, and 3) be useful to explain other puzzles which, until now, have been inexplicable.

Indeed, discerning an ultimate meaning and love beyond natural happenings is not contradictory in itself, it does not contradict other known facts, and it can explain other puzzles concerning the past, present, and future of the human and natural world. However, would such a speculative approach sufficiently help an agnostic to understand a believer's certainty of living in and with God, or would it rather lead to a sense of being tricked?

Let us use instead a more Pascal-like existential approach, which can be summarized in two sentences:

1. If humankind is the object of God's love, then nature serves as a tool in his hands to express his love through Creation, and all subsequent events in the universe and on earth.
2. To create and sustain such a world, God had to be "quite other," almighty, eternal, and ultimate.

The crucial question on which the validity of the argument depends, is whether the whole world, but especially all of humankind, is in fact the object of God's love. Discerning a clear affirmative answer to the first premise enables us to positively answer the second proposition as well.

Let us focus on the first premise: How do Christians discern being the objects of God's love?

Indeed, every Christian would rationally substantiate his or her personal conviction differently, based on personal experience. However, the knowledge of God's love as revealed in the Old, and even more in New Testament Scriptures, is common to all Christians. Even more important (and convincing) is a tangible feeling of God's love, experienced through a reciprocal relationship with God. Metaphorically, communication in this relationship can be compared to breathing. Christians are giving themselves to God and are receiving God's response in a way that is comparable to constant expiration and inhalation. They are "expiring," or giving themselves to God in faith, and "inspiring"—receiving God's love, peace, optimism and other gifts of faith through transempirical channels. The tangible God becomes this Supreme reality who is more real than the air we are breathing. Since such "breathing with God" produces real biblical, experienced effects, we could conclude: the more the one is able to "expire" faith, the more he or she is able to "inspire" God's love. Such a tangible union with the invisible God is the key to experiencing his love. It is Pascal's "Reason of the heart," which is equally—or even more—important (and not only to a mystic) than knowledge that stems from the Scriptures.

It definitely concerns transempirical evidence. If one experiences tangibly being the object of God's love—regardless of whether he or she is a value-discerning physicist, mathematician or astronomer, a biologist or physiologist, a religious physician, anthropologist, or historian, a theologian, a psychologist or a sociologist or an average person like all of us—then he or she can easily agree with the wholeness of the revelation, despite the fact that sensorial perception always and everywhere discerns only natural events. For someone who feels and knows beyond doubt that he or she is the eminent object of God's love, it becomes evident that God regulates events in the universe, on the earth and in human life purposefully, and out of love for the objects of his salvation. As the human body's behavior, gestures and love express the human mind and soul, for a person of faith, the "quite other" God's love is clearly expressed by the "natural world," and in the existential reality of humankind living in a God-created environment.

Indeed, for such a person it is self-evident that an almighty, ultimate, and eternal power was needed to create the universe, which from the start was created and programmed purposefully, as implementation of God's volition, choice, and benevolence towards humans. He, whose power is sufficient to create such a universe in order to establish and sustain human existence, and realize his own kingdom as the completion of his love, had to be almighty, eternal, and ultimate. God's love in creating and sustaining the world, experienced by people of faith, is the proof of his omnipotence.

According to Fritz Rotschild, to the Jewish mystics—students of the kabbalah—"Everything hinted on something transcendental." Thus, "The presence of God was a daily experience."[3] Here, we see the same experience of God directing all events in the world, realized through believers' transempirical discernment. If everything that happens in this world expresses the nature and will of God, and if everything happens by his plan, decision, choice (or at the very least, by his permission), then we really live in a miraculous world! God is in everything and behind everything. All things happen so that God's ultimate plan will be fulfilled.

33.4. Discussion

The first question may be:

> Despite your point that the relationship between God and nature is quite different than that between the human mind and the body, is it realistic to compare the complexity of the human body (which is directed by mind) with the universe (which is directed by God)?

Norman Geisler quotes the words of the agnostic astronomer Carl Sagan as follows: "The genetic information in the human brain expressed in bits is probably comparable to the total number of connections among neurons: about 100 trillion." Thus,

> If written out in English, say, the information would fill some 20 million volumes, as many as are stored in the world's largest libraries. The equivalent of some 20 million books is stored in the heads of every one of us. "The brain is a very big place in a very small space," Sagan said. [4]

I would like to add to this comparison the fact that the 100 trillion nerve connections are not static like books in a library. Every second, the average synapse transmits five to seven impulses. In the human mind, however, this unimaginable causally-regulated "traffic" that occurs during an action (such as in previously used example of hugging a loved child, wife, or parent) is coordinated toward the fulfillment of a mindful, teleological-psychological purpose: the expression of love. Indeed, if we are dealing with the expression of Christian love, then the mind, brain, nerves and muscles, and the whole person is expressing a teleological purpose set by the soul and Spirit.

Just as cause-and-effect regulation in particular brain processes, nerves and muscles is organized to enable the expression of human love, "natural happenings in the world" participate in the expression of God's love for us. Believers realize God's love not only through his inexplicable miracles, but also beyond his regulation of "natural" worldly processes toward a certain purpose: God's kingdom. Whether such a comparison seems realistic depends on whether one holds a value-discerning (or a value-blind) attitude. Nevertheless, for those Christians who transempirically experience that "Nothing is closer to man than God, and nothing is stranger than living in a godless world" (in the already-quoted words of Mauriac), and to whom everything in nature points toward God (as the Jewish mystics asserted)—the tangible presence of God beyond the natural world is not only plausible, but is an experienced fact of reality.

Then, again, the devil's advocate could argue:

> Could all this "expression of God's love," enabling and sustaining the universe, the planet Earth, human existence, and everything God does to sustain his kingdom, be the product of developmental and evolutionary processes of the "Eternal matter" that always and infinitely existed and evolved according to its own laws, and that humankind has mistakenly attributed to an omnipotent God?

We can respond with a counter-question: Applying the same logic, you would then have to discover beyond the affection and gestures of love from your dear wife, parents or children not loving persons, but nothing more than developmental processes of the same "Eternal matter" as well! That would mean discerning only the electrochemical processes in the brain and muscles of your wife, husband, or children as the real cause of the bodily expressions of love, affection, and devotion. Such a schizophreniform "depersonalization" and "de-realization" would then declare mere "objects," instead of people and persons, to be real. Such extreme value-blindness is uncharacteristic of human reasoning. A comparable—and in currently fashionable reductionism—"de-personalization," and "de-realization" disable discernment of ultimate Biblical peace, love, joy, meaning, and God's personal closeness, beyond the natural world, in postmodern apathetic religious, agnostic and atheistic individuals.

However, this is not how healthy humans perceive reality. As thinking and feeling people, we abstract and discern a "personality" beyond the material bodies of loving parents, spouses, and children. Moreover, we discern responsible, creative, ambitious, or other personality types, beyond the "bodies" of our friends, and not only the materialization of the "creative forces of Eternal matter" nor only the visible, touchable, and measurable physical-chemical-biochemical-neurological processes that regulate their behavior. Value-discerning believers have an even higher level of understanding as they realize the "quite other" love of an "Almighty, Eternal, and Ultimate Person" beyond the realities of the natural world. The natural world, to a believer's mind, is the expression of God's love even if bad things may happen in it, especially because good people overcome bad things by their union with (and in) the almighty, eternal, and ultimate love, who is God.

It is an answer to the question:

Why do non-believers have a different experience of the same "Ultimate reality?"

Both atheists and people of faith live in the same world. They recognize the same visible, touchable and measurable natural realities, but not the same goal and ultimate purpose in (and beyond) those realities. The interpretation of data (in light of an ultimate purpose, or without it) is what makes the difference between recognizing God's love and the value-blindness of agnostic reductionism, and self-deception that claims, "This is only nature, and nothing more."

The next question may be:

According to Jarosevski, at the dawn of our civilization some 6000 years ago, and through the ensuing millennia, the dominant way of thinking was "hylozoistic." That is, humans discerned a human-like activity beyond every natural event.[5] For example, even a Greek philosopher explained magnetism in terms of a loving attraction between metals. In this paradigm, not only nature was thought to have a human-like personality and behavior, but the gods, as well. After 300 BC, with the progress of Greek philosophical thought, this paradigm changed, and autonomous inanimate powers were also acknowledged as regulators of natural phenomena. However, from that point and on, human thought evolved in two divergent directions. Christians recognize autonomous natural forces, directed by God. Atheists do not discern any "quite other" absolute almighty, eternal and ultimate person beyond nature. How can this cognitive gap be bridged?

We have already discussed in detail which functions of recognition enable us to take a stand on this issue.

The different areas of competency of transempirical and sensorial-scientific recognition ought to be respected. We need to keep in mind that sensorial, scientific, or cognitive functions cannot recognize ultimate meaning purpose, but only transempirical functions of purpose can. As noted earlier, scientific, cognitive and sensorial recognition functions can neither efficiently prove Biblical love, meaning or faith, as some apologists have tried, nor disprove them, as some atheists have attempted. God's personality can be discerned and becomes experiential only transempirically, through introspection, reflection, and mystical functions or functions of purpose.

Agnostics are extrapolating their own "transempirical blindness." Instead of serving the soul, they promote slavery to the instinct and senses, and replace Christian conscience with an "internal inhibitor," like the superego. Consequently, agnostics and atheists may live in such way that they feel unworthy to be known by God, and God seems unworthy of being known to them. Such distortion of the proper hierarchy within a person inevitably causes subsequent value-blindness. Value-blindness is not expressed only toward God, but also the external world and reality reflecting God's person, closeness, love, and providence. It is a key pastoral-psychological problem of our time that, because of different value-discernments, believers and non-believers virtually do not live in the same world. It seems me that no act of charity and love is more important in our time than that of producing genuine "gifts of faith," and that of true Biblical discipleship. Only witnessing discipleship, the consequence of "being known to God," can prove the love of God to the world and open the eyes of the value-blind.

The last question: "Are we the only intelligent creatures in the universe?"

True biblical discipleship also means that we may or may not presume that the universe was created only for the sake of us humans. We do not know if other "objects of God's love," like humans, exist in the universe. But, we do know that if humankind is the object of God's love, then we are (or are among) the central figure(s) in the created world! Undoubtedly, the universe was then created as it is for our sake (or for sake of the humankind as well). What is even more important, however, as John Paul II wrote, is that we find ourselves at the center of the history of salvation.[6]

Notes

1. René Le Trocquer, *What is Man?* (London: Burns & Oates, Hawthorn Books, 1961), 37.

2. Adalbert Rebic, *Biblijska Pra Povjest* (Zagreb: Krscanska Sadasnjost, 1972), 86-99.

3. Abraham J. Heschel, *Between God and Man* (New York: The Free Press, A Division of Simon & Shuster, Inc., 1959), 3.

4. Norman L. Geisler, *Baker Encyclopedia of Christian Apologetics* (Grand Rapids, MI: Baker Books, 2000), 680.

5. Mihail Jarosevski, *Istoria Psihologii* (Moskva: Izdateljstvo Misl, 1966), 8-9.

6. John Paul II, *Crossing the Threshold of Hope* (New York: Alfred A. Knopf, 1994), 67.

Chapter 34

The Phenomenon of Jesus Christ: The Common Experience Behind the Biblical and the Transempirical

According to Marijan J. Fucak, Jesus was probably literate.[1] However, we do not have any document written by him. Because of that, we can learn about Christ's ministry only by examining the Scriptures, which reflect the faith and witnessing of his inspired disciples, as well as the early church's teachings and traditions. Here we reconstruct the history of early witnesses.

Jesus ascended to heaven probably around AD 30. The earliest document of the New Testament, Paul's First Letter to the Thessalonians, was written around AD 50. The first period of Christian witnessing encompasses those twenty years. It was characterized by the fervent oral teaching and preaching of his disciples. Jesus' message was spread from the Aramaic- and Hebrew-speaking regions into the Greek, and later, the Roman world. The first Christian centers were established in Jerusalem, Antioch, Damascus, Alexandria, Corinth, Rome, and other cities, but we have no written information about the oral teachings (*kerygma* and *didache*) of the apostles before the year AD 50. We can only indirectly and partially reconstruct their message according to Acts 1-10 (Peter's preaching), and Paul's mention of the tradition in 1 Corinthians 11:23 and Romans 1:2.

The first written information by the apostle Paul is dated between AD 49 and 69. His letters were often written in haste and were intended to respond to a particular challenge confronting local churches. Although it is sometimes difficult to place and date St. Paul's letters exactly, by reading them we get an idea of what life was like in the first Christian communities and the difficulties they faced, as well as their experience of faith.

Between approximately AD 69 and 80, the eyewitnesses of Jesus' ministry got old and slowly died out. According to Fucak, by that time, Jairus' daughter—if she was still alive—must have been around eighty, and the youngster from Mark 14:15 would have been eighty-five or eighty-six. Since it became obvious that the Lord was not returning as soon as some had expected, an urgent need arose to record the recollections of Jesus' witnesses for future generations. Three apostles, Mark, Matthew, and Luke, recorded their accounts in three different social and geographical locations, remembering different things from Jesus' ministry. Memorabilia were thus created as the martyr Justin in the second century called these first reports. Despite having been written by different people to different audiences, despite describing different recollections and responding to different needs, these first three gospels were synoptic in the main facts of their witnessing.

The later sources of the *evangelion,* such as John's gospel and letters, pastoral letters like 2 Peter, and The Revelation, were written between approximately AD 80 and 100. By that time, the Christian doctrine had become more defined and structured, as it had to respond to its first challenges: heresies internally, persecution externally.

The first written documents, as well as the entire subsequent history of the church along with later Scriptural interpretation and understanding, are a response to one central phenomenon—the teaching and preaching of Jesus Christ himself. The effects of dropping a stone into clear water can symbolize this process. Jesus Christ's ministry was the phenomenon that initiated all other "waves." The oral tradition between the years AD 30 and 50 represents the response to the "Phenomenon of Jesus"—the first wave. Paul's letters presented the second wave: a response to the actual problems of the early Christian communities. The synoptic Gospels (Mark, Matthew, and Luke) represent the third. St. John's writings stand for the fourth wave, the Acts of the Apostles the fifth, and so on. We can illustrate the process by which the Scriptures were formed with concentric circles as in Figure 34-1.

Figure 34-1

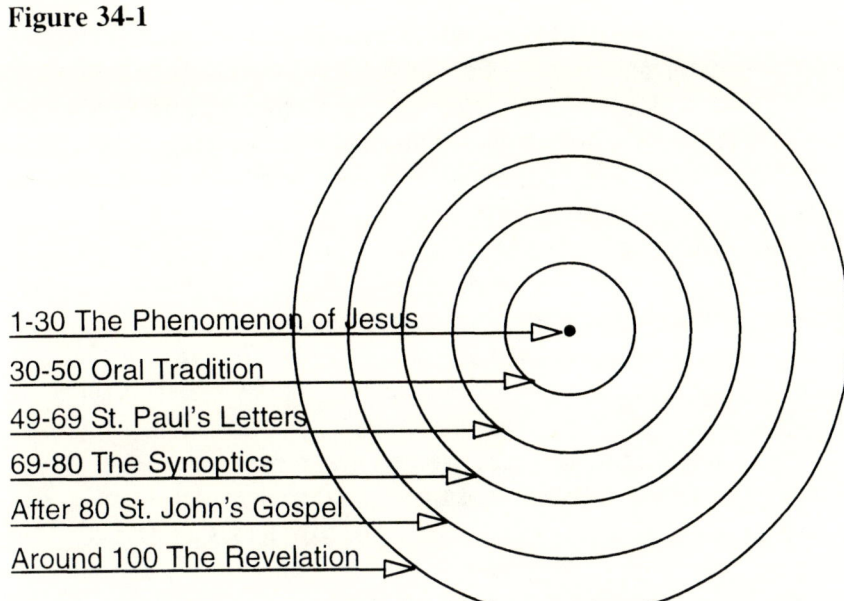

1-30 The Phenomenon of Jesus
30-50 Oral Tradition
49-69 St. Paul's Letters
69-80 The Synoptics
After 80 St. John's Gospel
Around 100 The Revelation

In the history of these waves there is for us postmodern people only one beginning: the Phenomenon of Jesus. But there is no end in sight. The early and Medieval church, the faith that characterized the Reformation and Counter-Reformation, the faith of the Enlightenment, pietism, orthodoxy, liberalism, existentialism, and all other "waves" are consequences of the phenomenon of Jesus Christ. They are also responses to problems confronting this first impetus.

Modern people's search for union with Jesus Christ also occurs in this context. Even the writing of this book, as well as its reading, are responses to this central impetus given by Jesus. The phenomenon of Jesus causes waves of reaction to his teachings almost 2000 years later.

The fidelity of the church expressed in these waves of witness is indeed surprising. However, the church is not built only on its fidelity to the Scriptures, ecumenical councils, and tradition as a record of the phenomenon of Jesus but also, and probably even more so, on Jesus' and the Holy Spirit's permanent presence among God's people.

How are Jesus, the Father, and the Spirit permanently present to people of faith? How does tangible union with the invisible God become experiential to Christians?

God always takes the first step in establishing a relationship. He is the unavoidable reality—the "quite other" person, addressing calls which are impossible not to hear or respond to. If we observe history from this perspective, we realize that even Immanuel Kant's keen interest in finding a solution to humankind's ultimate philosophical dilemmas; J. S. Mill's feverish atheism; Teresa of Avila's vision of the angels; Ivan the Terrible's religious fanaticism; Abraham's firm trust in Yahweh; the conversions of Saul and Thomas; the doubt of Descartes; Peter's message in 1 Peter 4:13-14; or postmodern people's religious apathy, are all special formulations of particular individuals' responses to God's call. Ultimately, all human behavior, and all of humankind's behavior, is a response to God's call.

For a psychiatrist, psychologist, or a theologian it remains a mystery why some answer God's calls positively, while others escape into irrationalism, agnosticism, communism, atheism, or religious indifference. The formulation of a personal response to God's call is the most important choice in each believer's life. The subject's assessment of the worth of his or her own life depends on this response. This response entails either the experience of an ultimate meaning and purpose behind work, love, death, and the whole of human existence, or a chronic estrangement from God and consequently, suffering having *bios*, but not *zoe*. This mysterious, fundamental choice determines whether one will recognize merely the sensorial-scientific reality of the world or will also transempirically know God and become known by God.

A positive human response to God's call evokes his swift reply: biblical peace, love, joy, hope, courage and other gifts of faith. The more the believer receives such gifts of faith, the more he or she will turn to Jesus; the more one exhales faith the more he or she will inhale God's love. Through such communication (including both God's speaking and silence), God's personality becomes a paramount, experienced, and evident reality. More and more, the believer tangibly recognizes the "quite other," infinitely loving programmer, who places humankind in a situation where a choice between the lure of the world and faith in an invisible God cannot be avoided. Human life, in fact, is a test situation. The intensity and depth of biblical gifts of faith and the overcoming of worldly suffering, boredom, and estrangement verify that the right choice is faith.

Thus, the experience of the presence of the biblical and transcendental God becomes a more substantial personal evidence than any sensorial, scientific, or cognitive discernment. From this point on, the cycle of faith will revolve more and more determinedly, always with bigger and faster turns: faith brings meaning and joy, joy makes faith strong, and strong faith brings more meaning, joy, and love in one's life. This is the typical experience for people living in union with Jesus.

The dynamics of this faith experience is illustrated in Figure 34-2.

Figure 34-2

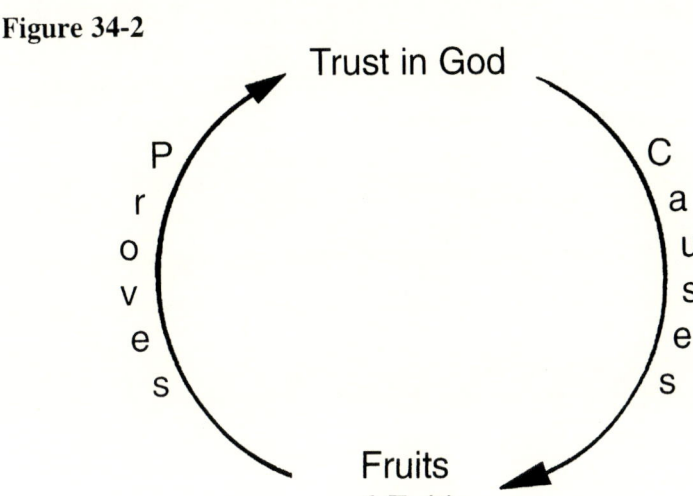

Despite all ups and downs, all roller-coaster-like setbacks and progressions, this angelic cycle of faith will continue unbroken, and turn ever faster. If the trend and general orientation of one's fundamental option in life centers in Christ, then real and tangible union with the almighty, eternal and ultimate love (i.e., God) is achievable.

Faith, the experience of communication with God, and the evidence of believers' union with Jesus, are verbalized in different terms through church history. However, the essence of the experience of union with the almighty, eternal, and ultimate loving God, is the same. The wording is different, but the experience is the same today as it was when the foundation of the Scriptures was laid.

On the other hand, this non-sensorial internal, reflective, and mystical evidence, substantiated by the Holy Spirit himself, is the substantiation of the human experience of the mystery we call faith. Jesus' disciples saw Christ, they saw his miracles and healings, they heard him speak and teach. Perhaps some of us envy them, and think, "If I had witnessed Jesus' miracles, it would be much easier for me to have an unshakable faith." However, sight does not make faith. Jesus' disciples, despite witnessing his deeds, experienced and relied on the same evidence of their psychological functions of purpose—conscience, soul, the father, the Spirit, and Jesus—that we, his modern disciples, rely upon. Their task of discerning faith in Jesus was no easier than ours today.

The experienced union with Jesus, to which the disciples and their followers were always faithful, is the reason for and explanation of why past and current challenges faced by the church could not, and indeed, cannot erase God from human hearts. This justifies hope in a new integration of God's people.

Note

1. Marijan Jerko Fucak. *Dogadjaj Isus Krist* (Zagreb: Institut Za Teolosku Kulturu Laika, 1989), 5-8.

Chapter 35

Conclusion

To humans living some ten thousand years ago, it seemed obvious that gods did exist and that they ruled from the upper world. Almost no one doubted that. An earthquake, a thunderstorm, or even a calm breeze were all considered signs of the gods' activities, proof of their presence in the world. The only question was whether they were good, benevolent, and helpful, or dangerous and vengeful gods?

After Abraham's appearance, the uncertainty for his followers was solved. Abraham believed that God is good. He received gifts of faith as proof both of God's goodness and of his own faith in this good God. This is the reason we respect him today as the Father of Faith.

Subsequently, Jewish spirituality changed. Many Jews believed that Yahweh was invisible and untouchable even though the visible consequences of his presence seemed obvious to them. He granted them military victory if they were obedient to him or punished them with defeats or even captivity (as in Babylon) for their sins. Good health, wealth, worldly success, and all good things, in fact every pleasure in their lives, were signs of God's benevolence and love; and poverty, sickness, or lack of success in this world were his punishments. Thus, God's presence for many Hebrews was obvious, and the relationship between him and his people was self-evident, proven by experience.

With the birth of Jesus and the proclamation of God's kingdom, people's relationship with God changed again. We read in Romans 14:17, "For the kingdom of God is not a matter of eating and drinking, but of righteousness, peace and joy in the Holy Spirit, ..." Clearly then, the kingdom of God does not exist only to serve our worldly welfare, as do food and drink. We experience God's presence, joy, peace and holiness not only outside of ourselves as riches, victory, or worldly success are experienced, but within the deepest part of our being. God and his kingdom are close to us. Nothing is as close to us as the Almighty, but at the same time, nothing can be as far away.

Despite great prophets, saints, martyrs, and scholars, naïve belief requiring sensorial-scientific reasons and worldly gains to prove faith has survived to this day. Many modern people are often still in search of visible and touchable proofs of living with God and in God, like people who lived several thousand years ago.

Such a search—the need for visible, touchable advantages or at least some speculative/philosophical evidence of God—has always been one of the characteristics of Western spirituality. For more than a thousand years, Christian Europe tried to find some kind of compromise between God's presence, experienced transempirically, and naïve belief. Until the sixteenth century, for example, the Western world generally believed that angels moved the stars in the heavens. The movement of the sun, observable to everyone, clearly demonstrated and made obvious God's presence. God maintained the function of the world; he had put us in the center of the universe, and was taking visible, measurable, and almost touchable care of humankind.

Some one thousand years ago, the famous scholar St. Anselm tried to find an argument for proof of God's existence, proof that would permanently resolve every doubt regarding this issue. By his ontological proof, he hoped to logically and irrefutably demonstrate God's existence. The history of the Middle Ages was full of such attempts. St. Anselm failed in his attempt to prove God's existence once and for all and to everybody independent of one's previous knowledge, background and experience. However, in 1632, the Italian astronomer Galileo succeeded in his attempt. He supported and expanded a heliocentric theory, earlier promulgated by the astronomer Copernicus, namely, that the earth revolves around the sun just like other planets, and the perceived revolving of the sun around the earth is regulated by pure physical and astrophysical rules.

Now-a-days it may be surprising that this astronomic discovery disturbed Galileo's contemporaries so much and caused them to struggle against the heliocentric theory and its supporters. Is it not all the same to us today whether the sun revolves around the earth, or vice versa?

The significance of Galileo's discovery was not just its opposition to certain theological concepts (e.g., the understanding of the Bible and the biblical description of Genesis favored in the Middle Ages). Neither was Galileo's significance only in scrutinizing naïve religious beliefs (and even interpretation of Scriptures) with the help of astronomy and science as criteria for truth of interpretation. A more important consequence that was later deduced from his groundbreaking discovery was the general philosophical uncertainty, skepticism: If the earth is not in the middle of the universe, then our earth is just an insignificant spot in space. If this is the case, then the universe was not created for our sake alone, and our good God in heaven does not move the rest of the universe around us just for our benefit. In fact, could it be that such a heavenly Father does not actually exist at all? This was the real danger of Galileo's theory.

Astronomical facts—that the earth, despite not being the center of the universe, is at least one of its focal points, where billions and billions of known and unknown cosmic influences converge, making life possible and proving God's care for the inhabitants of this planet—did not lessen such anguish. The year 1632 meant the end of an era in the history of humankind. It was the end of trying to imagine God's kingdom as something obvious, and something easily and readily observable in nature. It meant the end of understanding God and God's kingdom through sensorial, scientific, and in general cognitive functions. It also meant the beginning of the end of the flourishing of speculative/theoretical/philosophical theology. Something new began.

With Galileo, and especially with Descartes, an avalanche of justified and unjustified skepticism started to roll. At first, in the 17th and 18th centuries, many different schools of suspicion and doubt started to spread like a brushfire (like extreme rationalists, empiricists, solipsists and others). These schools of distrust were followed in the 19th and 20th centuries by modern reductionism, scientism, and other nihilist caricatures and exaggerations of Cartesian (Descartes') skepticism such as those held by extreme Darwinians, according to whom we are nothing more than highly evolved animals. Later came Karl Marx's dictum that religion is an opiate for the masses. Then we had the theories of Sigmund Freud, who proclaimed, "Religion is possible neither to prove nor to disprove."

From here on it was only a small step to the next, even greater challenge, for Christians typical of the postmodern mentality: Losing trust in human thought and acknowledging only what is sensory, visible, touchable and measurable. August Comte proclaimed—and postmodern Zeitgeist readily accepted—a positivist approach to life, faith, and God.

Postmodern skeptics wish to have proof, to be able to see, touch, grasp the "quite other" God, to use him for pragmatic and worldly purposes and not merely acknowledge the reality of his existence through a transempirical, reflective or mystical experience of a tangible union with the loving, suffering and glorious Jesus. In fact, before Galileo it was obvious to everyone that God does exist, and that he rules from the "upper world." But after Galileo's turnover, everyone has to choose between trust in an invisible God or in a visible world.

Postmodern humanity lives in a world of scientism that kills off the remainder of its religious beliefs based on naïve, cognitive proofs. In our time, naïve religiosity is slowly dying. On the other hand, agnosticism and religious indifference are exponentially multiplying. The post-modern western world is suffering a common and widespread syndrome: chronic loss of God!

What is to be the response to post-modern religious apathy?

This book's title gives the concise answer. Believers need a tangible union with the invisible God today more then ever in history! The paramount convincing power of a transempirical communication with the almighty, eternal and ultimate love, receiving his biblical gifts, is what makes or breaks faith for our positivist contemporaries. If we are the salt of the earth and the light of the world then there is no more important task than to become, every day, more Jesus-like in reflecting biblical meaning, joy, peace, love, hope, trust, and others gifts of faith, and to help our contemporaries to hear and positively respond to God's calls. Postmodern believers need evidence that their union with God proves the biblical message, and, in turn, that the Bible proves their union with God. Believers' factual living in God and with God, equally compelling as that which the authors of the Bible lived, is the most efficient answer to religious apathy and agnosticism and the most efficient tool in building God's kingdom.

We are living at a historical turning point. Naïve religiosity is slowly disappearing, while religious apathy is spreading. However, neither is faith static; it is evolving before our very eyes. History has demonstrated that the decline of faith and estrangement from God were always followed by a revival and a new theology and spirituality. Throughout Christianity's history, from the bloody persecution under the Emperor Diocletian, to Constantine's conversion in 313, through the Middle Ages' power struggle between popes and emperors, to the establishment of schools of distrust in the Enlightenment, to the estrangement between the church and society during secularism and modernism, to ideological persecutions during the rise of fascism and communism—in short, in spite of changing times, and continual challenges, Christianity has carried on its mission. The Church has overcome worse challenges than those presented by modern scientism, positivism, and religious apathy. The question that interests all believers concerns the Holy Spirit's intent: Will the current religious apathy get much worse or will a transempirical turn-around occur soon? Must the spiritual situation get much worse, or is it bad enough today to give fresh momentum to future spirituality, enabling a widespread tangible union with the invisible God?

In any case, a great historical watershed is taking shape now, right before our very eyes. We can assert that the believers and the Church of the future will either live in a tangible union with the invisible God or not exist at all. Since Jesus promised that the Church will persist and the gates of hell will not overcome it, our task is only to resist courageously all that threatens our faith. With the Spirit's help, time is on the Church's side, as it has always been.

May God help us in this quest!

Bibliography

Allen, R. E. *The Concise Oxford Dictionary*. Oxford: Clarendon Press, 1990.

American Psychiatric Association. *Quick Reference to The Diagnostic Criteria From Diagnostic and Statistical Manual of Mental Disorders*, IV. Washington, DC: The American Psychiatric Association, 1994.

Aquinas, Thomas, St. *Basic Writings of Saint Thomas Aquinas, Volume One*, ed. Anton C. Pegis. New York: Random House, 1945.

Augustine of Hippo. St. *Confessions*. Grand Rapids: Christian Classics Ethereal Library, 1999.

Barbour, Ian G. *Religion in an Age of Science*. San Francisco: HarperSanFrancisco, 1990.

Barnes, Robert. *Theories in Counseling*. Abilene, TX, Department of Counseling and Human Development, Hardin-Simmons University, 1994.

Bitter, Wilhelm. *Psychotherapie und religioese Erfahrung*. Stuttgart: Ernst Klett, 1965.

Blondel, Maurice. *L'Action. Essai d'une critique de la vie et d'une science de la pratique*. Paris: Premiers ecrits, 1950.

Bouyer, Louis. *The Church of God*. Chicago, IL: Franciscan Herald Press, 1982.

Brown, R. E., J. J. Castelot, J. L. McKenzie, and others. *The Jerome Biblical Commentary*. Englewood Cliffs, NJ: Prentice Hall, 1968.

Callahan, E. R. "Conscience." in *New Catholic Encyclopedia, Second edition,* Volume 4. Washington, DC: Thomson Gale in association with The Catholic University of America, 1993.

Copleston, Frederick. *A History of Philosophy, Volume IX*. Paramus, NJ: Newman Press, 1975.

Cross, F. L., and E. A. Livingstone, eds. *The Oxford Dictionary of the Christian Church*. New York: Oxford University Press, 1974.

Donne, John. *The Complete Poetry and Selected Prose of John Donne*, ed. Charles M. Coffin, New York: Modern Library Classics, 2001.

Durant, Will. *The Story of Philosophy*. New York: Washington Square Press, 1953.

Durrant, Michael. *The Logical Status of "God" and the Function of Theological Sentences*. Edinburgh: Macmillan, St. Martin's Press, 1973.

Erdody, Janos. *Requiem Firenceert*. Budapest: Szepirodalmi Kiado, 1980.

Erickson, Millard J. *Christian Theology*. Grand Rapids, MI: Baker Book House, 1995.

Eric, Ljubomir. *Strah, Anksioznost i Anksiozna Stanja*. Beograd: Institut Za Strucno Usavrsavanje I Specijalizaciju Zdravstvenih Radnika, 1972.

Fenichel, Otto. *The Psychoanalytic Theory of Neuroses*. New York, London: W. W. Norton, 1972.

Feuerbach, Ludwig. *Das Wesen der Christentums*. Samtliche Werke. Stuttgart, Philosophischer Verlag, 1903.

Flannery, Austin. *Vatican Collection Volume I; Vatican Council II: The Conciliar and Post-Conciliar Documents*. Northport, NY: Costello Publishing Company, 1992.

Frankl, Viktor E. *The Unconscious God*. New York: Simon and Schuster, 1975.

———. *The Doctor and the Soul. From Psychotherapy to Logotherapy*. New York: Vintage Books, A Division of Random House, 1986.

———. *Ärztliche Seelsorge*. Wien: Franz Deuticke, 1965.

———. *Antropologische Grundlagen der Psychoterapie*. Bern, Stuttgart, Wien: Hans Huber, 1976.

———. *Man's Search for Meaning (Revised and Enlarged Edition.)* New York: Washington Square Press, 1984.

———. *The Unheard Cry for Meaning*. New York: Washington Square Press, 1985.

Franzen, August. *Kleine Kirchengeschichte*. Freiburg: Herder Bücherei, 1968.

Freud, Sigmund. *The Future of an Illusion*. London: Hogarth Press, 1922.

Fucak, Marijan Jerko. *Dogadjaj Isus Krist*. Zagreb: Institut Za Teolosku Kulturu Laika, 1989.

———. *Biblijski Teologija Novogzavjeta*. Zagreb: Notes of an unpublished presentation at the Institut Za Teolosku Kulturu Laika, 1986.

———. *Evandjelje Ljubljenog Ucenika*. Zagreb: Institut Za Teolosku Kulturu Laika, 1986.

Geisler, Norman L. *Baker Encyclopedia of Christian Apologetics*. Grand Rapids, MI: Baker Books, 2000.

Gilson, Etienne, Thomas Langan, and Armand A. Maurer. *Recent Philosophy: Hegel to Present*. New York: Random House, 1966.

Hague, William J. *Evolving Spirituality*. Edmonton, AB: University of Alberta: Department of Educational Psychology, 1995.

Hardy, Daniel W. "Joy." In *The Oxford Companion to Christian Thought*, edited by Adrian Hastings, Alistair Mason, and Hugh Pyper. New York: Oxford University Press, 2000.

Hastings, Adrian. "Schism." In *The Oxford Companion to Christian Thought*, edited by Adrian Hastings, Alistair Mason, and Hugh Pyper. New York: Oxford University Press, 2000.

Hauser, Arnold. *Socijalna Istorija Umetnosti i Knjizevnosti*. Beograd: Kultura, 1966.

Hebblethwaite, Brian. "Soul." In *The Oxford Companion to Christian Thought*, edited by Adrian Hastings, Alistair Mason, and Hugh Pyper. New York: Oxford University Press, 2000.

Hugo, Victor. *Les Misérables*. London: Penguin Books, 1976.

Hyman, Arthur and James J. Walsh, eds. *Philosophy in the Middle Ages*. New York, Evanston, IL, and London: Harper & Row Publishers, 1967.

Heschel, Abraham J. *Between God and Man*. New York: The Free Press, A Division of Simon & Schuster, 1959.

Jarosevski, Mihail. *Istoria Psihologii*. Moskva: Izdateljstvo Misl, 1966.

Jeanrond, G. Werner. "Love." In *The Oxford Companion to Christian Thought*, edited by Adrian Hastings, Alistair Mason, and Hugh Pyper. New York: Oxford University Press, 2000.

John of the Cross, St. *Ascent of Mount Carmel*. Grand Rapids, MI: Christian Classics Ethereal Library, 2000.

John Paul II. *Crossing the Threshold of Hope*. New York: Alfred A. Knopf, 1994.

Jung, Karl G. *Man and His Symbols*. New York: Bantam Doubleday Dell Publishing Group, 1968.

Kardos, Lajos. *Behaviorizmus*. Budapest: Gondolat Konyvkiado, 1970.

Kasper, Walter. *The God of Jesus Christ*. New York: The Crossroad Publishing Co., 1992.

Kierkegaard, Søren. *Philosophical Fragments Johannes Climacus*. Edited and Translated by Howard V. Hong and Edna H. Hong. Princeton: Princeton University Press, 1985.

Kohan, P. S. *Istorija Zapadnoevropske Knjizevnosti*. Sarajevo: Veselin Maslesa, 1967.

Kubler-Ross, Elizabeth. *About Death and Dying*. New York: Macmillan, 1969.

Léon-Dufour, Xavier, Jean Duplacy, George Augustin, Pierre Grelot, Jacques Guillet, and Marc-Francois Lacan. *Rjecnik Biblijske Teologije*, Josip Turcinovic, ed. Zagreb: Krscanska Sadasnjost, 1988.

Le Trocquer, René. *What is Man?* London: Burns & Oates, Hawthorn Books, 1961.

Locke, John. *Essay Concerning Human Understanding*. London: 1894.

Lukas, Elizabeth. "What is Special about Logotherapy?" *A Presentation of Casuistic Elements with Case Studies*. Paper read at the Tenth World Congress on Logotherapy, Dallas, TX: July, 1995.

Mendez, Maria. *Life with Meaning, Guide to the Fundamental Principles of Viktor Frankl's Logotherapy*. Victoria, BC: Trafford, 2004.

Murray, Andrew. *With Christ in the School of Prayer*. New Kensington, PA: Whitaker House, 1981.

Nemeshegyi, Peter. *Egy Hit, Sokfele Teologia*. Budapest: Magyar Papi Egyseg, 1998.

O'Hear, Anthony. *Experience, Explanation, and Faith: An Introduction to the Philosophy of Religion*. London: Routledge & Kegan Paul, 1984.

O'Collins, Gerald. "Redemption." In *The Oxford Companion to Christian Thought*, edited by Adrian Hastings, Alistair Mason, and Hugh Pyper. New York: Oxford University Press, 2000.

Packer, J. I. *God's Plans for You*. Wheaton, IL: Crossway Books, 2001.

Peterson, M., W. Hasker, B. Reichenbach, and D. Basinger. *Reason and Religious Belief: An Introduction to Philosophy of Religion*. New York: Oxford University Press, 1991.

Quinn, Philip L. "Theories of Atonement." In *The Oxford Companion To Christian Thought*, edited by Adrian Hastings, Alistair Mason, and Hugh Pyper. New York: Oxford University Press, 2000.

Rahm, Bernard. *Principles of Reading the Bible—Hermeneutics*. Grand Rapids, MI: Baker Books, 1970.

Rahner, Karl. *Spirit in the World*. Montreal: Palm Publishers, 1968.

Ratzinger, Joseph. *Behold the Pierced One: An Approach to Spiritual Christology*. San Francisco, CA: Ignatius Press, 1986.

———. *Truth and Tolerance: Christian Belief and World Religions*. San Francisco: Ignatius Press, 2004.

Reardon, Martin. "Unity." In *The Oxford Companion to Christian Thought*, edited by Adrian Hastings, Alistair Mason, and Hugh Pyper. New York: Oxford University Press, 2000.

Rebic, Adalbert. *Biblijska Pra Povjest*. Zagreb: Krscanska Sadasnjost, 1972.

Russell, Bertrand. *Why I am Not a Christian and Other Essays on Religion and Related Subjects*. New York: Simon and Schuster, 1967.

Sartre, Jean-Paul. *La Nausée*. Paris: Bibliothèque des idées, Gallimard, 1938.

———. *L'Être et le néant*. Paris: Bibliothèque des idées, Gallimard, 1943.

Schnackenburg, Rudolf. *The Gospel According to St. John*. New York: Herder and Herder, 1968.

Schwarz, Joseph. *Argumente für Gottes Existenz*. Eisenstadt, 1988.

Staric, Aldo. *Susret S Kristom U Sakramentiam Crkve*. Zagreb: Institut Za Teolosku Kulturu Laike, 1988.

Stefanovic, Stanoje. *Tragedija Genija*. Beograd: Nolit, 1976.

Stojiljkovic, Srboljub. *Psihijatrija sa Medicinskom Psihologijom*. Beograd: Medicinska Knjiga, 1975.

Szabo, Ferenc. *Az ember es vilaga*. Roma: Self-published, 1969.

Teilhard de Chardin, Pierre. *Le Milieu Divin*. Paris: Seuil, 1957.

Teresa of Avila, St. *The Collected Works of St. Teresa of Avila*. Translated by Kieran Kavanaugh and Otilio Rodriguez. Washington, DC: Institute of Carmelite Studies Publications, 1976.

Thonnard, F. J. *A Short History of Philosophy*. Paris: Publishers of the Holy Apostolic See, 1955.

Tomic, Celestin. *Prapovijest Spasenja*. Zagreb: Provincijalat Hrvatskih Franjevaca Konventualaca, 1977.

Ungar, Maria. *Viktor Frankl's Meaning-oriented Approach to Counseling*. Edmonton, AB: Doctoral Dissertation. Department of Educational Psychology, 1999.

Vaihinger, Leo. *Die Philosophy Des Als Ob*. Berlin: Reuther & Reichard, 1911.

Vitz, Paul C. *Faith of the Fatherless: The Psychology of Atheism*. Dallas, TX: Spence Publishing Company, 1999.

Walsh, William Thomas. *Saint Teresa of Avila*. Rockford, IL: Tan Books and Publishers, 1977.

Wells, Herbert George. *A Vilagtortenelem Alapvonalai*. Budapest: Genius, 1925.

Weismayer, Josef. *Dogmatik, VII Kapitel: Hofnung Auf Vollendung*. Fernkurs Fur Theologische Bildung. Wien, 1985.

Williams, C. "Conscience." In *New Catholic Encyclopedia, 2nd ed.* Washington, DC: Thomson Gale in association with The Catholic University of America, 1993.

Zagorac, Vlado. *Sakramenti*. Zagreb: Institut Za Teolosku Kulturu Laika, 1968.

Index

Religious Experience, 118
Jeanond, G. W., and God's person,
72-73
Jeremiah, and kings' relationships
with God, 22-23
Jerome Biblical Commentary, The ,
and kingdom of God, 34
Jesus Christ. *See also* God's person;
Ascension of, 65-70; blessings
of, 59-60; and conquering of
Satan, 39-40; death and resurrection of, 36-37, 45-46, 53-
55, 65-70, 85-90, 91-106, 175,
316; Ecumenical Synods and,
10; and God's person revealed,
33-46; ministry of, 34-37, 42,
375-380 (*See also* Galilee);
miracles of, 60-63; person of,
10, 35-38, 40-42, 71; phenomenon of, 375-380; as "son of
man", 35-36, 41; suffering by,
53-59; symbols of, 43-44; and
work in Galilee, 34-36, 38-40
Jewish religion. *See also* Hebrew
history; and kingship, 22-23; sin
and atonement in, 54-55
John of the Cross: and *Ascent of
Mount Carmel*, 251; and *Dark
Night of the Soul*, 251
John Paul II, Pope: and *Crossing the
Threshold of Hope*, 181-182;
and denominational plurality,
258; transempirical experience/
recognition and, 7
John the Baptist, imprisonment of,
34
joy, 202-206, 218-225; Christian
understanding of, 206-211; and
faith, 211-214; Holy Spirit and,
52; kingdom of God and, 211-
212; meaning of, 198-202, 205-
206; and suffering, 50-51; in

transempirical discernment,
198-202; and transempirical
experience/recognition, 228-
229, 251-253
Joy, 211-212
Jung, Carl Gustav: and *Man and His
Symbols*, 13; and relationship of
kings and gods, 17

Kant, Immanuel: and *The Critique of
Pure Reason*, 116-117; metaphysical philosophy of, 116-
117, 353
Kasper, Walter, and definition of
God, 10
Kierkegaard, Søren A.: and angst,
316; and "paradoxical logic",
117; and *Philosophical Fragments—Johannes Climacus*, 10
king or kingship: god's relationship
with, 15-17, 21-24; primary
concerns of Jewish, 22-23
kingdom of God, 34; and Creation,
365-368; *Jerome Biblical
Commentary, The* and, 34; and
joy, 211-212; and love, 369;
meaning of, 33-35; New
Testament and, 33-35
Knorzer, Wolfgang, and kingdom of
God, 34
Kohler, Wolfgang, behaviorist, 3-4

La Nausée—Nausea, 173-174
L'Action, 118-119
language, of non-believers, 137-140
Last Supper, 43-44
Le Trocquer, René, and *What is
Man*, 114-115
Leibniz, Gottfried W., 108
Leo the Great, Pope: and fourth
ecumenical synod, 244; and
Vandals from North Africa,

About the Author

Dr. Paul Ungar completed his medical studies at the University of Belgrade in 1974. One of his first patients was a young man who was in a comatose state after a suicide attempt. When the patient regained consciousness, he surprised Dr. Ungar asking, "Why did you save me? Why must I live?" After his discharge from the hospital, he made a second attempt—and this time he succeeded. Dr. Ungar was haunted by the question: what should I have said to this young man? He went on to specialize in neuropsychiatry, but learned nothing about the answer the suicidal patient needed to hear. After obtaining his Master's Degree in Psychoanalysis, he pursued his Ph.D. studies with Dr. Victor Frankl of Vienna. He researched the topic, "What gives patients a purpose to live for?" and realized that nothing in medicine, psychology or philosophy answers this question satisfactorily but only trust in God. Therefore he turned to theology and earned a graduate degree in this discipline. The last twenty years he spent teaching intermittently at medical, psychology, and theology schools, as well as working in private practice as a psychiatrist and a psychologist. His interest was focused on how to achieve a synthesis between Biblical revelation and human experience. He published two books in this area—a textbook, *Pastoral Psychopathology*, in Djakovo, Croatia, in 1985 (in Croatian), and a manuscript, *Arguments for God's Existence*, in Eisenstadt, Austria in 1989 (in German). He has also published around thirty articles in the areas of medicine and psychiatry.